Lighting the Western Sky

Phoebe Hearst
during her middle years as a wealthy widow and businesswoman

Lighting the Western Sky

The Hearst Pilgrimage and the Establishment of the Bahá'í Faith in the West

Kathryn Jewett Hogenson

GEORGE RONALD
OXFORD

George Ronald, Publisher
Oxford
www.grbooks.com

A catalogue record for this book is available
from the British Library

ISBN 978-0-85398-543-3

Cover design: Steiner Graphics
Printed in Great Britain by the MPG Books Group

Contents

For Gary, Mary & Elizabeth
with love

and

For the long-suffering, stalwart Bahá'í community of Egypt
whose forefathers' dedicated, loving efforts were essential
to the successful rise of the Faith in the West

O Thou Provider! Thou hast breathed over the friends
in the West the sweet fragrance of the Holy Spirit,
and with the light of divine guidance Thou hast lit up the Western sky.
'Abdu'l-Bahá

Foreword

For more than a century the story of the first pilgrimage of Western believers to the Holy Land has fascinated Bahá'ís, especially those from North America and Europe. Golden names of those who took part – Lua Getsinger, May Bolles (Maxwell), Ella Goodall (Cooper), Robert Turner, Mary Virginia Thornburgh-Cropper, among others – have entered the pantheon of Bahá'í heroes and heroines and evoke feelings of awe, respect and gratitude. The journey of those fifteen souls during the winter of 1898–1899 has come to be recognized as a pivotal event in the history of the Bahá'í Faith; more than a pilgrimage – a turning point that would have far-reaching implications many centuries into the future for millions of people.

That historic pilgrimage has been recounted in snippets and summaries, but never told in its entirety, because it is complicated. The members of the pilgrimage did not travel together as a one group and several did not even meet for the first time until it was over. Each pilgrim had his or her own private personal experience during that sojourn in the Holy Land. And so, what has been published heretofore has only provided brief glimpses of the story, usually from the viewpoint of one particular participant.

As the Bahá'í world prepared to celebrate the centenary of its founding in 1944, there was a surge in interest in the first Western pilgrimage, especially in the United States. With the passage of time the historic importance of the Hearst party's visit was beginning to be appreciated. Many people turned to the one among the few surviving members who was best able to set out her recollections, Ella Goodall Cooper of California, a believer who had made service to the Cause the primary aim of her life, and pressed her to tell the story.

Mrs Cooper, a wealthy, childless matron, hired a stenographer to assist her in typing and compiling the notes and journals from her youth, with the goal of producing a publication about the first Western pilgrimage. She wrote to Anne Apperson Flint, another remaining pilgrim, and solicited her memories through a questionnaire. Unfortunately Mrs Flint, an elderly widow, was not capable of providing many of the answers sought by her old friend. Mrs Flint related to Mrs Cooper that her own papers from her youth were in inaccessible storage and her memory was dulled from years of troubles and ill-health. Both ladies had lost contact with the only other surviving pilgrim, Julia Pearson Hunt. Mrs Cooper also corresponded with the daughters of Helen Hillyer Brown and Agnes Lane Leonard to inquire about any papers their mothers might have left behind which could shed light on the pilgrimage. One indication as to how little knowledge the members of that illustrious group had about the pilgrimage is that neither Mrs Cooper nor Mrs Flint knew the first name of the eldest pilgrim, Mrs Harriet Thornburgh. At the time of the pilgrimage they had been in their twenties and Mrs Thornburgh had been in her sixties, and so, because of the prevailing rules of etiquette, they had only addressed her as 'Mrs Thornburgh'. Mrs Cooper lightheartedly noted that that lady would have to go down in history as 'H. Thornburgh'. Fortunately, that comment would prove to be incorrect.

Mrs Cooper's notes, journals and correspondence, even though they did not congeal into a publication during her lifetime, have nonetheless become an invaluable resource for posterity. They underpin this work.

Shoghi Effendi, in his seminal history of the Bahá'í Faith *God Passes By*, published for that same centenary in 1944, considered the first Western pilgrimage to be of such great consequence that he devoted considerable space to it, as in the following passage:

> By 1898 Mrs. Phoebe Hearst, the well-known philanthropist (wife of Senator George F. Hearst), whom Mrs. Getsinger had, while on a visit to California, attracted to the Faith, had expressed her intention of visiting 'Abdu'l-Bahá in the Holy Land, had invited several believers, among them Dr. and Mrs. Getsinger, Dr. Khayru'lláh and his wife, to join her, and had completed the necessary arrangements for their historic pilgrimage to 'Akká. In Paris several resident Americans, among whom were May Ellis Bolles, whom Mrs. Getsinger had won over to the Faith, Miss Pearson, and Ann Apperson, both nieces of Mrs. Hearst, with Mrs. Thornburgh and her daughter, were added to the party, the number of which was later swelled in Egypt by the addition of Dr. Khayru'lláh's daughters and their grand-mother whom he had recently converted.
>
> The arrival of fifteen pilgrims, in three successive parties, the first of which, including Dr. and Mrs. Getsinger, reached the prison-city of 'Akká on December 10, 1898; the intimate personal contact established between the Center of Bahá'u'lláh's Covenant and the newly arisen heralds of His Revelation in the West; the moving circumstances attending their visit to His Tomb and the great honor bestowed upon them of being conducted by 'Abdu'l-Bahá Himself into its innermost chamber; the spirit which, through precept and example, despite the briefness of their stay, a loving and bountiful Host so powerfully infused into them; and the passionate zeal and unyielding resolve which His inspiring exhortations, His illuminating instructions and the multiple evidences of His divine love kindled

in their hearts – all these marked the opening of a new epoch in the development of the Faith in the West, an epoch whose significance the acts subsequently performed by some of these same pilgrims and their fellow-disciples have amply demonstrated.

'Of that first meeting,' one of these pilgrims, recording her impressions, has written, 'I can remember neither joy nor pain, nor anything that I can name. I had been carried suddenly to too great a height, my soul had come in contact with the Divine Spirit, and this force, so pure, so holy, so mighty, had overwhelmed me . . . We could not remove our eyes from His glorious face; we heard all that He said; we drank tea with Him at His bidding; but existence seemed suspended; and when He arose and suddenly left us, we came back with a start to life; but never again, oh! never again, thank God, the same life on this earth.' 'In the might and majesty of His presence,' that same pilgrim, recalling the last interview accorded the party of which she was a member, has testified, 'our fear was turned to perfect faith, our weakness into strength, our sorrow into hope, and ourselves forgotten in our love for Him. As we all sat before Him, waiting to hear His words, some of the believers wept bitterly. He bade them dry their tears, but they could not for a moment. So again He asked them for His sake not to weep, nor would He talk to us and teach us until all tears were banished . . .'

. . . 'Those three days,' Mrs. Hearst herself has, in one of her letters, testified, 'were the most memorable days of my life . . . The Master I will not attempt to describe: I will only state that I believe with all my heart that He is the Master, and my greatest blessing in this world is that I have been privileged to be in His presence, and look upon His sanctified face . . . Without a doubt 'Abbás Effendi is the Messiah of this day and generation, and we need not look for another.' 'I must say,' she, moreover, has in another letter written, 'He is the most wonderful Being I have ever met or ever expect to meet in this world . . . The spiritual atmosphere which surrounds Him and most powerfully affects all those who are blest by being near Him, is indescribable . . . I believe in Him with all my heart and soul, and I hope all who call themselves believers will concede to Him all the greatness, all the glory, and all the praise, for surely He is the Son of God – and "the spirit of the Father abideth in Him."'

Even Mrs. Hearst's butler, a negro named Robert Turner, the first member of his race to embrace the Cause of Bahá'u'lláh in the West, had been transported by the influence exerted by 'Abdu'l-Bahá in the course of that epoch-making pilgrimage. Such was the tenacity of his faith that even the subsequent estrangement of his beloved mistress from the Cause she had spontaneously embraced failed to becloud its radiance, or to lessen the intensity of the emotions which the loving-kindness showered by 'Abdu'l-Bahá upon him had excited in his breast.

The return of these God-intoxicated pilgrims, some to France, others to the United States, was the signal for an outburst of systematic and sustained activity, which, as it gathered momentum, and spread its ramifications over Western Europe and the states and provinces of the North American continent, grew to so great a scale that 'Abdu'l-Bahá Himself resolved that, as soon as He should be released from His prolonged confinement in 'Akká, He would undertake a personal mission to the West. Undeflected in its course by the devastating crisis which the ambition of Dr. Khayru'lláh had, upon his return from the Holy Land (December, 1899) precipitated; undismayed by the agitation which he, working in collaboration with the arch-breaker of the Covenant and his messengers, had provoked; disdainful of the attacks launched by him and his fellow-seceders, as well as by Christian ecclesiastics increasingly jealous of the rising power and extending influence of the Faith; nourished by a continual flow of pilgrims who transmitted the verbal messages and special instructions of a vigilant Master; invigorated by the effusions of His pen recorded in innumerable Tablets; instructed by the successive messengers and teachers dispatched at His behest for its guidance, edification and consolidation, the community of the American believers arose to initiate a series of enterprises which, blessed and stimulated a decade later by 'Abdu'l-Bahá Himself, were to be but a prelude to the unparalleled services destined to be rendered by its members during the Formative Age of His Father's Dispensation.

No sooner had one of these pilgrims, the afore-mentioned May Bolles, returned to Paris than she succeeded, in compliance with 'Abdu'l-Bahá's emphatic instructions, in establishing in that city the first Bahá'í center to be formed on the European continent. This center was, shortly after her arrival, reinforced by the conversion of the illumined Thomas Breakwell, the first English believer, immortalized by 'Abdu'l-Bahá's fervent eulogy revealed in his memory; of Hippolyte Dreyfus, the first Frenchman to embrace the Faith, who, through his writings, translations, travels and other pioneer services, was able to consolidate, as the years went by, the work which had been initiated in his country; and of Laura Barney, whose imperishable service was to collect and transmit to posterity in the form of a book, entitled 'Some Answered Questions,' 'Abdu'l-Bahá's priceless explanations, covering a wide variety of subjects, given to her in the course of an extended pilgrimage to the Holy Land. Three years later, in 1902, May

> Bolles, now married to a Canadian, transferred her residence to Montreal, and succeeded in laying the foundations of the Cause in that Dominion.
>
> In London Mrs. Thornburgh-Cropper, as a consequence of the creative influences released by that never-to-be-forgotten pilgrimage, was able to initiate activities which, stimulated and expanded through the efforts of the first English believers, and particularly of Ethel J. Rosenberg, converted in 1899, enabled them to erect, in later years, the structure of their administrative institutions in the British Isles. In the North American continent, the defection and the denunciatory publications of Dr. Khayru'lláh (encouraged as he was by Mírzá Muḥammad-'Alí and his son Shu'á'u'lláh, whom he had despatched to America) tested to the utmost the loyalty of the newly fledged community; but successive messengers despatched by 'Abdu'l-Bahá (such as Ḥájí 'Abdu'l-Karím-i-Ṭihrání, Ḥájí Mírzá Ḥasan-i-Khurásání, Mírzá Asadu'lláh and Mírzá Abu'l-Faḍl) succeeded in rapidly dispelling the doubts, and in deepening the understanding, of the believers, in holding the community together, and in forming the nucleus of those administrative institutions which, two decades later, were to be formally inaugurated through the explicit provisions of 'Abdu'l-Bahá's Will and Testament.[1]

Unfortunately, the information available to Shoghi Effendi was as incomplete as it was for Mrs Cooper, and so the account reproduced above contains minor factual inaccuracies. Nonetheless, that passage from *God Passes By* is the touchstone, the lens through which the pilgrimage should be examined.

In truth, the pilgrimage is not easy to summarize because it involved a large number of people, occurred over a period of about five months, and included Ibrahim George Kheiralla, who would almost destroy the American Bahá'í community less than a year after the pilgrims returned to the United States. A primary goal in setting forth the story of the pilgrimage has been to provide a fuller comprehensible picture of it. In addition, this work seeks to correct the historical record as to its particulars. The passage of time, while erasing some traces, has made other information more accessible, especially relevant government documents now available through the Internet. Biographies of several of the principal members have been compiled. The context of the pilgrimage, that is, the first years of the Bahá'í Faith in the United States, has been ably researched and recounted, primarily by Dr Robert Stockman, in books, articles and websites. Undoubtedly, more details will come to light in the future, but the basic elements of the story can now be set forth accurately.

The story is not a mere recounting of history, it is a tale that inspires and instructs. Those privileged to take part in the first Western pilgrimage were, in the main, ordinary people with extraordinary spiritual insight. With almost no resources available to them, they took what they gained from their time in the Holy Land, established the Faith on a firm foundation in Europe and reestablished the American Bahá'í community on a proper, rock-solid foundation. Their achievements will remain an inspiration to all future generations.

The pilgrimage is also a cautionary tale. Not all those who took part in it made the most of the inestimable gift they were given. Bounties and blessings come with a cost; those who receive are tested. Not all lived up to the hopes and expectations generated by the pilgrimage. One can learn from this story the importance of perseverance in the face of tests, of gratitude and forgiveness and, above all, of the necessity of steadfastness.

Undoubtedly many readers will see themselves mirrored in particular members of the first pilgrimage. Other readers will relive their own experiences as pilgrims to the most Holy Places of the Bahá'í Faith through the journey of these spiritual forefathers. Each Bahá'í is part of a continuum of believers that reaches back into the past and stretches forth far into the future, called upon to carry out the tasks set before his own generation, while conscious of the contributions of those who came before.

Above all, the Hearst pilgrimage provides a window on – a brief glimpse of – 'Abdu'l-Bahá Himself and how patiently, lovingly He nurtured those from America and Europe whose religious background and ethnic culture were so different from the main body of Eastern believers at the time. The lessons he taught during that winter, the messages he conveyed through those early ambassadors of the peoples of the Americas and Europe, still resonate today, for he saw the end in the beginning. These were not simply fifteen pilgrims; they were the vanguard of waves of the whole of humanity which would lap at the shore of divine bounty and wisdom for ages to come. After the pilgrimage, the world would never be the same again.

Preface and Acknowledgements

Hand of the Cause of God 'Alí-Akbar Furútan, speaking informally to pilgrims one evening at the Haifa Pilgrim House during my first pilgrimage in 1981, talked about the many problems the hadíths had caused to Islam; that is, the oral sayings of the Prophet Muhammad, most of which could not be authenticated. This great servant and scholar of the Bahá'í Faith reiterated over and over to the listeners huddled about him that evening that in the Faith there are no hadíths; we rely upon the multitude of written Holy Texts, not on 'pilgrims' notes'. The memories of those who were privileged to meet a Central Figure of the Faith are instructive and inspiring, but should not be considered as providing definitive answers to theological issues.

Many of the teachings of 'Abdu'l-Bahá set forth in this book are pilgrims' notes; consequently they should not be given the same credence as the published works of the Master, even though some of the excerpts, especially those taken from *An Early Pilgrimage* by May Maxwell, are familiar because they are quoted frequently in Bahá'í literature. Therefore I have often given only the gist of many of the talks of 'Abdu'l-Bahá, rather than quoting exactly what a pilgrim recorded that He said. The reader should keep in mind that the quality of translation into English available to the first Western pilgrims was problematic. In a few cases, more than one pilgrim wrote about a particular talk of the Master. Where the two records do not agree, the one that sets forth the talk most clearly is used and noted as the source in the references.

Much of this work relies upon handwritten journals and letters, the majority of which have never been published previously and were never written with the idea that anyone other than immediate family members or intimate friends would ever see them. In fact, Harriet Thornburgh, at the close of most of her letters to Phoebe Hearst, requests that the letter be burned because she was afraid of the roving eyes of servants. (Fortunately, this wish wasn't carried out in every instance.) The only writing among the original sources that was ever prepared for publication was Ella Goodall's 1899 pilgrimage journal, which she arranged to have typed out and edited in the 1940s. I have used both the typed version of this journal as well as the original handwritten version. Many of these original documents are not always easily legible, especially when read as fuzzy photocopies or on microfilm. Further, many of the writers made use of common handwritten devices to maximize the use of limited space and to speed the time it took them to write, and so their abbreviations and jumbled prose make for slow reading.

The originals also include many misspellings and unclear punctuation.

Given these difficulties with some of the original documents and because this work is aimed at a general audience, the strict reproduction of extracts from letters and journals has been sacrificed for the ease of the reader. For example, marks that appear to be dashes are used by a number of the writers where modern scribes would use a full stop (period) or comma. When these dash marks appear the appropriate modern punctuation is used unless it is obviously supposed to be a dash. Furthermore, liberty has been taken in breaking some longer passages into paragraphs; this is noted where it occurs. Egregious spelling errors have been corrected. None of this editing has changed the meaning of the sources quoted and those who wish to study the originals will be able to gain ready access to them through the archives which hold them.

The letters sent to the early American believers by the Master were sometimes translated twice within the space of less than ten years as more competent translators became available. Nonetheless, most of these have yet to be translated with the care that modern translations of the Bahá'í Writings receive under the auspices of the Universal House of Justice. (In some cases, the original Tablet in Persian or Arabic has not been preserved.) These 'unofficial' or 'provisional' translations should be viewed as just that – interesting but not as authoritative as officially published translations. When known, the name of the translator and the date of the translation have been provided.

Ibrahim Kheiralla figures so prominently in the contemporaneous writings quoted that I use in most passages this old spelling rather than *Ibrahim Khayru'lláh*, the one prescribed by Shoghi Effendi for the Bahá'ís to use in transliterating Arabic and Persian words and names into western languages using the Roman alphabet. I have chosen to use the English spellings of Kheiralla and also of Anton Haddad; spellings they themselves used and which were used by those who knew them.

Etiquette in nineteenth-century middle- and upper-class America frowned upon the use of first names unless those using them were intimate friends or family members. If the person was a relative, the first name had to be preceded by the familial relationship such as Aunt Mary, Cousin Jane, and the like. The use of a first name when addressing a substantially older person was the ultimate *faux pas*, unless that person was a servant. Nonetheless, in writing this work, despite my strict upbringing in Olde Virginia manners, I have chosen to use first names for the main characters because I want twenty-first-century readers to be able to keep track of them as the story unfolds and to also feel a familiarity with them.

This book is truly a group project – I feel that I have only been the captain of a team. It is impossible to adequately express my gratitude for those who have so willingly and selflessly assisted in the production of this work. Time and again, I found that many people I have encountered, even if not directly involved, were enthralled by the topic, and their genuine enthusiasm and encouragement has been much appreciated; a number have provided me with new insights.

Roger Dahl, Archivist of the United States National Bahá'í Archives for many decades, is owed special thanks not only for his unfailing, prompt retrieval and conveyance of documents but especially for selflessly sharing his own research into the life of Robert Turner. No one is better equipped to be Robert Turner's biographer than Roger. I also appreciated the help of his assistant, Lewis Walker.

I wish to also extend a particular note of gratitude to Susan Thomas, Head of Resource Services at James Branch Cabell Library at Virginia Commonwealth University, to my sister, Nell Jewett Chenault, and to their staff at the Cabell Library for their assistance in providing access to the Phoebe Apperson Hearst Papers and for helping to locate other materials.

The staffs of the Bancroft Library at the University of California at Berkeley, especially Susan Snyder; of the Library at the University of Delaware; and of the Houghton Library at Harvard University were cheerfully helpful. Erin Chase at the Huntington Library assisted with photographs.

Heartfelt appreciation goes to Violette Nakhjavani and Nell Golden, co-literary executors of the estate of Amatu'l-Bahá Rúḥíyyih Khánum, for not only sharing some of the materials from the estate papers, especially the papers of May Bolles Maxwell, but for their love and encouragement. Mrs Nakhjavani was especially selfless in sharing information from her forthcoming book on the Maxwell family of Montreal as well as for offering valuable comments about my early draft.

Ali Nakhjavani's insights and guidance were invaluable. Ian Semple and Penelope Graham Walker kindly reviewed the entire manuscript, providing important suggestions and catching many mistakes both great and small. I am more grateful than I can express given the great demands on their time.

Mae Nieland provided provisional translations of documents in French, which was a great assistance.

The staff at the Bahá'í World Centre, especially in the Research Department, the Archives Department, and the Audio-visual Department were cheerfully helpful and enthusiastic about the project.

I wish to extend special thanks to Eileen Maddocks, to my husband Gary Hogenson and to our daughter Elizabeth Hogenson for their careful proofreading of the manuscript. They have saved me from embarrassment and improved the final product immensely. Other friends read early drafts and gave helpful comments, including our daughter Mary Hogenson, Kiser Barnes, Eric Mondschein, Carolyn Wade, Mae Nieland, Dicey Hall, and Ladan Doorandish-Vance.

My cherished long-time friend, Arlene Jennrich, proved me with housing and support during my time in Wilmette while conducting research at the National Bahá'í Archives. Kiser and Nancy Barnes, Peter and Janet Khan, Hooper Dunbar and Paul Lample have also provided encouragement and guidance. Suzanne Henck did research for me on Julia Pearson at Cornell University, for which I am very grateful. I am also grateful to Ethel Rosenberg's biographer Robert Weinberg and to the eminent historian Moojan Momen, for their willingness to consult with me about my research and to share their knowledge, especially of the early days of the Bahá'í Faith in the United Kingdom.

Tom Mann assisted with issues relating to some of the photographs, as did Ron Hillel of the Haifa Museums.

The grandsons of Helen Hillyer Brown, Anthony P. Brown and James Brown, graciously and enthusiastically assisted with providing a photograph of their grandmother and with stories from their memories of her, as well as granting permission to quote excerpts from her book *For My Children and Grandchildren*. Their friend Eric Holub of Hillside Press was also very helpful.

I'd like to express special thanks to Robert Stockman who first sparked my interest in this period of Bahá'í history more than two decades earlier when he pioneered the research into the origins of the Faith in America as a young graduate student. All future American Bahá'í historians will stand on his shoulders. His encouragement of this project and willingness to answer questions and to offer advice has been very helpful.

It is impossible to adequately convey my gratitude to the team at George Ronald: May Hofman, Erica Leith and Wendi Momen for their unwavering interest in this project from its early days and their competent, loving assistance in seeing it to completion. May's extensive knowledge and years of experience were invaluable, as was her patience as my editor. This book was in very good hands indeed!

This work would have never come about without the constant love and support of my husband, Gary Hogenson, who patiently listened as I again and again recounted the story to others, and who carefully checked my grammar and wording in the manuscript. His undying enthusiasm for the project has provided the underpinning that made this book a reality.

Kathryn Jewett Hogenson
Haifa, Israel
December 2009

One day in about 1896, 'Abdu'l-Bahá humorously said to Ḥájí Muḥammad-Ismá'il-i-Yazdí, 'I have had a dream and you must interpret it for me.'

The Ḥájí responded, 'But how am I to interpret my Master's dream?'

For the second time, in humour, 'Abdu'l-Bahá insisted that the Ḥájí was to give the meaning of His dream, but the Ḥájí again held his tongue.

Thereupon, the Master related:

Last night the Ancient Beauty appeared in my dream and said, 'I have guests that have never been here before. I want you to receive them most befittingly.' I related Bahá'u'lláh's command to the Greatest Holy Leaf, and together we went to the storage area and retrieved the set of fine china that the Khán's son (that is, the honoured Ḥájí Mírzá Muḥammad-'Alíy-i-Afnán) had sent from China, and got it ready.

After jesting with the Ḥájí some more, 'Abdu'l-Bahá explained the meaning of the dream: 'The standard of the Faith has been raised in America. A number in that country have embraced the Faith and will come here soon for pilgrimage to the Sacred Shrine of Bahá'u'lláh. These friends have never outwardly been here and will now come and share in this blessing.'

This was two years before the coming of the Americans.

– *Memoirs of Mírzá Habíbu'lláh Afnán*

CHAPTER 1

Expectations

Only the low steady pulse of the engine deep within the ship disturbed the stillness of the evening as the steamer, *S. S. Achilles*, pushed steadily northward up the coast of the Levant, that fabled sliver of land between Turkey and Egypt. The sea was calm and the voyage had been routine and uneventful. Five hours earlier the sun had disappeared beneath the sea of the western horizon sending most passengers and crew retreating from the decks to the warmth of cabins to escape the chill air of early winter, but a young American couple remained outside, too restless and excited to go below. Lua and Edward Getsinger strode up and down along the length of the deck, pausing occasionally by a railing at the side of the ship to peer into the blackness; searching for any sign of the coastline they were passing.

Hidden in the dark was the Holy Land, Palestine, biblical Israel, the place that the Getsingers had imagined ever since their childhood days in Sunday Bible School in the United States.[1] Children far away in America regarded the Holy Land as a magical place where God talked directly to man and performed miracles. The land which provided the setting for Bible stories was now thinly populated, desolate in many sections, little influenced by the technological advances of the age, thus there were few lights along the coast north of the small port of Jaffa to hint at even their location much less to illumine the reality of the Holy Land. So the Getsingers turned their gazes heavenward and marvelled at the dazzling sky. Edward, for one, would always remember the stars as he observed them that evening. There seemed to be countless more than in the night sky back home in Michigan. Jupiter in particular was especially brilliant on that clear night. Low on the horizon, its light was so intense that their fellow passengers mistook it for the beacon of a lighthouse as it cast a beam across the water.[2] Surely the unusual brightness of that planet was auspicious – a good omen leading them safely to a blessed spot as had the star of Bethlehem nineteen hundred years earlier. It was Thursday 8 December 1898, a night they would always remember because it marked the beginning of their time in the Holy Land, their spiritual home, the centre of their world. They were not typical travellers, not tourists or businessmen. They were pilgrims. Bahá'í pilgrims.

Edward Getsinger, with his short sandy-blonde hair, dark blue eyes and trimmed beard, was not a very big man at five and a half feet tall.[3] He considered himself a scientist despite his lack of academic credentials; and so for many years he had eked out a barely adequate living giving lectures on scientific subjects. The stars and planets that filled him with awe that evening had fascinated him ever since he was a boy.[4] At the age of 32 he, like most Americans of his day, was inexperienced at travelling outside his native land, which only added to his excitement. By his side was his petite, winsome wife Lua, with dancing blue eyes and a dimpled chin, her soft brown hair swept up onto the top of her head – pleasing to look at if not beautiful. She was almost six years Edward's junior[5] and even less experienced at travel than her husband. They had been married for barely more than a year – and what a year it had been. Their conversion to a new religion had radically changed their lives and set them on a new course that was now taking them to the remote section of the Syrian province of the Ottoman Empire – the Holy Land.

At about 10 p.m. the long, unbroken ridge of Mount Carmel began to loom visibly along the starboard side of the ship where it abruptly broke the cascade of stars, creating the illusion of a giant shadow. The mount thrust into the Mediterranean forming the lower tip of the half-moon bay where the ship would soon anchor. Activity on deck picked up as the crew began to prepare for the next port-of-call, Haifa. Myriad thoughts flooded the minds of the Getsingers as they anxiously peered into the darkness searching for the first view of their final destination – anticipation, fear, hopes, memories, practical anxieties, and fleeting images of the others who longed to be with them at that moment, but could not. They must have thought as well of the eleven other believers back in the United States and Europe who were anxiously awaiting news from them – to learn that the Getsingers had arrived safely and whether or not they too would soon be able to make the same pilgrimage. Lua and Edward were the fortunate ones, the first of their countrymen privileged to arrive at the place many others yearned to attain.

Almost three months earlier the Getsingers had left California by train. They had crossed the North American continent and then the Atlantic Ocean in the company of a few other members of their group. After a sojourn in Paris they had left their fellow pilgrims behind and proceeded south overland to Naples, Italy, and from there to Egypt by sea. The previous day they had boarded the *Achilles* at Port Said for the last lengthy leg of their trip. The beauty of the day just ended had added to their happiness as they approached their objective. However, this brief description of the previous three months does not adequately depict their travels. In reality, they had been on this journey all their lives, and they anticipated, indeed hoped, with every inner strength they could muster, that they were about to fulfil their deepest desires. They would not be disappointed.

Religious pilgrims like the Getsingers had been making long, treacherous journeys to the western edge of Asia for millennia. That strategic crossroads joining three continents had long held sway for millions of devout believers as the spot where they could most closely commune with their Creator. It was the nest of the prophets, the setting of many of the greatest dramas of three of the dominant religions of mankind. Jews came to worship at the site of their ancient temple in Jerusalem. Christians sought to walk in the footsteps of Jesus and to pray at the Church of the Holy Sepulchre in Jerusalem, the holiest spot of Christendom. Muslims, for whom pilgrimage was one of the five pillars of their Faith, travelled to worship at the Dome of the Rock in Jerusalem, the third most sacred place in the Islamic world.[6] Lua and Edward would have empathized with the spiritual yearnings that drew countless pilgrims from a variety of creeds to the hallowed places of the Holy Land throughout the ages, although they themselves represented something new. The Getsingers were Bahá'ís, followers of the latest of God's messengers, and their goal was not ancient Jerusalem of Mount Zion but the New Jerusalem of Mount Carmel. They had endured the hardships of lengthy travel not just to worship at the new Qiblih at Bahjí, though that would have been reason enough, but also to seek spiritual enlightenment from the duly appointed successor of the one whom they believed to be the source of all knowledge, of Bahá'u'lláh, God's messenger for the new age.

Their trip had been arranged by Thomas Cook & Son, the English travel agency established in the 1840s which pioneered the leisure travel business. From 1868 on, the Cook agency organized the visits of European and American Christian pilgrims to the Holy Land, a special interest of Thomas Cook who was himself a devout Baptist. Haifa was one of the ports it used for its clients because it provided easy access to nearby Nazareth, where Jesus grew up, and to other regional sites of the Galilee favoured by the long-ago presence of Jesus.[7] Haifa served merely as a way station, not as a point of interest. The Getsingers, however, were not the usual Cook clients. They would travel only to the Haifa Bay area, forgoing the Galilee, Jerusalem and the itinerary of the average American tourist or pilgrim. Their true purpose was a closely guarded secret.

The ship changed course from due north and headed toward the northeast as it rounded the point of the mountain and entered Haifa Bay, the best natural port along the eastern Mediterranean. The ship first slipped past the sleeping German colony and then the small city of Haifa, both nestled along the southern shore; but there were very few lights visible on land to mark those settlements. Candles and lamp oil were too expensive to be used at such an hour by farmers and tradesmen, so most residents continued the age-old habit of rising and retiring with the sun. The ship at last dropped anchor directly in front of the eastern suburb of the city, between the mouth of the Kishon River and Haifa's eastern wall, the usual landing area for many decades. The deck was transformed from the solitary refuge it had been an hour earlier to a hectic centre of commotion as orders were shouted in both Arabic and Turkish. There were practical concerns to attend to. Where was their luggage? Were their travel papers in hand? Skiffs, each commanded by a handful of oarsmen, rowed out to retrieve the passengers and cargo.[8]

Guided by the soft light from small lamps and flickering torches, the Getsingers gingerly made their way down a precarious rope ladder into a bobbing boat, Lua gathering her full skirts and Edward catching his wife and seating her safely. Clutching their belongings, they huddled next to each other in the little boat as the oarsmen rhythmically rowed toward the modest wooden pier that jutted out into the sea just beyond the breakers. Haifa still lacked proper port facilities; those wouldn't be built until ten years in the future. Only six weeks earlier, the city had been honoured by a brief visit from another Thomas Cook client, Kaiser Wilhelm II of Germany, when he passed through Haifa on his way to Jerusalem as a Christian pilgrim. The city had been spiffed up in preparation for the royal visitors, including the construction of a new short pier outside of town at the end of the main street of the German colony.[9] Nonetheless, ordinary travellers such as the Getsingers still had to come ashore at the back of the bay near the old customs house.

There remained one final potential hurdle to traverse that evening – gaining the approval of local Ottoman border officials to enter the territory. Even though the Getsingers had obtained the necessary travel documents in Egypt, it was always possible that some minor potentate might cause them trouble and they would be refused admittance into the Holy Land. Ottoman officials, especially in remote provinces like Syria, were notorious for their demands for *baksheesh* – payment for services rendered as the locals saw it, or bribery as Westerners viewed it.[10] The Getsingers' most critical concern was not to reveal the real reason for their visit, lest they jeopardize the safety of their Host or their access to Him. They entered the customs house and nervously awaited their turn to have their papers and baggage examined. Fortunately, that inspection passed without incident.

As they left the customs house, the Getsingers were relieved to find that they were indeed expected. The one who had taught them about the Bahá'í Faith in Chicago, Ibrahim George Kheiralla, was waiting for them along with two or three unfamiliar gentlemen whom, judging by their attire, they immediately surmised to be Persians. They had met Persian Bahá'ís in Egypt the day before and recognized the long, flowing outer cloak, called an *'abá*, and the tall headdress kept in place by yards of wound cloth, called a *táj*, that set them apart from the Arabs and Turks. The Turks in particular were easy to spot with their fezzes, like the one worn by their teacher. Ibrahim Kheiralla, as a native of a small village near Beirut, the next port city of any consequence north of Haifa, was quite at home that night. The Getsingers smiled as they were introduced to the small welcoming party. They knew no Persian or Arabic and their local hosts spoke no English, but words were not necessary to convey the excitement and warmth they each felt at this their first meeting. The group made its way up the beach past the wharf and warehouses, Kheiralla serving as translator, as the Persian friends led the way into the sleeping town.

It was about 10:30 in the evening when they disembarked from the *Achilles*. Despite the lateness of the hour and the rigours of the just completed journey, their hosts were not ready to simply deposit the Getsingers at their hotel and be off to bed. The Getsingers were unaware just how avidly their fellow believers in Haifa had anticipated their arrival. For the past several years the small group of Bahá'ís resident in the Holy Land had heard rumours that their precious Faith had spread to the Great Republic of the West, the United States.[11] But who could really believe such a thing in the Middle East where wild rumours had their purposes? Now, by the grace of God, the first of the Western believers had actually come, come to pray at the Holiest of Shrines and to visit the Master. What a miracle! What a cause for rejoicing! These friends all understood the dangerous consequences if the true purpose of the Getsingers' visit became known to the enemies of their Faith, and a number of them lurked about Haifa. The Bahá'ís knew only too well from numerous painful experiences that it was impossible to be certain who could be trusted. Nevertheless, the safe arrival of the first Americans was so important, so historic, such cause for celebration, that the Haifa Bahá'ís could not wait to see them. Their yearnings to witness this red-letter event overrode their usual caution, so it had been stealthily arranged that Lua and Edward would first be taken to a particular coffee house near the port where the local believers could at least get a glimpse of the Americans. Who would suspect friends simply enjoying a late cup of tea at their favourite gathering place?

At the time Haifa was walled on three sides facing the land, with the remaining side along the sea kept open. The small group entered the densely built little city through either the eastern gate near the customs house or from the beach. Most of the businesses and government offices were situated along the main street, Jaffa Road, which ran close by and parallel to the water between the 'Akká Gate on the eastern wall and Jaffa Gate on the western wall. The land rose quickly to meet the base of Mount Carmel and so the houses were jumbled close together with the upper ones seeming to be almost on top of the others. The population of about 10,000 was now spilling out of the walls: a Muslim suburb was expanding toward the east and a Christian suburb was spreading toward the west. The city had both minarets topped with crescent moons and modest cupolas adorned with crosses with no one type of house of worship dominating its skyline because the numbers of Christians and Muslims were almost equal. The business district in the centre of the city provided a subtle buffer between the neighbourhoods of the two religious communities. The city also had a small but growing population of Jews who were beginning to create their own neighbourhood up the slopes of the mountain just outside the southwestern city wall.[12]

As the Getsingers were led through narrow, unpaved streets, they could barely discern any of the features of Haifa in the darkness. In only a few minutes they arrived at the unimposing coffee house owned by a Bahá'í and located near the beach. The lamplight inside was so dim that at first they could not see, until their eyes adjusted, that there were people already seated in the establishment. Coffee or tea houses were the pubs of the Middle East, providing not only light refreshments but also a public gathering place for men as a welcome alternative to overcrowded households. Customers could while away hours squatting on low stools or sitting cross-legged on mats on the floor, sipping the thick bitter black coffee for which the region was famous or puffing on tobacco through elaborately decorated water pipes. Tea was also available in tiny handle-less glasses and always served with plentiful cubes of sugar. Furthermore, the coffee house served as a place of entertainment where the patrons often listened as storytellers and poets recounted the mythical heroic tales of the region, enjoyed music, and gambled – usually playing the favourite game of the area, backgammon.[13]

That evening tea was ordered for the Getsingers, the perfect antidote to the cool night air. They tried to look inconspicuous, as did all those who were there to catch a glimpse of the Americans. Lua especially must have been a rare sight to the patrons because women from good families seldom visited coffee houses, or for that matter, openly socialized with men. Western women in the 1890s were much freer in their associations than their Arab sisters and, as 'unmannered foreigners', could get by with behaviour frowned upon by local custom, though there were limits. In the future, Lua would come to learn Middle Eastern rules of etiquette for her sex through close tutoring and painful experience to the point where she could easily be mistaken for a native Christian woman.[14]

The awkward silence was broken when an elderly Persian man rose from his seat, saluted the Getsingers, and then with the unaffected dignity born of high breeding approached the couple and welcomed them warmly in a language they did not understand but which nonetheless resonated deep within their souls. At that moment Lua and Edward had no clue as to the identity of the greeter, but all the other Bahá'ís present understood what an honour it was for the Americans to be officially received on behalf of their host by Mírzá Muḥammad-Qulí. An unimposing, quiet man in his sixties with a long graying beard, this eminent believer had suffered much because of his unwavering devotion to the Faith. He was the younger half-brother of Bahá'u'lláh, the uncle of the One the Getsingers had come to meet and His most important surviving adult male relative. Though of aristocratic birth and raised with the advantages of wealth, Mírzá Muḥammad-Qulí had never chafed under the hardship and poverty that became his lot in the path of service to Bahá'u'lláh. He had been the one to pitch the tents during the trying march of the band of Bahá'í exiles as they were removed under military escort from Baghdad to Istanbul. It was he who had served the tea and performed the menial tasks of the household that made the hardships of imprisonment easier for his companions to bear.[15] Edward Getsinger was startled once he was able to get a better look at Mírzá Muḥammad-Qulí in the low light. He recognized that elderly gentleman as the very man he had seen in a vision several years earlier, the vision that had led him to the Bahá'í Faith. Lua would later write that never before had she beheld a face more full of love and kindness. As a man of few words, Mírzá Muḥammad-Qulí then took his leave, saying that he must depart very early the next morning for the city on the other side of the bay, 'Akká,[16] to report their safe arrival to his Nephew.

As the honoured guests returned to sipping their hot tea, Ibrahim Kheiralla began to speak in hushed tones, filling them in on much of what had transpired since he had left them and the other Western pilgrims in Paris. A burly fellow with a handle-bar moustache, he was the only one among the believers who really looked as though he belonged in an Arab coffee house that evening, the others were predominantly foreigners. Aged 49, he had just spent seven years in the United States where he had converted a number of people to his religion, all the while honing his English. He had become the father figure of the American Bahá'ís – a role he promoted and relished. The Getsingers were two of his best students, especially Lua, who had not only given her whole heart to the Bahá'í Faith but who also possessed an innate ability to draw others to it. Both Lua and Edward had helped him to rapidly expand the number of American adherents and had even established new communities of believers, such was their fervour to spread the infant Faith. Because he was a native of the Levant, he had been sent ahead of the first group of Western Bahá'í pilgrims to prepare the way for them. Permission to come to the Holy

Land had been given contingent upon the Americans not arriving together as one large group, in order not to draw the attention of the enemies of the Faith and raise the suspicions of Ottoman officials. So that December evening their fellow pilgrims were either en route to Cairo or impatiently marking time in France or New York City.

When Kheiralla had arrived in the Haifa Bay area almost a month before, he was overwhelmed by the honours and love bestowed upon him for his role in spreading the Faith to the West. He could never adequately articulate all that had happened, nor did he wish to disclose everything to the Americans. After his years of living and travelling in the West, the pilgrimage was also a homecoming for Ibrahim Kheiralla. He had been reunited with his two daughters in Cairo, and one of them had accompanied him to Haifa. Lua and Edward had met the other daughter in Egypt when they changed ships. Soon the Getsingers would see for themselves all of the wonders of which he spoke.

At last the hotel manager arrived to escort the Getsingers by lamplight to his establishment; but unable to tear themselves away from the Americans, Kheiralla and several others accompanied them on the walk to their accommodations. It was well past midnight when these last stragglers said their goodnights and allowed the Getsingers to settle into their room. Everyone present knew that they had been privileged to be part of something monumental; an event that would be remembered well into the future, especially the Getsingers who were exhilarated by all they had experienced. They assumed that surely they would meet the One they had come so far to see the very next morning. Sleep was out of the question.

The young couple arose and dressed at dawn to be ready for the moment they were summoned, but the hours dragged on without any word from across the bay.

In the daylight Lua and Edward could finally survey their new surroundings and discovered that they were situated in one of the loveliest spots imaginable. Low mountains provided an enchanting backdrop for the dramatic sweep of the bay. In the clear air of early December, the blue-gray hills of the Galilee toward the north and east were a reminder of the venerable history of the area, especially its associations with the early years of Jesus. That thought alone – that they were literally walking in the footsteps of Christ – would have thrilled them. If the day was particularly clear, they would have spied at the back of the mountain range to the north the majestic form of Mount Hermon capped with early snows, which would have also been visible to the residents of Damascus on its other side. Distances in the Levant were slight compared to what they were accustomed to in the United States. Haifa was located in the open, rolling meadows and deep *wadis* that separated Mount Carmel from the sea. The countryside was barren, with large patches of rock and scrub broken only by the occasional palm tree or olive grove. The starkness of the terrain only added to its elegant loveliness. Close to the shore were wide fields of rich dark-brown soil newly planted with grain, with rows of bright green shoots already visible. Though it was the beginning of winter, the two travellers from America could have easily confused the season with early spring, for winter in the Holy Land marked the coming of rains that revived the land parched by six months of uninterrupted heat and drought. Purple and pink crocuses and wild pale yellow narcissus were blooming on the hillsides, bringing patches of colour and life back to the landscape which only weeks before had been sun-baked a wilted brown. On the steep slopes in the distance they could probably see flocks of sheep and goats picking their way through scrub and feasting on the fresh emerald growth of newly sprouted grass, tended by shepherds whose appearance was unchanged from that of their distant ancestors. Assuredly, it must have seemed a sight straight out of the Bible.

Haifa, a relatively new city given the millennial standards of the Levant, had a chequered past. The walled town had been entirely rebuilt in the middle of the eighteenth century to provide an alternative to the port of the ancient city of 'Akká, its sister across the bay, whose harbour had silted up making it inaccessible to the larger steamships of the modern age. Before that time, the small settlement on the southern shore of Haifa Bay had been a refuge for pirates and brigands who preyed on ships that made the mistake of anchoring on that deserted shore. The southeastern coastline had also been a favourite spot for smugglers who wished to avoid the customs officials stationed in 'Akká, earning Haifa the unflattering nickname 'Little Malta'. During the 1760s the tiny settlement had been forcibly removed by its Ottoman overlords to its current site about two miles to the east just outside the swamps of the Kishon River delta, and below the remains of a small decaying castle perched on a small knoll. Despite its new location and confinement within narrow stone walls, Haifa remained untamed and dangerous. One did not casually venture out at night, because of the indiscriminate firing of guns, usually just to make a ruckus.

During its first decades, new Haifa was a backwater of a town. But as its port increased in importance to the grain and cotton merchants who brought their goods from the interior of the country through the Jezreel valley and the pass that opened onto the plains of 'Akká, the town began to grow rapidly, magnifying economic opportunities for ambitious entrepreneurs. The city started attracting immigrants from the hinterland and surrounding countries and thereby became less provincial. The regional seat of government was transferred from 'Akká to Haifa in the 1880s. For centuries the region had been under the rule of the Ottoman Turks and their proxies. Now, in the waning days of that all-but-dead empire, the decay of political decline was evident everywhere, in the lack of infrastructure and other government services and in the general corruption and lawlessness, despite Haifa's increasingly robust economy. Within a few short years the building of a spur of the Hijaz railway to Haifa and the erection of new port facilities would transform the city into a booming metropolis and would change the ethnic and religious mix of its population.[17] Simultaneous with the emergence of Haifa, the Ottoman Empire would breathe its last breath, following the overthrow of the Sultan in 1907 and the breakup of its remnants at the conclusion of World War I. The Getsingers arrived just in time to observe the fleeting last moments of an ancient way of life that was soon to vanish.

Haifa was not the only community on the southern shore of the bay. Situated outside of Haifa, about a mile and a half to the west, was a small colony of German Christians who called themselves the Temple Society, or 'Templers'. Their tidy, plastered homes with gabled, orange-tiled roofs had been constructed in straight rows with ample space left between, making the orderly German community easily distinguishable from the hodgepodge of tightly connected Arab-style stone buildings with flat roofs in Haifa. During the late 1860s and early 70s, close in time to the arrival of Bahá'u'lláh, these Templers had arrived at the gently sloping plain stretching from Mount Carmel to the sea, and there recreated a German farming village at the foot of the mountain. They were a devout Protestant sect that believed, based upon close study of scripture, that the return of Christ was imminent and that they would find Him near Mount Carmel. They had come to wait for Him, bringing not only their theology but their German habits of industry and knowledge of agriculture, medicine, new technologies and commerce. By the time the Getsingers arrived thirty years later, the Templers had established a prosperous agricultural community that was diversifying by establishing other businesses such as road building. It would be fair to say that these Germans had raised the general standard of living of the region.[18] An English writer who took up residence among the Templers wrote, 'Thanks to the efforts of the [German] colonists, it [the Templer settlement] has become an oasis of civilization in the wilderness of Oriental barbarism, where the invalid in search of health, or the tourist on the lookout for a comfortable resting-place on his travels, will find good accommodations, and all the necessaries, if not the luxuries, of civilized life.'[19]

The year 1898 had already been a banner year for that German community of about 700 souls, because in October it had had the honour of hosting Kaiser Wilhelm II when he arrived in the Holy Land. With much fanfare and ceremony, the Kaiser had disembarked from his ship not at the eastern end of Haifa but at the German colony itself at the beginning of the main street of their community, which at that time started at the beach.[20]

Because Edward Getsinger was the son of German parents who had separately emigrated to the United States before they met and married, it would have been easy for locals to assume that he had come to Haifa because of the Templers. (In fact, Edward's father was from Württemberg, the same state in Southern Germany where the Temple Society was founded and headquartered.) The hotel where he and Lua were staying at the outset of their time in the Holy Land was probably situated in or near the German Colony.[21] They would spend much time in that German community during the coming months and learn of its associations with Bahá'u'lláh.

Towering over both Haifa and the German Colony was Mount Carmel, whose apt name means 'Vineyard of the Lord'. Though hardly more than a steep limestone hill by the standards of those who, like the Getsingers, were familiar with the much higher Rocky Mountains of the American West, its association with stories of the Old Testament enveloped its desolate, rocky slopes with the haze of divine mystery and promise. It was on that very mountain that the prophet Elijah sojourned after he had successfully challenged the priests of Baal to determine whose was the One True God. According to tradition, a cave at the lower northwest point of the mountain had not only sheltered Elijah but had served the Greeks as a shrine to Adonis.[22] The Getsingers could observe a single long pathway carved into the side of the mountain rising at a steep angle and aimed at the promontory where Mount Carmel jutted into the Mediterranean Sea. At the top of the trail was the fortress-like stone monastery of the Carmelite order where monks worshipped and waited expectantly for the return of the Messiah. Ironically, Bahá'u'lláh visited that monastery during the last year of his life, but the monks did not recognize that He was the one whose advent they were earnestly praying to hasten. During the coming months the Getsingers would come to appreciate that that holy mountain held great significance for Bahá'ís, as well as for Christians and Jews.

Undoubtedly, as Lua and Edward ventured forth from their hotel to explore, they strained their eyes to take in any visible details of the small town of 'Akká at the edge of the bay on the opposite shore. 'Akká was the home of 'Abdu'l-Bahá, the son of Bahá'u'lláh, and their journey's end. Perhaps they observed caravans of camels and donkeys laden with sacks of grain or cotton making their way along the beach, which served as the highway between the two ports. Though only about nine miles by land, the distance was more easily traversed along the shoreline than by way of the poorly maintained roads.

They must have longed to follow that beach to the distant white city, but they had to wait to be summoned.

As morning became midday, the chanting of muezzins issuing the call to prayer from the minarets of the Haifa mosques must have entranced the Getsingers, especially Lua, who loved to sing. The high-pitched, loud, melodic chanting that echoed through the *wadis* was unlike any sound they had heard before, quite different from the tolling of church bells. It was a Friday, the Muslim day of rest, and so all Muslim-owned shops were closed.[23] Lua and Edward might have seen groups of the faithful from among that community scurrying toward the mosques for the Friday midday services as noon approached; while in the Christian part of town business continued as usual. Over time the Getsingers would adapt to these rhythms of the Levant.

Noon became afternoon and the sun was moving close to the water, soon to disappear into the sea, though the mountain blocked the view of the sunset on the Haifa side of the bay. Their first day in the Holy Land was drawing to a close and still no word had come. To be so near to the One they sought, to be able to see where He lived but yet not be allowed to go that last short distance, was indeed slow torture. No doubt, they did not dare stray far from the hotel lest they miss any message from their Lord. Nightfall came and still there was no word.

Nevertheless, they had received an invitation from one of the local believers, Ḥusayn Effendi Tabrízí, to come to his home for dinner that evening. This devoted, trustworthy gentleman, the son-in-law of Mírzá Muḥammad-Qulí, had been residing in Haifa for some years in order to assist the Bahá'í pilgrims passing through that city.[24] As soon as the Getsingers arrived at his home he imparted the good news they had been waiting for. He had received word from the Master that they were to go to Him the next morning and 'that His heart longed to see the first American pilgrims'. That evening the relieved Getsingers were overwhelmed by the kind hospitality of their host and hostess, who spared no effort to entertain them and who constantly told their special guests that they should consider their home to be the Getsingers'. After a delightful visit, Lua and Edward returned to their hotel radiant and full of great expectations. They sat together late into the night recounting their many blessings.

Again, sleep was impossible.

The approach to Haifa from the Mediterranean Sea, with the German Colony in the foreground. The dock constructed for the visit of Kaiser Wilhelm II in August 1898 is visible. Photograph by Edward Getsinger

Disembarking in Haifa Bay at the end of the 19th century

The dock at Haifa, photograph by Edward Getsinger during the first pilgrimage. It was apparently unchanged since the time of Bahá'u'lláh

Courtesy of Dr Y. Rimon

Street scene in Haifa, 1912. Photograph by Leo Kahan

Tea house in Haifa, possibly the one frequented by the Bahá'ís. Photograph by Edward Getsinger

A wedding party approaching down a Haifa street

The German Colony, viewed from Mt. Carmel. Photograph by Edward Getsinger

Two Templer buildings in the German colony. The larger house was visited by Bahá'u'lláh in 1891. The foundations of the Shrine of the Báb can be seen halfway up the mountain. Photograph by Edward Getsinger

The German Colony, end of the 19th century. Photograph by Alice Oliphant

Looking back at Haifa from the beach

'Akká, approaching from Haifa by way of the beach

The harbour of 'Akká, viewed from the Crusader tower in the water

Looking across the city of 'Akká toward Mt. Carmel

CHAPTER 2

A Seed Sprouts in America

What went through Lua's mind that interminable Friday in Haifa as she and Edward impatiently fidgeted and paced while awaiting the summons to finally meet her Lord face to face? Did she think back to all that she had experienced since the fateful day in 1893 when she first became aware of the name Bahá'u'lláh? The story of her devotion to the newest of the world's great religions spans almost the entire period of the establishment of the Faith in the West. How appropriate then that the one who would attain the honour of being named 'Mother Teacher of the West' herself first inhaled the faint fragrances of the new blossom just as it began to open. The remarkable story of how the Getsingers came to be in the Holy Land cannot be told without going back in time to the arrival of the Bahá'í Faith in the Americas. It is the tale of how the nascent Faith was transformed from what was ostensibly an obscure Middle Eastern sect to a dynamic world religion.

It would be difficult to find a major religion more organized and systematic in its approach to expansion than the Bahá'í Faith; so the serendipitous manner in which it was first introduced to North America was decidedly uncharacteristic. It was as if the breath of God gently blew a seed across the ocean, where it landed in the fertile heartland of a continent and sprouted unnoticed and untended. During the twentieth century, the Bahá'í Faith would be established in almost every country and territory, usually through deliberate, sacrificial action undertaken in response to guidance from the Head of the Faith, but not so in the United States in the beginning. The American Bahá'í community was initially established through seemingly insignificant actions, almost as if brought about by chance, and carried forward by the most unlikely of people.

The first Bahá'í to come to the United States had embraced the Cause only weeks before his arrival; consequently, he had very little accurate knowledge of his new faith, and so he proved to be too timid to openly introduce it to others during his first stay. This traveller, whom historians of the future will honour as the first Bahá'í to set foot in the New World, was Anton Haddad,[1] an unassuming businessman and professional translator, slight of build, with an olive complexion, dark hair and eyes, and a moustache. He was born in a small village near Beirut, Lebanon,[2] where he was raised as an Orthodox Christian. He acquired a working knowledge of English through a solid education, probably provided by Western Protestant Christian missionaries who established a number of schools in Lebanon during the nineteenth century. The tottering Ottoman Empire offered few opportunities for advancement based solely on merit, and so, like many of his fellow Lebanese Christians, he migrated from coastal Syria first to Egypt and then, a few years later, on to New York City in search of opportunities to make his fortune. By all accounts, he was a man of upright character with a wife and two young children, whom he had to regretfully leave behind near Beirut until his finances allowed him to send for them. At approximately the age of 30 he arrived in New York in late June of 1892. He initially hoped to earn his way by selling inventions concocted by his older business partner, good friend and fellow-countryman, Ibrahim George Kheiralla, the one who had introduced him to the Bahá'í Faith. Both would have a profound influence upon the development of the Faith in the West, one for good and the other, well, it would be true to say that his motives were primarily self-centred.[3]

Ibrahim Kheiralla was born on 11 November 1849 in the village of Bhamdoun on Mount Lebanon near Beirut and not far from Haddad's home village, 'Ayn Zhaltá. While still an infant he lost his father and was raised by his widowed mother. His family had been members of the Orthodox Melkite Christian Church of Antioch for generations, but his mother chose instead for him to be educated primarily in schools run by western Protestants. He had had the good fortune to receive a well-grounded schooling from his earliest years, including a university education at the newly established Syrian Protestant College[4] in Beirut; in fact, he was a member of its first graduating class. This school, established by American Presbyterian missionaries, had as its primary mission the betterment of the Arab world through education. But beneath that noble purpose lurked the natural desire to convert Arabs, even those who were already Christians, to the Protestant branch of Christianity. Because Kheiralla had been educated from his childhood primarily in Protestant schools, he had come to identify with that Christian theology, rather than with the Orthodox teachings of his family. However, the Syrian Presbyterian College was unique among educational institutions established by Westerners in the region, because from its earliest years it did not disdain the local Arab culture and heritage but in fact promoted the use of the Arabic language. Because of this liberal approach and philosophy, many of the college's students became leading proponents of Arab nationalism. Nonetheless, practical realities required that much of the instruction be conducted in English.[5] This training would provide Kheiralla with two important tools when later teaching the Bahá'í Faith in the United States: fluency in English and an intimate understanding of American Protestant Christian ideology and culture. During the time he attended the college, it offered only two tracks of study, medical training or a more general 'literary' one, that is, a liberal arts education. Kheiralla chose the latter.[6]

Jobs for English-speakers were more abundant in Egypt than in Beirut, because during the last years of the nineteenth century Egypt was a British colony in every respect except in name,[7] so like many of those educated in mission schools of the Levant, Ibrahim Kheiralla and Anton Haddad migrated to Cairo seeking work and it was there that they met for the first time – drawn to each other by their shared culture from their home villages on Mount Lebanon. Haddad worked for many years as a translator for the Egyptian government. Kheiralla first found employment as a teacher and then tried his hand at business. He worked in both the cotton and sugar industries, and became prosperous enough to own businesses and a large tract of land. It was during this time that he first married and established a family. After his wife died in childbirth, leaving him with two young daughters and a son to raise alone, he remarried. The second marriage was unsuccessful and so, following a divorce, he ventured into marriage a third time.[8] His run of bad luck did not end with his family life; he lost his wealth through a lawsuit. Perhaps because of these misfortunes, Kheiralla began a spiritual quest that initially focused upon the occult, especially magic. He was convinced that he possessed special powers and wanted to learn to enhance them. This search led to a man who told him that he was looking in the wrong places, that rather than pursue 'black' magic, he should pursue 'white' magic, and he directed Kheiralla toward a person who could help. That man was 'Abdu'l-Karím-i-Ṭihrání, a Persian businessman who was also one of the leaders of the small Egyptian Bahá'í community. It took some effort on Kheiralla's part to gain access to 'Abdu'l-Karím and to get him to agree to speak to him of spiritual truths, because the Egyptian Bahá'ís were ever cautious, wary lest their group be infiltrated by one who meant them harm. The first thing 'Abdu'l-Karím told Kheiralla was to burn all his books about magic. Only then would he be willing to teach him.[9] This was probably in 1889. For the next two years Kheiralla would be an ardent student, coming to him daily for lessons on the teachings and history of the Bahá'í Faith.[10]

During the late 1880s the tiny Cairo Bahá'í community was composed almost exclusively of Persians who wished to be geographically close to the centre of their Faith, because Bahá'ís had to receive special permission from Bahá'u'lláh or 'Abdu'l-Bahá to reside in or near 'Akká. This nearby community of Egypt provided essential services to Bahá'u'lláh, and later the Master, such as purchasing necessary supplies, assisting pilgrims on their way to and from the Holy Land, and channelling sensitive communications away from the watchful eyes and machinations of the many enemies of the Faith in the postal and telegraph offices in the Levant. Like the Bahá'ís of Cairo, Kheiralla was also a stranger far from home and so was befriended by this group of expatriates.

Kheiralla was an eager student, but there was a problem – language. 'Abdu'l-Karím knew very little Arabic and Kheiralla knew no Persian. The common language was English, which neither knew in depth. Like many migrants, the believers in Cairo spoke their native tongue among themselves and learned only the little Arabic that was necessary to get by in the wider community. A few spoke French, which would prove useful when Western believers began to arrive in Cairo. At the time, 'Abdu'l-Karím's limited knowledge of English was apparently unique among the friends in Egypt. Even published works were of little help to Kheiralla's investigations, because few of the massive volumes of Writings of the Báb, Bahá'u'lláh, and 'Abdu'l-Bahá had been printed, and those scant few books were primarily in Persian. So despite his many hours with his teacher, Kheiralla's understanding of Bahá'í principles never advanced beyond a superficial level. Another problem that would become apparent as Kheiralla began to spread the teachings of the Faith himself was that his own teacher was a convert from Islam and had many incorrect understandings of the Faith which he then passed on to his student, including the erroneous belief that the Bahá'í Faith accepted reincarnation.[11]

The most beneficial aspect of the education Kheiralla obtained from the Cairo friends was the stories.[12] He would listen attentively, with his teacher providing broken-English translations, as the Persian friends sat together either sipping sweet tea or bitter, thick coffee from small ceramic cups and passed the time recounting tales from the early years of their Faith. These surely touched his heart and inspired him. Undoubtedly they included heart-wrenching stories of persecution and martyrdoms that had taken place in their native land of Persia, the cradle of the Faith. It must have been instilled into Kheiralla that he should always exercise caution; no one could readily detect who was a spy or who among the friends would be willing to betray his fellow believers. This last lesson would never be forgotten, even in the land of religious freedom, the United States.

In 1890, after about two years of study, Ibrahim Kheiralla formally converted to the Bahá'í Faith. Writing years later about his investigation and acceptance, he recounted:

> ['Abdu'l-Karím] delivered to me the message of this great truth and proved it from a Mohammedan standpoint, which is not sufficient to convince

> one grounded as I was in Christian doctrine and belief. His earnestness, however, commanded my deepest attention and respect. After receiving from him the announcement of the Manifestation of God, I commenced studying the question from a scientific and biblical standpoint, at the same time praying fervently to God for enlightenment and guidance to the truth.
>
> My prayers were answered and my researches proved fruitful, for I discovered that all Spiritual truths are reasonable and capable of clearer demonstration than material facts.[13]

There being no formal method of enrolment, Kheiralla wrote directly to Bahá'u'lláh, as was the custom at the time, stating his acceptance of the Faith, and received a letter (Tablet) from Him in reply. Though no authoritative copy of that Tablet exists, in the translation of it published later by Kheiralla, Bahá'u'lláh made a prophetic promise that '. . . Verily We heard your supplications, and granted them to you, and remembered you with such remembrance whereby the *hearts will be attracted to you . . .*'[14]

During these same years Kheiralla developed his close friendship with the young Anton Haddad and introduced him to the Bahá'ís. In the beginning, Kheiralla maintained the secrecy of the Faith by only teasing his friend with hints of what he was learning. He let Haddad know that the teachings had to be kept in the strictest confidence and only divulged to those sincere seekers who were first thoroughly vetted. This, not surprisingly, piqued Haddad's curiosity and he begged to be allowed to become part of the exclusive group. After some time passed, he was finally taken to meet 'Abdu'l-Karím. As soon as they met, 'Abdu'l-Karím remarked to Kheiralla, 'He looks to me to be like unto a piece of pure gold that only needs to be cleaned and polished.'[15] Haddad was immediately drawn to the teachings of the Faith and converted to it around the time of the passing of Bahá'u'lláh, in the spring of 1892.

Haddad and Kheiralla had dreams of improving their lots in life and both concluded that the best opportunities for doing so were to be found in the West. Kheiralla, an imaginative fellow, had devised several inventions and obtained patents for them through the foreign embassies in Egypt. Several of the Egyptian believers, including 'Abdu'l-Karím, were willing to provide the two with capital to travel to the West to sell his contraptions and even to care for Kheiralla's family in Cairo while they were gone. Haddad initially hesitated to leave his steady employment as a translator for the Egyptian government, but was swayed because of 'Abdu'l-Karím's enthusiasm for the enterprise and his willingness to back the venture financially.[16] 'Abdu'l-Karím also provided them with a most precious parting gift – copies of several Tablets of Bahá'u'lláh.

Less than a month after the Faith suffered the devastating loss of its Founder, the two new believers set sail from Alexandria, going in two different directions – Haddad heading to New York and Kheiralla to St Petersburg where he hoped to sell his design for military boots on stilts to the Russian army. Later Haddad summed up all that he knew about the Faith at the time he departed for America: God had been made manifest in the person of Bahá'u'lláh and he (Haddad), as a former Christian, had been taught new interpretations of certain Biblical prophecies. As he was about to depart, 'Abdu'l-Karím also told Haddad the Greatest Name of God which was used as a sort of mystical password and greeting among the believers.[17]

The interweaving of mysterious divine forces, mixing the destinies of these two men with other, seemingly unrelated but fateful events, now started to unfold. Part of Kheiralla's attraction to the United States was the Colombian Exposition which was about to open in the city of Chicago to celebrate the 400th anniversary of Columbus's first expedition to the New World.[18] Nations from around the globe had been invited to participate in the fair, so ambitious foreigners rushed to Chicago where they hoped to make their fortunes by taking advantage of that unique opportunity. One of Kheiralla's patents was for a ticket that had space on it for advertisements and he felt certain that the promoters of the Exposition would be willing to buy the rights from him to use it. Selling the ticket was the hopeless mission assigned to Haddad, who realized after much fruitless effort that no one in the United States was willing to pay for such a simple idea. Despite the failure of this business venture, the Exposition itself would add the second element of the story of the spread to the Faith to the Americas because the first public address in the United States to mention the Faith would be given at that fair on 23 September 1893.[19]

The Colombian Exposition, also known as the Chicago World's Fair, was held on the shores of Lake Michigan enveloped by Chicago, 'City of the Big Shoulders'[20] – the city in America with the tallest skyscrapers and most progressive ideas that best exemplified modernity in the late nineteenth century. From its stockyards and railroad termini to its innovative educational and social institutions, it was the nerve centre of the heartland. 'Chicago is the place to make you appreciate at every turn the absolute opportunity which chaos affords,' wrote the young academic John Dewey shortly after his arrival in the city in 1895, ' – it is sheer Matter with no Standards at all.'[21]

The scientific wonders and cultural achievements of the age showcased at the Colombian Exposition provided the attendees with a glimpse of foreign countries and unfamiliar ways of life through authentic exhibits sponsored by the governments of the participating nations. One example of how progressive the Fair was in promoting social reforms was the exhibition hall dedicated to the accomplishments of women, a significant, albeit small, achievement contributing to the attainment of the equality of the sexes. Thus the Exposition provided the perfect context in which to announce to the Americas the advent of the world-embracing Bahá'í Faith with its far-reaching, revolutionary teachings about the oneness of mankind and the need to eliminate all barriers between peoples.[22]

A highlight of the Colombian Exposition was the World Parliament of Religions, one of a number of assemblages held as part of the Exposition. This Parliament, which convened at one of the Fair's pavilions on 11 September 1893, was the first attempt ever to bring together representatives of the diverse religions of the world in one forum. Organized primarily by Protestant Christians of more liberal convictions, the Parliament included speakers representing Buddhism, Judaism, Hinduism, Islam, the Parsi religion, Shintoism, Confucianism, Taoism, and Jainism. While the programme was dominated by Christian speakers who hoped to persuade those present of the superiority of their own beliefs, it was nonetheless a major historic leap forward in interreligious tolerance and brotherhood. The Parliament has been widely considered by historians and scholars of religion as marking the beginning of both the interfaith and ecumenical movements and the reasoned academic study of comparative religion in America.[23]

The speech in question, which signalled the public announcement in the Western Hemisphere of the coming of Bahá'u'lláh, drew upon the work of an orientalist at Cambridge University in England, Edward Granville Browne. He was a young student of the Persian language and culture who had travelled extensively through Iran and surrounding regions, where he came into contact with the Bahá'í Faith. He was impressed by the accounts of the Báb and His teachings and so actively pursued His followers in order to record information about this fledgling religion. He presented a series of talks about the Bábí Faith in England in 1889[24] and subsequently was granted a meeting with Bahá'u'lláh, the only Western scholar to be given that privilege; in fact, he was Bahá'u'lláh's guest at His home at Bahjí for five days. Browne's written account of that memorable encounter would, at this historical moment, be shared with the attendees of the conference.

On 23 September 1893, a paper written by Dr Henry H. Jessup – a Presbyterian American missionary to Syria, one of the founders of Ibrahim Kheiralla's *alma mater*, the Syrian Protestant College,[25] and a prolific author – was read to the thousands of attendees. While the paper, entitled 'The Religious Mission of English Speaking Nations', had nothing to do with the Bahá'í Faith, it ended with Browne's published account of his first audience with Bahá'u'lláh. Dr Jessup felt that the sentiments expressed by Bahá'u'lláh were compatible with Protestant Christianity and well expressed the noble ideals underpinning the Parliament. Here is how the talk concluded:

> In the palace of Behjeh, or Delight, just outside the fortress of Acre, on the Syrian coast, there died a few months since a famous Persian sage, the Babi Saint, named Beha Allah – the 'Glory of God' – the head of a vast reform party of Persian Moslems, who accept the New Testament as the Word of God and Christ as the deliverer of men, who regard all nations as one, and all men as brothers. Three years ago he was visited by a Cambridge scholar, and gave utterances to sentiments so noble, so Christ-like, that we repeat them as our closing words:
>
> That all nations should become one in faith and all men as brothers; that the bonds of affection and unity between the sons of men should be strengthened; that diversity of religion should cease and differences of race be annulled; what harm is there in this? Yet so it shall be. These fruitless strifes, these ruinous wars shall pass away, and the 'Most Great Peace' shall come. Do not you in Europe need this also? Let not a man glory in this, that he loves his country; let him rather glory in this, that he loves his kind.[26]

Three of the nineteen people who would be honoured with the title 'Disciple of 'Abdu'l-Bahá'[27] heard of the Faith for the first time because of that address. Listening closely in the audience that day was a 36-year-old Canadian-born Chicago businessman, William H. Hoar. The mere mention of Bahá'u'lláh's name was enough to capture his attention, spurring him to search for more information. He would become an active, staunch believer. There is also reason to believe that Lua, then a 21-year-old unmarried dramatic-arts student, was there as well. If not, she read the talk in one of the many publications that printed it.[28] Another restless seeker of religious truth, 46-year-old American Civil War veteran and insurance executive Thornton Chase, did read it in a newspaper. He was likewise intrigued and began to investigate through libraries. Miraculously, all three would find their way to Kheiralla, by then the only believer on the continent.

Anton Haddad never made it to Chicago and its Exposition because he ran low on money. Despairing of ever selling any of Kheiralla's inventions, Haddad wrote to him imploring that he join him in America. Kheiralla had had no success in Russia either, so he sailed for New York from Germany, arriving on 20 December 1892. Haddad struggled to make a living in America for another year, but finally gave up and returned home to Lebanon during April of 1894. Kheiralla was left alone, the only Bahá'í in all of the Western Hemisphere. He had no better luck selling his inventions than his partner had, and so instead switched to selling oriental items in partnership with a Lebanese immigrant he had met in New York. Kheiralla finally left New York and headed west, hoping to reach Chicago and perhaps find another way to make money from the opportunities available because of the Fair. He discovered that he could sell more oriental wares if he incorporated lectures about the Levant into his sales pitch. Americans, a provincial people sheltered by two oceans, were fascinated by tales of faraway places they could only dream of visiting. He must have conjured up for them visions from the Arabian Nights, taking advantage of the surge of interest in the Middle East throughout Western Europe and the United States during the late nineteenth century.[29] These talks gave Kheiralla experience with American audiences and, as an insightful man, he quickly learned how to appeal effectively to them. Utilizing this approach to commerce, he moved from town to town until he reached his destination in February of 1894. He was too late; the Exposition had already closed.

Until Kheiralla arrived in Chicago, it seems that neither he nor Haddad had made any deliberate attempt to spread the joyful news of the advent of another Messenger of God. But when he settled in the Chicago area, Kheiralla detected a keen interest in religion among its citizens – an unusual openness and broadmindedness that was in large measure due to the Congress of World Religions; he therefore decided to add religion to his lecture topics.

Selling oriental wares, even when the sales pitch was preceded by a talk on Middle Eastern culture, was not providing Kheiralla with an adequate living, so he had to try a new tactic. His timing was terrible. The Chicago Fair had been so successful that about 27 million people attended it, equivalent to half the population of the United States at the time; but when it closed, the thousands of people employed by the Fair were suddenly without work; a high percentage of them were foreign immigrants. This created a social disaster for the city of Chicago; consequently, in late 1893 it became the epicentre of a nationwide economic depression. There were thousands of men wandering Chicago seeking employment, much as Kheiralla was.[30]

Despite all of 'Abdu'l-Karim's tutelage and warnings that he should put aside his quest to develop powers other than spiritual virtues, Kheiralla remained determined to develop and use supernatural powers he thought he possessed, among them the ability to heal merely by touching the sick. Surely that gift could be exploited for money. He found an unscrupulous employee at a medical school who was willing to provide him with a certificate conferring upon him the title of medical doctor for the then exorbitant sum of thirty dollars.[31] From that point on, he added 'Doctor' to his name[32] and opened an office in the premises of a Masonic Lodge in Chicago. His patients were probably the desperate, those who had given up on conventional physicians and were willing to try any approach that might cure their chronic or terminal illnesses. Kheiralla, with his charm, exotic background and unscrupulous intelligence, found many willing to pay him for cures even though these were based primarily on superstition.

American literature and folklore have long included the comic figure of the charlatan salesman, the oily character, or smooth-talking pitchman selling 'snake oil' or patent medicine to gullible, unlettered frontiersmen. Americans generally view the world optimistically and want to believe the best of people. They also understand and even admire those who concoct far-fetched schemes for making money, though no story of a rogue is ever complete without the come-uppance in the last chapter. A favourite example of this character is the phony Persian peddler in the Rodgers and Hammerstein musical *Oklahoma*. The audience knows he is a fake, but it also knows that deep down he is not all bad, just someone trying to make a living. Other well-known examples include the Duke and the Dauphine in Mark Twain's classic novel *Huckleberry Finn.*[33] It is easy to place Kheiralla in any of those roles. But unlike the snake-oil salesman, when he began to sell religion he was peddling ideas which sprang from deep truths. As Edward Getsinger would later remark about Kheiralla, 'it does not matter what kind of a pipe pure water flows through, if the water is pure, that is sufficient'.[34]

It did not take Kheiralla long to find people interested in what he had to say about spiritual matters. By June of 1894 he was able to gather his first little study circle of four inquirers in the parlour of a home in Chicago for their first meeting. That tiny group would have certainly been astonished that evening if it had recognized itself as the embryo of a movement that would attract millions of people in the future. Present were William F. James, a 36-year-old grain broker; his friend Thornton Chase, mentioned previously, who heard about Kheiralla through James; Edward Dennis, a small-business owner; and Marian Augusta Miller,[35] an unmarried Englishwoman, aged 33, who most likely first met Kheiralla when seeking medical treatment, though she also had dabbled in astrology and mysticism and so may have become acquainted with him because of that mutual interest.[36] Marian was the daughter, granddaughter and niece of Anglican clergymen, and so must have been immersed in conventional religious training during her formative years.[37] Educated and of at least modest independent means, when she arrived in the United States and why she was in Chicago remain mysteries.

It is worth a detour to discuss the nature of those persons who filled the chairs in Kheiralla's classes. It has often been remarked that Americans as a people are truly a new race of men. Over time this became literally as well as figuratively true, as intermarriage between the diverse ethnic groups that populated the country through immigration created a people of very mixed parentage representing all of the races of mankind. The United States was the first nation on earth composed primarily of the middle class, without an official aristocracy. This vast country, with its expansive and undeveloped spaces, unbridled markets and democratic government, has allowed the widest possible expression of the human spirit. This has often led to excesses both good and bad. But the freedoms enjoyed by Americans, coupled with their material prosperity, had created by the 1890s a generous and broadminded people who were not easily understood by those who remained behind in the countries they left for the New World. This difference in thinking, in spirit, was perhaps best exemplified in the American attitude toward religion. There were Christians in other parts of the world, surely, but American Christians didn't think like them.[38]

A small but significant percentage of the first Europeans to colonize North America came to escape religious persecution or to establish utopian religious communities. These were primarily various Protestant sects, especially those based upon the teachings of John Calvin, though Judaism also found the United States to be a hospitable climate. The colonists who came essentially for religious reasons had a disproportionate influence upon the development of the English colonies, especially in the northern New England region. These were the ones who established the first enduring educational institutions, usually to promote their religious teachings. As the spiritual descendants of Calvin, they emphasized the Old Testament over the Gospels, especially the passages about God's 'chosen people', which they believed they were. Just as Moses had led the Children of Israel to the Promised Land, so they saw themselves as the new Children of Israel settling in a new Promised Land that would be a light unto the nations. This heavy emphasis upon studying the Bible required a literate public and so New England could boast the highest literacy rate in the world in the seventeenth and eighteenth centuries. Well into the first decades of the twentieth century, many Americans knew the Bible intimately, and had probably been taught to read through it.

In the early eighteenth century, the English colonies along the east coast of North America underwent a social revolution dubbed 'The Great Awakening'. This period of religious fervour was so widespread that it affected multitudes up and down the various colonies along the Atlantic Coast, and Roman Catholics as well as all Protestant denominations. One of its primary spokesmen was the great philosopher and theologian Jonathan Edwards, who preached the importance of God's love as well as His wrath, thereby providing a creed well suited to colonists who had come to create unencumbered new lives in a new country.[39] This period from about 1730 to 1750 would have long-lasting and far-reaching implications for America, not least of all that it made the majority of the population religious churchgoers for the first time, even in colonies where religion had not been a key reason for the migration to the New World. While the European teachings of the Enlightenment were creating deists out of the better educated in North America, the emotionally charged meetings that characterized the Great Awakening were transforming the middling folks of the colonies into Baptists and Presbyterians (and, later, Methodists). The historian Paul Johnson summarizes it as follows:

> The Great Awakening was thus the proto-revolutionary event, the formative moment in American history, preceding the political drive for independence and making it possible. It crossed all religious and sectarian boundaries, made light of them indeed, and turned what had been a series of European-style churches into American ones. It began the process which created an ecumenical and American type of religious devotion which affected all groups, and gave a distinctive American flavor to a wide range of denominations. This might be summed up under the following five heads: evangelical vigor, a tendency to downgrade the clergy, little stress on liturgical correctness, and even less on parish boundaries, and above all an emphasis on individual experience. Its key text was Revelation 21:5 'Behold, I make all things new' – which was also the text for the American experience as a whole.[40]

After that period of religious fervour waned, the colonists, newly unshackled from religious dogma and European religious authorities, next turned to freeing themselves from the bondage of European governmental authorities. The latter half of the eighteenth century was a period of political upheaval surrounding the American Revolution, during which the religious groups that had benefited from the Great Awakening consolidated their gains. As representatives of a newly emancipated people derived from European societies with state-sponsored religions upheld by the force of law, little wonder that in the spirit of the Great Awakening those politicians who drafted the documents which would underpin the new government added a legal right to religious freedom. As the writer Jon Meacham puts it, those 'Founding Fathers' who wrote the Declaration of Independence and drafted the Constitution of the United States were implicitly making the following declaration:

> that Americans respected the idea of God, understood the universe to be governed by moral and religious forces, and prayed for divine protection

> against the enemies of this world, but were not interested in establishing yet another earthly government with official ties to a state church.[41]

The first amendment of the Bill of Rights of the Constitution forbade the government at the national level from either endorsing a particular religion or giving it privileges (that is, establishing a state religion) or preventing the free exercise of any religion, Christian or otherwise.[42] This lack of a state religion had the ironic effect of making Americans more religious, not less. Religions were forced to compete in the market-place of ideas and became stronger for it. Half a century after the adoption of religious freedom as a right enshrined by law, President John Tyler remarked:

> The United States have adventured upon a great and noble experiment, which is believed to have been hazarded in the absence of all previous precedent – that of total separation of church and state. No religious establishment *by law* exists among us. The conscience is left free from all restraint and each is permitted to worship his Maker after his own judgment . . . The Mohammedan, if he were to come among us, would have the privilege to worship according to the Koran; and the East Indian might erect a shrine to Brahma if it so pleased him. Such is the spirit of toleration inculcated by our political institutions.[43]

As the nineteenth century dawned and it appeared that the infant nation might indeed live, a new wave of religious revival ignited by emotionally charged 'camp meetings' swept the nation, beginning primarily in the rural Appalachian mountain regions.[44] Americans began to look back at the brief history of their country in awe and wonder. Surely it was the Hand of God which had brought their forefathers to those shores and aided them to conquer a wilderness. Surely it was the aid of the Almighty that had made it possible for a rag-tag army, comprised of farmers and artisans, to defeat the best professional army in the world. Surely it was a Gift of Providence that they had been blessed with wise, extraordinary leaders during the birthing of their nation. Their liberty, their benign government, their widespread prosperity had never before been seen in the world. Surely God was smiling upon their enterprise. But all this Divine Grace and Bounty would be lost if they did not become worthy. A second Great Awakening took hold of much of the United States. This time it not only led to increased religious fervour, but to greater morality, as those affected strove to become deserving of God's favours.[45] Thus a natural outcome was not only increased religiosity but also social reform movements, especially those seeking universally available public education for children, the eradication of alcoholic beverages with their accompanying domestic violence, rights for women and the abolition of slavery.

This Second Great Awakening spawned not only renewed religious zeal among the general population but also groups expecting the imminent return of Christ based upon close study of the Biblical prophecy. Most notable were the Millerites who identified 1844 as the year of Christ's return, which corresponded with the year that the Bábí Faith (or movement), the immediate precursor to the Bahá'í Faith, began in Iran.[46]

This religious free-for-all in the United States during the early nineteenth century also led the intelligentsia away from the mystical religious experiences of the Second Great Awakening toward an intellectual, wholly rational approach to religion that even left room for doubts about the very existence of a deity. As children of the Enlightenment who were tempered by influences of nineteenth-century Romanticism, these Christian intellectuals, who called themselves Unitarians, 'drained Christianity of so much spiritual content that little remained except a catalog of urgent social agendas'.[47]

With its religious freedom and immense geographic wealth that allowed those who were less conventional to simply pull up stakes and move, the United States provided the perfect incubator for sects and offshoots of the major Christian denominations. By the time Kheiralla arrived in the United States, these various religious currents swirling through the general population had become less fervent and fanatic, and had become an integral part of accepted American patterns of thought.

Most of those sitting in the chairs at Kheiralla's Chicago classes were the products of this peculiar religious heritage. Would it come as a surprise that even in this most unorthodox of countries, those who were initially attracted to the Bahá'í Faith were often themselves unusual – even well-nigh eccentric? A number had been attracted to mystical or occult teachings, just as Kheiralla had been in Egypt. In fact, one common thread among those first drawn to his teachings was a connection to activities held at the Chicago Masonic Temple,[48] especially one mystical, secret group of businessmen, the Order of the Magi. Just as Kheiralla had been told by his Bahá'í teachers in Cairo to renounce his interest in the occult, so those early seekers of truth would ultimately have to shun secret societies and the occult as their faith in the Bahá'í teachings was strengthened.

Lua was the second of those affected by the mention of the Faith at the Chicago Exposition to find Kheiralla. She and her brother William, a medical student studying homeopathy, were boarders at the home of a homeopathic physician,[49] Dr Chester Ira Thacher,[50] who had his medical office in the same Masonic building as did Kheiralla. Dr Thacher was apparently a member of the Order of the Magi and fascinated by astrology and mysticism, an interest that Lua shared with him.

On the surface, Lucinda Louisa Aurora Moore[51] (known to everyone she grew up with as 'Lulu' and to her later friends simply as 'Lua') had the stereotypical American upbringing at a time when the United States was a primarily agrarian, small town society. She was born on 1 November 1872 near Hume, New York,[52] the sixth child of a farming family with nine children. Her father, Reuben D. Moore, had worked hard all his life, first as a lumberman, drover of sheep and cattle and hired farmhand, then purchasing and running his own farm at Mills Mills, the year after Lua was born.[53]

Allegany County, where she was raised, was in the region of western New York State sometimes referred to as the 'burnt-over district' because the flames of religious zeal of the Second Great Awakening burned over the region so thoroughly that there were no souls left to be saved by evangelical preachers. During the days when the embers of the Awakening were still glowing, Reuben Moore, a young man in his twenties, had undergone a religious conversion and joined the Baptist Church, leaving aside the Quaker Faith of his mother, so all his children were raised to be Baptists.[54] The region was not only filled with Methodists and Baptists but was the spawning ground of groups such as the Millerites[55] and the Mormons.[56] Some of the social reforms that grew out of the Awakening were also first set in motion in that same area, including the movement for women's rights.[57] It is impossible to know the degree to which this highly charged milieu directly affected the Moore family, but it seems probable that Lua imbibed many progressive ideas because of where she grew up.

Her sister said of young Lua that, 'Lua had lovely reddish brown hair. It fell in waves about her face, and was so long she could sit on it. Her skin was fair. Her eyes were large and blue. She was as straight and slender as a white birch.'[58]

Lua's patiently enduring father was twenty-five years older than her mother, Ellen McBride Moore,[59] who was an unconventional farm wife. She had a keen, questioning mind that rebelled at the light fare offered to the ordinary churchgoer of rural America. Her inability to silently accept church dogma got her into trouble with the local clergy. Lua grew up to be much like her mother and seemed to those who watched her bloom into young adulthood to hold the promise of success in life because of her great capacities. One of her gifts was a lovely singing voice. A natural performer, she decided to train for the stage – a most unlikely choice at that time for a farm girl who had only a basic village-school education. But if that were not surprising enough, she was drawn not to nearby New York City with its world-famous theatres and schools of dramatic arts, but to far-off Chicago, the 'Second City', always second to New York. This decision was based upon a gut feeling that she could neither articulate nor resist. So off she went to Chicago to study acting.[60] When she arrived and what she did there during her first years in the Midwest remain a mystery. What is known is that during this period she went from church to church, searching for a religion she could believe in, but like her mother, she did not find the answers to her inner yearnings.

As soon as Lua began to attend Kheiralla's classes, she was vivified like a dry sponge that immediately sprang to life through the healing moisture of the few Bahá'í teachings he imparted. For the first time in her life, she discovered spiritual teachings that rang true, that she could accept wholeheartedly. She understood, at last, why she had had the inner prompting to go to Chicago. On 21 May 1897 she was formally inducted into the Faith by receiving the Greatest Name.[61] She soon was one of Kheiralla's star pupils, cautiously, though zealously, bringing many others to him.

By the time that Lua became a confirmed believer in 1897, Kheiralla had taught the Bahá'í Faith to slightly fewer than sixty people. First to convert were the members of his earliest group, William James followed by Marian Miller. The third and fourth were Thornton Chase and Kate Ives. Over time, these last two came to be considered the first American male and female believers because neither James nor Miller remained in the Faith. Nonetheless, Kheiralla's ability to attract Americans to the new religion was remarkable, especially because his classes were advertised only by word of mouth. Truly, Bahá'u'lláh's prayer that Kheiralla would attract hearts had born fruit. Kheiralla was careful to maintain his position as the exclusive chief teacher and guide to his growing congregation, and he encouraged his more devoted students, such as Lua, to carefully bring inquirers to him for instruction.[62]

Kheiralla tinkered with his teaching approach until at last, about a year after his first class, he had devised a series of thirteen lessons. All lessons were conducted in a secretive manner as though the student was being inducted into an exclusive secret society like the Masons. The first sessions combined his knowledge of science with his study of the Bible and so seemed both logical and spiritual. His expositions upon Biblical prophecies were designed to lead the student to the conclusion that it was time for the coming of a new divine messenger, an idea which had already taken hold in the United States during the Second Great Awakening and which was gaining further momentum in the lead-up to the turn of the century. The Bahá'í Faith and Bahá'u'lláh, referred to as 'the pith' of the course, were only introduced once the student got to the eleventh lesson. Furthermore, the lessons were constructed to build up to the greatest, most powerful of all spiritual secrets, the true name of God

– the 'Greatest Name'. The Greatest Name is 'Alláh-u-Abhá' which means 'God is Most Glorious'. This would be revealed only during the final lesson once Kheiralla had judged the inquirer ready to receive it. By accepting the Greatest Name and saying it, the student was initiated into the Bahá'í Faith and entered onto the membership list kept by Kheiralla's secretary, Maude Lamson. The final requirement was for the new believer to write a letter setting forth his declaration of faith and post it to 'Abdu'l-Bahá in 'Akká.[63]

These theological lessons provided Kheiralla with patients for his medical practice. The spiritual teachings were given free of charge; the medical sessions, of course, cost money. By late 1896 Kheiralla was giving free 'open' public lectures at which he would present some of his introductory material, and that same year he produced a pamphlet entitled *The Identity and Personality of God*.[64] These publications further helped with his recruiting for both his classes and his medical practice.

During her years in the Thacher household, Lua met someone else who would become very important in her life, Dr Edward Christopher Getsinger.[65] Like Thacher, Edward was a homeopathic physician, which probably explains how they knew each other. He would occasionally travel to the Chicago area to give lectures on scientific topics, and it was apparently during one of those visits that he first met Lua. They encountered each other a number of times before she began her studies with Kheiralla. Most likely, Lua attended some of Edward's lectures. But Edward was a student of science, not of religion, and he did not share her desire to find answers to spiritual and metaphysical questions, though he had some knowledge of those topics.[66]

Edward grew up in the predominantly German, small community of Frankenmuth, Michigan,[67] the fifth of the six sons of Johann and Theresia Göetzinger, Lutheran immigrants from Württemberg and Saxony, respectively, in Germany. He recounted in his memoirs that he was 'reared to be a German in America'.[68] His father initially worked as a tailor but then turned to saloon-keeping,[69] a not uncommon profession for German immigrants skilled in the art of brewing beer. While few details of Edward's first three decades have survived the passage of time, when he was a child he had the unusual advantage of being mentored and taught daily by a university professor from Heidelberg.[70] His constantly expanding, insatiable interest in the natural world drew him as a young adult to the western wilderness of the Rocky Mountains where he lived among backwoods mountaineers for some years.[71] Though he lacked a strong schoolhouse education,[72] throughout his life he continued to acquire knowledge through self-study. It was this approach to learning through focused reading that gained him a profession. After extensive reading about the medical field of homeopathy, followed by the required hospital residency, he was granted a licence to practice as a homeopathic physician by the State of Michigan.[73] Looking back, Edward concluded that his parents' experience as pioneers on the American frontier and his own experiences in the untamed West had taught him the values of industriousness, trust in his fellow citizens, and appreciation for truth and justice. He was a restless soul who earned his living as a travelling lecturer and writer about science, rather than from a fixed medical practice. He had actually heard of Kheiralla while giving public lectures in Kalamazoo, Michigan, because Kheiralla had remained briefly in that city on his way to Chicago;[74] but Kheiralla's teachings held little interest for him at the time.

Edward represents another, less common but nonetheless significant, thread of thought about religion that was beginning to take hold, especially in academic circles: that is, scepticism about the existence of a Divine Creator. It was an age when ground-breaking scientific insights were revising the way that all aspects of nature and the order of the world were viewed. One result of this revolution in knowledge was that many scientists concluded that there was no place for God in the grand scheme of the universe. Charles Darwin's *On the Origin of Species*, published in 1859, was earth-shaking not because it demonstrated that living species evolve over time, a view many scientists already held, but that evolution occurred by chance, not design. There was no great master plan devised by a supernatural being unfolding. As the distinguished professor and writer, Louis Menand, describes Darwin's explosive masterpiece:

> The purpose of *On the Origin of Species* was not to introduce the concept of evolution; it was to debunk the concept of supernatural intelligence – the idea that the universe is the result of an idea.
>
> For a belief that species evolve is not incompatible with belief in divine creation, or with belief in intelligent design. Progressive adaptation might simply be the mechanism God has selected to realize his intentions. What was radical about *On the Origin of Species* was not its evolutionism, but its materialism.[75]

Even if Darwin did not mean it to be, the book was taken as a direct assault upon belief in God. Numerous great thinkers at prestigious universities turned away from theology and towards science, deciding that it was natural laws alone that determined human behaviour, not a deity.[76] Edward, as a scientist, was very much affected by these ideas, which would have permeated the books and journals that he pored over. He came to believe that the term 'God' was just another way of describing the forces of nature, that there was no supernatural, All-Powerful, All-Knowing Entity. He referred to himself as an unbeliever and pantheist.[77] Public espousal of atheism was possible in the United States because it was one of the few countries during the nineteenth century where the choice to believe anything or nothing was a matter of law. Freedom of religion allowed for freedom from religion.

When Edward again returned to Chicago, most likely in 1897, and renewed his acquaintance with Thacher, Lua and her brother, he noted that both Chester and Lua had lost enthusiasm for astrology and the occult, subjects which had previously occupied their minds. They were on to some new mysterious interest – apparently a religion – which they spoke of in hushed tones only among themselves. Both had concluded that Edward would not be interested in their secret.

Thacher owned a farm in the countryside outside Chicago and invited Edward and the Moores to visit as his guests. The fresh air and greenery made it a relaxing place, away from the hubbub of the city. There Edward had a strange experience that would transform his life.

He was sitting alone in a chair in the parlour early one morning contemplating a difficult point of chemistry for an upcoming lecture when suddenly it seemed as if the wall before him gave way and he began to see a distant place.[78] All the while conscious that he was fully awake with his eyes wide open, a wondrous scene unfolded before him. He watched himself walk about in some unknown Eastern country – his first thought was that it must be Egypt. There was a sea and beside it a small oriental city with hills in the background. He had always wanted to travel to Egypt because he believed that there he would be able to find a wise man who could impart to him the ancient knowledge of the East, who would be able to explain to him the mysteries of immortality. Perhaps this was the place he would find such a man. Then, as suddenly as it appeared, the vision was gone.

A confused Edward resumed his preparation for the next day's lecture when about twenty minutes later the vision reappeared. He again had the extraordinary experience of observing himself, this time near a city he would later discover to be 'Akká. His *doppelgänger* walked toward a small hill that he would later realize was Tel Napoleon, the site of the ancient settlement of Ptolemais (the original site of 'Akká).[79] In the distance was a large building he could barely make out because of 'the intense rays of light which shed their radiance away up into the heaven with such brilliancy that it was brighter than the sun or brighter than the daylight'.[80] He watched as his double clambered up the hill and from there beheld the beautiful, glowing building. Was this the place where he would find the teacher he sought? The other Edward reached the top of Tel Napoleon where he could get a better look, but the brightness of the building was such that he still could not make it out clearly, though he would later identify it as the Mansion of Bahjí, the final residence of Bahá'u'lláh. A man in Persian garb came out of a door in the outer wall which surrounded the edifice and sat down on a stone as though waiting for someone. Edward later recognized Mírzá Muḥammad-Qulí as the man in the vision. In the vision, he tried to get to that place of light by descending the hill and beginning to traverse the distance of several miles that separated him from his goal, but just then the vision disappeared.

Still sitting in his chair, Edward pinched himself. He was indeed fully awake. Somehow, deep inside he knew that he must go to that faraway place to find the hill and the house which shone like a beacon. With these thoughts racing around and around in his head, he tried mightily to refocus on chemistry and the preparation of his lecture. After another twenty minutes the vision appeared for a third time. This time, Edward found himself walking toward the mansion of light. He watched as his double approached the old gentleman, who arose and, with his hands crossed upon his breast, bowed to him and asked in a strange language, 'Are you of us?' He could not make out what his double replied, but the old gentleman must have found the answer to be satisfactory for he then went and knocked on a large metal door which was opened from the inside. Muḥammad-Qulí led him through a wonderfully beautiful courtyard, with a fountain and flowers, to a large room where fine damask curtains were hung. Lovely woven carpets adorned the floor and there were divans on two sides of the room. The chamber was unoccupied. The two men stood together in silence for a few moments and then a loud voice said in English, 'This is where God lived (or lives) and his son (the name was unintelligible) is now here, and when you come again you shall see him.' As these words were spoken, Edward experienced for the first time in his life what he could only describe as a religious feeling. His double and his companion exited through the same court, and as they did so the vision vanished as quickly as it had come.[81] Edward resolved then and there to find that place.

Unable to shake off the memory of the three weighty visions, Edward joined the Thacher family and their guests at the breakfast table, listening with one ear as his friends spoke in veiled language about their own mysterious knowledge which they judged him unready to hear. As he turned over the morning's experiences in his mind, he began to think about the Bible and its prophecies regarding Christ. Having rejected religion, he had not read the Bible since he was a boy, therefore his first resolution was to purchase one as soon as possible. He also decided to inquire of his friends what it was that made them so tight-lipped.

From that morning on, Edward began to engage his companions more and more in discussions about spiritual matters. He wrote of how he finally brought up his new ideas with Thacher.

> We arrived at our eating place and sat together at the dinner table still talking upon religious subjects when I . . . said, 'Doctor, I can tell you what you believe. You believe that there is a God who came in the flesh in an Oriental country and who died a saint and his son is now living in that same city. You believe that this is the end of a period or cycle and that the great advent of the Christians who expect Christ to come down from the clouds . . . is now fulfilled and that many strange things are going to happen.' While I was telling the Doctor this his eyes became larger in utter astonishment, and he asked me who told me about these things, but he would not admit that this was what he really believed, because he had been forbidden, as well as all others who had been taught by Dr Kheiralla, that they must not speak one word of it to anyone without his permission, but must bring the inquirers to him personally and he will judge them as to whether they are worthy or not. Dr Thacher then said that I must certainly go and see this man . . . who could tell me many things.[82]

Thacher agreed to make an appointment with Kheiralla for Edward. When the two met for the first time a week later, they sized each other up. Edward took an immediate dislike to Kheiralla but decided that, regardless, he held the key to his visions. Apparently the feeling was mutual; Kheiralla had decided that the visions were made up by Thacher and the Moores to cover up their disclosure to Edward of his teachings. Despite Kheiralla's evasive approach to teaching about the Faith, requiring lesson after lesson covering material of little interest to Edward – nonsense to him – in order to gain 'the pith',[83] he nevertheless persevered because he believed that this was the only course to a correct understanding of his visions. After weeks of suspense, Edward finally heard about the coming of God's newest messenger, Bahá'u'lláh, Whom, after some study, he accepted completely. His name was entered on the membership list on 26 October 1897.

Even before his final conversion to the Faith, Edward had decided that, rather than continue teaching science, he would redirect his energies to spreading religious truths, and he began to urge many of his own students to study with Kheiralla. Lua and Edward had been attracted to each other for some time and now found a point of common interest – a desire to zealously serve their new-found faith. They decided to marry without further delay. The simple wedding took place on 26 May 1897, in the Chicago home where Kheiralla's classes were then being conducted. The bride was 24 and the groom was 31.[84] Lua had formally accepted the Faith just a few days earlier. Theirs was the second Bahá'í marriage in the United States since Kheiralla had taken a fourth bride, one of his first students, Marian Miller, on 8 June 1895 at the home of another member from that first class, William James.[85]

After Edward's formal acceptance into Kheiralla's group, the newly-weds travelled to Edward's home state of Michigan and then on to Hume, New York to visit Lua's family. They were able to teach the Faith to her mother, Ellen Moore, and four of her siblings. Her brother William, who had remained back in Chicago, had already become a Bahá'í a few months earlier. Lua's mother, after a lifetime of search, had finally found a religion she could accept without reservation. The Getsingers then went to the town of Ithaca, New York, where they quickly attracted people to a Bahá'í study class. They were even able to convince Kheiralla to briefly visit the area in January 1898 in order to assist them.[86]

While in Ithaca, Edward had a second unusual experience. He happened upon an article in a newspaper that spoke highly of a wealthy woman who was a great philanthropist, who had given generously to universities, hospitals and other charities. At that moment, a strange feeling overwhelmed him and he had an inexplicable sense that he must seek out the woman and tell her about the new religion, but the article gave no clue as to her whereabouts. The inner command to find that lady played upon his mind to such a degree that he could not sleep that night. The next morning Edward confessed to his new wife the source of his distraction and his determination to meet the heiress and give her the message of the Faith. Lua had always acted upon impulses and hunches, so she understood and supported him in this quest. Edward began to make inquiries and discovered that the lady had homes in Washington, D.C., New York City, and San Francisco, California. He wrote to her Washington address and found out that she was not there. He made inquiries in New York City, but she was not there either. That left only one other place, far-away California. [87]

Edward left Lua with her family in January of 1898, and set off to cross the continent. The object of his quest was no ordinary person but arguably one of the most powerful women in the country, certainly among the wealthiest in her own right. It was none other than Phoebe Apperson Hearst.

CHAPTER 3

The Good Fairy

Edward's irresistible impulse to seek out Phoebe[1] Elizabeth Apperson Hearst seems, with the advantage of hindsight, to have been truly inspired. Her entrance into the story of the Bahá'í Faith in the West would have far-reaching consequences because she inadvertently changed the course of the American Bahá'í community, thereby heading it onto the right path. She herself was almost too good to be believable. For many decades Phoebe's own contributions to the betterment of mankind have been overshadowed by the accomplishments of the multitude of others whose achievements she quietly made possible. Undoubtedly, future generations will give her a closer look and then bestow upon her much deserved laurels. A brief overview of her life leaves no doubt as to why some of her friends referred to her as their 'fairy'.[2]

Phoebe, like Lua, was a farm girl from a backwoods area.[3] She was born in Franklin County, Missouri, near the small town of St Clair on 3 December 1842, and was raised in a humble log cabin with a lean-to for a kitchen not far from the Meramac River. That county is located in the hardscrabble Ozark region of the state with hills, deep ravines and caverns. Her parents, of English and German stock, had migrated west to the Missouri territory from the mountains of Virginia and South Carolina and brought along with them many of the opinions and conservative gentility of the rural antebellum South.[4] Randolph Walker Apperson and Drucilla Whitmire Apperson first made a living by running a general store and then by farming. While biographers differ in their assessment of the Apperson family's financial status,[5] there is no doubt that the Appersons valued formal education and somehow provided their daughter with better than average schooling for a girl raised on the frontier. When she was young, Phoebe and her father shared a love of poetry; both wrote poems and together created notebooks full of not only their own writings but also literary works that they found meaningful. In many ways, as the only surviving child in the family until her brother was born when she was eight, Phoebe was as much a son to her father as she was a daughter; they were very close. Her father taught her many things about both business and life, lessons that normally were reserved for sons.[6] Her family's financial difficulties also taught her the value of money, that it should be husbanded judiciously and spent frugally. When Phoebe was a teenager she was sent by her parents to Steelville Academy, a coeducational boarding school run by the Presbyterian Church, located not far from the regional centre, St Louis; there she did well.[7] Young Phoebe was known during her Missouri childhood as highly intelligent, intellectually curious and an insatiable reader. What she did not gain through her formal education she acquired through serious study and reflection on a variety of subjects, prompting one who knew her as a middle-aged matron to describe her as 'Refined and high-minded by nature, through her extraordinary acquaintance and contact with the world, her thoroughly ordered and well-balanced intellect [she] has gained an education that schools and colleges could not give.'[8] She was also well liked even though she was innately shy and reserved. As one of her biographers noted, 'Phoebe had a rare quality of presence, an "aura" about her that people did not forget.'[9]

The Appersons were members of the local Cumberland Presbyterian Church where her father was a church elder, an important lay position.[10] As a young man, he had undergone a religious conversion. It was said of him that 'His life has been consistent with his profession of religion, for, by precept and practice, he has shown his love for the Master [Christ].'[11] Phoebe's aunt was married to the community's Presbyterian minister, so the family was naturally involved in all local church affairs. The congregation they belonged to was an offshoot of the Presbyterian Church and a direct product of the Second Great Awakening, described previously, as well as an indirect legacy of the First Great Awakening that began the rift within the American Presbyterian Church. Lacking doctrinal stringency, this small Christian denomination born in rural Appalachia was especially notable for its early ordination of women ministers,[12] and its progressive teachings regarding African Americans and other minorities.[13] Even though Phoebe did not remain an active member of the Cumberland Presbyterian Church throughout her life, her upbringing within it instilled in her reverence for the Bible, high moral standards, and a strong sense of the importance of being a good neighbour.[14]

This charming young lady stood only five feet tall, had a trim figure, wavy dark hair and blue-gray eyes that attracted many a prize-suitor; but serious Phoebe was not interested. She became a teacher when only about 16 or 17 years old and quickly rose from being the mistress of a small country schoolhouse at Reedville to a teacher in a school for the children of the workers at the Meramec Iron Works in the next county, to finally being a private tutor for a well-to-do family. This last employer helped to open her eyes to the wider world and instilled many socially progressive ideas in young Phoebe.[15]

Phoebe Elizabeth Apperson had been named in part for a Franklin County neighbour and close family friend, Elizabeth Hearst, to whom she was distantly related. This cousin had a son, George Hearst, a bachelor more than twenty years older than Phoebe who had headed west in 1850 to seek his fortune during the California gold rush of 1849. George had briefly studied mining and worked in the lead mines near his home as well as in the copper mines owned by his father. The West, however, offered the opportunity not to just eke out a bare living in farming and mining, but to become rich. Word spread throughout the country that gold, silver and other valuable metals and minerals were being discovered in abundance in the raw wilderness of the western mountains of the United States. George had the extreme good fortune to be a young man at just such a moment, because of his peculiar inborn talent for finding minerals.[16] Shawnee Indians who knew him as a young man in Missouri bestowed upon him the apt name 'Boy-That-Earth-Talked-To'. 'Gold Fever' took him over; he could not resist the call to join the thousands who rushed to the gold fields of California. Despite his uncanny ability to understand geology – to look at a hill and know what was beneath the dirt – he spent almost a decade wandering the West, failing at everything he tried. His fortunes finally changed when he acquired an interest in a mine in the Sierra Nevada Mountains that produced what became known as the Comstock Load, one of the greatest veins of silver ever found. Suddenly, he was wealthy.

Despite his new riches, George forever remained an affable, kind, simple miner at heart, much more at home around a campfire with rugged, unschooled men than in well-appointed parlours or elite social clubs. To the end of his days, he was generosity personified, especially to old miners down on their luck. And he never shrank from hard work, even when he could afford servants.

At the age of 41 he returned to Missouri to settle a business matter and to tend to his ailing mother. He found that during his long absence the neighbour he had carried on his shoulders when she was a young child had blossomed into a lovely woman of 18 – the belle of the neighbourhood. George decided that this sprite was for him and began to court Phoebe persistently. They were an odd couple. Lanky, scraggly, six-foot-tall George seemed to be twice her size. He could barely read or write despite his intelligence, and he lacked her genteel manners. To make matters worse, he was a rejected suitor of her mother and was old enough to be her father. But he was handsome in an uncouth sort of way and he had the ability to give Phoebe a bigger world than rural Missouri. He had a lively sense of humour coupled with an honest and upright character.[17] Despite the reservations of her parents who thought that he was too old for her, Phoebe and George were married by a Presbyterian minister with little fuss at the home of a friend on 15 June 1862, within ear-shot of a skirmish being fought nearby as part of the American Civil War. Four months later the newlyweds slipped through the wartime perils of Missouri and made their way to New York City from whence they set sail for Panama. They crossed the narrow isthmus and then boarded another ship sailing up the Pacific coast to the burgeoning, untamed, circus of a city that was young San Francisco.[18] By the time they arrived, Phoebe was noticeably pregnant.

The natural beauty of the San Francisco area in the 1860s must have thrilled the young bride coming from the landlocked farming country of the Midwest.[19] The city was situated on hills overlooking a deep blue bay interspersed with islands and coves. In the distance, other hills provided a delightful backdrop to complete the beautiful panorama. Originally established as a small Spanish mission outpost, the discovery of gold in the nearby mountains in 1849 had changed its character virtually overnight. Will Rogers expressed it well by calling San Francisco 'the city that was never a town'. As the primary deep-water port of that region, the city sprang up so rapidly that during 1849 alone a hundred new buildings a month were constructed.[20]

As a rough, booming, dirty city full of energy and vice, San Francisco must have been both repulsive in its bawdy manner yet alluring and exciting to the adventurous young wife who, up until her marriage, had only known the pleasures and restrictions of rural life. The wealth to be made from the immense untapped natural resources of California was attracting all manner of people from many parts of the world – Europe, the eastern United States, Mexico, and even China – and Phoebe did not hesitate to take advantage of the best San Francisco had to offer, especially its exuberant showcasing of the arts. The shiny coins in men's pockets attracted vaudeville acts and opera singers, dance-hall girls and ballerinas. There were also numerous booksellers and even a few libraries. Later, she would be among those who would work to refine the raw new city by promoting institutions for education, charity and high culture. The city also offered her one particular advantage – no native-born, local aristocracy. The *nouveaux riches* were the city's gentry, and she was one of them. In the San Francisco of the 1860s there were few barriers to inhibit the ambitious.

In April of 1863, before she was even settled in her new home, Phoebe gave birth to her only child, William Randolph Hearst, whom she called 'Will'. From that day forward to the end of her life, he was the centre of her world.

George often left his family for long stretches of time to travel to his growing empire of mines and real-estate holdings. Occasionally Phoebe would leave young Will behind and accompany her husband on horseback to crude mining camps. Their alliance was a partnership if not a romance. From the earliest days of their marriage, George recognized his wife's intelligence and good sense and so not only kept her abreast of his business dealings but also solicited her advice about his affairs.[21] George was an honest and fair businessman, but he was also a gambler, consequently – just as with his high-stakes poker games – his risky business deals did not always succeed. At one point a law suit almost ruined him. Another time he suffered such financial reverses that they were forced to sell the family home and many of their possessions. But with his intuitive knack for mining, George was always able to recoup his money – usually at a much greater magnitude than before the loss. After he struck it rich with a gold mine, his economic fortunes never wavered again. As a man away from home for weeks or months at a time, rumour had it that George was not always faithful to his wife, but their marriage weathered that storm as well. In George there was much to forgive but also much to like. The Hearsts prospered and bought a mansion on the wealthy heights of San Francisco's Nob Hill –also derisively referred to as 'Snob Hill' – and established their niche in California high society.

Phoebe longed for other children, especially a daughter, but none came.[22] So she directed her inexhaustible energies toward her son and civic activities, throwing her talents and resources behind many good causes. She also developed the family's social standing among the upper crust of California society by becoming a renowned hostess, which also served to promote her husband's business and political ambitions. But her *soirées* were never simply social affairs; they often showcased artistic talent or promoted intellectual ideas. She was becoming known as a grand society lady.

Ever since he was a young man, George had been drawn to politics. He was able to parlay his wealth and social position to gain first a seat in the California state legislature and finally, in 1886, a seat in the United States Senate, a position attained through a gubernatorial appointment to fill an unfinished term rather than by election. The Hearsts, by then among the wealthiest people in America, added to their holdings a mansion in Washington, D.C., where Phoebe quickly became a dominant force in the social life of the capital. Her lavish balls were a highlight of the society calendar and well reported in the newspapers. The Hearsts were invited by the President to dine at the White House. Their social circle encompassed the great and powerful of the world, not just of California.

Phoebe disdained politics; nonetheless, she played the role of dutiful wife by assisting her husband and later her son to attain their political ambitions through her efforts to raise and maintain the family's social standing both in California and Washington, D.C. The extravagant *soirées* and balls held at the opulent Hearst mansion in the nation's capital made her queen of Washington society.[23] Nevertheless, she drew the line at direct involvement in politics. She confided her thoughts on the subject in a letter to an old friend.

> . . . I hate politics so that it is difficult for me to mention the subject. Mr. Hearst expects to be elected to the Senate for six years but the matter cannot

> be decided until the Legislature meet and elect whoever may be their choice. There is a democratic majority and it is thought they must elect Mr. Hearst but I have no faith in politicians. One can never depend on them . . .
>
> I like Washington, but could enjoy more there if not in political life. A Senator's wife has her trials, I assure you, and I don't consider that there is much honor in politics.
>
> You know I am always obliged to carry all social responsibilities. Will don't like society, and I need not tell you how I have to manage Mr. Hearst to keep him ever near the right thing.[24]

The Hearst household gained a new member during the Washington years: Phoebe's niece, Anne Drusilla Apperson. Anne, the daughter of Phoebe's only sibling, Elbert, came from California early in 1887 to live with the Hearsts because of her parents' marital problems.[25] She was only nine years old at the time. The arrangement was supposed to be temporary but proved to be permanent and Anne became the daughter Phoebe had longed for.[26] Attractive if not a beauty, very fair in complexion with golden brown hair and blue eyes, Anne was much indulged by both her aunt and uncle, who provided a rich milieu of educational and social activities for her. For example, they made it possible for her to attend the exclusive boarding school for girls in New York City, the Spence School. Anne, however, could be difficult and sometimes fought with her aunt.[27]

During those same years, Phoebe also began to mentor a number of other young women, including two who will figure prominently later in the story, May Bolles and Helen Hillyer. She would take these and other young ladies with her to society functions and ensured that they were exposed to good schooling and high culture.

An article in the society column of a California newspaper reporting the visit of one of Anne's school friends to the Hearsts' Washington residence provides a good example of the publicity Phoebe received during her years as a resident of the nation's capital. The writer waxed enthusiastic about Anne's charming manners and then went on to say that this was the result of Phoebe's own 'well bred cordiality' which made her hospitality 'a thing to remember. It is so simply honest, – so sincere, so very genuine that you appreciate the real desire of your hostess to make you both welcome and happy.' The writer did not stop there in extolling Mrs Hearst but went on to say that 'to do good in the world in the best way – to make many, many people happy, – that is an ideal which Mrs Hearst has set for herself, and for once, an ideal is realized.'[28]

As the vibrant, wealthy wife of a Senator, Phoebe used the prestige of her position to promote many worthy causes, especially those related to education. She co-founded the prestigious Cathedral School for Girls in Washington, D.C. to which many of the leaders of the country have sent their daughters over the years. She worked to establish free kindergartens for the poor and to promote the idea of early childhood education in Washington, D.C. and California. Notably, she established free kindergartens not only for white children, but also for African American children – a radical accomplishment for a white woman at a time when widespread racial prejudice led to the neglect of that segment of the population.[29]

Mrs Hearst was a co-founder of that quintessential American institution, the Parent-Teacher Association (PTA), originally called the National Congress of Mothers, which, more than a century later, remains the most influential and widespread organization for the promotion of education in the United States. As a former schoolteacher, she valued all stages of education and gave generously of her time and funds to the University of California at Berkeley.[30] She was rewarded by being named the first woman to ever serve as a Regent of the University of California, a very controversial appointment at the time because of her sex. She also established free libraries in several mining towns in order to help the workers, many of them new immigrants, improve themselves through self-study.[31]

Many of the causes that Phoebe chose to support had an underlying theme – the advancement of women. She was a firm believer in providing opportunities for women to support themselves financially at a time when social and legal barriers made it difficult for them to obtain well-paid work. For example, Mrs Hearst viewed kindergartens not only as a means of providing early childhood education that would thereby elevate society, but also as respectable employment for women as teachers. Her libraries provided women with jobs through which they could develop management skills. A number of her gifts to the University of California at Berkeley were for the benefit of its female students who at the time were shunted aside on campus – no place was allocated to them to live or study on the university grounds. Instead, the women students were assigned only a washroom within which to congregate socially, so Phoebe rectified this humiliating situation by constructing a social hall exclusively for the female students of Berkeley. She was also an ardent supporter of the Young Women's Christian Association (YWCA), an organization that promoted wholesome, educational and athletic activities for girls and young women. And while she did not approve of some of the extreme methods used by the women's suffrage movement, she did, nonetheless, quietly provide financial support to organizations promoting women's right to vote, especially after the death of her husband.[32]

The scope of her activities and influence was remarkable. Phoebe was a leading promoter of the effort to build the Washington Monument in the nation's capital as a befitting tribute to George Washington. She was credited with the restoration and preservation carried out in the 1890s of Washington's home, Mount Vernon, a national treasure. She promoted advances in medicine by not only funding major research but also by establishing hospitals. She had a special interest in homeopathy and helped to establish the first hospital of that nature in San Francisco. Her enthusiasm for the emerging field of anthropology led her to underwrite archaeological research and excavations in the southwest of the United States, Greece, Egypt, and Peru, among other locations. A number of the greatest archaeologists of the time were in her employ.[33] She also collected many rare and significant antiquities which would become the heart of the collection of the anthropology museum she founded at the University of California in Berkeley. Phoebe's generosity also assisted many promising artists, doctors, architects, and scholars, not only through monetary gifts but also through promotion of their work. For example, she was in part responsible for launching the career of Julia Morgan, the first major American woman architect. She was exceptionally generous during times of catastrophe, such as following the earthquake in Charleston, South Carolina, and, of course, the great 1906 earthquake and fire in San Francisco.

An interesting side note to Phoebe's largesse was her interest in a retreat facility in Maine. She became acquainted with another strong-willed lady, Sarah Farmer, perhaps through their mutual interest in promoting education. Sarah Farmer had a lifelong dream of creating a conference centre in Maine within easy distance of Boston where the great thinkers of the day could gather, give lectures and promote new ideas, especially about spirituality. This appealed to Phoebe and so she provided most of the funding for the establishment of that retreat, Green Acre. Years later, with Phoebe's tacit blessing, this property would be turned over to the Bahá'í Faith by Sarah, who became a believer independently of Phoebe.[34]

Phoebe's charitable work was not solely a matter of writing cheques; she also took a sincere personal interest in the people and organizations that she helped. During her early years in San Francisco, Phoebe began to make discreet inquiries about deserving young people who lacked the means to gain an education and then quietly provided the necessary funds. Although much of her giving was done anonymously, she sometimes became so personally involved that she could well have been accused of trying to run the organizations she was assisting. She received untold 'misery letters' from friends, distant relatives, and strangers seeking money, employment or other forms of assistance. She considered each request and wrote a short note to her secretary at the top of each letter as to what action should be taken. Phoebe was soft-hearted but she was also just and knew that her funds were not unlimited; she could say 'no'. It was not unusual for a person receiving her financial support to receive a letter from her with accusations of spending her money unwisely. The recipient would pen a hasty reply begging forgiveness, which she always gave, but the lesson had been put across and in the future funds would be more carefully husbanded.[35]

Phoebe always seemed to be thinking of others. Her kindness and generosity were manifested not only through her charity. Wonderful illustrations of her thoughtfulness were the numerous times friends would be delighted by the surprise delivery to their door of a box of flowers or grapes grown on her estate.

Phoebe's thoughts, nonetheless, never strayed far from her adored son William, who grew up to be a most unusual man. He was a strange mixture of light and darkness, quiet like his father with the refined manners and gentle courtesy of his mother and an intelligence honed through his mother's careful tutelage. Through Phoebe he had acquired a taste for the arts – though more plebeian than hers – and collecting. Will, as he was known to most people, exasperated his mother because he was amoral, in stark contrast to her above-reproach morality, and his scandalously open affairs with various women – especially showgirls – would be long remembered as a key element of his biography. If he had failed to acquire his mother's sexual morals[36] he did at least inherit her social conscience, for he strongly sympathized with the underdog and the oppressed and saw himself as their champion. Like his father, he harboured unconcealed political ambitions, aiming unabashedly to become President of the United States. And, like both parents, he was very honest and a fair employer. He was kind and generous, but his soft, almost effeminate appearance and voice (despite standing more than six foot tall) masked a man with an aggressive self-confidence. Will knew how to get his way. Not surprisingly, he had been excessively spoiled as a child and had developed a strong will and a mischievous streak that got him expelled from Harvard University after one too many extravagant pranks coupled with inattention to his studies.

George Hearst was exasperated that his only offspring exhibited no interest in carrying on any of the family businesses, which at the time included many of the most important gold, silver and copper mines in the country and large real-estate holdings in the western United States and Mexico. Only one Hearst asset attracted young Will. George had acquired a failing San Francisco newspaper, the *Examiner*, as part of the settlement of its debts, and he intended to use the paper to promote his own political career and the Democratic Party.[37] The newspaper business had captured Will's undying devotion during his

Harvard years. While a student, he had turned around the finances of the insolvent student publication, *The Harvard Lampoon*,[38] and made it profitable. He used holidays from school to spend time observing at the offices of the great newspapers in New York City and Boston. He seemed to have printer's ink for blood – and begged his father to let him run the *Examiner*. George was hesitant. So Will took a job with Joseph Pulitzer's *World* newspaper in New York to prove his sincerity to his father. At last George relented, and so at the age of 23 William embarked on establishing what would become one of the most important media empires in the United States through the financial backing of his family's mining and real-estate fortune. Will proved that he had the same intuitive feel for the news business that his father had for finding minerals, immediately devising many innovations that would be copied by competing papers; but he also had enough of his parents' business acumen to figure out how to run a newspaper profitably, because within three years the *Examiner* went from consistently losing money to making a profit. George was proud, and not a little surprised.[39]

Senator George Hearst died of cancer in 1891 while serving in Congress, making Phoebe at the age of 48 one of the wealthiest widows in the United States. His will left everything to her.[40] This unusual disposition of the estate was contrary to the general custom of America in the nineteenth century that dictated that adult sons should inherit family businesses and in turn provide for their widowed mothers out of a spirit of filial responsibility and largesse. At the time, many people were shocked and felt that Will was the rightful beneficiary.[41] George's disposal of his huge fortune is a measure of the degree to which he took his wife in as his business partner and respected her judgement – a view toward the role of women that subsequent decades would consider exceptionally enlightened for that time. Suddenly Phoebe had full control of a massive business empire which at the time was valued at nineteen million dollars – and considered by some biographers to be a vast underestimate of the true value of the holdings. This heavy responsibility did not cause her to curtail her already busy schedule of civic organizations and society engagements; it just reduced her sleep. Her grandson later remembered how his grandmother would sit at her desk after the rest of the household retired and work well into the early hours of the morning on her business affairs.[42] From that point on she always appeared to be tired, and the bouts of ill health she had experienced throughout her adult life seemed to recur with greater frequency. Even though she employed competent managers, Phoebe was very much involved with her businesses, directly overseeing accounts and making many of the decisions herself. During the remaining decades of her life, the Hearst empire would retain its value under her watchful and prudent care.[43]

The early months of 1898 marked a turning point for the Hearsts because it was during that period that Will became widely recognized as one of the most influential and powerful men in the United States. Will had begun to gain national notoriety during the 1896 presidential election because of his support for William Jennings Bryan, the candidate of the Democratic Party.[44] The pro-Bryan stance of his newspapers was credited with making the outcome much closer than it otherwise would have been. Even though Bryan lost to William McKinley, the Hearst papers increased in circulation and became the primary voice of the Democratic Party because of that hotly contested election. Following closely on the heels of the presidential election, Will turned his attention to the cause of the oppressed people of Spanish-controlled Cuba, trumpeting their plight through his newspapers. Consequently, he was widely considered the one person most responsible for precipitating the Spanish–American War.[45] That conflict brought about not only the final expulsion of Spain from the Americas after centuries of domination, but also the acquisition of the United States's first colony, the Philippines. In addition the war also had another repercussion of even greater importance: the United States was accorded the status of a great international power for the first time in its more than one-hundred-year history as a republic. And one ancillary by-product was that the war set in motion the political career of Theodore Roosevelt. Certainly Will's newspapers (by then he owned a second one in New York City, the *Journal*), at his express direction, had whipped up the anti-Spanish sentiment and war fever that made the war unavoidable. By the spring of 1898, William Randolph Hearst was a national public figure both admired and reviled.

This was just the beginning of an extraordinary career. William's widespread influence would affect the course of American history for decades.[46] And the only person who could control William was Phoebe, because she firmly held the purse strings and decided whether to provide him the capital necessary to expand his publishing empire. Even though Will owned his papers, he could not improve or expand them without large infusions of cash from his father's estate, so in reality he was always beholden to his mother, who treated all business transactions with him as though they were arms-length affairs. He had to beg, cajole, and barter with his mother. She tried to use this power over his finances to temper his behaviour, especially his choice of young women, but she hated to deny him anything. This battle of wills wore her down and broke her heart.

It is the inherent nature of newspapers to become embroiled in political affairs; in fact, since the earliest days of the Republic, most American newspapers were founded to promote a particular political party or public issue and made no pretence of detached objectivity. The Hearst papers were no exception, and served as mouthpieces and champions of the Democratic Party. But Will took them one step further. He believed that newspapers should not just report events; they should shape events. This new approach became known as 'yellow journalism' because his New York newspaper and that of his primary rival, Joseph Pulitzer, which quickly followed suit, both ran the Yellow Dog comic strip. After whipping up anti-Spain sentiments, Will was not going to quietly report the war he helped to start from a desk in New York City. He personally led a large contingent of his staff to Cuba and onto the front lines, where he experienced at least one close call during a shell attack. One can only imagine what his mother thought of his serving as a war correspondent. Will remained in Cuba during the spring and summer of 1898, while his mother retreated for a time to the enormous Hearst ranch in northern Mexico, where she could escape news of the war.

This, then, was the great lady that Edward Getsinger was seeking. He left no record of the details of his travels as he crossed the United States. Certainly the long trip by train and coach would have afforded him ample time to think about how he would approach such a woman. How could he persuade her to meet him? What would he say? Should he tell her about the Bahá'í Faith immediately, or first gain her confidence through a circuitous path? He finally settled upon requesting that she assist him with gaining employment at one of the California universities.

Meanwhile, Lua waited back in Ithaca. In February she wrote to a Bahá'í friend in Chicago of her continuing success in attracting people to the Faith, and went on to say, 'I am rather lonesome since Mr. Getsinger went away still – I do not mind it as I thought I would. This glorious truth fires up all voids and takes away all sorrows.'[47]

Edward was not only lonely but ill. The arduousness of the travel had worn him down and his funds were running low. He arrived at the small agricultural town of Pleasanton, set in a valley some thirty-four miles east of San Francisco, and inquired after Phoebe but found that she was in Mexico. There was nothing to do but wait. He stayed in that little town for weeks, which turned into months, fending off his ill health and hoping that Phoebe would soon return. Undoubtedly he walked the country road between the town and the great estate to inquire after the owner many times. One can imagine him returning again and again to the main gate that separated the road from the winding drive that led up the hill to the main house, trying to convince one of her staff to tell him when she would return.

Following the death of her husband, Phoebe built a country mansion for herself on a hillside with a scenic view of the Armador–Livermoor Valley and christened it 'La Hacienda del Pozo de Verona', after the antique Italian well-head that graced its grand entrance.[48] It was a magnificently luxurious 1,900-acre estate that had been originally purchased by George to be a horse ranch. She had only just completed the main house the year before Edward's arrival. Its style has been difficult to categorize – a cross between a Spanish castle and a Moorish villa on the Mediterranean – with towers, patios and verandas. Its fifty-three rooms were decorated with art treasures, books, tapestries, antiques, the products of years of careful, eclectic collecting from all over the world. The mansion – really a comfortable museum – had forty guest rooms, each with a fireplace and sunken marble bath. The sixty-by-forty-foot music room was large enough to serve as an auditorium or ballroom and had an elevated stage at one end. There was one large room devoted to the storing and processing of gifts for the one thousand and more people she remembered each year at holidays and birthdays. There was a two-storey playhouse for children and kennels for her collies and setters. It would later have California's first indoor swimming pool. The estate also had its own train station and telephone line.

The estate was also a well-equipped, self-sufficient, working business office and farm with arbours and orchards and such massive flower beds that there were more than enough flowers to ship bouquets to hospitals and charitable events throughout the San Francisco Bay area. Her grounds were so exquisitely laid out with such a variety of plants and trees that they made a great impression upon the renowned botanist, Luther Burbank, who noted that 'everything had a place and everything had a use besides its ornamental value which is so rarely seen any where else . . .'[49] One visitor remembered that 'The whole place had a sense of pink and light.'[50]

Finally, Edward's patience and persistence were rewarded, and he was escorted to the main house of the Hacienda to see Phoebe. One version of this first encounter that circulated among the Hearst family was that the butler, Robert Turner, informed Phoebe of Edward's persistence (and probably that he judged Edward to be harmless), so she instructed that he be brought in and invited to join her other guests for dinner. He must have been awestruck as he passed the manicured lawns and opulent rooms. At long last, he was presented face-to-face with Phoebe herself. According to the Hearst family accounts of that dinner, Phoebe was so interested in what he had to say that she sat listening to him most of the evening, without paying much attention to her other guests.[51]

Though many people have speculated over the years as to exactly how Edward met Phoebe and what he said to her, that moment cannot be reconstructed accurately because Edward's is the only known written account, and it leaves many details to the imagination:

> Finally after two months Mrs. Hearst arrived and I was able to see her and told her that I had come to endeavor to receive a professorship in the University of California of which Mrs. Hearst was one of the regents. I explained to her my fitness for such a position and it seems that her niece had read of me some time before of some of my discoveries and had mentioned my name and my discoveries to Mrs. Hearst which also made it easier for me to receive consideration at once. On the next visit I told that I had left my wife in the East and if it was possible for me to receive encouragement that I would send for her, have her come to me to which she also agreed.
>
> When Lua arrived she gave Mrs. Hearst the Message and she became a believer. During this time I was quite ill, although not in bed, nevertheless I was quite unfitted to do any kind of mental work but had to rest my brain in order to overcome my difficulties. During this time Mrs. Hearst was very kind to both of these servants and attended to all our needs and requirements. With such great kindness and generosity that these servants have never forgotten her and never failed to appreciate her noble qualities.[52]

Phoebe still considered herself to be a Presbyterian. She had attended church services frequently during the early years of her marriage and sent her young son to the Sunday School of the Presbyterian Church in San Francisco. Over the years her interest in spiritual matters did not wane, but her church attendance did. While in Europe she had become better acquainted with other Christian denominations and even had a brief audience with the Pope in Rome.[53] Her husband, on the other hand, came from a less religious family than his wife and took pride in never joining a church.[54] She often jokingly recounted the following incident from Will's childhood that summed up the family's religious leanings. The Hearsts had failed to have Will christened as an infant. This greatly agitated his Irish Catholic nurse who was certain that the child's immortal soul was in jeopardy. So one day she snuck Will into a Catholic church while his parents were not at home and had him properly baptized. When Phoebe heard about this she exclaimed, 'But, I am a Presbyterian!', to which the nurse replied, 'No matter, madam. The baby is a Christian!' This incident always amused Phoebe.[55] She was as broadminded in her views about religion as she was in her other opinions and read a wide variety of thinkers on the subject; for example, her personal library included a complete set of the published works of Emanuel Swedenborg. She occasionally included churches and religious organizations among her charities. A case in point was the time when Phoebe discovered that a small town where one of her husband's mines was located had many saloons but only one tiny Catholic chapel. She paid for the establishment of a Methodist church in that locality. But she herself had never sworn unwavering allegiance to any religion, which did not mean that she felt religion to be unimportant. On the contrary, she thought deeply about spiritual matters.[56] With the coming of the Getsingers, she finally found a faith that completely resonated with her.

Phoebe was not the only one at the Hacienda interested in what the Getsingers had to say about religion. During their years in Washington, D.C., the Hearsts had employed a young man to serve the senator. Most likely born into slavery on a farm near Norfolk, Virginia on 15 October 1855,[57] Robert C. Turner became the right hand of first George and then Phoebe. There were stories of how young Robert would patiently stand near the senator as he ate so that he could clean up the mess that the unrefined George would make all over the elaborately set table by fidgeting with bread. Robert would then unobtrusively provide him with another piece.[58] After George's death, Robert was almost always with Phoebe serving as her butler, an important household position, especially considering the size and number of her residences. Most likely his responsibilities included the supervision of other staff. When, as a widow, Phoebe again made San Francisco her primary residence, Robert moved with his wife, Malissa, to California from Washington, D.C. Some months after her husband's passing, Phoebe penned this tribute to Robert:

> And who reigned over my kitchen dominion and kept the machinery oiled and quiet? Well, the most glorious, the most important, the most absolutely indispensable, was Robert, my faithful servant, for if he has a marked fault, it is his aptitude to extend, to swell, far beyond the need and size of the occasion.[59]

As one of the people she trusted the most, it is likely that Robert was inconspicuously standing close to Phoebe when she met with Edward for the first time. Robert's heart was moved by what he heard of the new Faith and he became a devoted believer, the first African American to accept the Cause.

That June, Anne Apperson returned home to the Pleasanton estate from a stay in Paris, where she had been studying, to discover the Getsingers already staying there. She too was attracted to the new religion they enthusiastically espoused and became a believer.[60]

Another of Mrs Hearst's protégées, Helen Adelaide Hillyer, was also staying at the Hacienda that summer. Twenty-six-year-old Nell, or Nellie, as she was known to her friends, was Phoebe's foster child. Her parents Munson Curtis Hillyer and Martha Elizabeth Lowe Hillyer had, like George Hearst, moved to California during the gold rush to seek their fortune in mining. Apparently the Hillyers were living at the 'Lick House', a famous San Francisco boarding house, when the Hearsts stayed there as newlyweds. In addition to the Hillyers and the Hearsts, other future stars of California such as the Leland Stanfords[61] and Mark Twain (Samuel Clemens)[62] were also residing at the Lick House at the time.

Tall with gray eyes and brown hair, Nell was born in San Francisco on 12 July 1872.[63] Her father first ran a flour mill and then turned to his real interest – mining. She was the youngest of four children, only two of whom had survived. Her sister was much older and she married by the time Nell was four, so Nell grew up as an only child, much indulged and pampered. When she was seven, the family moved from San Francisco to Virginia City, Nevada, and later to Silver City where her father was a superintendent of mines. Those mining towns made San Francisco seem refined by comparison. But as the daughter of an important person in the mining industry, her lot was above that of most of the residents of those rough places, and her father's position brought her special privileges such as meeting President Rutherford Hayes and holding the hand of President Ulysses S. Grant as he toured the mines.

When Nell was 11 years old, tragedy struck the Hillyer family. Nell's mother became seriously ill and so the family returned to San Francisco. Phoebe, a long-time friend of Nell's mother, offered for young Nell to live with her while Martha Hillyer received care at a residential facility.[64] Mrs Hillyer died a few years later; consequently Nell continued to live with Phoebe off and on while her restless father pursued mining and other business interests in Alaska and Colombia. It seems that Phoebe surmised that Nell's upbringing in Virginia City had made her deficient in manners and gentility. She took Nell under her wing and exposed her to polite company, throwing a 'coming out' ball for her in Washington, D.C., and sending her to Europe on a year-long tour for cultural edification and to study French at the Berlitz Language School in Paris.

When Nell returned to the Hacienda from France during the summer of 1898, she was quickly drawn to the Getsingers and what they had to say about religion. Nell was a free spirit – spunky, audacious, and adventurous. Her childhood religious education is unknown and was most likely as spotty as her formal schooling; but her maternal grandfather was a clergyman and her father's parents had been devoted members of the Congregational Church, the American remnant of Puritanism, and so undoubtedly she was influenced in some way by that background. With the same high-spirited enthusiasm she exhibited towards most of life, Nell plunged into study of the Bahá'í Faith.[65]

Phoebe began to tell her friends and relatives about the new religion and arranged for Lua to conduct a small study class, which met first at her country mansion, the Hacienda, and then in downtown San Francisco in Phoebe's apartment at the top of the Examiner Building on the corner of Third and Market Street.[66] Lua used the same lessons that Kheiralla had developed. The first class member to become a confirmed believer was 29-year-old Californian Henrietta Emogene Martin Hoagg, the wife of John Ketchie Hoagg who had made a fortune through flour mills. Emogene, as she was generally known, had been searching in vain for a religion that would satisfy her inner yearnings, and while visiting Phoebe at Pleasanton she immediately responded when Lua told her about the Bahá'í Faith. Looking back on her conversion, Emogene said, 'My interest augmented from lesson to lesson. The first commune, "O my God, give me knowledge, faith and love", was constantly on my lips, and I believe those words from the Fountain of Eternal Light awakened my soul and mind to a faith that has never wavered.'[67]

Nell interested her friend, Ella Francis Goodall, in Lua's classes. It seems that the two had first met while taking a philosophy class together. Ella was born on 12 January 1870 in San Francisco,[68] and came from another well-to-do family. Her English father, Edwin Goodall, was a partner in a successful shipping business.[69] Of average height, slender and erect, with hazel eyes and dark hair which was already beginning to show strands of white, Ella was then 27 and an avid student of music, having even tried her hand at composing; her works had been performed at amateur musical productions.[70] She lived with her parents and younger brother in an imposing 'gingerbread house' with elaborately carved wooden decorations that had been custom-built for her family in the city of Oakland, the little sister of San Francisco across the bay. Ella was a lady in the nicest sense of that word – dignified, poised, well-mannered, courteous, thoughtful, and kind. She was accustomed to elegant social occasions even though she herself was never extravagant. She was listed on the San Francisco Social Registry for many years and often had her name printed in the society pages of newspapers. Nonetheless, she was always approachable and friendly to people from all walks of life. One of her friends later recounted, 'Everyone felt Ella's happy exuberance when she entered a room. She had a charm and a beautiful, loving spirit which drew friends to her.'[71]

Nell invited Ella to join her one evening at the Hearst downtown penthouse. At that time, Lua still taught the Bahá'í lessons in the same secretive manner as Kheiralla had taught them. Consequently, because Ella was not yet an initiate, she was required to remain in another room while Lua took her more advanced students through the evening's lesson. Finally at 1 o'clock in the morning, Lua came into the room where Ella had been kept waiting for hours and at once began her spiritual instruction. They were famished from the long evening, and so, despite the late hour, sent out to nearby Gooby's Saloon for an oyster loaf, which they washed down with wine.[72] Even though

Ella must have felt ignored most of the evening, Lua did not tell her anything of substance about the Faith during her first lesson. 'The pith' never came until lesson eleven. So Nell shortly thereafter took it upon herself to jump ahead and tell Ella about Bahá'u'lláh. Ella, fortunately, had the insight to see that there was a great truth behind the little information that Lua had imparted to her. Ella shared it with her mother, Helen Sturtevant Arey Goodall, a native of Maine and former schoolteacher.[73] Unfortunately, the Getsingers left San Francisco soon after Ella and her mother started their instruction in the Faith. The Goodalls became so impatient to know more of the new religion that in October they travelled by train across the continent to New York City in order to learn more from Anton Haddad, who had recently returned to the United States.[74]

Phoebe had more on her mind that summer of 1898 than the Bahá'í Faith and her son's war in the Caribbean. She probably arranged for the Bahá'í classes to be transferred from the Hacienda to her downtown apartment in order to remove her Hacienda visitors because she was preparing for another guest who was coming secretly – her light and mentor, Dr William Pepper. She had met Pepper in 1895 when that renowned surgeon was called in to attend to her after she suffered a heart attack. Thus began one of the most significant relationships of her life. In Pepper she found an equal – an exceptional person of many talents and interests. He shared her brilliance and energy, and saw in her someone open to new ideas and possibilities. She called him 'one of the best friends of my whole lifetime', and also said: 'His beautiful helpful sympathy has encouraged me in many ways.'[75] As president of the Archeological Museum at the University of Pennsylvania, he stimulated her enthusiastic curiosity about the origins of mankind and encouraged her to underwrite anthropological and archeological field work. He was himself a noted scientist who made many breakthroughs in the field of medical research and so stimulated her interest in funding those scientific pursuits. He was also a leader in the field of education, and his reforms while serving as provost at the University of Pennsylvania are still regarded a century later as in part responsible for the transformation of that school into the distinguished modern institution it has become.

Pepper, though only 54, was suffering from ill health that summer of 1898, so Mrs Hearst invited him to the Hacienda in the hope that the California sunshine would restore him. But while at her home his health took a turn for the worse and he died on 31 July. The strain of caring for him during his final illness and her grief at his passing sent Phoebe to bed for several weeks. This tragedy had followed closely upon the heels of her parents being ill – not to mention coinciding with her worries about Will, who was still in the midst of a war zone. Writing to her childhood friend and confidant, Mrs Clara Reed Anthony, on 22 August, she said, 'Dr Pepper came and his illness and death were very distressing. The shock and fatigue laid me up for a time.'[76] She added that she was therefore contemplating a trip abroad – her own usual cure for the stresses of life.

Phoebe had always been attracted to anything French, especially Paris. Even as a teenager in Missouri she had learned passable French and as a young housewife in California she had gone to great lengths to continue her study of it.[77] She had taken her son, while still a boy, to Europe several times to visit its great museums and historic sites. It would be fair to say that her European trips were the means whereby she attained the equivalent of a university education. She did not just tour the European attractions for pleasure; she visited them for intensive study.[78] In addition to providing her with longed-for intellectual stimulation, Europe, and especially Paris, was where she could relax away from the daily press of her weighty responsibilities.

By the end of August Phoebe had decided to go first to her apartment in Paris and then to winter in Egypt where she would host a party of friends on a Nile River cruise. She wanted to meet the archaeologist George Reisner while in Egypt to determine if she should fund his pioneering research into ancient Egypt – a fitting way to carry forward the work that had been promoted by Dr Pepper. Her time in Egypt would be followed by a second cruise along the Eastern Mediterranean coast with a stop in Istanbul. She of course planned to travel in her beloved Europe after the cruises and would cap off the trip with the formal presentation of her niece, 21-year-old Anne, at the Court of St James in London; the event would mark Anne's formal 'coming out' into the upper echelons of society.

Pilgrimage to the Holy Tomb of Bahá'u'lláh at Bahjí and sitting at the feet of 'Abdu'l-Bahá had become topics of great interest to the American believers following the return of Anton Haddad to the United States in mid-December of 1897. During his return to his home in Lebanon, he had had the privilege of making a pilgrimage to 'Akká and meeting the Master. His description of that visit was widely circulated among the American believers:

> Oh my dear brother heaven is there & the paradise of God. Everybody would desire to be a servant in that place. I cannot explain to you the dignity & respect appearing on the faces of the favorites. The appearance of glory & besides these attributes the signs of kindness & generosity, love, & happiness for the human race. On account of this he ['Abdu'l-Bahá] cannot sleep nights, people not leaving him a minute. Everybody goes to him for help & he never rejects them. His time is spent enlightening

> all – rich as well as poor, it makes no difference to him. His knowledge, understanding & high attributes are his characteristics & he is really the spirit & son of God . . . There is paradise & happiness . . . He said great blessings were coming to the U.S. He said 'If God wished it will be the happiest country in the world.'[79]

Haddad's return to New York also marked another important change in the nascent American Bahá'í community because he presented the believers with an alternative to Kheiralla as a source of information about the Faith. Kheiralla immediately began to worry that his position as unchallenged, unofficial head of the American believers would be undermined. His dilemma was complicated by a lie he had told his followers – that he had actually met Bahá'u'lláh and 'Abdu'l-Bahá. He begged Haddad not to expose this deception, justifying his actions by saying that he had seen them both in visions and visions were, in his estimation, the same as reality.[80]

There is no record of how Phoebe decided to add a pilgrimage to 'Akká to visit 'Abdu'l-Bahá to her winter itinerary. Perhaps Lua or Edward suggested it after reading Haddad's glowing account. The idea must have had added appeal because of the death of William Pepper. He had been one of the tiny handful of people she genuinely looked up to, that she was close to; consequently, she must have felt rudderless after his passing. Perhaps a spiritual teacher like the Master could lighten her heart and fill the empty places in her soul.

Phoebe, a seasoned traveller, was accustomed to taking along an entourage, so the Getsingers were invited to accompany her. Probably at the urging of Lua, Phoebe also decided to invite Mr and Mrs Kheiralla, even though she had not yet met them.

Ibrahim Kheiralla had not been idle during the months that the Getsingers were in California. As Americans are wont to do, a number of his Chicago students had moved and spread the Faith to other communities. By the end of 1898 there were groups of believers in New York City, Washington, D.C., and Kenosha, Wisconsin in addition to Chicago, Ithaca and San Francisco. Kheiralla had visited New York City and Kenosha. He was also busy writing an introductory book to the Faith entitled *Beha'U'llah*, and had taken up residence in Maine. He was absorbed in that work when he received the cable from Lua conveying Phoebe's invitation. Of course, he could not refuse, so he hastened to finish his manuscript and rushed to Chicago and Kenosha to ensure the steadfastness of those communities during his absence.[81]

Other members of the Hearst Nile cruise party included Phoebe's niece Anne, as well as a young cousin, Agnes Lane, who like Anne was another of Phoebe's protégées.[82] Robert Turner, of course, would come. In addition,

Phoebe would bring one of her maids, Amalia Maria Bachrodt, called 'Emily' by the Americans. Emily, who was 47 years old, industrious, single, and thoroughly reliable, had arrived in the United States from her native Germany at the age of 23. She had worked for Phoebe for a long time as a 'ladies' maid', and had accompanied her mistress on at least one previous trip to Europe.[83] She too accepted the Bahá'í Faith. Phoebe's cousin, Joe Clark, and other close friends such as the artist Orrin Peck, a 'second son' to Phoebe and the Hearst family's 'court jester',[84] would round out the group that would holiday with her in Egypt.[85]

Emogene Hoagg, an outstanding pianist and vocalist, had spent most of the previous year in Milan studying singing. She was about to return to Italy for further voice study and was invited to accompany the group at least as far as Paris. While not part of the pilgrimage to 'Akká *per se*, she was keenly interested in it and was a peripheral member. Emogene would spend much time in the Holy Land in later years, beginning with her first pilgrimage in 1900.[86]

Phoebe wanted a travelling companion for herself. Since all the other travellers were young enough to be her children or were her employees, she invited her childhood friend residing near Boston, Clara Vance Anthony, to accompany her, but Mrs Anthony had to decline the invitation because of family responsibilities.[87] One can only speculate how the course of the development of the Faith in the British Isles would have been altered had Mrs Anthony been able to come along because the friend Phoebe then turned to as an alternate was living near London. The substitution of Mary Virginia Thornburgh-Cropper (more about her later) as Phoebe's travelling companion would prove to be a fateful change that resulted in the establishment of the Faith in England.

Most of the party left California by train around 10 September 1898 – probably in Phoebe's private rail car – and arrived in New York City about the 15th, where she and some or perhaps the entire group stayed at the luxurious Astoria Hotel.[88] Phoebe then took her companions on a side trip for a few days to her home in Washington, D.C.[89] Writing to Mrs Anthony from Washington, she again talked of her overwhelming fatigue: '. . . how I shall live through the next three days I do not know. If I can get on the steamer I will sleep all the way to Cherbourg.'[90]

While in Washington, Phoebe hired another employee to accompany the group during the months abroad: a tutor for Agnes who would be missing school because of the trip. Agnes suffered most of her life from chronic health problems that at times required the use of a wheelchair, so choosing her teacher was a delicate matter. One of William Pepper's protégées at the University of Pennsylvania, Dr Alonzo Taylor,[91] recommended the sister of one of his classmates from Cornell University. The young woman, Julia L. Pearson, was also a Cornell graduate and Dr Taylor vouched that she was a hard worker. Julia was born in Chicago on 10 November 1876 to a middle-class family, and in 1898 was residing in Philadelphia.[92] Her schoolteacher mother, Lucy Pearson, had a remarkable ability to stimulate a desire for learning, and consequently Julia came from a family of high academic achievers.[93] Twenty-one-year old Julia had received her degree in philosophy only a few months before the Getsingers established the Faith in Ithaca, where Cornell was located.[94] Julia was attractive in a business-like sort of way, of medium height and build with gray eyes and light brown hair. During the trip, she would assist Phoebe with correspondence in addition to her duties with Agnes. Julia would also become a Bahá'í and a pilgrim.

Undoubtedly, the brief stay in New York City afforded the Getsingers and the new California believers an opportunity to meet with the Bahá'ís in that city. Mr and Mrs Arthur Pillsbury Dodge had learned of the Faith in Chicago, and then moved to New York where they had played a major role in establishing that Bahá'í community. Dodge was a self-made man of many talents: a lawyer, magazine publisher, and inventor who during his lifetime made and lost a number of fortunes. He would later be named a Disciple of 'Abdu'l-Bahá. With the assistance of Anton Haddad, he was conducting Bahá'í meetings and attracting many New Yorkers to the Faith.

There was undoubtedly envy among the believers who were staying behind and one in particular expressed his feelings about not being part of the pilgrimage. Ibrahim Kheiralla had taken the liberty of inviting Thornton Chase to come along (probably at his own expense), but Chase could not obtain time off from his employer. Chase wrote to Kheiralla that, 'I am heart broken to learn that you are going . . . and it is impossible for me to join you.'[95] Thornton Chase, like many others, resolved to travel to 'Akká at the first opportunity. However, all agreed that it was befitting that Mr and Mrs Kheiralla should accompany Phoebe; after all, Kheiralla had been the one to introduce and establish the Faith in the United States. Besides which, he had told this flock that he had actually met both Bahá'u'lláh and 'Abdu'l-Bahá, and so everyone assumed that his prior experience and native Arabic would prove useful to the American pilgrims. The Kheirallas met the Californians for the first time in New York and met Phoebe for the first time on board ship.

The last evening before their departure, the New York believers turned out to wish their teacher *bon voyage*. One of them, James Brittingham, wrote the following account of that evening and of Kheiralla's parting message.

> . . . he called all the believers together down on 14th Street New York at the home of Mrs. Jones, who was a believer and Dr Kh[e]iralla told us . . . he

> had called us to him to give us a warning. He told us to remember always that the Message he had given us was the truth and we must never allow ourselves to be weaned from it, and he warned us to be on our guards and he said 'I want to tell you that a great teacher in this country was going to fall, but we must not fall with him ['] – and even if it was Kheiralla who fell, we must not fall with him for he had given us the truth.[96]

Kheiralla's words would prove to be prophetic, but not in the way in which he probably intended.

At last the Hearst party with its new additions and great expectations set sail for France, on Thursday 22 September aboard the German ocean liner *S.S. Fürst Bismarck.*[97] The first Bahá'í pilgrims from the West were on their way.

CHAPTER 4

Paris and the Dawning of the Faith in Europe

Mrs Mary Bolles was surprised to learn that her friend and benefactress, Phoebe Hearst, was about to arrive in France. Even though the two ladies had been friends for years, Mary could not always anticipate Phoebe's whims. During the fall of 1898 Mary and her two adult children were enjoying Phoebe's extended hospitality in that they were residing in Phoebe's Paris apartment while Mary's son, Randolph, was studying architecture. There was little time to prepare for Phoebe's arrival; her decision to come had been somewhat hasty and, as usual, she was bringing an entourage that included a few unfamiliar names. Preparing the grand flat on the fashionable Quai d'Orsay for its owner would take some work. Phoebe had put as much care into furnishing her Paris accommodations as she had her other homes; after all, Paris was one of her favourite places – a retreat of sorts. It was inevitable that that apartment would also be filled to overflowing with items from her collections of art and antiquities. Mary and her family had had the pleasure of enjoying these treasures in exchange for the minor inconvenience of assisting with the management of the suite when its mistress was absent. Now Mary set the necessary steps in motion. There were unused rooms to open and air, pantries to fill and additional servants to engage. Having visited with Mrs Hearst only a year before at her new country estate in California, Mary was well acquainted with both her friend's high housekeeping standards and expectations of propriety.

How Mary Ellis Martin Bolles came to know Phoebe Hearst remains a mystery.[1] Certainly, since Mary was the daughter of a well-to-do bank president from New York City, the two ladies belonged to the same elite social strata, but before living in France her world had been primarily the East Coast of the United States. She had married another New Yorker, John Harris Bolles, on 7 October 1868. It had seemed a promising match since John's father was a well known, prosperous New York physician and John was an engineer who also worked for a while in the financial industry; but the marriage was short-lived, perhaps because John and Mary had opposite temperaments. Whereas she loved the gaiety of an active social life, he preferred solitary, serious activities.[2] A few years after their two children were born, the Bolles went their separate ways despite their continuing affection for each other. They never divorced, but neither did they ever live together again as husband and wife. John headed west where he ended up in Colorado, probably working with his entrepreneur younger brother who became rich through silver mining and land development, and Mary moved with their small children to her parents' home in Englewood, New Jersey.

The Martin household in which the Bolles children grew up was no longer wealthy, not only because Mary's father was by then retired but because of an unforeseen calamity. One evening in 1869, thieves broke into the Ocean National Bank and took all of the money in its vault. As a result, the bank failed. Her father, David Randolph Martin had founded that bank and managed it as President for years, so it was the primary source of his income. To compound that disaster, the receiver appointed by the government to oversee the liquidation of the bank proved to be dishonest. Lawsuits and even a Congressional investigation went on for more than a decade, during which Randolph Martin was repeatedly called to testify.[3] It is a measure of his character that he paid off at least part of the bank's remaining debts to its depositors out of his own pocket. Gone were household luxuries the family had always been accustomed to, and the grandchildren remembered wearing hand-me-down clothes from their more prosperous New York cousins. Nonetheless, it must have been an active household, which at times included Mary's older brothers, who were slow to marry. The eldest brother, Benjamin, was not only a surgeon but also a well-known author of books and magazine articles on a number of subjects, especially travel in England and France, so it is easy to deduce that the Martin home must have provided an intellectually stimulating environment for the grandchildren.

While nothing is known for certain about the Bolles/Martin family's religious leanings, though one friend said that they were Unitarians,[4] the peculiar choice of a clergyman to officiate at Mary and John's wedding may hold a clue. The Reverend O. B. Frothingham[5] was perhaps one of the most radical, liberal, free-thinking, outspoken Christian ministers in the United States at the time, and it is unlikely that he would have been chosen to conduct the wedding if at least one of the couple did not approve of his ideas. Originally a Unitarian who was part of the transcendental and the abolitionist movements, Rev. Frothingham believed that Christianity had run its course and was dying from corruption of the spirit. He sought a more ecumenical spiritual fellowship that embraced even followers of faiths other than Christianity. He earnestly believed that a great 'Religion of Humanity' was about to be born. Frothingham broke with the Unitarian church and became the president of the Free Religious Society. He was a gifted, popular orator and a widely read author.[6] It can be assumed that he had some influence upon the thinking of the Martin and Bolles families.

Mary and her children were living in Paris in 1898 so that Randolph could study at the famous École des Beaux Arts, then widely considered the finest school of architecture in the world. Paris, as the turn of the century approached, offered a lively social circle for American expatriates because it was the acknowledged cultural capital of the world. Many Americans had taken up residence in Paris and many more visited. It was a place to see and to be seen among the American elite, whose Parisian social affairs were reported extensively in the *New York Times*. The Yanks in Paris primarily socialized with each other rather than with the French because they were overwhelmingly Protestants and most of the French were Catholics.[7] Nonetheless, there was always an abundance of friends and acquaintances from back home to fill a calendar with social engagements.

While Randolph made friends at school and enjoyed Paris, his older sister, May, spent most of her time at the apartment, coping with chronic ill health. When the Hearst party arrived at the beginning of October, 28-year-old Mary Ellis Bolles, known simply as 'May',[8] was bedridden; in fact, there were well-founded fears that she was dying but no doctor could adequately explain why or put a diagnostic name to her ailment. Her delicate condition was evident in her appearance. A mere wisp of a figure often assumed to be younger than her age, she had wide blue eyes peering out of an ethereal face framed by soft brown hair. May had not always been plagued with poor health. The onset of the malady at around age 20 had circumscribed her world and, it seems, plunged her into depths of depression and feelings of hopelessness. She occasionally rallied; nevertheless, during periods of relapse she would become exhausted and breathless after short physical exertions.

Even before her illness, May had not been like other children; she had always been inexplicably drawn to religion. At the age of 11 she had the first of a number of unusual experiences. While sleeping, she saw a light so bright that she physically became blind for an entire day. This strange occurrence was followed some time later by a dream in which angels were carrying her through space. She realized that they were showing her the earth as it would be seen from far above, and she noted that it had been marked by seals with one word spread over its surface. When she awoke, all that she could remember of the word was the first letter B and the letter H; but deep within herself she knew that the dream held profound significance for the course of her life. At another time she had a vision of a majestic figure robed in Eastern clothing who beckoned to her from across the Mediterranean Sea. Her first thought was that it must be Jesus, but she would come to recognize that it was 'Abdu'l-Bahá. Despite the educational opportunities provided by her family, including a period in a French convent school, May at the age of 14 announced that she was finished with formal schooling. As she later remarked, 'I felt very distinctly there was another way of acquiring knowledge.'[9] Her life was in essence one long spiritual quest until the day Lua Getsinger walked into her bedroom. As May's daughter would often remark many years later, God chose the weakest vessel in Europe to spread His Cause.

While the Bolleses were preparing for its arrival, the Hearst party was 'crossing the briny deep'. Lua was keeping a journal, apparently a gift to her from Nell Hillyer, inscribed from 'Helen of Troy' to 'the dear little messenger that brought the gladtidings to me with love and gratitude'. Except for a couple of days of bad weather that brought on bouts of seasickness among the group, the crossing was blessed with fair weather and moonlit evenings. Lua noted that 'our last dinner on board was very nice and we had a jolly time', although she later added in a letter to Thornton Chase that 'The sea has its charms – but the land has more by far.'[10] Kheiralla must have passed the time on board ship getting to know the new believers from California and imparting further lessons. Phoebe, if her stated intentions were achievable, used the brief week away from cables and letters to rest. The ship docked at Cherbourg and the group travelled overland to Paris, arriving on 29 September. Undoubtedly the Getsingers tried to soak in everything they passed by as they got their first look at Europe.

Soon after arrival, Edward was called upon to look in on May. Certainly it was assumed that he could be of help as a homeopathic physician. He spent a few minutes with the patient and then came out of her room looking for his wife. His conclusion was that May did not need a doctor, she needed spiritual help. Lua went to May and in the first moments of their time together changed May's life forever by telling her about Bahá'u'lláh. May was so overcome by what Lua said about the coming of a new Messenger of God, so thirsty for that spiritual truth, that she at once raised herself up from her pillow and exclaimed, 'I believe! I believe!' and then like a proper Victorian lady, promptly fainted from the emotion of the moment.[11] May's heart had undoubtedly been prepared for the spiritual teachings by years of suffering and it took only that little spark from Lua to set it aflame. With her heart filled with newfound faith, May's health improved.

The day after her arrival, Lua penned a letter to Thornton Chase back in Chicago, a letter really meant for all the members of the Chicago Bahá'í community, in which she spoke of her feelings of destiny, of the great moment that was upon them, and beseeching him and the other believers remaining behind in the United States to remain steadfast during this period when their primary teacher, Kheiralla, was absent.

> I feel almost selfish when I think of the rest of you – who have been working in the cause so much longer than I have – still debarred from enjoying what your dear hearts most long for – and that the great blessing has been bestowed upon me. I do not and cannot feel that it is because I am more worthy of it – for I have done very little – but in my heart I have truly loved, and do love my God – and have had no doubts whatever. You know I asked in my letter last Spring that I might be the humble instrument of assisting Dr. K – financially to make the journey – and I feel this is the direct answer to my supplication – which God in His Infinite Mercy and wisdom saw fit to consider. I think it was answered more for Dr. K.'s sake than mine. We are not going to Acca when Dr. K. goes – he goes ahead alone – and if he succeeds in getting an invitation for Mrs. K, Mr. G and myself we will follow later. I will surely write you from there and I am going to keep a diary making a record of everything I see and hear.

Lua goes on to urge them to put all petty jealousy and gossip out of their midst and not to focus on the faults of others. There must have already been rumblings against Kheiralla because she warns them to not speak negatively of their teacher. She ends with these stirring words:

> Oh my brother – and all dear believers – stand firmly together – helping one another, and loving one another – thus showing to the world that we are in reality – children of God! My love is with you, and my prayers are for you all.
>
> May God bless you and comfort you
>
> With sincere affection I am your Sister in the glorious cause. Lua M. Getsinger[12]

Having never visited any of Phoebe's other homes, the reaction of the Kheirallas when they first eyed her luxurious Paris apartment may well be imagined. But they did not linger for long. Within a few days of their arrival in France, Marian Kheiralla left for London to visit her family and to arrange, if possible, for the aunt who was her substitute mother, Marianne Brown, to join the party heading for 'Akká.[13] This aunt had accepted the Faith several years earlier when Marian had taken her new husband to England to meet her family. Kheiralla himself had other business of a personal nature to attend to, and so he left within a fortnight for Egypt from whence he would proceed on to 'Akká to prepare for the arrival of the rest of the group.

The Hearst party was counting upon Kheiralla to carry out one important task. Permission had not yet been sought from 'Abdu'l-Bahá for them to be allowed to come to 'Akká. Kheiralla was to deliver the request. Lua wrote the supplication on behalf of them all in the most eloquent, Biblical and flowery style she could muster – decidedly un-American – which she must have thought was required for such an important document.

> In God's Name –
> To the Greatest Branch
>
> My Lord, My Lord – from my heart I send Thee greetings and beg Thee to accept my life as sacrifice to Thy Will and wish. Oh my Lord, I praise God my Beloved that my supplication has been heard and I have been permitted to approach this near unto Thee – but oh Prince of the world my heart yearns for the exaltation of Thy presence and my eyes long to behold the glory of Thy beneficent face – therefore I am enabled to once more feel encouraged to come unto Thee as a child, pleading for consideration.
>
> I beg of Thee, oh best Beloved of the Father – that you will specially bless my dear Teacher – who has guided me to the Blessed Tree of Life and who so kindly bears to Thee – oh Blessed one – this humble message – and oh Ruler of the House of David and King of the world – will you ask God the Mighty, the most High to cleanse me from mine iniquities and make my heart pure that I may be made worthy of completing the journey to The Holy City and kneeling before Thee to kiss the dust beneath Thy Holy Feet. Also I beg thee this blessed privilege be conferred upon my husband and the rest of our party who have thus far accompanied our Beloved Teacher. I salute Thee by the Name of Abha and humbly await Thy pleasure,
>
> Thy unworthy Servant
> Oct. 10th, 1898[14]

Lua included a list of names with her petition, many of which are puzzling because, in addition to some of the members of the Hearst party, there are other names whose identity and connection to the Faith remain a mystery.[15] Were they people in France who had shown an interest? Friends made on board the ship perhaps? Even more confusing is the omission of several members of the Hearst party. In any case, once it was dispatched, there was nothing to do but bide their time while awaiting an answer.

The friends tarrying in Paris were soon joined by a mother and daughter from California who resided in England – friends of Phoebe – who not only would be valuable members of the pilgrimage group, but also important to the establishment of the Faith in Europe. When Phoebe's life-long friend, Clara Anthony, declined the invitation to join the trip as Phoebe's travelling companion, Phoebe extended the same offer to another friend, 41-year-old Mary Virginia Shepherd Thornburgh-Cropper. This change in travelling companions would result in the founding of the British Bahá'í community.[16] Just as a young American invalid would establish the Bahá'í Faith in France, so God chose two of the most dejected, rootless ladies in England to carry forth His work.

Virginia Thornburgh-Cropper,[17] known to most people as 'Minnie', was a Californian, even though she had lived all of her adult life in England. Her parents were among those settlers who streamed westward during the Gold Rush. Her father, William ('Bill') B. Thornburgh, had migrated to the California gold fields to seek his fortune from his boyhood home near Harper's Ferry, Virginia.[18] He made money from a number of professions: he farmed, he served as sheriff of Yuba County for a time, and had his hand in California mining and real estate. When Minnie, his first and only child, was born, he was part owner of a local brokerage business, Cheeseman, Jewett & Thornburgh in Marysville. Minnie's mother, Harriet ('Hattie') Frances Burtis, was from Kentucky originally.[19] Prior to her marriage in 1856,[20] she had been living in Johnson Creek, near Marysville, where Bill Thornburgh's brother had a prosperous business as a grocer. Hattie was only 17 when she became a wife and 18 when she became a mother. When Minnie was a toddler, her parents owned a sizeable farm in Marysville which employed a number of workers, in addition to her father's other business dealings. A few years later, the family moved to Virginia City, Nevada, where her father established the Paxton & Thornburgh Bank and was also involved in the mining industry.[21] About 1863 or 1864 the bank was dissolved and the family returned to California.[22]

Hattie and Bill Thornburgh idealized England; perhaps theirs was the natural sentiment of descendants of immigrants who view the ancestral homeland with romanticized (and usually unrealistic) longing. When they moved back to California from Nevada, they bought 13,000 acres of prime land at the point where Berkeley and Oakland meet, and built a replica of an English castle on a site on the side of a hill with a breathtaking view of the bay and San Francisco. In order to enjoy the English sport of foxhunting, they not only raised hounds; they imported English foxes and hired English grooms to tend their stables of pedigree horses. At some point Bill, the prosperous entrepreneur, moved his family from the 'castle'[23] to San Francisco where they acquired another fine home in the exclusive Nob Hill neighbourhood on Pine Street, the same avenue where the Hearst home graced a corner lot.

Like Phoebe, Hattie's world revolved around her only child. Minnie grew up to be a willowy young lady with chiselled features, soulful blue eyes and light brown hair. Unlike her mother, who was of average stature, Minnie was exceptionally tall for a girl, almost six feet; years later she would repeatedly bemoan her 'accursed height'. Nothing is known about either Minnie's or her mother's educational backgrounds, but both shared an interest in the arts, especially music, and were avid readers.

Into this little American family of anglophiles came the welcome addition of an English youth, Edward Denman Cropper, known as 'Denman'. Englishmen of means were charmed by the 'social ease and naturalness' of American women, while young American ladies were attracted to the seeming sophistication and chivalrous manners of upper-crust Englishmen.[24] There is nothing to tell us how the young people met or what attracted them to each other, although Minnie and her mother had travelled back to the United States from England on the same ship with Denman in December of 1873. There was much to like in Minnie. She was intelligent with an inquiring mind, could sing, enjoyed taking part in amateur dramatic productions, and was well-mannered, self-effacing and considerate. Denman and Minnie were married in San Francisco on 4 June 1874 by the Episcopal Bishop of California when she was only 17 and he was 20.[25] Accompanied by her parents and a few servants, Minnie and Denman sailed to his ancestral hometown of Liverpool from New York City in November of 1874 to meet his illustrious family and to begin her new life in England.[26] Undoubtedly there must have been dinners and parties to show off the new bride and her wealthy parents to the groom's Dingle Bank[27] friends and relatives. The Thornburghs and the Croppers surely must have been pleased that their children had made such a match. He brought a British pedigree to the marriage and she, as the only child of well-to-do parents, brought the prospect of a sizeable inheritance. Her new husband demonstrated how proud he was of his marriage, at least in the beginning, by applying for a new coat of arms and adding the name Thornburgh to his own surname.

Denman came from a high-minded, accomplished, prosperous family. His paternal grandfather, James Cropper, went from being a yeoman farmer to a wealthy man through his partnership in a shipping business, whose vessels included packers sailing to and from the United States. James, a staunch Quaker and proponent of strict morality, was well known for his social conscience and his philanthropy. According to one story circulated about him, when someone wrote a 'misery letter' asking for assistance and addressed the envelope with only the words to 'the most generous man in Liverpool', the post office delivered it to James Cropper. Denman's grandfather was also well known for his outspoken advocacy of the abolition of slavery, actively collaborating with the leader of that movement, William Wilberforce. This was a most courageous stand for a shipowner in a port which derived much of its income from the fruits of slavery. He was also a forward-thinking man who was involved in the early development of railroads. Denman's distinguished maternal grandfather, Thomas Denman, was Lord Chief Justice of England and another active proponent of abolition. Denman's mother, Margaret Denman Macaulay, was a widow at the time his father Edward Cropper took her as his third wife. Her first husband was the son of another of the founders of the abolitionist movement, Zachary Macaulay, and the brother of the famous author, historian and politician, Thomas Babington Macaulay. Denman's parents actively continued the work of their families in the movement to eradicate the blight of slavery and even hosted the American author and famed abolitionist Harriet Beecher Stowe at their home during her tour of England when he was a small boy. A number of the extended Cropper family had strong religious leanings, with many of its members adhering to the Quaker (The Society of Friends) movement. There were also Anglican clergy among his relatives.

Edward Cropper, Denman's father, was a successful businessman whose enterprises included slate mining, railways, and telegraphy. His prosperity allowed him to move his family from Liverpool to Kent where he bought the large early nineteenth-century Tudor-style manor house, Swaylands, in 1859. It can be assumed that after Minnie, her husband, parents and the servants disembarked at Liverpool and paid their respects to friends and relations in that city, the newlyweds then proceeded to Kent and took up residence at the Cropper family estate.[28]

When the Thornburghs returned to California, they must indeed have pictured in their minds the happy image of their only daughter as the mistress of a grand English country house, happily married with a brood of children at her knee and a life filled with garden parties, teas, and dances in the company of the most refined, high-minded, and elite of British society. But it was not to be.

Denman was nothing if not courageous. He had received a fine upper-crust education at Eton followed by a year at Cambridge University. But he was not drawn to the learned professions or to business, unlike most of his family; instead he chose a career in the British army and it appears that he pursued the profession for which he was best suited.[29] One of his many awards was for saving a drowning man from San Francisco Bay in 1878. He served as an officer in the British Army during the Zulu War and would die of pneumonia as a result of being wounded in 1901 while serving in the Boer War in

South Africa, posthumously being elevated to the rank of Lieutenant-Colonel and honoured with yet another award for distinguished service. His private life, on the other hand, was not as stellar.

Denman's father died in 1877 and Minnie's in 1878, changing their financial fortunes, and Swaylands was sold. The couple took up residence in the same area of Kent at Ovenden House. There are hints that the young husband was not always faithful to his marriage vows.[30] In 1881, he left her.[31] The fairy tale was transformed into a nightmare.

During the first year of the separation, Denman continued to at least provide financial support to his wife, but that too changed. Only after many years of keeping a painful memory to herself did Minnie confide what happened to her mother, who in turn entrusted it to Phoebe in a letter.

> – 'oh how I long for a home to feel at rest & no uncertainty [said Minnie to her mother]. I have had nothing but uncertainty since the day I went to the paper man.' What paper man I asked! 'at Sevenoaks. The newspapers did not come. I sent a message, still they did not come. I drove to his place, Walter told him to come out. I said I had been much inconvenienced & asked why he had not sent the papers – he stammered [&] got red, at last said, I think Mam I had better show you a letter I received. He brought it out & I read "we are requested by Mr. Thornburgh-Cropper to say he will not be responsible for any debts incurred by Mrs. Thornburgh-Cropper after this date" signed by his solicitors. I told him to send the papers as usual & his bills would be paid weekly. I have not known the security and protection of a home since that day early in '82.[32] The same kind of letters were sent to the tradespeople & to the servants.' This was the very first intimation I ever had of the above – you nor I will ever know half of that fiend's brutality.[33]

By the age of 25, Minnie found herself adrift and alone in a foreign country, far from her mother and relations, childless, with the legal restraints of marriage but without any of its benefits, and in increasingly straitened circumstances. She began to live out of residential hotels, especially the 'family' hotel, The Crown, in Westerham, Kent,[34] and tried to keep up the appearances of wealth without having it, because to do otherwise would have taken her out of the social circles to which she was accustomed.[35] She became adept at maintaining a happy façade, all the while slowly dying on the inside.

Meanwhile back in California, her mother, widowed by the age of 40, faced another problem. William Thornburgh left an estate that should have allowed his wife and daughter to live comfortably,[36] but the estate became embroiled in a lawsuit and the Thornburgh side lost. Hattie demonstrated her strong sense of justice by firmly refusing on principle to settle the suit, despite Minnie's tearful pleas to her mother to do so.[37] This financial calamity was compounded by Harriet Thornburgh's firm conviction that a great injustice had been done, that witnesses had lied in court and documents had been forged. She could not let go of this hurt. Years later she confided to her friend Phoebe, 'I work all the time – anything & everything. I wash & iron all the handkerch[ie]fs. I can't be idle. The moment I am not occupied I go over the trial in all it minutest details – it seems harder & harder to bear each day I live.'[38]

In 1895 Hattie moved in with her daughter in England, where she abhorred the dreary, cold climate and lack of California sunshine, conditions her daughter had long before accepted. The letters to Phoebe from this plain-spoken, forthright daughter of the frontier also indicate that she continued to mourn her husband's death almost two decades later. Hattie was content to remain in the background, content to play the supportive role in her daughter's efforts to make her way in the well-to-do levels of British society, content to stay at home in their rented rooms while her daughter travelled to the continent or went off for extended visits to friends. They were not destitute, but their primary assets were not liquid and were based in the United States. They suspected, probably with good reason, that the men who were supposed to be looking after their affairs were not doing so. Former business partners of William Thornburgh were cheating his widow and daughter out of their fair share of profits. Out of desperation, they repeatedly turned to the one friend willing to help – Phoebe Hearst. For years she assisted them financially by buying items they needed to sell quickly, by lending them money and through outright gifts of cash. She also sent them presents, usually items such as a new fan, a necklace, or gloves that an elegant lady in high society needed but which they could no longer afford. They in turn knitted her gifts such as shawls. She was their 'fairy godmother', their true friend in their hour of need, and they addressed her as 'fairy' in their letters. But had not Phoebe herself also looked into the abyss of marital infidelity, lawsuits and financial ruin?

Minnie struggled for years with the dilemma of the broken marriage. She was the one with the grounds to initiate a divorce based upon adultery and desertion at a time when divorces were difficult to obtain. Some of her friends urged her to remarry, but she was painfully aware of the stigma attached to divorce in Victorian England. She writes to Phoebe about the Prime Minister, the Archbishop of Canterbury, and others who railed against divorce as a moral scourge upon society at large. But she was becoming increasingly desperate, and at least a final agreement with her estranged husband might put her on firmer financial footing. The stress of this situation, especially the drawn-out process of making a decision to end the marriage legally, was such that by the mid-1890s she was miserable and suffering so much from what her doctors called 'nervous exhaustion' that her hands became almost completely paralysed. She sought rest and treatment at spas on the continent, but there was suspicion that 'taking the waters' only worsened rather than improved her health. Her normally well-ordered handwriting provides silent testimony to her poor health – it went from being beautiful to an almost illegible scrawl.

According to an announcement in the *New York Times* in February of 1897, a London court finally granted Minnie a divorce.[39] That was not the end of her troubles. She wrote to Phoebe on 4 February 1897, 'My life is being slowly crushed out under this torture of debt & uncertainty – not that this wld signify if by so doing my obligations would be honestly settled.' Her letter then goes on to give her friend a complete accounting of her assets with a plea for Phoebe to help her by buying a valuable tapestry that was being stored in California and some land she owned in Fresno. On 20 April 1897 she again wrote to Phoebe, 'Each day brings fresh difficulty which I have no way of meeting – or staving off. Everything seems lost, my courage lies fainting at my feet.'

Lest it appear that her life was all gloom and despair, it should be added for balance that Minnie and her mother did have a social life in England, even if not extensive, with a few well-placed friends. They excelled at hiding their troubles. Both were avid readers and interested in the happenings of the day, and both loved high culture such as opera and concerts of serious music. Minnie compensated for her childlessness by taking temporary responsibility for young girls from the United States who were studying in England – a sort of aunt during their school holidays[40] – and became very attached to these young ladies. Her mother joked in a letter about how one of Minnie's young charges taught her to ride a bicycle and that her very proper daughter enjoyed it! Minnie and Phoebe commiserated in their correspondence about the travails of caring for adolescents in the role of foster mother without being the actual parent.

After learning about the Bahá'í Faith from the Getsingers, Phoebe wrote to Minnie in England that she had found a new religion that Minnie might be interested in and promised to tell her more, without disclosing any particulars in the letter. At around the same time, most likely the summer of 1898, Minnie came across a mention of the Báb while looking up something else in an encyclopaedia.

> A short time later I was searching in the encyclopaedia for some information about King David, about whom I had had an argument. In turning over the pages, my eye was caught by a name, 'Bab'. I read on after the

> name, and found it to be the history of a messenger of God Who had been martyred in Persia, after bringing a new interpretation of truth to the Muslims. There was something in this story of a martyr for His faith that so moved me that I went to the British Museum to search for further information regarding Him, and His teaching. [41]

Imagine Minnie's delight when she discovered that the religion touted by her good fairy was also the one she was investigating independently. Her mother was visiting the United States at the time, but undoubtedly Minnie shared this first gleaning about the Bahá'í Faith with her when Hattie returned to England in October.[42]

Mother and daughter travelled across the English Channel to rendezvous with Phoebe. There they were introduced to the Getsingers and joined Lua's class. The party of the first Western pilgrimage was almost complete.

The growing group of friends in Paris had plenty of free time, all except Phoebe, who had business to attend to as a Regent of the University of California at Berkeley.[43] They continued to wait for a reply from 'Abdu'l-Bahá to the petition for permission to come to 'Akká. The interlude was put to good use by Lua, who began study classes in the Hearst apartment. She wrote about it to the believers in Chicago and, in her most elegant handwriting, enclosed the following list of the study class membership:

> Students in Paris
>
> Mrs. M. V. Cropper Cal.
> Mrs. Harriet Thornbourg
> Miss Julia L. Pearson Wash. D.C.
> May E. Bolles New York
> Mr. R. C. Turner California
>
> This last student is a colored man – and a most ardent believer
>
> Give my love to all the Believers in Chicago. I wish they were all going with us to Acca.
>
> Yours very truly!
> Mrs. E. C. Getsinger[44]

This list is significant not only because it contains the names of a number of people who would adorn the pages of the early history of the Bahá'í Faith in the West, but because it demonstrates the liberality of the group. After the social reforms of the twentieth century, it is difficult to appreciate fully how revolutionary it was for a group of white Americans from the upper social strata of society to sit and study with an African American butler in 1898. This seemingly simple act required putting aside deeply engrained racial and class prejudices. From the beginning of the British colonization of the Americas, the enslavement of Africans was America's 'original sin' that had ultimately been resolved through the massive bloodletting of a civil war little more than thirty years earlier. The price the United States paid in lives and treasure to end slavery is beyond description. Hattie had lived through the years of that war as a young adult. Robert probably had childhood memories of slavery and the war. In the 1890s, the wounds were far from healed. Even among those enlightened enough to feel great sympathy for the former slaves and their progeny, there remained deep-seated feelings that black Africans were an innately inferior people. In fact, there was a widely accepted school of thought that the races of mankind were separate species; this was touted as scientific fact in a popular science book co-written by the primary professor of science at Harvard University.[45] Robert, too, would have had to overcome any lingering feelings of resentment toward the white race for the unspeakable crimes it had committed against his own people. Aside from racial prejudices, it was unheard of at the time for a servant to sit down with his employer's friends and family as an equal to study religion, or to study anything together, for that matter. This little group of the young and the middle-aged, women and men, black and white, master and servant, represented the dawn of a revolution in human interaction, brought about by the coming of God's Messenger for this day, Bahá'u'lláh.

The weeks of waiting turned into almost two months. The Getsingers, the least travelled of the group, were taken on sightseeing outings by Mrs Hearst. Lua recorded that one day was spent visiting the Eiffel Tower and Napoleon's tomb and driving through the immense scenic park, the Bois de Boulogne, on the outskirts of the city. Another day she went with Marian Kheiralla and Phoebe (who by then she was referring to as 'Aunty') to see the famous Tuileries Gardens. On Sunday 9 October, some of the group visited the Cathedral of Notre Dame. That famous Paris landmark evoked deep feelings of resentment toward the older religious establishments of Christianity that must have been smouldering within Lua, because she wrote in her journal that the visit 'made my blood boil and my heart to be kindled with fury. When will this deception and hypocrisy cease and God's creatures cease to be vultures that prey on poor suffering humanity?' The last Sunday of October the Getsingers and May, upon whom Lua had bestowed the pet names 'Viola' and 'Violet', spent a delightful day enjoying the autumn beauty of the Bois de Boulogne again and the charms of the evening lights along the Champs-Élysées. At the end of that halcyon day Lua wrote, 'I was most happy.'[46]

Of course, the group also went shopping. For many Americans, the cultural attractions of Paris were nothing when compared to its stores. The ladies all had new gowns made by the best Parisian dressmakers, at Phoebe's expense. Kheiralla had led them to believe that 'Abdu'l-Bahá lived in a grand palace; and consequently they assumed they needed fine attire to be received by Him. This was logical since most high ecclesiastical figures of the time, from the Roman Catholic Pope to Protestant bishops, lived in princely fashion. They also purchased costly gifts to present to the Head of the Bahá'í Faith.

It was a most exciting time to be in Paris. The city was preparing for the 1900 Paris World's Fair and exhibition halls that would become integral parts of the city's renowned beauty were under construction, as was the Paris subway system.[47] Historians have referred to this period in the United States as 'the Gilded Age' because of the rise of *nouveau riche* families through the accumulation of vast fortunes, a byproduct of the Industrial Revolution. It was also the 'Age of Empire', best epitomized by the splendid celebration of Queen Victoria's Diamond Jubilee only a year earlier just across the Channel in London, the world's capital of the time. Britain alone controlled about a quarter of the world's land mass and about the same percentage of its peoples. France, Germany and the other European powers were eager to match it. The United States was on the cusp of entering the contest for overseas colonies. To be a European was a very heady identity at the close of the nineteenth century and brought with it feelings of superiority. Paris itself was preparing to extol its own grandeur as the capital of the French empire through its forthcoming World's Fair that would herald the turn of the century with a celebration of modern achievements much as the Colombian Exposition in Chicago had done seven years earlier.

European historians also refer to the last years of the nineteenth century as 'La Belle Époque', that is, the Beautiful Age. It was a time of peace on the continent – a rarity – when there was easy movement between the countries of Europe. Standards of living were rising and the middle class was growing. The arts were flourishing. Educational institutions were producing intellectuals and scientists who were expanding available knowledge at a rapid pace. If London was the centre of political power, Paris was the undisputed cultural centre for this period. But France in 1898 was in the grip of a controversy that laid bare the ugly side of the beautiful age. The Dreyfus Affair, involving the conviction of a Jewish army officer for treason, had exposed the corruption and anti-Semitism underpinning French society. At the time the Americans arrived from California, Emile Zola's famous essay *J'accuse* had been published just months before and all of France was embroiled in arguments about the role of the army, the Catholic Church, the trustworthiness of the government, and the place of French Jews in French society. It is impossible to believe that the American Bahá'ís in Paris were untouched by this raging controversy.[48]

Lua passed her twenty-sixth birthday on 1 November while they were still biding their time in Paris.

> My birthday!
>
> Twenty six years old today and I feel so much younger and look it too. Still I am 26! Have had a perfectly lovely day riding with my husband – the very best and dearest man in the world . . . A year ago today I was in Ithaca, N.Y. and today in Paris. I wonder where I shall be next year? Doing good, I hope wherever I am. My birthday presents were beautiful and best of all I had tea at 5 p. m. with my own 'Queen Anne'. . .[49]

Finally, the long-awaited reply arrived from 'Akká. 'Abdu'l-Bahá's response to the request for permission to come had been translated into garbled French, probably by one of the Persian believers residing in Egypt. In it He says that He has 'read your recent letter requesting permission to visit this faraway land in the company of a few Servants of God'. He then goes to the heart of the matter and replies, 'O Servant of God, [although] wisdom dictates otherwise, we permit you to come (with the other women) on condition that you arrive in pairs and remain for a few days (only) because the ignorant plot and the [unintelligible] scheme.'[50] They must have all been very happy with the answer even though it clearly evinced the dangers encircling 'Abdu'l-Bahá at the time.

Phoebe knew that May was longing to go to 'Akká too, because she began to sell her jewellery to cover her expenses. Phoebe generously offered for May to make the trip as her guest despite her poor health. She also invited Hattie to accompany May to 'Akká. Then Phoebe's thoughts turned to her protégée back in the United States, Nell Hillyer, and she decided to invite Nell as well. Edward shot off a hasty telegram to Nell inviting her to take part in the pilgrimage, which she received gratefully on Thanksgiving Day. This was followed by a letter to her from Phoebe herself, which did not arrive until mid-December. Nell was ecstatic.

Even before receiving Phoebe's own invitation to join the pilgrimage, Nell (without intimating to Phoebe that she had gotten Edward's cable, lest it was a mistake), wrote to her mentor on Phoebe's birthday about the joys of their new Faith.

> 112 E. 56th Street
> New York City
>
> My Dearest Dear
> Have been thinking of you all day long and have been travelling with you down through France and into Italy. This is the first birthday that has passed over your blessed head since you have come into the new and true life, and I am sure you do feel as though you were born again. I know God will spare your life to us here in this world where we need you for many years to come and I hope you feel as though you wish to remain. Your last letter made me so happy to know the glory of the Truth was still shedding its light upon you. I trust the Sun of Light and Truth will ever continue to shine upon you and that the blessing and gifts you most desire will be given you. What a new world and life is opening out to us both and you can well imagine with what anxiety I await your letter after reaching Acca. Will you send me a few lines dear?[51]

At the time, Nell was in New York City with Ella and her mother Helen Goodall. The Goodalls had only been able to receive two lessons from Lua before the Hearst party left California. Even though Lua had really told them little about the Faith, the few prayers that were shared with them and the snippets they heard were enough to enkindle their hearts. They left California in late October and reached New York City on 19 November, where Nell had already arranged for them to become pupils of Anton Haddad. Having actually spent time with 'Abdu'l-Bahá, Anton should have been a better source of information about the Faith than Kheiralla; however, Haddad read from the Kheiralla lessons without comment. The Goodalls were eager students who had memorized the few prayers they were given even before leaving home, and said them daily, finding that even those few words of Sacred Text had great effect. When the lessons were complete, Haddad 'gave the Great Message, or, as it was then called, the "Pith" of the Teachings, and then bestowed upon them the Greatest Name'.[52]

Even though Nell had visited the Holy Land before, she naturally wanted someone to travel with her and Ella was the logical choice. Ella couldn't believe her good fortune that so soon after her acceptance of the Faith she would be able to go to its holiest spot and meet with its Head. Her mother wanted to go as well but was having health problems that made such a long trip out of the question. Ella's father could well afford to provide the funds to cover her expenses; thus she was the only member of the pilgrimage group whose costs were not covered by Phoebe. In fact, Ella had not yet met Phoebe. A second message was sent to 'Abdu'l-Bahá asking permission for Nell and Ella to be added to the Hearst pilgrims and the reply came back as a cable which said simply, 'yes but secretly'.[53] Ella resolved not even to tell her father and brother her full itinerary.

Nell wrote to Phoebe on 22 December about the pilgrimage once she had received an invitation from Phoebe herself.

> Of course you must know how happy I am to think with your consent and wishes it is made possible for me to visit the favored spot. There is nothing else in this world that I desire more; and when I think that I have really received the word from you to go I can hardly realize it. I wonder what I have ever done to deserve all these great privileges.
>
> I am indeed glad that Mrs. Thornburg[h] and Mrs. Cropper have become so interested and of course I shall be only too glad if May Bolles wishes and can go when I do. I will aid her all I can to make the journey comfortable for her.[54]

Phoebe had proposed that Nell arrive in 'Akká in February along with May and Hattie in order to comply with the wishes of 'Abdu'l-Bahá that they keep the groups small. Nell assured Phoebe that she would try to keep her itinerary a secret and that she would not even tell her only close relative, her sister. Nell lost no time in making travel arrangements.

> I went to the steamship office today and was told that the line of steamers sailing weekly from Naples is by far the best for us to take to Alexandria. $50.00. And that I can cross from New York to Genoa on the German line of steamers for $100.00 making the trip from New York to Alexandria $150.00 which I think is quite reasonable. If I can arrange with Miss Bolles to meet me at Genoa of course I will go this southern way as I really do not need or care to go to Paris now. I will ask Miss Bolles if she knows anything of Mrs. Thornburg[h]'s plans . . .

Nell continued on in her letter introducing Ella to Phoebe. 'Ella is a dear girl and looks upon life just about as I do. I am sure you would like her.' She also comments upon Agnes, 'always the same sweet dear child' and the transformation apparent in Anne since she accepted the Bahá'í teachings.

> . . . I am so delighted Anne has changed as she has. I had a short note from her the other day that you would hardly believe could have been written by her. She could not have written it a year ago. Certainly the teaching[s]

> have done wonders for her. I shall be so glad to have her go to A. ['Akká] with me and only wish little Agnes could go too, but that will come a little later on.

Nell cannot express enough to her benefactress her happiness at being enabled to go to 'Akká: '. . . when I think of the joy and peaceful pleasure in store for me, I am happier than if a fortune had been laid at my feet.'

That same Thanksgiving in Paris, the Getsingers were celebrating that most American of holidays with their fellow countrymen, Minnie and Hattie.[55] It was the day before Lua and Edward were to finally depart for 'Akká after almost two months of waiting. Apparently Lua had some unfinished business with the mother and daughter. She was following the Kheiralla lesson plans and perhaps had not yet gotten to the last lessons about the coming of Bahá'u'lláh as the messenger of God for this day. Lua recorded what transpired in her journal:

> Thanksgiving Day Nov. 24, 1898
> I have been very busy packing and getting ready to leave Paris today, but accepted an invitation from Mrs. Cropper to eat Thanksgiving dinner with them at their Hotel Belmont. We spent a very pleasant evening together – during which I delivered to them the Glorious Message of the Coming of the Kingdom of God which they rec'd with great joy!
>
> We leave for Haifa tomorrow and I am anxious for the morrow to come my heart yearns to be in the <u>land</u> of all <u>lands</u>.[56]

The Getsingers were the first of the Americans to depart from Paris for the Holy Land.[57] They left on Friday, 25 November, heading south overland through France to Italy where they boarded a steamer at the port of Naples. On 3 December Lua made the following entry in her journal:

> We have journeyed from France, stopping at Florence and Rome, and now we are in sight of Mt. Vesuvius and about to set sail for Alexandria on the 'Regina Margarheita' [sic] – every day brings us nearer the Holy Place – although we have seen many interesting things the days pass much too slowly![58]

Three days later they reached the port of Alexandria, Egypt, where they changed to the steamer that would take them on the last leg of their journey. Egyptian Bahá'ís were waiting for them. One can only imagine how thrilled they were, after sending off Kheiralla and Haddad six years earlier, to see two

'Abdu'l-Bahá, at Lincoln Park, Chicago, 3 May 1912

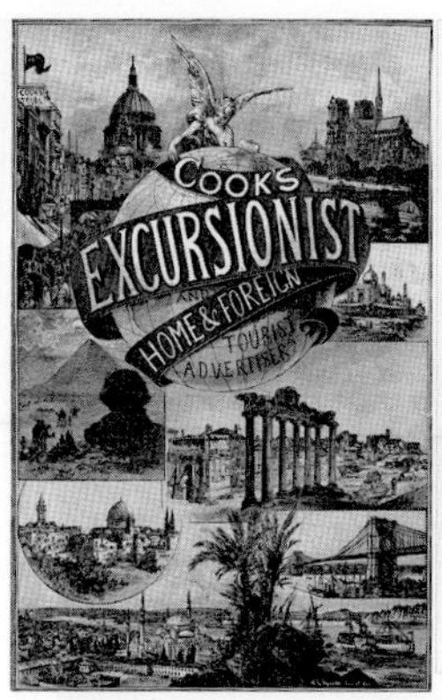

HAMBURG-AMERICAN LINE.

THE GREATEST STEAMSHIP COMPANY IN THE WORLD.

New York, Cherbourg (Paris), Southampton (London), and Hamburg.

FAST LINE TO

LONDON AND THE EUROPEAN CONTINENT.

SHORTEST SEA ROUTE TO PARIS.

The Twin-Screw Express Steamers of this Line, "AUGUSTE-VICTORIA," and "FÜRST BISMARCK" are of 13-16,000 Horse-power, and are unsurpassed for SAFETY, SPEED and COMFORT. These Steamers do not carry cotton. This is the ONLY LINE carrying Cabin Passengers exclusively by Twin-screw Steamers.

THE HAMBURG-AMERICAN LINE'S STEAMERS

Belong to the fastest plying between New York, Cherbourg (Paris), Southampton (London), and Hamburg, having accomplished excellent time on this route. Passengers leaving New York on Thursday are landed in Cherbourg or Southampton on the following Thursday, reaching Paris or London on the same day, thus making the trip from NEW YORK to PARIS or LONDON in less than a week, and to Hamburg, Berlin, etc., in less than 8 days.

PARIS. The Express Steamers of the **HAMBURG-AMERICAN LINE** land passengers at Cherbourg, and a Special Train in waiting upon the arrival of the steamer will convey passengers to Paris in about 6½ **hours**. The great convenience offered by this new port of call in reaching Paris will undoubtedly be much appreciated by the traveling public.

LONDON. The distance by rail between Southampton and London by the **HAMBURG-AMERICAN LINE'S** Special Train is about **2 hours.**

HAMBURG. The most important commercial centre of Continental Europe, and one of its most beautiful cities, has an excellent Express Train Service with all parts of the interior.

HAMBURG-AMERICAN LINE, **37 BROADWAY, NEW YORK.** Cor. LA SALLE AND RANDOLPH STS., CHICAGO

Travel brochures, courtesy of the Thomas Cook Archive. The American edition of Cook's Excursionist for August and September 1898 included information about tours to Egypt and Palestine, and an advertisement for the Hamburg-American Line's steamer Fürst Bismarck, *on which Phoebe Hearst hoped to 'sleep all the way to Cherbourg'* *(see p. 55)**. The 1898-99 brochure, given to all travellers who had bought tickets, includes information on the boat and train travel undertaken by the Getsingers, Helen Hillyer and Ella Goodall, while the 1891 Handbook on Palestine and Syria gave useful advice and information for travellers.*

Egypt and THE NILE

PROGRAMME of COOK'S International Tickets To EGYPT and the FIRST & SECOND CATARACTS of the NILE

THOS COOK & SON

LONDON.

SEASON 1898-9

PRICE SIXPENCE. POST FREE.

28 THE NILE.

The steamers of the Messageries Maritimes leave Marseilles for Alexandria and the Syrian Coast every Thursday at 4.0 p.m.

The steamers of the Italian General S. N. Co. leave Naples every Wednesday, reaching Alexandria on Sunday. Another Service leaves Venice every alternate Tuesday, and Brindisi alternate Fridays, reaching Alexandria on Monday.

The "Regina Margherita" of that Company, so justly appreciated by passengers last winter, leaves Naples every Saturday at 3.0 p.m. from November 5th, and arrives at Alexandria on Tuesday at 6.0 a.m., returning every Tuesday at 5.0 p.m., reaching Naples at 8.0 o'clock on Friday morning. First Class cabins only contain two berths, and the meals are served as on English Steamers by English-speaking assistants.

The North German Lloyd's steamers to China and Australia leave Genoa and Naples fortnightly for Port Said, Ismailia, and Suez.

From Alexandria to Cairo three Express Trains run daily in three hours and a-half, and Ordinary Trains in six hours. Trains on the Suez Canal Company's light railway, carrying passengers, run twice daily in each direction between Port Said and Ismailia, in connection with trains to and from Cairo.

Trains leave Ismailia for Cairo every day at 1.13 p.m. and 7.0 p.m., due in Cairo 4.45 p.m. and 10.30 p.m. Our representative meets all steamers and trains at Port Said and Ismailia; at the latter station he will attend to the passing of passengers' baggage through the Customs, transport of baggage from quay to railway station, &c., for an inclusive fee of 2s. per passenger.

The foregoing times of steamers and trains are subject to alteration.

Tickets for any Route can be obtained at our Offices in London, and at the Offices of the Company in Alexandria, Port Said, and Cairo.

COOK'S

HANDBOOK FOR PALESTINE AND SYRIA.

Introductory.

PRACTICAL INFORMATION FOR TRAVELLERS.

SEASON FOR EASTERN TOURS.

SPRING is the best time for a tour through Palestine. Travellers who are intending to visit Palestine as well as Egypt, cannot do better than select December, January, or February for their Nile journey, and March, April, or May, the most genial months of the year, for Palestine. If this is inconvenient the months of October and November are considered by many travellers to be very favourable for Palestine, in which case the Palestine Tour should be commenced at Beyrout and terminate at Jaffa, and the Nile trip might be made on the return journey in December.

BENEFITS OF ASSOCIATED TRAVEL.

Apart from the question of expense, travelling in the East, either alone, or with only one or two companions, is not desirable. In Egypt, Palestine, and Syria, the mode of life, language, and customs of the country are altogether different from anything to which the European traveller has been accustomed; the modes of travelling are novel, and the difficulties

6 INTRODUCTORY.

For Egypt every Friday evening, *via* Brindisi.
" " " alternate Thursday evening, *via* Marseilles.
" " " Thursday morning by Austrian Packet.
" " " alternate Saturday evening by Italian Pckt.
For Syria (Jaffa, Jerusalem, etc.) the same as for Egypt.
For Smyrna daily, *via* Constantinople.
" " every Friday evening, *via* Brindisi.
" " alternate Thursday evening and Friday morning, *via* Marseilles. Postage to the above-named places, 2½d., not exceeding ½ ounce.

Letters by Brindisi to Alexandria take six days in transit, by Marseilles seven days.

There are daily mails from Alexandria to Cairo, Suez, Ismailia, and Port Said. Letters for Upper Egypt are forwarded daily.

For the Syrian Coast and Palestine. Letters are delivered in nine days, *via* Brindisi; the French mails take from ten to twelve days.

To most of the above-named places letters can be registered at a charge of 2d.

Money Orders are issued on Egypt at the following rates—for £2, sixpence; for £5, one shilling; for £7, one shilling and sixpence; for £10, two shillings.

BACKSHEESH.

Everywhere, from morning till night, the traveller will be tormented with applications for backsheesh, which has been called the alpha and omega of Eastern travel. It is the first word an infant is taught to lisp; it will probably be the first Arabic word the traveller will hear on arriving in Palestine, and the last as he leaves it. The word simply means "a gift," but is applied generally to a gratuity or fee, and is expected no less by the naked children who swarm around the traveller when he arrives in a village, than by the enlightened officials of the Custom House, or other public institutions. If each traveller would make it a rule never to give backsheesh, except for some

CAMP LIFE. 7

positive service rendered, *worth the sum given*, he would confer a boon upon the people and upon future travellers. It should be remembered also that to most applicants a piastre or two represents an enormous sum of money.

CAMP LIFE.

When the camp arrangements are as they ought to be—and this is always guaranteed under the management of the dragomans engaged by Messrs. COOK & SON—camp-life is delightful. Friends make up little select parties of their own, and share the same tent or tents. Each tent is designed to accommodate two or three persons, and is well furnished—that is to say, it has an inner lining of chintz, which gives it a gay and bright appearance, and Turkey or Persian carpets are laid over the floor; it is fitted up with neat iron bedsteads, with the cleanest of clean linen, and good comfortable beds; round or against the tent-pole is a table, with washing-basin; and on the pole are strapped pegs for holding clothes, etc.

In the centre of the encampment the Saloon is pitched—a spacious tent, constituting the *salle à manger* and drawing-room of the "travelling hotel."

Each tent bears a number or some distinctive sign, and the traveller's luggage is marked with a corresponding number or sign, so that every day, when he comes to the camping-place, he finds his tent pitched and all his belongings to hand.

The daily arrangements are generally as follows:—Early in the morning the dragoman's whistle is sounded to summons the camp-followers, and then two or three men go round to all the tents, beating a tattoo on a tray, ringing a bell, etc., to make noise enough to thoroughly rouse the heaviest sleeper. In half an hour dressing and packing must be finished, and in that time breakfast is ready, and the attendants are at work taking down tents, folding up beds and bedding, and getting ready for the start. However early the start may be made there is always a good breakfast ready, and plenty of time

8 INTRODUCTORY.

allowed to do justice to it. The *menu* includes tea, coffee, and milk, with boiled eggs or omelette; then follows a course of hot chicken, or cutlets. After breakfast, every cup and plate is washed and packed in large cases. Everything needed for the journey has to be carried on mules—tents, poles, cords; stores for the four or five weeks' provisions; plate, glass, knives and forks, tent furniture, the cooks' stoves and fuel, the treasure chest—all has to be packed on the backs of mules, and carried over some of the most rugged and difficult roads in the world. The alacrity with which the work of packing and unpacking is done will astonish the traveller the first time he sees it, and will be a continual source of amusement day by day.

After breakfast the start for the day's journey is made; and, each day's programme having been announced the day before, travellers generally spend any leisure time in reading up the places they will visit. At some convenient and interesting spot, previously fixed upon, luncheon is served; this has been specially conveyed on mules, and consists of one dish of cold meat and one of poultry, sardines, eggs, bread and cheese, and two kinds of dessert.

An hour and a half to two hours is generally allowed for luncheon time, which can also include a "nap" if needed.

About six or seven in the evening the journeying for the day is over, and every day the traveller has the unexpected but extreme satisfaction of finding tents all pitched, and the cooks busy at work beside the glowing camp-fire. There is time to have a leisurely "wash-up," to unpack the portmanteau, and then the dinner-bell rings. The table of the saloon is generally gay with flowers gathered en route, and the general aspect of the social board is such as might be expected in the neighbourhood of the Italian Lakes, but not in the wilds of Syria. The bill of fare usually comprises soup, mutton, or lamb, chicken or turkey, a capital pudding, cheese, and dessert.

After dinner travellers amuse themselves according to the bent of their inclinations; the muleteers gather round the

MESSRS. T. COOK & SON'S TOURS. 9

camp-fire and smoke their narghilies; and about ten or eleven o'clock there is quiet in the camp for the night.

TRAVELLING ARRANGEMENTS OF MESSRS. THOS. COOK & SON.

The travelling coupons issued by THOS. COOK & SON are now so well known and universally used, that it is unnecessary to enter into particulars about them. Suffice it to say that they have been found to be advantageous to all European travellers, and in the East, where travelling is under greater difficulties in every respect, their system is indispensable to those who are unable to grapple with the obstacles presented by not being acquainted with Oriental languages, and with having to deal with dragomans and others, whose demands are invariably exorbitant.

In Palestine, more than anywhere else in the East, it is desirable, for the comfort and pleasure of a trip, that all arrangements respecting contracts with dragomans, tents, and equipments, backsheesh, Bedouin escorts for unsafe districts, charges for visiting mosques and sacred places, etc., should be undertaken on behalf of the traveller, and this Messrs. T. COOK and SON are prepared to do. They have made such arrangements in the East, that the most inexperienced travellers may avail themselves of them without fear of not being able to get on as well as in the beaten continental routes. They issue tickets for individuals, or for small or large parties, and every season they organise parties who travel under the personal superintendence of one of their experienced staff of conductors.

It will be only necessary here to indicate some of the arrangements which they have successfully carried out in past seasons, and will be improved as each fresh season ensues. Every year they publish a little book (price 6d.), giving details of their Personally-Conducted, and Independent Eastern Tours, and to this the traveller is referred, as the cost of a tour varies according to circumstances, and general arrangements are liable to variation.

Americans who embodied the spiritual pay-off on their investment, even if Kheiralla's money-making schemes had borne no fruit. In a very real sense, Kheiralla's achievement – opening the West to the Faith – also belonged to the Egyptian Bahá'í community.[59] In her last journal entry for the trip, Lua recounted the brief stopover in Egypt on 6 December:

> Arrived at Alexandria this morning and was met at the steamer by Salim Effendi – who is a friend of Dr. K's and he was very kind to help us with our baggage etc. We transferred to the steamer 'Achille' bound for Haifa and shortly before sailing Dr. Kheiralla's daughter Labiba came on board. We were very pleased to see her and she informed us that her eldest sister was in Haifa which pleased us very much also – as she speaks English and would be of great service to us in our meeting those whose every utterance is a precious gem.[60]

The Getsingers, symbolically representing all the peoples of the West, were at long last approaching the Holy Threshold – the spot their hearts yearned to attain.

CHAPTER 5

The Master and Kheiralla

While Lua and Edward waited anxiously across the bay to be summoned, a crowd was forming in a large courtyard in 'Akká. The scene unfolding that morning would be witnessed by the Getsingers many times in the years ahead and would always move their hearts. In the compound of a large building bound on three sides by a high stone wall, a growing group of ragged people were milling around, obviously expectantly waiting. The open area in front of the old structure was more than an acre in size, with plantings of vegetables, flowers and small fruit trees near the walls and one large tree in its centre, but otherwise open and barren. Earlier that morning the ground had been lovingly sprinkled with water to reduce the dust from the anticipated crowd. Despite the large size of the yard, the crowd began to fill every available space. The gathering of the city's poorest, most desperate citizens in front of the residence of 'Abdu'l-Bahá on the Muslim sabbath was a weekly Friday ritual.

More and more people poured through the gate at the southeast corner of the wall – the only opening onto the narrow lane fronting the complex.[1] There were young widows clutching babes in one arm while holding the hand of another child, the lame and the ill, orphans and workmen too elderly and infirm to continue earning a living, and those who could not escape poverty for a multitude of reasons. They all were coming to see the one person who cared about them, who could help them. On Friday mornings they visited Him, but more often He visited their homes – usually in the early hours before the sun was fully up when He did not yet need to turn His attention to His other duties, or in the darkest moments of the night when they urgently needed Him. He had prayed for and with them. He had fed them spoonfuls of nourishment when they were ill and cleaned their homes Himself when they were unable to do so. He had listened patiently to them as they wept and recounted their troubles. He had seen to the education of their children and sent physicians to them without ever letting anyone but the doctor know the identity of their benefactor. He was their kind father in all things.

At the appointed time, the Master Himself strode into the yard through the main gate, having just returned from His many errands in the town. The crowd immediately enveloped Him, each one shouting to Him and trying to touch

Him in order to gain his attention. He commanded them to be seated. His lieutenants quickly organized the crowd of 60 or 70 – some weeks it reached 200 – into two rows and directed them to sit down. Then the Master Himself passed from person to person, not missing anyone in the queues. He lovingly caressed the heads of the children and patted the shoulders of many. He took some by the hand as he looked deep into their eyes and whispered words of comfort. He pressed a coin into the palms of most of His visitors, except those of the children, because He did not want to instil in them dependence upon charity. He also did not give alms to any able-bodied men who were unwilling to work, no matter how dire their circumstances, for He did not reward laziness or mendacity and thereby hoped to correct character. Finally, after He had greeted everyone, He dismissed them collectively and the crowd arose and headed back out through the same gate by which they had entered the compound.

As the poor departed, a member of the Master's household stepped forward with a washbasin in his hands and a clean towel draped over one arm. The Master washed carefully, having just taken the hands of many of who were diseased. That precaution completed, he turned his attention to a well-ordered group of twenty or more children, who had remained in the yard and formed a line according to height. These were the pupils of the school He had established. First He conferred briefly with their teacher, and then He proceeded to speak to each child. One by one, they held out their work for the week, which He examined thoroughly as He went down the line of budding scholars. He would make corrections on their papers with a reed pen and give each student praise, encouragement, loving admonitions and instructions as to what needed to be done to improve during the course of the next week. He also inspected each youngster from top to bottom, giving special attention to the cleanliness of their hands. When He was finished evaluating their progress, He gave the pupils a gentle, uplifting but edifying talk. At last, He again passed down the line, presenting each child with a small coin, entertaining them all with humorous stories as He went along. Their wide smiles were proof that all the children loved Friday mornings with the Master.

'Abbás Effendi, as He was known to the citizens of the region, was not only father to the poor, but was considered an exceptional sage whose door was open to high and low alike. When He was not ministering to the downtrodden, He was likely to be engaged in assisting the officials of the city in resolving difficult issues. They frequently sought His advice and counsel. So did ordinary citizens. Had He been proclaimed governor or mayor, it would have been a demotion. This high regard and admiration for Him, held tightly in the hearts of the citizens of 'Akká, was remarkable considering that he had arrived in that penal city in 1868 as a reviled prisoner.

The futility inherent in attempting to adequately recount the story of 'Abbás Effendi, known to posterity as 'Abdu'l-Bahá, becomes self-evident when one ponders that one of the titles given to him by Bahá'u'lláh is 'The Mystery of God'. 'Abdu'l-Bahá made no claim to prophethood, nor to being the messenger of God for this day; that station belonged alone to His earthly and spiritual father, Lord and Master, Bahá'u'lláh. Instead, upon His assumption of the role of Head of the Faith following His father's passing, He bestowed upon himself a new name – 'Abdu'l-Bahá – Servant of Glory, and He revelled in His servitude. There has never been a human being quite like Him throughout the whole of the recorded history of mankind, for He was created by God Almighty to be the perfect spiritual man, the exemplar for mankind to study and emulate for ages to come, one who demonstrated how to live by the teachings of a messenger of God. One apt description of 'Abdu'l-Bahá states:

> His humility was not due to any *diffidence* or other failing. Nor did it imply any self-abasement or self-deprecation. What it meant was the obliteration of the personal self. His separate ego had no existence at all save only as an instrument of expression of the higher self that was one with God.[2]

'Abbás Effendi was born shortly after midnight in Tehran, the Persian capital, on the very night that the Bahá'í Faith was born in the city of Shiraz. It was 23 May 1844, the day that the Báb declared to His first follower, Mullá Ḥusayn, that He was the Promised One from God that all of mankind was awaiting.[3] Two quiet, private events in the darkness of that one night, a conversation and a birth, would remake the entire world.

'Abbás Effendi's father, Bahá'u'lláh, immediately accepted the Báb as a messenger of God as soon as He was informed of Him. At the time, 'Abbás Effendi was a baby; thus, He was raised as a Bábí, not as a Muslim. His early life mirrored the turbulent history of the short ministry of the Báb.

It did not take long for the Báb to attract multitudes to His Cause and consequently to arouse the enmity and envy of the clergy and government officials. He was arrested and moved from place to place as a prisoner until He was finally executed on 9 July 1850 in the market square of the city of Tabriz at the age of thirty. During this period of immense upheaval 'Abbás Effendi was a young child growing up in his father's wealthy household in Tehran, the place that became the eye of the storm for the Báb's followers. His father hosted many of the illustrious early believers and sheltered them when circumstances became dangerous. One of those under his care was the renowned poetess and champion of the education of women, Ṭáhirih, who would hold the toddler 'Abbás Effendi on her lap as she spoke from behind a screen to the learned men who came to hear her expound upon abstruse religious topics.

'Abbás Effendi, who was also called 'Áqá', 'the Master', by everyone in the household at the insistence of his father, displayed remarkable qualities from the first days of his life. He was brilliant, wise far beyond his years, and generous to such a degree that his father would joke about the need to restrain his tendency to give things away lest he give himself away. He did not receive a formal education; instead, his own father taught him the basics of reading and writing. His favourite pastime became reading the Writings of the Báb. He was a skilled horseman like his father, and also shared his father's delight in animals, nature and children. While still a child, he contracted tuberculosis and suffered seriously from it for some time.

When he was about eight years old, the first of a lifetime of calamities beset his family. A deranged follower of the Báb, distraught at the Báb's execution ordered by the highest levels of the government, attempted to assassinate the Shah of Iran. Fortunately, the shot only wounded the Shah, but the assassination attempt provided the excuse its enemies needed to unleash a torrent of persecution against the nascent Faith.

Bahá'u'lláh, though completely innocent of any complicity in the attempt on the Shah's life, was arrested and thrown into the most loathsome dungeon in Tehran, where He languished for months, watching as daily one or more of His fellow believers were led out of the prison to be executed. His health deteriorated with each passing day until He was close to death. At the time of His arrest, mobs attacked and looted His Tehran residence, forcing His household members to flee for their lives. 'Abbás Effendi, along with his younger sister and brother, went into hiding under the care of their courageous mother, clutching the few remaining possessions they could salvage. During those fearful days, young 'Abbás Effendi would venture into the streets to undertake errands on his mother's behalf, but as soon as other boys spied him, they would chase him and pelt him with stones, such was the hatred generated by the ignorant toward the followers of the Báb. One day, this persecution became so unremittingly terrible that 'Abbás Effendi hid for hours until nightfall in the shelter of a doorway. When darkness came and he thought it safe to sneak back to his mother, he found his tormentors still patiently waiting for him. As the months of uncertainty dragged on, his family's plight became so desperate that on one occasion all his mother could offer him to eat was a handful of flour.

'Abbás Effendi convinced a loyal servant to take him to see his father in the prison. As the boy was being led down the stairs into the dungeon, a voice that he recognized as his father's rang out and ordered that he not be brought any further into that hell-hole. He did, however, witness his father's wretched state when Bahá'u'lláh was brought outside for brief exercise. His beloved noble father was hardly recognizable. At that moment 'Abbás Effendi knew that his father was the one foretold by the Báb, the one the Báb referred to as Him Whom God Shall Make Manifest, the Messiah, the Messenger of God for this Day. 'Abbás Effendi, at the age of eight, gained the distinction of being the first to believe in Bahá'u'lláh, the Glory of God.[4]

After several agonizing months, the Russian and British ambassadors interceded on behalf of Bahá'u'lláh, preventing His execution and gaining His release from the dungeon. He was ordered into exile; thus, after the few weeks respite granted Him to regain enough health to travel, He and His family began the arduous trek under armed guard over high mountains to Baghdad. It was mid-winter. The exiles had been stripped of most of their belongings and were ill-prepared for the forced march. The youngest son, Mírzá Mihdí, had been tearfully left behind with relatives because he was not strong enough for the journey. 'Abbás Effendi's mother, the saintly Ásíyih Khánum,[5] also of noble, wealthy birth, was pregnant. During that long, harsh journey, 'Abbás Effendi suffered from frostbite.

When they at last reached Baghdad, the fabled, ancient city on the Tigris River which centuries before had been a centre of high culture and learning, the family settled into inadequate, miserable quarters. Other followers of the Báb had already fled to that city, but the constant fear of renewed persecution prevented easy interaction among the believers. The followers of the Báb were leaderless and some of them had begun to act in ways contrary to the spiritual and moral teachings of their martyred prophet. This spiritual vacuum caused a crisis to begin brewing among the little band of exiles. Bahá'u'lláh determined that the best way to deal with the disunified Bábí exiles was to remove Himself and let events unfold without His involvement. He slipped out of town without even telling His own family where He was going and headed to the mountains to the northeast in the region of Kurdistan, where He lived in a cave and roamed the hills in solitude dressed as a dervish.

During Bahá'u'lláh's absence, the lives of 'Abbás Effendi, his mother and younger sister were miserable. The baby born soon after their arrival in Iraq died because one of Bahá'u'lláh's half-brothers, Mírzá Yaḥyá, was afraid to summon a doctor into the home to tend to it lest the doctor report his whereabouts to the authorities. This same uncle kept the family virtual prisoners because of his own paranoia and cowardice. That they survived that terrible period seems nothing short of a miracle. Finally, after two years, Bahá'u'lláh returned to His family in Baghdad in response to the appeals of His family and friends when they learned of His whereabouts. When He entered the house, 'Abbás Effendi threw himself at his Father's feet and wept.

With the return of Bahá'u'lláh to Baghdad, not only did the family's situation improve immeasurably, but the Bábí exiles began to accept His guidance, leading to the transformation of the morals and behaviour of those around Him. Other believers began to make the long pilgrimage from Iran to see 'Abbás Effendi's Father because, even though the same perfidious uncle who confined them during Bahá'u'lláh's absence was titular head of the faith of the Báb, Bahá'u'lláh was the only one who displayed true spiritual power and insight.

While 'Abbás Effendi was still a boy, his Father entrusted him with important responsibilities, once even assigning him the task of answering a difficult theological question posed by one of the believers. His answer was so profound, so erudite, that it astonished both the recipient and many others who read it. Despite his youth, 'Abbás Effendi was increasingly included in deep theological discussions in the presence of the learned and leaders of the community.

The Muslim clergy of Iran had hoped that the exile of the remaining leaders among the followers of the Báb would lead to the final demise of the new religion. But Bahá'u'lláh's guidance, sagacity and influence not only gained new adherents to the Faith in Iran and Iraq, but totally revitalized and energized it. The obvious recourse needed to check the growth of the Cause was to remove Bahá'u'lláh further from the Iranian border. The Sultan of Turkey agreed to take Him; consequently Bahá'u'lláh was commanded to leave Baghdad and take up residence in Istanbul, again proceeding into further exile under an armed escort.

Bahá'u'lláh left His Baghdad residence for the last time and made His way with majestic dignity through the narrow lanes of the city that had adopted Him as one of its most cherished citizens, down to the banks of the Tigris River where He boarded a small boat and crossed over to a private garden on the opposite shore. Multitudes of citizens turned into the streets to witness His departure and to bid Him farewell. Many were in tears, distraught at losing the one who had become not only dear to them, but their guiding star, their loving father. At some point during that fateful, heart-wrenching day, Bahá'u'lláh made known to some of His companions that He was the Promised One of the Age, the one that the Báb had told them to watch and wait for. The well-kept secret, that the child 'Abbás Effendi had been the first to penetrate with his deep spiritual insight those many years earlier in Iran, was now unveiled. That day in April 1863 marked the outward beginning of Bahá'u'lláh's ministry and is celebrated as the first day of the Festival of Riḍván. A day marked by the sorrow of separation became transformed into a day for rejoicing that would be remembered always.

It took the family and small entourage of followers about five months to travel from Baghdad to Istanbul by land and sea. Eighteen-year-old 'Abbás Effendi seemed to never tire as he rode ahead of the caravan to farms and villages to procure provisions for the exiles. He relished opportunities to ride beside his Father and always kept a watchful eye that everything was in order. From the period of that journey until his Father's passing, the Master took care of the daily necessities of life so that his Father need not worry about such matters. He became his Father's liaison with government officials. He took responsibility for most business affairs. He was the first to meet the pilgrims and to prepare them to be received by his Father. Toward the end of His life, Bahá'u'lláh often remarked that the Master had 'made Himself Our shield',[6] and for that He was truly grateful.

Bahá'u'lláh and the Master had a unique relationship. They certainly had the close intimacy often found between a father and son, but the relationship was far deeper, far more complex than that of family ties. Of all human beings, 'Abdu'l-Bahá had the most perfect understanding of His Father's nature and powers as the Manifestation of God, as well as of His purposes for humankind. This understanding and His absolute devotion to Bahá'u'lláh were reflected in everything He did and said. For example, in later years, as the Master rode His donkey toward His Father's residence at Bahjí, He always dismounted when He came within sight of the Mansion, and would continue on foot. Bahá'u'lláh, for His part, would eagerly await the Master's coming and would send the men of the household out to greet Him and escort Him. One has only to read the Tablets that Bahá'u'lláh revealed in honour of the Master to obtain a glimmering of the love He had for His eldest son, of the confidence He placed in Him and the joy that His mere presence gave Him.

The Master passed His young adult years first in Istanbul, that teeming, ancient capital of the Ottoman Empire at the entrance to the Bosphorus Strait where East and West met and mixed, and then in the small city of Adrianople,[7] where His Father was further exiled. The band of exiles enjoyed a modicum of freedom in that town, though they lived in straitened circumstances, far below the level they had been accustomed to in Iran. 'Abbás Effendi became much loved by the people of Adrianople, including the local governor. So when the machinations of His Father's enemies finally convinced the Sultan to exile Bahá'u'lláh and His little band of followers to a worse place of exile, it was 'Abbás Effendi's firm insistence and influence that persuaded the government officials to overturn the first order from Istanbul that required the dispersal of the household of Bahá'u'lláh and, instead, to keep the family and companions together.

With the few possessions they could carry after insufficient time to dispose of everything else, the exiles were escorted, again under harsh conditions, to the port of Gallipoli, where they were put on a steamer and sent south through the Dardanelles and past the Greek islands to Egypt and then from Port Said north up the coast to the Holy Land. That voyage of late summer 1868 quickly became a nightmare because they had not been given adequate time to purchase provisions, including food, and the steamer itself was overcrowded and filthy. After about ten days of travel they arrived sick and exhausted at the port of Haifa, where they were first taken to the local jail to be counted. Then they were sent on the last miserable leg of their journey across the bay to the prison city of 'Akká. It was 31 August, the height of the summer's heat, and that day there was no wind. The small sailing boat took eight hours to sail cross the bay, at least three times longer than normal. They had no water to drink and no food, as they were baked by the sun out on the waters of the bay.

Their landing late that afternoon was probably the worst moment of their lives. The boat was unable to draw close to the sea gate entrance of the town, thus the prisoners had to wade ashore, holding high their possessions to keep them dry. Most of the population had turned out onto the city walls to watch, jeer and taunt the 'God of the Persians', the derisive name by which they had heard Bahá'u'lláh referred to by the authorities. It was 'Abbás Effendi who prevented one indignity that day. The ladies were expected to be carried ashore on the backs of men – a great humiliation for noblewomen accustomed to living in cloistered surroundings away from the gaze of men who were not related to them. Somehow 'Abbás Effendi procured a chair and then used it to have each woman carried ashore, held aloft by several men. The exiles were then marched through the narrow streets to the Citadel. This imposing compound had a northwest tower originally built as a palace, but many years later it had been transformed and expanded into a large army barracks with its four wings surrounding a central courtyard. After years of neglect, the facility had become so dilapidated that it was unfit for human habitation. As soon as they arrived, 'Abbás Effendi's noble sister, Bahíyyih Khánum, collapsed, probably from dehydration. The only water available to revive her was the muddy water used by a local potter.

Still lacking food and water that terrible first night in their new prison surroundings, the 68 exiles – entire families including infants – still found reason to celebrate. They had not been separated from each other or from Bahá'u'lláh!

The Master, then aged 24, was so revered by His fellow prisoners that they felt that they had to be on their best behaviour while in His presence. In the close quarters of the prison's tower, He did not want His fellow inmates to be uncomfortable; therefore He requested that He be given a space of His own away from the rest of the group. The only place available was the basement, the room used as a morgue. It was damp and exceedingly cold in winter. But as He later recounted, His two years in that abysmal room provided Him with an opportunity to do something He had long wished to do: read and study the Qu'rán in its entirety. The bad climate of that room also caused Him to develop rheumatism, which would plague Him the rest of his life.

Bahá'u'lláh was too prominent, with too many well-placed friends, to be disposed of through execution. 'Akká provided a more sinister means toward the same end. The city was so foul that it was proverbial that a bird flying over it would drop dead from the stench. In fact, the Turkish city was built on top of a warren of tunnels constructed by the Crusaders hundreds of years before. These would fill with water that became putrid in the summer heat and evaporation created a visible haze of bad air over the town. The well water was brackish because of the town's proximity to the sea and good water required a long trek into the countryside. The city was also surrounded by thick walls constructed with the intent to keep out European invaders once the last of the Crusaders had been expelled from the city. In fact, the walls were so impregnable that they had thwarted Napoleon Bonaparte in 1799 when he laid siege to 'Akká. It was the perfect place to send the worst prisoners of the Ottoman Empire. All but the hardiest usually took sick and died shortly upon arrival. It was undoubtedly hoped that the same fate awaited Bahá'u'lláh and His companions.

The enemies of the Faith soon had their wishes fulfilled. Within a few weeks, almost the entire group was deathly ill with dysentery and typhoid. 'Abbás Effendi was one of the only two who did not succumb, so he nursed his family and companions night and day for three months. Three of the exiles died. Finally, Bahá'u'lláh wrote a prayer and asked everyone to recite it, and the sickness subsided. As others regained their strength, the Master Himself at last fell ill with dysentery. When He recovered, He resumed His position as the one who oversaw the daily details of their lives. Furthermore, the Bahá'ís began to gain the trust of the guards and local officials as they observed that the Bahá'ís were high-minded people of good character rather than the miscreants they had been told to expect; consequently, the prisoners were allowed to send a few men to the market with a guard to buy better-quality food. The Master would wait at the gate and inspect each purchase to ensure that nothing that would make anyone sick was brought in.

The greatest tragedy of this period was not the harsh living conditions, not even the deaths; it was that God's Messenger was not able to get God's Message out into the world. This relentlessly weighed upon the minds of the prisoners. This torment was aggravated by watching helplessly as Bahá'í pilgrims, who had travelled on foot all the way from Iran, strained their eyes as they stood beyond the city walls, hoping to catch a fleeting glimpse of their Lord as he acknowledged them from a prison window by waving a cloth.

One evening in June of 1870, 'Abbás Effendi's younger brother Mírzá Mihdí, called the 'Purest Branch', was pacing the roof of the prison, where he could enjoy the cool sea breezes of sunset. Twenty-two-year-old Mírzá Mihdí was handsome, with soulful eyes. He was taller than his older brother and slender. This devoted believer had experienced the trauma of being separated from his parents at the tender age of four because he was judged too young and frail to endure the hardships of the mountain journey to Baghdad. After seven years of being cared for by relatives in Tehran, he was reunited with his parents in Baghdad at the age of eleven. He was a kind and gentle soul whose job it was to make copies of the Writings of his Father in his exquisite penmanship. That early evening Mírzá Mihdí became so focused upon the verses of God he was reciting that he forgot to pay attention to his steps and fell through a skylight onto a wooden crate. The crash sent everyone running to his side. When the Master saw the situation, He went down on His knees in front of His Father and tearfully begged Him to use His powers to spare His brother's life. Bahá'u'lláh privately tended to His young son and offered him the possibility of a full recovery and normal life. But Mírzá Mihdí rejected it and begged his father to let his life be a sacrifice so that the pilgrims would be able to attain Bahá'u'lláh's presence. Bahá'u'lláh granted His son's wish and the next day the youth died.

Within a few months, the sacrifice of the Purest Branch had its desired effect and the government removed the prisoners from the barracks. Most of them were allowed to establish normal lives within the walls of 'Akká. Bahá'u'lláh and his immediate family, however, remained under house arrest and were moved from house to house until, after about ten months, they were settled in the vacated home of a Christian wine merchant near the western city wall by the sea. When they first occupied the eastern side of the building, the section referred to as the House of 'Údí Khammár, there were so many people crowded into that small home that at one point thirteen people were sleeping in one of the rooms.

It was during the time in the House of 'Údí Khammár that Bahá'u'lláh revealed his most important book, the Kitáb-i-Aqdas, the book of laws and exhortations for this day. It was also during this time that the Master's life took a new turn.

The Master had grown up to become a very charming, intelligent, handsome man of the best of character. When well into His twenties, people wondered why He had not yet married. Many a young lady tried to capture His attention. Daughters were offered and politely declined. From His childhood, as was the custom at that time in Iran, it had been agreed by His family that He was to marry His first cousin, the daughter of one of His Father's brothers. During the years in Baghdad, that uncle had travelled all the way to Iraq to meet with Bahá'u'lláh and during the visit gifts had been exchanged to seal the engagement. Back in Iran, the young lady was very happy about the prospect. But the uncle died and other members of the family, who disapproved of Bahá'u'lláh and His religion, thwarted the marriage by arranging for the promised young lady to marry another against her will. She did not live long after her forced marriage and it has been said that her fatal illness was brought on by a broken heart.

A new bride was chosen from a wealthy, noble family of staunch believers residing in the city of Isfahan. Her birth seemed little short of miraculous since her parents had found it difficult to conceive children. One day her father was privileged to be dining with the Báb, who inquired after him and his family. When He learned of the couple's difficulties in having children, He took some food from his own plate and passed it to her father, instructing him to eat some and to take the remainder home to his wife. Her father complied and within the year a daughter was born. This child grew up to be lovely of face and of character and a very ardent, firm believer. It was arranged in accord with the wishes of Bahá'u'lláh that she and her younger brother should travel together to 'Akká without intimating either the purpose of their travel or their destination. En route they visited the widow of the Báb (who took great delight in the company of the young lady), performed the requirements of Muslim pilgrimage to Mecca, and then finally made their way to the prison city.

The young woman and her brother had been instructed not to disembark from the ship when they reached 'Akká until someone came to the port to fetch them. Time passed, no one came, and it looked as though the ship would sail with them still aboard. At the last moment, Bahá'u'lláh's next-door neighbour, a Christian named Ilyás 'Abbúd, breathlessly arrived to retrieve them. 'Abbúd had realized that, as prisoners, Bahá'u'lláh and His family were not allowed to bring people into 'Akká; and consequently he took the responsibility upon himself to vouch for the new arrivals and to tell the officials that they were his guests, the guests of a free and prominent resident of the city. The Master observed all this from afar, watching undetected as His intended bride entered the city.

Bahá'u'lláh gave His future daughter-in-law a new name, Munírih, which means 'luminous'. He was obviously pleased with her, but yet the wedding did not take place. Months dragged on until at last the next-door neighbour again intervened to assist the family. 'Abbúd realized that the overcrowded space of the House of 'Údí Khammár, with no private rooms, was unsuitable for a newly married couple. He cut an opening in the wall between his home and that of Bahá'u'lláh's and then offered a room from his own house for the young couple. With that problem solved, the marriage took place almost immediately during the summer of 1872.

'Abbás Effendi and Munírih Khánum[8] adored each other. They had nine children but only four survived to adulthood. Three were lost as infants, a son died at about age four and a daughter died at age fifteen. The four children who survived into adulthood were all daughters. This lack of a male heir was a source of worry and contention for many of the believers, since Persian families placed great value on sons and, more importantly, because many Bahá'ís were uneasy about the line of succession of the Faith. The Master, however, was unperturbed and refused the oft-proffered solution of taking a second wife.[9]

When 'Abbúd moved his family to a new residence, he offered his side of the house to Bahá'u'lláh. It was more spacious and grand than the House of 'Údí Khammár and had a fine balcony that overlooked the sea. The family and other members of the household spilled into the remaining spaces of the building, filling it to capacity as more and more people came under their care.

During this period of the late 1870s and early 1880s, the Master continued to take responsibility for His Father's business affairs and to serve as His liaison with government officials. He had also become the champion and helper of all of the poor and needy in 'Akká. As the believers slowly gained the trust of the local population, transforming in their eyes from criminals to respectable fellow citizens, it was the Master's conduct, especially, that brought about this change. Over the years, He became the most revered citizen of 'Akká, the one everyone turned to for advice and assistance, from governors and high officials to the destitute and reviled. On the other hand, Bahá'u'lláh ended His public life from the time of His incarceration in the prison of 'Akká. Even after His release from the confinement of the Citadel to house arrest, He continued to stay clear of the public eye, meeting only with His followers and occasionally with public officials. He left the work of associating with the local society of the Levant to His eldest son.[10]

Bahá'u'lláh Himself wrote of the high station and qualities of that son. In the Súriy-i-Ghusn (Tablet of the Branch) He stated:

> There hath branched from the Sadratu'l-Muntahá this sacred and glorious Being, this Branch of Holiness; well is it with him that hath sought His shelter and abideth beneath His shadow. Verily the Limb of the Law of God hath sprung forth from this Root which God hath firmly implanted

in the Ground of His Will, and Whose Branch hath been so uplifted as to encompass the whole of creation. Magnified be He, therefore, for this sublime, this blessed, this mighty, this exalted Handiwork! . . . A Word hath, as a token of Our grace, gone forth from the Most Great Tablet – a Word which God hath adorned with the ornament of His own Self, and made it sovereign over the earth and all that is therein, and a sign of His greatness and power among its people . . . Render thanks unto God, O people, for His appearance; for verily He is the most great Favour unto you, the most perfect bounty upon you; and through Him every mouldering bone is quickened. Whoso turneth towards Him hath turned towards God, and whoso turneth away from Him hath turned away from My Beauty, hath repudiated My Proof, and transgressed against Me. He is the Trust of God amongst you, His charge within you, His manifestation unto you and His appearance among His favoured servants . . . We have sent Him down in the form of a human temple. Blest and sanctified be God Who createth whatsoever He willeth through His inviolable, His infallible decree. They who deprive themselves of the shadow of the Branch, are lost in the wilderness of error, are consumed by the heat of worldly desires, and are of those who will assuredly perish.[11]

And in other Tablets Bahá'u'lláh wrote further about the Master:

The glory of God rest upon Thee, and upon whosoever serveth Thee and circleth around Thee. Woe, great woe, betide him that opposeth and injureth Thee. Well is it with him that sweareth fealty to Thee; the fire of hell torment him who is Thine enemy.[12]

We have made Thee a shelter for all mankind, a shield unto all who are in heaven and on earth, a stronghold for whosoever hath believed in God, the Incomparable, the All-Knowing. God grant that through Thee He may protect them, may enrich and sustain them, that He may inspire Thee with that which shall be a wellspring of wealth unto all created things, an ocean of bounty unto all men, and the dayspring of mercy unto all peoples.[13]

Nine years after the exiles arrived in the prison city, Bahá'u'lláh began to make statements about how He longed to see the countryside. Ever since His arrival in the Holy Land, He had been confined unremittingly within the city walls of 'Akká, an urban landscape devoid of trees, even of grass. 'Abbás Effendi took His Father's comments to be a cue that it was time to demonstrate His

Father's true freedom – no earthly king can thwart the will of God by imprisoning His Chosen One. Even though the Sultan of Turkey never rescinded his order that Bahá'u'lláh be incarcerated for eternity, the local officials of 'Akká had long ceased to treat Him as a prisoner; indeed, most held Him in high regard. 'Abbás Effendi made arrangements for His father to move to a house in the countryside with the approval of both the local officials and the head mufti of the region. Many members of the family and household moved with Him, but the Master and His family, His mother, and His devoted sister Bahíyyih Khánum stayed behind in the House of 'Abbúd in 'Akká. Bahá'u'lláh continued to reside with 'Abbás Effendi in 'Akká during the winter months, but He spent the warmer months just outside the city, first at the Mansion of Mazra'ih and later at the Mansion of Bahjí.

It is difficult to believe that one so perfect, the embodiment of kindness and humility, should have enemies; but so He did. The accolades the Master so well deserved served to harden some hearts that were filled with envy and jealousy or which feared the growth of the new religion He espoused. More shocking still, some of those who harboured ill-will toward Him were from His own family. To understand this it is necessary to examine family patterns of the Orient during the nineteenth century.

The Holy Qur'án allowed Muslim men to take up to four wives. In nineteenth-century Iran, as was true throughout much of the world, women were under the control first of their fathers and, after marriage, of their husbands. Especially in upper-class Persian households, it was the common practice to keep women and girls away from the public eye where men who were unrelated to them could see them. This of course meant that women were completely dependent on their male relatives for economic support because they could not easily leave their homes to earn a living. Women's chastity was highly valued and it was assumed that men were unable to control their urges around them, so even the hiring of a maidservant was not permitted unless the owner of the house married her. If a man died, it was expected that a male relative would marry the widow to ensure the support of the deceased man's family. Marriages were arranged by parents, usually with complete disregard for the wishes of the couple. In theory, the first wife had a say in the taking of additional wives, but in practice this prerogative was not often extended to her. Marriage had evolved to become primarily a means of controlling the breeding and care of offspring and was entered into based upon practical and financial considerations rather than on emotions. It was the particular duty of men of means to take multiple wives because they could afford to assume responsibility for a number of women and children. This arrangement of many children with one father and different mothers was a recipe for family jealousy and intrigue, as each wife vied for the affection and material resources of the one head of the household.[14]

Before He began His ministry, Bahá'u'lláh acceded to the customs of His homeland and the Islamic Faith and took three wives. All three marriages were arranged. He married the mother of 'Abbás Effendi when only 18 and she was between the age of 12 and 16. Ásíyih Khánum, known as Navváb, and Bahá'u'lláh were deeply devoted to each other. About thirteen years later, responsibility for marrying his first cousin, Mahd-i-'Ulyá, fell to Bahá'u'lláh because her first husband had died and he had been a close friend of her late husband. This second marriage took place when 'Abbás Effendi, the eldest surviving child of Bahá'u'lláh, was about seven or eight. The second wife was jealous of 'Abbás Effendi from the beginning. Her sons could never assume His position in the family as the eldest son while 'Abbás Effendi lived, and it did not help her feelings of envy that He was also a perfect child in every way. This jealousy was passed on to her children. She and Bahá'u'lláh together had six children, four of whom lived to be adults – three sons and a daughter. When Bahá'u'lláh moved to the countryside outside 'Akká in 1877, he took Mahd-i-'Ulyá and her children with him, in part because of the growing enmity between that segment of his family and that of his first and primary wife. (It was natural that, as a married man whose primary responsibilities had to be carried out in the town of 'Akká, the Master would continue to reside in the town.) During Bahá'u'lláh's lifetime, this family tension was concealed from all but the most intimate members of the household.[15]

On 28 May 1892 Bahá'u'lláh, the Glory of God, the Supreme Manifestation of God, passed away after a brief illness at Bahjí at the age of 74. 'Abbás Effendi was with him at the end.[16] Even before Bahá'u'lláh could be laid to rest, the pent-up jealousy of Mahd-i-'Ulyá's children and some of 'Abbás Effendi's cousins began to ooze out. 'Abbás Effendi responded by acting as though they were still His well-wishers, by concealing their misdeeds, and by continuing to shower them with love and kindness. It was at this time that the Master took for Himself the name 'Abdu'l-Bahá, Servant of Bahá, to set forth as clearly as possible that He considered himself a servant of the Cause of God, even as He assumed the leadership of it.

To His followers, the Ascension of Bahá'u'lláh was a calamity, a major earthquake that shook them and plunged many into deep despair. Their only comfort was the clear instruction in Bahá'u'lláh's Will and Testament, the Kitáb-i-'Ahd, to turn toward 'Abdu'l-Bahá, referred to by His Father as the Most Mighty Branch.

> It is incumbent upon the Aghsán, the Afnán and My kindred to turn, one and all, their faces towards the Most Mighty Branch. Consider that

> which We have revealed in Our Most Holy Book: 'When the ocean of My presence hath ebbed and the Book of My Revelation is ended, turn your faces toward Him Whom God hath purposed, Who hath branched from this Ancient Root.' The object of this sacred verse is none other except the Most Mighty Branch ('Abdu'l-Bahá). Thus have We graciously revealed unto you our potent Will, and I am verily the Gracious, the All-Powerful.[17]

The Master's role as successor of his father had been indicated years earlier in the Kitáb-i-Aqdas:

> 'When the ocean of My presence hath ebbed and the Book of My Revelation is ended,' proclaims the Kitáb-i-Aqdas, 'turn your faces toward Him Whom God hath purposed, Who hath branched from this Ancient Root.' And again, 'When the Mystic Dove will have winged its flight from its Sanctuary of Praise and sought its far-off goal, its hidden habitation, refer ye whatsoever ye understand not in the Book to Him Who hath branched from this mighty Stock.'[18]

'Abdu'l-Bahá's three younger half-brothers refused to accept Him in their hearts as the sole head of the Faith even though, in the beginning, they feigned loyalty to Him. They lost no time after the passing of their Father in beginning to secretly plot and scheme, to spread malicious rumours, and to generally make life for 'Abdu'l-Bahá as miserable as possible. For example, they began to insist that 'Abdu'l-Bahá supply them with luxury items and cover their lavish living expenses from the funds contributed to Him by the believers for the work of the Faith. 'Abdu'l-Bahá sought to pacify them by giving them what they demanded even though it meant that His own household, which was a paragon of frugality already, was deprived of even basic necessities. His half-brothers would then lie to local government officials, complaining to them that 'Abdu'l-Bahá kept the funds of the Faith for Himself while leaving them impoverished. They even used the funds 'Abdu'l-Bahá gave them to bribe government officials in order to undermine the Master's standing in the community.[19]

For the first four years after the passing of Bahá'u'lláh, 'Abdu'l-Bahá continued to endure the trials brought on by His brothers silently and patiently, concealing them from the body of believers in the hope that these family members would realize that they were violating the letter and spirit of Bahá'u'lláh's teachings and return to the straight path. But in 1896 the half-brothers, led by the eldest, Mírzá Muḥammad-'Alí, wrote to selected leaders within the Bahá'í community in Iran, appealing to their egos and trying to elicit their complicity in nefarious plans to supplant 'Abdu'l-Bahá as Head of the Faith. This open breaking of the Covenant of Bahá'u'lláh, that explicit pact He had made with His followers that they should wholeheartedly, unhesitatingly, follow His appointed successor after His passing, plunged the entire Bahá'í community into a crisis. Even though very few defected to the half-brothers, the grief that this open rebellion brought with it was too great to measure. For a time during 1897, the Master withdrew from the turmoil of 'Akká and Haifa and took up residence by Himself in a small building at the entrance to the Cave of Elijah at the northwestern most point of Mount Carmel.

The hindsight of history teaches that crises such as the rebellion of the Master's extended family serve a very useful purpose in carrying forward the Cause of God. Just as a violent storm brings down dead branches and trees that are weak at the core, these rebellions separate devoted believers from those who are spiritually dead, though outwardly they may appear to be the most sincere adherents. Those with strong egos, those who seek power for its own sake, have no place within the Cause of God; thus episodes of rebellion invariably serve to cleanse the Faith of such dead wood.

Losing the Light of the World, Bahá'u'lláh, was an affliction almost beyond endurance, but to compound that loss with the treachery of those who had been part of the family, who had been among the companions during the years of exile and imprisonment, who had given great service to the Cause in the face of the persecution of two powerful kingdoms, brought the little band of the faithful in the Holy Land to a very low ebb indeed. There was, however, one ray of sunshine to dispel the gloom – the rise of the Faith in America.

It is not known for certain if 'Abdu'l-Bahá or Bahá'u'lláh had any direct or indirect role in the encouragement and financial support given by the believers in Egypt to Ibrahim Kheiralla and Anton Haddad as they departed for the West, just at the time Bahá'u'lláh lay dying. The timing of their departure for the West within a few days of the passing of the Blessed Beauty and the establishment of His mighty Covenant in the person of 'Abdu'l-Bahá seems more than coincidence. Shoghi Effendi would later write in *God Passes By* that the United States was the community 'called into being through the creative energies released by the proclamation of the Covenant of Bahá'u'lláh . . .',[20] that Covenant which became fully known through the promulgation of Bahá'u'lláh's Will and Testament after His ascension.

'Abdu'l-Bahá did not intervene in the teaching work in the United States in any way during the first years. Even though the friends would each send a letter to 'Abdu'l-Bahá when they decided to become Bahá'ís, prior to 1899 He is known to have sent only one letter to any of the American believers and to have given neither direct guidance nor encouragement to Ibrahim Kheiralla. The first real guidance to the American community came from Anton Haddad, who related what the Master had told him to say to the Americans during his 1897 pilgrimage.

When Kheiralla arrived in 'Akká on his birthday, 11 November 1898,[21] and the day he described as the 'greatest of my life', the Master showered him with praise for the enormous accomplishment of bringing the Faith to the West. Indeed, at that moment there were about a thousand Bahá'ís listed on the rolls in the United States, in large measure due to Kheiralla's efforts. 'Abdu'l-Bahá bestowed upon him the titles 'Bahá's Peter', 'The Second Columbus', and 'Conqueror of America'.[22] Kheiralla was overwhelmed by the reception he received not only from 'Abdu'l-Bahá Himself but also from the believers in the Holy Land. He wrote from 'Akká to Anton Haddad on 17 November 1898 that

> . . . the Master (Moula) (May my soul be a ransom to the dust of His feet!) has shown me so much kindness and benevolence that it is beyond my power to express them either in writing or in speech. Not only the Master, but all the believers and the prominent and distinguished guides and grandees have paid me more deference than I am worthy of. This was no other than a Divine gift and a heavenly mercy. Exalted be He who gives to whom He pleaseth without merit.
>
> I now have thoroughly have [sic] realized the great station to which I have attained, and the Master has imbued my mind with a spirit of knowledge which I never expected to attain in this world.[23]

On his way to 'Akká, Kheiralla had spent almost three weeks in Egypt, where he was reunited with his daughters Nabitha and Labitha. He had been joyously welcomed by the Egyptian believers.

> Abdul Kerim Effendi Tehrani came twice from Cairo to Alexandria especially for the purpose of meeting me. Consider, my brother, what a great kindness and care is this? Also some of the prominent believers came and visited me. They told me that had my coming become known to the believers throughout Egypt, hundreds of them would have come to meet me.[24]

This brief period in mid-November of 1898 would turn out to be the brightest moment of Kheiralla's life. He was welcomed in the Holy Land as a hero, but he was about to tarnish his own lustre.

CHAPTER 6

Arrival in the Most Great Prison: 'Akká

Sunday morning, 10 December, the Getsingers awoke early following a second restless, seemingly interminable night of little sleep and much extolling in whispers of their great blessings and good fortune. They put on their best new clothes, the ones purchased in Paris for the express purpose of meeting their Lord. As Lua later recounted, they both felt at the time that the best attire they owned was not even 'half good enough' for the occasion at hand. The day they had anxiously awaited had arrived, and so they paced about in their hotel in Haifa until about 8:30 a.m. when at last a carriage pulled up to the hotel to take them, along with Kheiralla and his eldest daughter, around the edge of the bay to the ancient city of 'Akká – 'the place of all places, the New Jerusalem, the Holy Abode of the Most High, and the Dwelling Place of our Gracious Lord'.[1]

Lua later wrote the following vivid account of that morning of mornings for the believers in Chicago.

> It is about five miles[2] from Haifa to Acca – the road close to the sea – indeed in the sea, for the horses were walking in the water and at times the waves dashed nearly to the top of the wheels. After riding for about a quarter of an hour we could see the City in the distance. It was a beautiful morning and as we looked we could but think of the description in the Bible, 'a city all of gold beside the crystal sea'. It was bathed in a flood of golden sunshine and the splashing up against its walls sparkled with splendor! We gradually approached nearer and nearer until at last we passed 'the shed which serves as a coffee house outside the wall', and entered the city by its solitary gate and drove straight to the house of Abbas Effendi.
>
> We[3] entered the garden, ascended one flight of stairs, and were shown into a hall, or reception room, where we removed our wraps, and were welcomed by the uncle who told us to pass into the next room. Dr. K. went ahead, and by the violent beating of my heart, I knew we were soon to behold the Blessed Face of the Prince of the House of David, the King

> of the whole world. We reached the door and stopped – before us, in the center of the room, stood a man clad in a long raiment, with a white turban upon His head; stretching out one hand to us, while His face, which I cannot describe, was lighted by a rare, sweet smile of joy and welcome! We stood thus for a moment, unable to move; then my heart gave a great throb, and scarcely knowing what I was doing, I held out my arms, crying, 'my Lord, my Lord!' and rushed to Him, kneeling at His blessed feet, sobbing like a child. In an instant my husband was beside me, crying as only men can cry! He put His dear hands upon our bowed heads and said, in a voice that seemed to our ears like a strain of sweet music, 'Welcome, welcome, my dear children, you are welcome; arise and be of good cheer.' Then He sat down upon a low divan and we sat on one side almost facing Him, Dr. K. and his daughter on the other side, and He began to talk to us . . .[4]

Edward would always remember the intense emotions of that first meeting with the Master as well, but he also remarked in his memoirs of his astonishment at the directness, the simplicity of the event. They had expected a grand ceremonial entrance. What they experienced instead was love unalloyed.

That very same day, back in Paris, a second significant, though more public, event took place. Historians of the future would mark the end of the Spanish-American War as the beginning of what would become known as the 'American Century', the period during which the United States became the dominant world power. That same day, 10 December 1898, representatives of the warring parties signed the treaty that formally concluded the war instigated months earlier by Phoebe's son. The 'American Century' literally began the day the first American Bahá'í pilgrims arrived in 'Akká.[5]

The moment of their first meeting with 'Abdu'l-Bahá was, of course, a highlight of their lives for all the first Western pilgrims. Their reactions at the time varied from the highly emotional to the subdued to outright stupefaction. May Bolles, for example, recorded the following memory in her journal:

> In a moment I stood on the threshold and dimly saw a room full of people sitting quietly about the walls, and then I beheld my Beloved. I found myself at His feet, and He gently raised me and seated me beside Him, all the while saying some loving words in Persian in a voice that shook my heart. Of that first meeting I can remember neither joy nor pain nor anything that I can name. I had been carried suddenly to too great a height; my soul had come in contact with the Divine Spirit; and this force so pure, so holy, so mighty, had overwhelmed me. He spoke to each one of us in turn of ourselves and our lives and those whom we loved, and although

> His Words were so few and so simple they breathed the Spirit of Life to our souls.[6]

Years later, Minnie Thornburgh-Cropper penned a brief, almost mystical, description of her first encounter with the Master. She accompanied Phoebe to Haifa a week or more after the Getsingers arrived in the Holy Land, having been subjected to two much more trying Mediterranean voyages than Edward and Lua had experienced.

> Mrs. Hearst and I arrived in Cairo, Egypt, after a terrible storm at sea, and remained there for a few days until all had been explained to us regarding our actual journey into the prison city.
>
> We then took a small, miserable boat to Haifa. There was a storm here also, and we were beaten about unmercifully in our all too inadequate steamer. Upon arrival we went to an hotel, where we remained until nightfall as it was too dangerous for us, and for 'Abdu'l-Bahá, Whom we were to visit, for strangers to be seen entering the city of sorrow.
>
> We took a carriage after the night had fallen, and drove along the hard sand by 'way of the sea beyond Jordan', which led us to the gates of the prison city. There our trusted driver arranged for us to enter. Once inside we found the friends who were awaiting us, and we started up the uneven stairs that led to Him. Someone went before us with a small piece of candle, which cast strange shadows on the walls of this silent place.
>
> Suddenly the light caught a form that at first seemed a vision of mist and light. It was the Master which the candle-light had revealed to us. His white robe, and silver, flowing hair, and shining blue eyes gave the impression of a spirit, rather than of a human being. We tried to tell Him how deeply grateful we were at His receiving us. 'No,' He answered, 'you are kind to come.' This was spoken in a very careful English.
>
> Then He smiled, and we recognized the Light which He possessed in the radiance which moved over His fine and noble face. It was an amazing experience. We four visitors[7] from the Western world felt that our voyage, with all its accompanying inconvenience was a small price to pay for such treasure as we received from the spirit and words of the Master, Whom we had crossed mountain and seas and nations to meet. This began our work to 'spread the teaching', to 'mention the Name of Bahá'u'lláh, and acquaint the world with the Message'.[8]

Like May, Marian Kheiralla spontaneously fell to her knees at the feet of the Master, sobbing and kissing His delicate hands. She first met Him in His own small room where He was seated on a divan upon which were scattered writing materials. He patted her tenderly on her cheeks and shoulders and in His gentle voice told her that she was most welcome and should be at ease and happy.[9]

Ella Goodall's and Nell Hillyer's first meeting with the Master was perhaps the least dramatic of the group. After first being graciously received by 'Abdu'l-Bahá's two sons-in-law, they were ushered into the small anteroom where they both removed their wraps. They were then led into the modest sitting room where they found 'Abdu'l-Bahá seated in the corner of a couch. Both young ladies knelt before Him and kissed His hand. He directed them to sit beside Him and began to welcome them by making gentle small talk. Both ladies were so overwhelmed that throughout the first interview they were hardly able to answer His simple questions regarding their health, journey and the weather. Ella wrote to her mother, 'Truly, His presence is overpowering.'[10]

Most of these Western pilgrims had never seen a photograph of the Master before meeting Him. In fact, no photograph had been taken of Him since the period of exile in Adrianople when He was in his early twenties.[11] Now He was a vigorous man of full maturity at the age of 54. Perhaps Anton Haddad had given the pilgrims some intimation of what to expect, but otherwise they were venturing into the unknown. Ella wrote in her journal that when they rose to go with 'Abdu'l-Bahá to lunch, she finally plucked up the courage to look at Him. She later penned a description of Him for her mother:

> In looks He is a little older and greyer than I had pictured, rather short than tall, but with a majestic bearing that at times makes Him seem like a giant. He has wonderful soft brown eyes,[12] gray hair & beard, but very black brows, the sweetest smile in the world and a spirit shining out of His face that draws one like a magnet, and at times gives Him the expression of a martyr . . . [13] He wears the long, loose coat-like clothes of the Persian, also a white fez bound round with folds of soft, white muslin.[14]

Lua, after some months of being in the presence of 'Abdu'l-Bahá, wrote:

> The Face of the Master is gloriously beautiful. His eyes read one's very soul, still they are full of divine love and fairly melt one's heart! His hair and beard are white, but soft and fine like silk. His features are finely chiseled and very classical. His forehead high and full and His mouth supremely beautiful, while His hands are small and white like a woman's. Now I have tried to describe Him but you see it is a feeble attempt and I assure you it is inadequate in the extreme![15]

From 1871 until 1896 the Master had resided within the city walls of 'Akká in the House of Abbúd. He married in that house and His children were all born there. He penned His two books, *A Traveller's Narrative* and *The Secret of Divine Civilization*, within its walls. By 1896 His four surviving daughters had become adults and two were married; consequently the House of 'Abbúd was becoming overcrowded, not only with relatives but also with the growing number of people under the Master's care. To remedy the problem, He rented a section of a much larger building only half a block away from His old home and next to the prison where He and his family had suffered immeasurably when they first arrived in 'Akká. This newly-leased residence was the southwest section of a large square building with a central garden courtyard which had been built about 1817 by a young ruler of 'Akká, 'Abdu'lláh Pá<u>sh</u>á. It was designed to be an opulent residence – the governing palace of the city – but by the time the Master rented rooms in it the imposing complex was nothing more than a dilapidated old apartment building with other sections occupied by unrelated tenants. For example, the eastern section was rented by a Christian missionary doctor from England who used the lower eastern level as a medical clinic. The Master used one large room on the ground level as a reception room for meeting the public and pilgrims from the East.[16] Upstairs there was a private suite of rooms given to the ladies and young children which was off-limits to men who were not intimately part of the household. The House of 'Abdu'lláh Pá<u>sh</u>á was set off from the town on three sides by a high sandstone wall which created an outer courtyard within which the Master planted a garden. The building itself was entered through a large metal door studded with bolts that was like a city gate in miniature. To reach 'Abdu'l-Bahá's living quarters, it was necessary to cross the spacious inner courtyard, which had a modest ornamental garden laid out in a geometric pattern covering its southern half like a worn Persian carpet. Despite its decayed state, the local Bahá'í friends lovingly referred to the House of 'Abdu'lláh Pá<u>sh</u>á as 'the Palace'.[17]

The room where the Master first welcomed most of the Western pilgrims faced full west and had a commanding view of the sea and the ancient sandstone wall that separated the city from the water.[18] After climbing a long, treacherous flight of uneven, stone stairs which hugged an outside wall, they would have entered a small upper-level open court that provided light and air to the rooms surrounding it. Immediately to the right there was a door with a raised wooden sill that opened into a small anteroom with one window directly facing the very prison cell that had held Bahá'u'lláh thirty years before. To the left was the doorway and a step up to the reception room with its low couches placed straight ahead under the three western windows. During the winter months the Americans probably watched as large waves crashed against the outer wall, propelling sea spray all the way to those very windows. The room had a high ceiling, which made it seem larger than it was. It was a plain room, sparsely furnished. The Master had had it panelled with cedar to absorb the dampness that hung in the winter air of 'Akká and made His bones ache. 'Abdu'l-Bahá's home at the House of 'Abdu'lláh Páshá was far, far from being the magnificent palace the Americans had expected. Commenting some months later on the household of the Master, Lua said that the house and its surroundings were not so grand, that 'everything – even their manner of dress – is simplicity itself, but there is a dignity and grandeur in this simplicity that is quite beyond description'.[19]

One can only speculate about what was happening in the other rooms of 'Abdu'l-Bahá's household as the Master greeted each new contingent of Western pilgrims. Surely there was much excitement and great joy. Many of believers resident in 'Akká had endured years of deprivation and suffering because of their great love for the nascent Faith, and now God was sending them tangible proof that the might of the Shah of Persia and the Sultan of Turkey could not prevent the spreading of God's Message to the greater world. They must have been beside themselves with happiness, for the arrival of the Americans marked a great victory, especially after the recent traumatic years following the passing of Bahá'u'lláh. Yet these local believers would have had to temper their celebrations, for the Master was keen not to draw attention to the arrival of the American visitors lest the enemies of the Faith take notice and devise ways to turn this historic development into yet another calamity. The walls had ears. Phoebe's presence in the house, in particular, had to remain a carefully guarded secret because of her prominence. It is noteworthy that she and her two female companions, alone among the first Western pilgrims, were brought to the Master under the cover of darkness because of the real dangers posed by her coming. However, by the time the last of the Americans arrived in March, the local believers had become less guarded; they crowded around the entrance to House of 'Abdu'lláh Páshá to watch Ella and Nell enter.[20]

The Getsingers were allowed to stay only a few days in 'Akká before returning to Haifa. Accounts are not entirely certain, but there is reason to believe that Edward then returned to Egypt to fetch Phoebe. She, Minnie, and Phoebe's maid Emily Bachrodt arrived in Haifa probably around 20 December.[21] They stayed several days in 'Akká and then returned to the opulent Gezireh Palace Hotel in Cairo before the 25th, Christmas Day, where they celebrated the Christian holiday period with other friends and relatives assembled there for the cruise up the Nile River. Inexplicably, the Getsingers were allowed to remain in the Holy Land, though most of the time they had to reside in Haifa unless summoned to return to 'Akká. Ibrahim Kheiralla and his daughters also remained and so 'Abdu'l-Bahá arranged for them and the Getsingers to take up residence in a rented house in Haifa.[22] The members of the Hearst party in Egypt embarked on the Nile cruise on 2 January, the day after New Year's Day, and returned to Cairo in mid-February.

At some point in late December, Marian Kheiralla arrived alone from England to join her husband and meet her stepdaughters for the first time. She had brought her Bahá'í aunt, Marianne Brown, as far as Milan, Italy, but Miss Brown's health at age 71 did not allow her to proceed any further. That disappointed lady instead stayed behind in Milan with Emogene Hoagg, who was already engaged in teaching the Faith to her Italian singing instructor and others of her acquaintance.[23]

Meanwhile, back in Paris, May Bolles had wasted no time after the others departed for Egypt, introducing people to the Faith and preparing to depart for 'Akká. The first person to accept the Faith under her tutelage was an American artist from Ohio, Brenetta Herrman, in her early twenties,[24] who was in Paris to study painting. She wrote her letter of acceptance to the Master in January of 1899.[25]

May wrote to Phoebe on 2 January 1899 after Phoebe had completed her visit to 'Akká, asking among other questions what clothes would be appropriate for her visit to the Shrine of Bahá'u'lláh.[26] May also corresponded with Harriet Thornburgh about the arrangements for them to travel together. Hattie, who hated the cold British weather, was spending the winter in a boarding house in southern France near Marseilles while her daughter, Minnie, was travelling with Phoebe. The two ladies rendezvoused and sailed together from Marseilles on 9 February on the *S.S. Carthage*, arriving on 13 February at Port Said, Egypt, where they were met on board by several of the Egyptian believers, who undertook to prepare the two Americans for their pilgrimage.

> They did everything for us, got us rooms at the hotel, attended to our baggage, and during the time we were there came to us almost every hour of the day and evening, inviting us to their homes, taking us to drive, and indeed showing us a love and kindness such as we had never seen before. At the time we could not understand the spirit which animated them, but afterwards we knew that we were dead and they were living and were quickened with the love of God. On the afternoon of our arrival Núrulláh Effendi called for us and drove us to his house, where we met his dear wife and daughters with the same radiant faces and wonderful love that we had seen in our two brothers, and there for the first time we beheld the face of our beloved Master. I could not remove my eyes from this picture,

> and these friends gave us each a copy and a lock of hair of the Blessed Perfection. Then we were entertained with tea and many sweet cakes, and when we left, although not a word had been spoken except through an occasional interpretation of our brother, we were united in an indissoluble bond of love, and we felt that no language could have been more eloquent than that silence in which our hearts alone had spoken.[27]

After two days of waiting in Egypt, May and Harriet were escorted by their new Egyptian Baháʼí brothers to the small steamer that would take them up the coast to Haifa, arriving in the late evening of Thursday 16 February. Unlike the other groups, they did not stay in a hotel but in the house in Haifa which had been leased for the Kheirallas and the Americans and it was there that they met the Master the very next morning. Several Russians whom they had met on board the ship from Port Said came to the house early in the day, 'their faces shining with a great light as they entered His Presence'.[28] Speaking of that unforgettable morning, May wrote, 'We could not remove our eyes from His glorious face: we heard all He said; we drank tea with Him at His bidding; but existence seemed suspended, and when He arose and suddenly left us we came back with a start to life: but never again, thank God, to the same life on this earth! We had "beheld the King in His beauty. We had seen the land which is very far off." '[29]

On Monday 20 February, three more American pilgrims arrived in Haifa from Egypt. Anne Apperson was accompanied by Julia Pearson and Robert Turner and they met the Master in Haifa on that same day. But they did not see Him for long because within hours He had to return to ʿAkká because of business with the government. The next day, Lua, who by that time was beginning to serve as a hostess for her fellow pilgrims on behalf of the Master, arrived in Haifa from ʿAkká along with several of ʿAbdu'l-Bahá's daughters. The Master had instructed the five newly arrived Americans to be prepared to leave early Wednesday morning for ʿAkká. May related what happened next.

> On Tuesday night I told my spiritual mother that the Master evidently did not realize how ill and weak I was or He would never have expected me to leave with the others on Wednesday morning. Oh! We of little faith! No wonder she smiled and shook her head, saying, 'You will soon realize something of the power of ʿAbdu'l-Bahá.'
>
> It was about dawn when I awoke, feeling myself stirred by a breeze. I cannot describe what followed, but through my soul was flowing an essence; a mighty, unseen force was penetrating all my being, expanding it with boundless life and love and happiness, lifting and enfolding me in

> its mighty strength and peace. I knew then it was the Holy Spirit of God and that our Lord was praying for His servants in that blessed dawn, and I arose and prayed and was quite well. At an early hour we all met and set out in carriages for the holy city and the merciful spirit of God never left us as we drove along the shore, drawing ever nearer to the earthly abode of Him who was the Glory of God, His bounty descending like rain upon our souls. Our hearts were too full for words and in reverent silence we gazed upon the walled city as it lay white and clear and beautiful in the still morning light, with the deep blue Mediterranean at its feet and the dome of the luminous sky above. We crossed two streams which flowed from the land into the sea, the horses wading up to their sides, and reached at last the stone gates of 'Akká, drove through the narrow, picturesque streets where the early-rising oriental world was up and stirring, and arrived at the house of 'Abdu'l-Bahá.[30]

Last to arrive in the Holy Land were Ella and Nell, who had more adventures than the rest of the group during their travels. They bid adieu to their friends in New York and left their rented room on East 56th Street for the ship, only to find that its departure was delayed because of a breakdown of machinery. After waiting another six days at the home of friends, they used their connections in the shipping business to gain passage on an already overbooked steamer leaving for Italy. The Atlantic crossing was dreadful, with high seas that left them seasick much of the voyage. They left a porthole in their cabin open for air and consequently the entire cabin was flooded when a large wave hit. Their voyage across the Mediterranean on the Italian liner *Regina Margherita* was not any better. They were able to recover in luxury in the Gezireh Palace Hotel as Phoebe's guests in the rooms just vacated by Anne and Julia. Phoebe kept them up late one evening recounting her own experiences of her meeting with 'Abdu'l-Bahá.[31] Rested and charged by the stories they heard in Cairo from those who had already visited 'Akká, they left by train for Port Said on 1 March. During the confusion of embarking, they had not been informed that they needed to change trains at the southern end of the Suez Canal. Even the well travelled Helen was caught off balance by what happened next.

> . . . when we reached Ismalia we remained quietly in our compartment, bought oranges and dates out the window and of course were greatly interested in watching the crowd, a seething mass of humanity. Finally, we felt the train move, and after a few minutes I said to Ella, 'Something is wrong. We are going back toward Cairo,' and I pulled the bell cord on the side

of the car. Soon excited conductors came running along the outside step from both directions yelling, 'Q'est qui a? Q'est qui a?'[sic]. I said I feared something was wrong, that we wanted to go to Port Said where we had a steamer to catch and I realized we were going in the direction of Cairo. He said, 'C'est vrai, Madame,' but he said he would dump us out at the next station, where we could get a train back to Ismalia and then catch the next accommodations to Port Said. He did literally dump us out, but I could hardly call it a station. There was simply a platform and a couple of wooden benches in what seemed to us a portion of the Sahara. Soon however, up out of nowhere came men and children curious to know who and what we were. They spoke a little French and we soon made them understand we were waiting for a train to take us back to Ismalia.

After two or three hours' wait that seemed much longer, something on wheels came along that we boarded and we were once more on our way. It was well into the evening and quite dark when we reached our goal for the night, for of course no more trains were going to Port Said till the morning. There was a miserable little hotel in the station, and as the town did not look that we would fare any better going farther, we negotiated for a meal and night's lodging. We elicited quite a bit of curiosity having arrived at that hour and on that train, so quite a number of very queer people came snooping around even after we were shown to an apartment, which consisted of a very open-air bedroom with porches on two sides. We decided we would not undress at all, so crawled up onto the large bed that was well draped with mosquito netting and there we remained practically bolt upright all night.

We were called and left at an early hour on the first train to Port Said. When we arrived there, I was all primed for a heavy reprimand to the Thomas Cook's agent for having been so remiss as not to have informed us we should have changed cars the afternoon before at Ismalia, but when I saw the distressed look on his face change to one of relief when he found us, and when he said he had been wiring frantically to Cairo to know where we were and that he had had the steamer held for us till our arrival,[32] of course all was forgiven.[33]

After their trials and exploits, the two young ladies arrived safely at Jaffa on 3 March where, during a brief stopover, they met part of the Hearst group from Cairo and went aboard the *S.S. Auguste-Victoria* to see Phoebe again.[34] She was waiting to rendezvous there with the friends who had just concluded their pilgrimages to the Holy Land. From Jaffa they would embark together on a cruise of the eastern Mediterranean, including a stopover in Istanbul, as they made their way back to Paris. Late that evening, Ella and Nell arrived in Haifa. After spending a day exploring that city, Nell and Ella finally reached 'Akká on Sunday morning 5 March, the last of the Hearst party to arrive.

'Akká would have been a source of wonderment for the Americans had they not been overwhelmed by the purpose of their visit. As a new country, the United States had very few buildings that were even 200 years old, much less a thousand. 'Akká was one of the oldest continuously inhabited places on earth, with a rich and tragic history. As the only natural port along the coast of the Holy Land, many of the great personages of history had passed through it. 'Akká had hosted St Paul, St Francis of Assisi and Marco Polo, to mention but a few. Unfortunately, because of its strategic position some of its visitors also brought their armies with them. It had changed hands countless times and witnessed untold atrocities as a result. It was the bulwark and unofficial capital of the Christian Crusaders for 200 years. Many of the buildings still standing during the 1890s had been constructed 700 years earlier by those European warriors. The House of 'Abdu'lláh Páshá itself was built upon the warren of vaults left behind in 'Akká by the Crusaders. The Muslims who finally drove out the Europeans were determined that 'Akká would never again fall to foreign invaders and so its double walls[35] were reinforced to such a degree that they were considered impregnable.[36] The Ottoman Turks inherited the city when they became the overlords of the region after they captured Istanbul in the late fifteenth century. For a brief period in the eighteenth century, the local Ottoman officials in the Levant revived and rebuilt the ruined little port city. The best of 'Akká's buildings extant in the 1890s were constructed during that brief renaissance, including the principal mosque, which dominated the skyline.

The Ottoman use of 'Akká as a port was brief because its harbour had started to silt in well before the nineteenth century, making it impossible for large ships to come close; but those absentee overlords did find one good use for its impregnable walls – it made a perfect penal colony. There were only two ways in and out of the city, a sea gate by the port and a fortified land gate with the standard Near East zigzag design that prevented cavalry charges into the city. These massive wooden gates were firmly shut and bolted two hours after sunset every evening. Its foul air and brackish drinking water made it a despicable, unwholesome place. The Ottomans banished many of their worst trouble-makers to that historic city. However, with the arrival in 1868 of Bahá'u'lláh and his companions as prisoners, the city began to improve as if by magic. The winds seemed to shift, bringing better air, and when asked by a governor if a favour could be performed for him, Bahá'u'lláh requested that the city's old aqueduct, which had fallen into disrepair, be restored so that 'Akká could again have good drinking water. It did not go unnoticed among the local residents that, with the coming of the Baháʼís, their own living conditions improved.

When Baháʼu'lláh arrived in ʻAkká, He christened the entire city 'the Most Great Prison' even though it could be argued that the Tehran dungeon in which he had been held had been physically worse. ʻAbdu'l-Bahá lived most of His life within its walls and did not completely move His residence out of the city, even to Haifa, until 1910[37] when the Young Turk Revolution resulted in the release of the prisoners of conscience of the Ottoman Empire, including ʻAbdu'l-Bahá, and when the city's walls were finally breached to allow a normal flow of traffic in and out.

What was life like in the household of the Master there in the Most Great Prison? Ella wrote to her mother, 'The atmosphere of absolute love and affection that pervades the Holy Household is not to be equalled any where.'[38] May wrote in her journal of the loving-kindness extended to the February group during the period they were at the House of ʻAbdu'lláh Pá<u>sh</u>á.

> They took us to our rooms which, alas!, they had vacated for our sakes; they gave us every comfort, anticipated every need and surrounded us with care and attention; yet through it all shone the light of wonderful spirituality, through these kindly human channels their divine love was poured forth and their own lives, their own comfort, were as a handful of dust; they themselves were utterly sacrificed and forgotten in love and servitude to the divine threshold.
>
> During the three wonderful days and nights we spent in that sacred spot we heard naught but the mention of God; His Holy Name was on every tongue; His beauty and goodness were the theme of all conversation; His Glorious Cause the only aim of every life. Whenever we gathered together in one of the rooms they spoke unceasingly of the Blessed Perfection, relating incidents in the life of the Beloved, mentioning His words, telling of His deeds and the passionate love and devotion of His followers until our hearts ached with love and longing. There were some women in the household who were clad all in white and we learned that they were the wives of martyrs, and we heard the tragic and glorious histories of many of our Persian brethren.[39]

Two months into her pilgrimage, Lua wrote to Thornton Chase that 'there are no words in which to describe' life in the household of ʻAbdu'l-Bahá.[40]

> Truly, I feel like one in a dream, and now can scarcely collect my senses enough to write anything about this most wonderful and Holy Household.

> For the past two weeks I have been staying at Acca for the purpose of studying the Persian language, which Our Lord commanded both myself and my husband to learn as soon as possible. One of His daughters is my teacher and though I have studied such a short time, I am now able to read easy words and know one prayer by heart. The atmosphere of the place is wondrous, knowledge and understanding seem to float in the air! I am simply benumbed by the great privileges and blessings showered upon me daily, and so much so, that I feel myself to be a miserable worm of the dust unable even to crawl. One can't imagine such love and kindness as they continually show to be manifest upon this earth but it is true, and now I know that we Americans have only the semblance while they have the real thing.[41]

It was the Master's devoted sister, Bahíyyih Khánum, titled the 'Greatest Holy Leaf', who presided over the household, and not the wife of 'Abdu'l-Bahá, Munírih Khánum, whom the pilgrims called the 'Holy Mother'.[42] Lua wrote of how at their first encounter, the Greatest Holy Leaf took her in her arms and kissed her tenderly on both cheeks.[43] The Greatest Holy Leaf stood in rank in the Faith second only to her older Brother. Her loving but firm countenance, her tireless energy and her immense inner strength made her appear to be a very powerful person to the pilgrims, even though physically she was very petite. She had lived her life in the near seclusion of women's quarters, giving it over completely and unhesitatingly to service to her Father, her Brother, and the Faith. Remembering the Master's extraordinary sister years later, Ella recounted the following:

> We were among the first believers from the West to see her but the pilgrims of later years have had opportunities for longer visits and more intimate association with her great spirit, nevertheless her personality made an indelible impression upon us even then when we . . . understood almost nothing of its Teachings and still less about the Persian people. In fact, from all we were told about her before we actually met her the thought of her great station was quite awe inspiring. It surely was impressive to be told that Bahá'u'lláh had said that her spirit was so pure that her prayers would always be acceptable to God and this being known among the believers it was touching to see how they revered her and begged for her prayers in their behalf with absolute certainty that her supplications would be answered.[44]
>
> But when we actually met her, she was so simple – with the simplicity of the truly great – that she put us at ease at once, and we were delighted to

> discover that she had a keen sense of humor and her eyes were lovely blue. Like all the ladies of the Holy Household she showered us with her love and it was not long before we had the temerity to respond to that glorious character. Hers was the responsible position in the prison home – she seemed to be the center about whom all the women revolved not those of family alone but pilgrims and resident believers as well. It was evident that all instinctively conceded to her a spiritual authority second only to the Master.[45]
>
> In her room the gatherings of the household took place. It was the prized privilege of the visiting pilgrims to join the family there for the early morning tea, 'Abdu'l-Bahá being the only man present. His favorite seat was in the corner of the long divan where he could gaze out of the window over the fortress walls to the blue Mediterranean Sea. He often wrote or corrected and signed tablets while sipping His tea, having directed one of his daughters or a visiting Bahá'í lady to chant the prayers of Bahá'u'lláh. The little maid . . . at the samovar placed a . . . Persian rug in the middle of the floor. While the children were free to run in and out as they pleased and even the birds often flew in from the open court attracted by bits of sugar, which was their share of the heavenly table!
>
> The Greatest Holy Leaf, or Khanum, as she was called, which means, The Lady, being the chatelaine of the home, always carried her bunch of keys and never failed to oversee all domestic affairs of the household and under the most primitive conditions. She seemed to us to be always so perfectly balanced between the spiritual and the practical. You remember that when 'Abdu'l-Bahá was asked who was preferable, Mary or Martha,[46] His reply was to the effect that the women Bahá'ís should strive to be both – Khanum surely fulfilled that great ideal.
>
> Each day we loved her more and drew closer to her, in spite of the fact that she spoke no English. We seemed to sense despite our own ignorance that she knew all about us, understood our spiritual needs and longings, and coming down to our level without the slightest hint of superiority, penetrated to our awakening souls and drew them forth to meet her own in the spirit of the most loving kindness, and her flashes of charming humor.[47]

The Master took upon Himself the responsibility of caring for a number of people besides His own family and household attendants. In particular, those widowed or orphaned because of the persecution of the believers in Iran were taken under His protective care; some were residing in 'Akká in His household or in the House of 'Abbúd. Ella commented in her journal about her encounter with a woman who had lost her family because of the tyranny of the enemies of the Faith in Iran. She was very impressed with the widow's steadfastness in the face of unbearable suffering in the path of service to her Lord. Naturally, the tales they were told of the persecution and martyrdom of the Iranian believers in the Cradle of the Faith touched the hearts of all of the Americans.

The women among the American pilgrims were able to associate freely with the cloistered ladies of the household, especially the daughters of the Master who were close in age to many of them. (Men who were unrelated to the family by blood or marriage were generally denied access to the women's quarters of the household.[48]) Ella wrote eloquently in her journal of the lunch she and Nell were served shortly after their arrival and of some of the time they spent with the ladies of the household.[49]

> After lunch the Master left us. He had sat at table with us and served us with His own hand to everything. The little round table was set in European fashion for our benefit, for when the family are alone the women eat in their own room on a low table around which they sit on the floor. We were surprised to find how many of the dishes we could not only eat, but relish. The Persian cooking is very good. They use a great deal of rice and there is one particular dish of it they have for every meal (pilau).
>
> After lunch we went into the ladies' room and met the ladies of the household . . . The room is always full of believers and even the servants come in and kneel down on the floor to hear the Tablets read. They are believers with the exception of one old woman, who has served thirty years in the home because she loved the Manifestation so devotedly, and she also loves the Master in the same way. She is very ignorant and does not know anything except that they are holy people and she begs to be allowed to stay always. The atmosphere of the home is something unique, such love and affection as they show to everyone is scarcely to be believed; the way in which they greeted us, perfect strangers, and made us feel completely at home was a big lesson all in itself. They treat the servants just like members of their own family, and give constantly to the poor, money, food, medicine, and help of all kinds. Of course they are prisoners and are seldom out of the house so, as one of them said who did not feel very well, 'the body gets tired in the prison but the heart is not caged.' . . . They read [from the Bahá'í Holy Writings] several times a day and everyone listens with most intense interest, and those who remember Him [Bahá'u'lláh] always weep at certain passages. It was very interesting to see a little Christian Syrian girl who was there to teach the ladies English and who knows nothing of what they believe. She was so affected by one of the Tablets that she burst into tears and left the room. Upon her return they asked why she left, but she could only shake her head and say, 'Oh it was so beautiful, so beautiful.'[50]

The second afternoon that Ella and Nell spent in 'Akká was also spent with members of the household. Ella recorded the following in her pilgrimage journal.

> In the afternoon we went for a short walk with some of the ladies, accompanied by four or five of the young servants, girls and boys. Some of these children heard this message in India and begged to be allowed to come to the Holy Household to serve; and anybody who is accorded this privilege of serving in any way in the family considers himself blest indeed. They carried with them some pistachio nuts that had been roasted in the ashes and some dried fruit, and we sat down on the grass and ate them. They serve tea on all occasions, about five times a day – Persian tea. It is a cultivated taste, I think, quite good, only they have it a little too often and too strong! We had a beautiful view of the sunset from the ramparts over the superb Mediterranean Sea, with Mt. Carmel in the distance and a most gorgeous sky.[51]

One of the youngest members of the family made a special mark on Ella's heart – 'Abdu'l-Bahá's eldest grandchild, Shoghi Effendi, who had just passed his second birthday. She described the toddler in a letter to her mother as 'a perfect little picture & reminds me of the Old Master's [sic] children in the pictures'.[52] This child had been born at the House of 'Abdu'lláh Pá<u>sh</u>á during March of 1897 to the Master's eldest daughter and her husband, a relative of the Báb, making him the physical embodiment of the mystical connection between the two Divine Messengers. One memory of that little boy especially stood out in Ella's mind and she wrote about it years later at the time Shoghi Effendi became his Grandfather's successor as Head of the Faith, that is, assumed the role of Guardian.

> One day . . . I had joined the ladies of the Family in the room of the Greatest Holy Leaf for early morning tea, the beloved Master was sitting in His favourite corner of the divan where, through the window on His right, He could look over the ramparts and see the blue Mediterranean beyond. He was busy writing Tablets, and the quiet peace of the room was broken only by the bubble of the samovar, where one of the young maidservants, sitting on the floor before it, was brewing the tea.
>
> Presently the Master looked up from His writing with a smile, and requested Ziyyih Khanum to chant a prayer. As she finished, a small figure appeared in the open doorway, directly opposite 'Abdu'l-Bahá. Having dropped off his shoes he stepped into the room, with his eyes focused on

> the Master's face. 'Abdu'l-Bahá returned his gaze with such a look of loving welcome it seemed to beckon the small one to approach Him. Shoghi, that beautiful little boy, with his exquisite cameo face and his soulful appealing, dark eyes, walked slowly toward the divan, the Master drawing him as by an invisible thread, until he stood quite close in front of Him. As he paused there a moment 'Abdu'l-Bahá did not offer to embrace him but sat perfectly still, only nodding His head two or three times, slowly and impressively, as if to say – 'You see? This tie connecting us is not just that of a physical grandfather but something far deeper and more significant.' While we breathlessly watched to see what he would do, the little boy reached down and picking up the hem of 'Abdu'l-Bahá's robe he touched it reverently to his forehead, and kissed it, then gently replaced it, while never taking his eyes from the adored Master's face. The next moment he turned away, and scampered off to play, like any normal child . . . At that time he was 'Abdu'l-Bahá's only grandchild . . . and, naturally, he was of immense interest to the pilgrims.[53]

The pilgrims absorbed life lessons not just from watching but from the way they and others were treated. On the very first full day of May's and Harriet's pilgrimage, while still in Haifa, the Master announced to those assembled with them that He wished them to all accompany Him two days hence to the spot on Mount Carmel marked by cypress trees where Bahá'u'lláh rested and pointed out to the Master the place where a befitting mausoleum should be built in which the sacred remains of the Báb were to be interred. This invitation filled the hearts of the friends with great joy and anticipation. But the next morning May's ill health returned and she took to her bed. The Master came to her room to see her and, taking hold of both her hands, pressed His hand over her brow to check for fever. May said that the Master 'gazed upon me with such gentleness and mercy that I forgot everything but the love and goodness of God, and my whole soul was healed and comforted. I looked up into His face and said: "I am well now, Mawláná." But He smiled and shook His head and bade me remain there quietly, until He should return at noon.' She continued to have pain for some hours but by evening was better and able to have a restful night, which left her hopeful that she would be able to take part in the visit to Mount Carmel scheduled for the next day.[54]

> On Sunday morning we awakened with the joy and hope of the meeting on Mount Carmel. The Master arrived quite early and after looking at me, touching my head and counting my pulse, still holding my hand He said to the believers present: 'There will be no meeting on Mount Carmel

> to-day. We shall meet elsewhere, Insha'alláh, in a few days, but we could not go and leave one of the beloved of God alone and sick. We could none of us be happy unless all the beloved were happy.' We were astonished. That anything so important as this meeting in that blessed spot should be cancelled because one person was ill and could not go seemed incredible. It was so contrary to all ordinary habits of thought and action, so different from the life of the world where daily events and material circumstances are supreme in importance that it gave us a genuine shock of surprise, and in that shock the foundations of the old order began to totter and fall. The Master's words had opened wide the door of God's Kingdom and given us a vision of that infinite world whose only law is love. This was but one of many times that we saw ʻAbdu'l-Bahá place above every other consideration the love and kindness, the sympathy and compassion due to every soul. Indeed, as we look back upon that blessed time spent in His presence we understand that the object of our pilgrimage was to learn for the first time on earth what love is, to witness its light in every face, to feel its burning heat in every heart and to become ourselves enkindled with this divine flame from the Sun of Truth, the Essence of whose being is love. So on that Sunday morning He sat with us for awhile and we thought no more of the meeting on Mount Carmel, for in the joy and infinite rest of His presence all else was swallowed up.[55]

The Master was very busy and thus could not be with the Americans all the time even though most of the Western pilgrims were in ʻAkká for but a few days. When not with them, however, He never let them forget that He was always present in spirit. He would send them small tokens of love to remind them – a bouquet of violets, oranges from a Bahá'í garden – little things which were nonetheless precious to their grateful recipients. The gifts of flowers in particular were lovingly pressed and carried back to America to share with the believers who had not been able to be included in the pilgrimage.

There was much to take in, but the time was short for most of the American pilgrims and language barriers made it impossible to gain more than the spirit of the household of the Holy Family. But so powerful was that spirit that it touched all of the hearts of the Hearst party. None would ever forget the experience of being immersed in a home propelled by the power of love.

CHAPTER 7

Paying Homage at the Sacred Spot

The paramount purpose of Bahá'í pilgrimage is to offer homage and prayers at the resting places of God's most recent Manifestations;[1] however, this reason for visiting 'Akká was only dimly understood by most of the first Western pilgrims because their knowledge of the Faith prior to their arrival in the Holy Land was limited. There is some mention of their feelings of anticipation about visiting the 'Sacred Spot' but, in deciding to undertake the pilgrimage, the desire to find a spiritual teacher, as they did in the person of 'Abdu'l-Bahá, was uppermost in their minds. Perhaps this hierarchy of spiritual priorities reflected their Protestant upbringing, which down-played pilgrimages to sacred places and emphasized the spiritual teacher.

There were very few Bahá'í Holy Places to visit in the Holy Land in 1898, as many of the locations visited by later pilgrims were not yet built or in the possession of the Faith at that time. Thus the pilgrims visited only the Shrine of Bahá'u'lláh, the Riḍván Garden, and, of course, the House of 'Abdu'lláh Pá<u>sh</u>á. Their journals and letters make no mention of the House of 'Abbúd, though it must have been pointed out to them. Even though 'Abdu'l-Bahá continued to have control of the House of 'Abbúd, it was at the time the private residence of several families of believers who were in effect its custodians. The Citadel, where Bahá'u'lláh and his fellow exiles had been imprisoned for more than two years, could only be observed from a distance, but not entered, because it was still being used by the government. The future site of the Shrine of the Báb, half-way up the side of Mount Carmel overlooking the Templer Colony, was clearly visible throughout most of the Haifa area, but only Edward mentions actually visiting it. As noted previously, the February group was scheduled to visit that site with the Master Himself, but He postponed the excursion because of May's poor health and it appears as though the group never went.

The first full day in 'Akká, after a good night's sleep, was usually the day during which each group visited the resting place of Bahá'u'lláh at Bahjí. The pattern was to enjoy a leisurely morning with the household of the Master, followed by a visit to the Riḍván Garden after lunch. The pilgrims were given ample time to drink in the beauty and tranquillity of that Holy Place. After enjoying mid-afternoon tea in the Garden, the pilgrims would join the Master in the late afternoon at Bahjí.

While Bahá'u'lláh was still a prisoner inside the walls of the Most Great Prison, the Master had an opportunity in 1875 to rent a garden for His Father's use not far outside the city next to the Tel of 'Akká (Tel Napoleon). The garden had been created on an artificial island which had the shape of a ship. The Na'mayn River[2] had been diverted to create not only a pleasure island but also a mill pond for the local grain mill. The river was only about five metres wide on most sides of the island and about a metre deep, but that was sufficient to make it navigable by small boats. It had also been fully stocked with fish. Visitors entered the garden through a stone gateway at one end of a little wooden bridge which spanned the western branch of the river. The few steps it took to cross that short span transported the visitor into another world. One impressed visitor remarked that coming upon the garden 'suddenly it is like a scene in fairy land'.[3] The centrepiece of the garden was a lovely, scalloped, tiered fountain which sprayed refreshing jets of water cascading down its sides when a little donkey at the far end of the island turned a wheel that pumped water from the river. The water flowed from the pool at the base of the fountain into a stream that passed between intricately carved blue and white benches and then back into the river. The deep-seated oriental benches which allowed visitors to sit cross-legged, some overhanging the river, were shaded by two towering mulberry trees. The tinkling of the fountain mixed with the light playing through the trees; the general ambiance of the garden creating a refreshing refuge from the arid city of 'Akká.

Shortly after moving to the Mansion of Mazra'ih in 1877, Bahá'u'lláh made His first of many visits to the garden, which He named the Garden of Riḍván, that is, the Garden of Paradise. He also referred to it as His 'verdant isle'. He had always loved the greenery of the countryside; therefore this little oasis provided Him with a restful environment and a measure of happiness after nine years of being deprived of the joys of nature.[4]

The Master arranged for the garden to be improved, a process that continues even into the present. The pilgrims coming from Persia would bring plants and seeds, especially those known to have been beloved by Bahá'u'lláh in His homeland, such as a rare white rose with a golden centre. There were graceful willows along its river banks, pomegranate and other fruit trees lining its pathways, as well as glorious beds of flowers. Next to the small boat dock at one end of the garden was an unimposing house, with porches adorning its front, where Bahá'u'lláh would rest during the heat of the day, even sleep overnight during occasional extended stays in the garden.

In 1898 the gardener, Áqá Abu'l-Qásim, was the same person who had served there during the days when the garden was visited by Bahá'u'lláh Himself.[5] This devoted believer tended the garden with diligence and zeal for decades, and ensured that all who visited it enjoyed their stay. Áqá Abu'l-Qásim was a native of Manshád and had a brother who served as a gardener at Bahjí. This tall, gentle giant of a man took great pleasure in regaling the pilgrims with stories of the times that Bahá'u'lláh visited the garden.[6] He made a lasting impression upon the American pilgrims, several of whom wrote about their visit to the Riḍván Garden. May recorded the following:

> On Friday morning the Master told us that we would, that day, visit the Holy Tomb of Bahá'u'lláh. Accordingly, that afternoon, we all set out in carriages and drove through the narrow streets, out through the stone gates into the beautiful surrounding country in the direction of the Bahjí and the garden of Riḍván. It was a beautiful day, the sky was blue and clear, the sun shone with eastern warmth and splendour, a light breeze stirred and the air was perfumed with roses. After driving for about half an hour we reached the garden where Bahá'u'lláh spent much of His time during His long years of exile in 'Akká. Although this garden is small it is one of the loveliest spots we had ever seen. Bahá'u'lláh frequently said to His gardener, Abu'l-Qásim, 'This is the most beautiful garden in the world.' With its tall trees, its wealth of flowers, and its fountains, it lies like a peerless gem surrounded by two limpid streams of water just as it is described in the Qur'án; and the atmosphere which pervades it is so fraught with sacred memories, with divine significance, with heavenly peace and calm that one no longer marvels to hear of the traveller who, passing one day before its gates, paused and gazing in saw Bahá'u'lláh seated beneath the shade of the mulberry trees, 'that canopy not made with hands,' and remembering the prophecy in the Qur'án, he recognized his Lord and hastened to prostrate himself at His feet. We visited the little house at the end of the garden and stood on the threshold of that room where Bahá'u'lláh was wont to sit in hot weather, and one by one we knelt down, and with tears of love and longing kissed the ground where His blessed feet had rested. We returned to the garden, where Abu'l-Qásim made tea for us, and there he told us the story of the locusts. How that during one hot summer there had been a pest of locusts and they had consumed most of the foliage in the surrounding country. One day Abu'l-Qásim saw a thick cloud coming swiftly towards the garden, and in a moment thousands of locusts were covering the tall trees beneath which Bahá'u'lláh so often sat. Abu'l-Qásim hastened to the house at the end of the garden and coming before his Lord besought Him, saying: 'My Lord, the locusts have come, and are eating away the shade from above Thy blessed head. I beg of Thee to cause them to depart.' The Manifestation

> smiled, and said: 'The locusts must be fed; let them be.' Much chagrined, Abu'l-Qásim returned to the garden and for some time watched the destructive work in silence; but presently, unable to bear it, he ventured to return again to Bahá'u'lláh and humbly entreat Him to send away the locusts. The Blessed Perfection arose and went into the garden and stood beneath the trees covered with the insects. Then He said: 'Abu'l-Qásim does not want you; God protect you.' And lifting up the hem of His robe He shook it, and immediately all the locusts arose in a body and flew away. When Abu'l-Qásim concluded this story he exclaimed with strong emotion as he touched his eyes: 'Oh, blessed are these eyes to have seen such things; oh, blessed are these ears to have heard such things.' In parting he gave us flowers, and seemed, like all the oriental believers, unable to do enough to show his love. We then entered once more our carriages, and still gazing back at that lovely spot, we drove towards the Holy Tomb.[7]

Ella also recorded the story of the locusts[8] and added an additional story from Abu'l-Qásim.

> One day when he was feeling very tired Abul Kasim [sic] fell asleep near the entrance to the garden, sitting cross-legged on the ground. Suddenly he was awakened by feeling something touch his neck and cheek, and looking up saw the Manifestation standing beside him. 'Oh, Abul Kasim,' He said gently, 'You are tired, you have fatigued yourself in order to build this rough stone entrance to the garden. But in the future you will see that this rude entrance will be changed for another and a most beautiful one. When this takes place people will say, Abul Kasim was here, and used to open the gate for the believers to come and see their Lord.' At that time you will see and hear this and you will remember what I said to you. And a time will come when the stones of this building will be made of precious material, a few even of gold and silver; yea, even the soil of this divine garden will be sent to far countries as a most precious treasure. For although God created the earth and the whole world belongs to Him, yet this blessed spot differs from all other places, for He Himself designed it and planted it and chose it to be His special property and delight.'[9]

Lua especially remembered her visit to the room of Bahá'u'lláh in the little building at the far end of the garden.

> In one part of this place is a small cottage where the Manifestation used sometimes to stay, and we were permitted to enter this also, to go into

> the room which He always occupied, kneel before the chair upon which He sat, and to kiss the place upon which the soles of His feet rested! The spiritual atmosphere of this place was overwhelming; our tears fell like rain over our faces, and some of the Believers with us cried aloud. Indeed, to enter this room is a great blessing. I have felt nearer to God since that day! On the chair was a wreath of flowers, and some beautiful cut roses placed there by the Greatest Branch, who commanded that they should be given to us (my husband, Dr. K., his daughter and myself); also four large oranges, which were on a table opposite as we left that most sacred place.[10]

After their restful yet exhilarating interlude in the Garden of Riḍván, the pilgrims reluctantly left that delightful spot for the most important destination of their pilgrimage, Bahjí. This is the Qiblih of the Bahá'í Faith, the point of adoration toward which all believers turn as they say their daily prayers. When Bahá'u'lláh passed away in 1892, He was laid to rest in a building adjacent to the Mansion at Bahjí, His summer residence for the last almost thirteen years of His life. At the time, His daughter[11] and son-in-law were residing in that smaller house. His sacred remains were interred in the southwest corner room. To set that room apart and to strengthen and secure its walls, a stone façade was erected on its two outer walls as quickly as possible following Bahá'u'lláh's interment. Believers would prostrate themselves at the threshold of that hallowed room, but only 'Abdu'l-Bahá ever entered it.

Unfortunately, the unfaithful members of the Holy Family had retained control of the Mansion of Bahjí, with its chamber where Bahá'u'lláh ascended. Within less than a year after the passing of the Blessed Beauty, the Master's half-siblings were able to prevent Him from ever entering that sacred place again. As time went on, they became more and more belligerent when 'Abdu'l-Bahá, in the company of believers or even government officials, came to pray at the Sacred Tomb. They would stand on the upper level balcony of the Mansion to gawk and mock. The Americans had been apprised of this background by the members of 'Abdu'l-Bahá's household, no doubt to forewarn and prepare them.

After 'Abdu'l-Bahá was restricted from gaining access to even the lower level of the Mansion, he rented the far end of the same building which housed the Sacred Tomb in order to provide a place for the friends to rest and take light refreshments while at Bahjí.[12] There, the Americans were served tea and visited briefly with the Master. But this was a sidelight of the visit. Ella recounts her first visit:

> We drove to the little tea house near the Bahjí where we found the Master seated on the divan reading some letters just received from Persia. He

told us that a poor ignorant man who could neither read nor write had converted a very high official to the Truth and he in turn had given the teachings to twenty others and their letters (of supplication) had just been sent to our Lord. We had tea while he wrote a few Tablets, then gave the word to go to the Tomb . . . From the window of the tea house we had seen the procession of believers walking on ahead like pilgrims, and we soon followed them, going before the Master left.

There is some ceremony connected with the visit of the Tomb, and it is very affecting indeed. It is here that the pilgrims come to ask for special blessings and it is a great thing to have the privilege of making this visit. First taking off our shoes, we knelt and kissed the threshold of the entrance and again the doorsill of the inside room. The first court or rather the main part of the building is like a court with a little garden in the centre, filled with palms and shrubs and fenced with a low iron fence. Off from this court which is partly roofed with glass, is a sort of apse square, carpeted with a large Persian rug. There we were conducted first to wait a minute for the Master. He came in among the bowed heads of the people and opened the door of the Inner Tomb, motioning us to go in.

The sepulchre proper is sunk beneath the floor, and we knelt around the Persian rug which covers it.

There are also flower vases set upon the floor and a handsome candelabra at each corner, all gifts of devout believers. On the doorsill we left the flowers that had been given us from the Riḍván [Garden].

After a moment the Master came back with a taper in His hand with which He lighted the candles in the great chandelier over our heads. Then he beckoned to Nell and to me, and giving us each a lighted candle told us to light those of the other candelabras at the four corners of the sepulchre. After that we took our places again then soon went out into the court. The Master took us up into the apse and stood there facing the East while we all prayed silently for what our hearts most desired. I shall never forget His face as He stood there. He looked as though He were indeed communing with the Infinite and receiving blessings and instructions from His only Superior. Again, as He lighted the candles, the sweet calm of His face was the look of the joyful martyr . . . He did not shed a tear. But it is easy to imagine how He affected all of us. We finally followed Him out after kneeling once more at the Sacred Door . . .[13]

Writing to the believers back in America, Lua said about her first visit to the Shrine of Bahá'u'lláh that, 'you must excuse me if I do not enter into detail about this – I cannot find words to express myself. Suffice it to say that the

Greatest Branch let me walk in His footsteps and led me by the hand into this sacred place, where I knelt down and begged of God to cleanse my heart from all impurity and kindle within it the fire of His Love.'[14]

It was highly significant that the Master led the Americans into the actual room under which the Blessed Beauty was interred. This was a great honour that apparently had not been accorded to anyone during the entire period since the passing of Bahá'u'lláh, and signified the importance of their coming as the first pilgrims representing the peoples of the West.

May recorded that over one hundred Oriental believers were gathered at Bahjí the day that she and the February group made their visit to the Tomb of Bahá'u'lláh. 'Knowing that we were among the first American pilgrims to that Holy Spot they had come from all directions to behold our faces, and their own shone with love and joy which amazed us, and which we can never forget.'[15] She also remembered the words spoken by the Master to prepare them for the experience.

> By and by He came to the door of the tea-room, and the lightning of His glance fell on us and He said in a quiet, low tone: 'We are now going to visit the Holy Tomb. When you are praying in that divine spot remember the promise of Bahá'u'lláh, that those who attain this pilgrimage shall receive an answer to their prayers, and their wishes shall be granted.'[16]

May went on to recount her experience that unforgettable day in February 1899:

> As we entered, a door in the opposite corner opened and the ladies of the holy family arrived, thickly veiled; they came forward and greeted us tenderly. At the further end of the court is a door at one side, and within is the Holy Tomb. As we gazed upon this veiled door our souls stirred within us as though seeking release, and had we not been upheld by the mercy of God we could not have endured the poignancy of joy and sorrow and love and yearning that shook the foundations of our beings. The blessed Master was calm and radiant and led us to the open space at the end of the court beside the Tomb, where, in the mellow light of a stained glass window, we all stood in silence until he bade one of our group to sing *The Holy City*. No pen could describe the solemn beauty of that moment, as, in a broken voice, this young girl sang the praise and glory of God, while all were immersed in the ocean of the Divine Presence. The tears of the pilgrims flowed and strong men wept aloud. Then 'Abdu'l-Bahá led us to the door of the Tomb where we knelt for a moment, then He opened the door

> and led us in. Those who have passed that threshold have been for a brief moment in the presence of God, their Creator, and no thoughts can follow them. The Tablet of the Holy Tomb[17] was chanted by a young Persian, and when we left that blessed spot the oriental pilgrims entered slowly, until all had been within; then our Beloved closed the door, and after singing *Nearer, My God, to Thee*[18] at His request, we quietly withdrew.[19]

As they each stepped silently out of the Shrine into the light of sunset, somehow the world seemed different than it had before they entered that most sacred of places. Everything around them was more beautiful. Lua had the privilege of walking in the little garden beside the Shrine with the Master where He picked flowers and leaves and presented them to her to take to the other believers in America.[20] May never forgot the sight of the Master as they climbed into the waiting carriages.

> 'Abdu'l-Bahá, leaving us to follow slowly, walked to a slight rise in the rolling green fields before us and there stood against the soft background of the evening sky. Oh, most glorious form! Standing there in the gathering twilight with the sunset fading in mild tints from the western sky and the full moon rising above His divine head.[21]

There were few trees to block the wide vista of the open fields which separated the Galilee hills in the east from the sea in the west. There was a clear view of the prison city in the distance with Mount Carmel providing a backdrop. Ella wrote of the golden light which bathed the landscape as they rode by carriage back to 'Akká.

> It was the time of sunset, and the light that lay on this land of glorious color is utterly beyond description. The whole plain was suffused in it and the sun going down into that marvelous blue sea was a sight I shall never forget. This whole day was perfect. Truly this is God's own country, the real new Jerusalem. Such a great peace overshadowed us that it did seem as though our visit meant at least much comfort to our hearts and the certain belief that our prayers would be answered. It seems to me I was never so completely overcome.
>
> We walked part of the way home and enjoyed the balmy air and superb view while we let the carriages return for the Master as He had insisted that we should go first and we filled it to capacity. After we returned our Lord sent us the flowers that had rested in the doorsill of the inner tomb.[22]

These first visits to the Holy Shrine were capped with unforgettable evenings with 'Abdu'l-Bahá, as Lua recounted:

> That night He sat us all at the table and dismissed the servants, saying He would serve us Himself and He did so. He did not sit at the table with us, but waited upon us. At the conclusion of the meal He said, 'I have served you tonight, that you may learn the lesson of ever serving your fellow creatures with love and kindness.' He bade us good night and advised us all to rest early, so we went to bed and this night I had a long delicious sleep and rest.[23]

When Ella and Nell returned to the House of 'Abdu'lláh Pá<u>sh</u>á, members of the household told them that it had been a great honour and privilege to have been invited by the Master to light the candles within the inner room of the Shrine of Bahá'u'lláh.

> At dinner time we tried to express our gratitude for being accorded the great blessing of lighting the candles (we had been told that it was a rare privilege as it had only been done once before and never before had the Master asked anyone to assist in the ceremony.) He said that it was a symbol that meant a great deal. He hoped we would never forget it, and what did we think was its meaning. Nell said she thought we had been walking in the darkness of ignorance and we were now to find the light, or light was to be given us. I thought we were going to be allowed to diffuse the light of this Truth and light the candles of others. He smiled and said that both thoughts were good, but that it had another significance which would not appear now but in the future we would know. He wanted us to think about it much, and hoped we would prove ourselves worthy of it. Our emotions were too overwhelming to be expressed, and we did not try.
>
> He began to speak again about the Persians saying; 'You know that in Persia the art of poetry is reckoned among the highest attainments, and yet there are now among the believers there some very poor and entirely uneducated women who compose such beautiful poems that the most learned people listen eagerly to them. They are written in even a loftier style than those of Quarratu'l-Ayn,[24] [sic] though hers are more prized because, having died a martyr, her remembrance, personality and poetry are all invested with a special fragrance. When she embraced the Bábí faith her husband, children and all her relatives bitterly opposed her and even tried to kill her. But now, many of these same people go to her grave and weep and lament over it even taking the dust of the grave to make eye

water for the cure of diseases of the eye, so greatly is her memory hallowed because her life was given for the Cause of God.

'The Arabs divide tears into two classes, hot and cold. Hot tears are those that are caused by sorrow or anguish of the heart, and scald the eyes. Those called "cool tears" spring from emotions produced by great happiness, and they are healing to the eyes. This latter is the real meaning of the name Quarratu'l-Ayn, "Consolation of the eyes".'[25]

With so much to absorb, to experience, to feel, their days of pilgrimage were intense, overwhelming – the highlight of their lives, especially the days that they visited the Sacred Spot, the physical embodiment of the spiritual heart of the Bahá'í Faith. Those days were filled with 'cool tears'.

CHAPTER 8

The Master Speaks

No doubt a number of the pilgrims, like Lua,[1] made resolutions – even commitments – to record every detail of their historic visit. But how can one capture the sun on paper? Good intentions were abandoned when confronted with the hopelessness of the task. Some of the pilgrims may have felt that the Master's admonition to maintain secrecy demanded that they be cautious in putting pen to paper. Fortunately, three of the young ladies did find the time to keep daily journals and Marian took notes on at least one occasion, so posterity has not lost all of the teachings of the Master from that significant period.[2] But what tantalizes are the days and weeks of the pilgrimage for which there is no record of what transpired. The reader can follow Phoebe, Minnie and Emily up the stairs to the awaiting ephemeral figure of 'Abdu'l-Bahá in the lamplight, but once He ushers them through the door at the top landing we are not permitted to follow them further. And what of the approximately six weeks when only the Getsinger and Kheiralla families were in the Holy Land? Silence is all, except for a few intriguing hints.

The words of 'Abdu'l-Bahá to this first group of American visitors are especially significant because He treated them as emissaries of the peoples of the West. He knew that what He said would be repeated in assemblies and gatherings and spread by letter and word of mouth. These words would be, for most of those who encountered them, their first brief glimpse of the vast teachings of His Father, Bahá'u'lláh, and would serve to guide them down the newly laid spiritual path of the Bahá'í Faith.

What has been recorded of the Master's teachings to these first Western visitors is remarkable and demonstrates not only the range of His mind but His uncanny knowledge of current events and topics. He continually amazed the Americans. Ella told her mother, 'He Himself knows everything. When the high officials talk to him they are perfectly astonished as the extent of His Knowledge on every subject under the sun.'[3] Coming from one without a formal education, with no access to any but a few books, and living as a political prisoner in a backwater of a town, this seemed little short of miraculous.

Marian, who arrived alone in late December after her husband and the Getsingers were already in 'Akká, recounted her first interviews with the Master which touched upon a number of themes:

After lunch and a rest, I was called to have an interview with our Lord in another room, and Mrs. Getsinger, who had been the first to see me arrive and welcome me, went with me. I asked Him some questions, and He told me that I must live and work for the Cause – that He wished me to be as He is – to be absolutely indifferent to praise or blame, whether I eat or do not eat, sleep or not, am in comfortable or uncomfortable surroundings, with friends or enemies – all these things must be as nothing to me, for I must cut my heart from myself and from the world, and must look to my God only, and follow the example of my Lord in all things (who is loving to all in look, word and action, even to those who wish to harm and oppose Him), and that then I would receive great spiritual gifts and blessings. Many other things He said, but of course I cannot attempt to write everything, or this account would never go off; and besides, some things were too purely personal.[4]

When Ella and Nell met the Master for the first time, he launched into the subject of America as soon as they sat down to lunch with him, and then instructed them about the importance of faith. Both women recounted that memorable mealtime conversation in their daily journals. Ella wrote:

He began to talk to us about the 'far country' from which we had come, saying that we were blessed indeed for many who were nearer had longed for the privilege but had been denied, while we who were so many miles away were 'children of the kingdom' and had been received. He then spoke of the difference between Napoleon and Christ, the one had sacrificed over four hundred thousand lives simply for his own sake, to gain his personal ends and satisfy his vanity; whereas, though thousands had suffered in the cause of Christ, the good it had done humanity was incalculable and His name would shine forever and ever in the spiritual realms as well as on earth, while the other had never done anything for humanity, no good would come from his exploits and his name would only be remembered in a most material way for a comparatively few years.[5]

He then spoke of the persecutions of the Babis in Persia, and that at the time of the exile [of Bahá'u'lláh] it was so bitterly cold that water from a drink would freeze on their beards, and yet in their travels under such hardships not one of them felt the cold or suffered in body at all, for the fire of the love of God so burned in their hearts that they were happy in spite of everything. While still in Persia they were terribly persecuted by the government and were of course accused of every bad deed and

> wrong thought that is possible. They never complained, only kept quiet and bided their time; then when somebody was sent to examine them or try them to see if they were dishonest, drunkards, thieves, stingy, liars, etc. they always discovered that they were honest, clean, pure, truth-tellers, never touched liquor and were most generous. Then they would say, 'Well, we can find nothing against them, but it's a pity they are Babis.' When the cabinet [of Persia] met to discuss their affairs, (as in Mohammedan countries, it is the religion of the state) the Prime Minister goes on record as having said, 'Well, I do believe that if we had not persecuted these people their religion would have died a natural death, but we have so brought them into prominence by our actions that everybody is enquiring into their belief and they are making converts daily.'
>
> The difference between truth and error is that the truth must live and grow stronger by opposition where the weaker religions die out one by one. A Babi who had been condemned to death was being ridden through the town turned backward on a donkey and the people were running beside him, beating the donkey with sticks and shouting and mocking at him. They passed the hut of a hermit fire worshipper[6] who, hearing the noise, came out to see what was going on. They told him what they were doing with the Babi and he said, 'Well I think this must be the truth, else why do you make so much fuss about it? If you are so afraid of it that you must persecute it then it must be strong indeed.' So after investigating he became a convert and with him all the fire worshippers, for he was a high priest and taught them all.[7]

Mealtimes, especially the midday luncheon, became the primary time when the Master could talk with the Americans uninterrupted and instruct them, because He was otherwise engaged in a myriad of activities from before dawn until late into the night. He would pace about the small room with its window overlooking the sea and pause by each plate to spoon on more food, all the while followed by the fixed gazes of His entranced guests. Administering hospitality never distracted Him as He expounded in His mild, gentle voice and answered questions on a variety of topics.

Marian wrote of her first meal in the Master's household, of the loving atmosphere and what he said to the little group. He was very conscious that, while the United States was her adopted home, England was her native country and so He spoke of both.

> He helped us all to the various courses of food as they were placed on the table, and most lovingly and carefully looked after our needs. He talked

> much of America, and said that if the believers there will live in real love and harmony with one another, as one soul living in different bodies, that the greatest blessings are in store for that country, but that if they do not, the blessings will be deferred. His heart is very full of love to all the believers there, and He rejoices greatly, and all the Holy people with Him, when new applications arrive and new names are received into the Kingdom. He said also that England shall be blessed, and should receive the light from America, and that when her people learned the truth, they would be very solid in it. He has emphasized the condition of mutual love as being of the utmost importance if we wish to gain anything spiritually, and has spoken of its absolute necessity many times. In one conversation He said, that as everything we see around us in the material world of greatness, beauty and use, is the result of the combination of atoms united by the law of affinity or attraction, and that whenever this law ceases to operate at any point, dissolution and death ensues, so also precisely the same law holds in the spiritual world – unless each separate soul is united by love to the other souls, he or she is in a condition of death, out of harmony with and against the spiritual laws, and nothing they do will succeed. Without love we can attain nothing!![8]

Lua wrote of her first repast at the home of the Master to the friends in Chicago. It was the crowning event of an amazing day.

> In the afternoon they[9] read Tablets aloud, and told us many interesting things connected with the early history of the Babis. So swiftly did the time pass that we were quite astonished when dinner was announced. They served a special meal for us, as they eat much later than we do, but so anxious was I to see my Lord again that I begged He would at least come into the room with us. The request was more than granted [for He came] and sat at the table, seating me on His right and my husband on His left. I felt too happy to eat and sat with my eyes riveted upon His glorious face. He turned towards me and sweetly smiling said, 'The Love of God burning in your heart is manifest upon your face and it gives us joy to look upon you.' I then called His attention to St Luke, 14th chapter and 15th verse, 'Blessed is he who shall eat bread in the Kingdom of God.' He thereupon took up the loaf and brake[10] it and gave each one of us a piece of the same.[11]

Likewise, May would never forget her group's first luncheon with the Master at His home in 'Akká and penned the following description:

We all met again at table for dinner, and as we sat down to our first meal in the holy household a great light shone upon us, and the Master said: 'Blessed is he who shall eat bread in the Kingdom of God.' Then He told us that the prophecy of Christ was now fulfilled and that we should thank God unceasingly and with all our hearts for this great blessing which it was beyond our power at present to realize. He told us that the meal was composed of two parts, spiritual and material. That the material food was of no importance, and its effects only lasted twenty-four hours, but the spiritual food was the life of the soul, and that the effects of this meal which we were enjoying would last for ever and ever. During the dinner our Master talked to us and taught us, referring to Christ, quoting His utterances and prophecies, and always speaking with a clearness and simplicity which any child could comprehend; yet His symbols and metaphors, drawn always from nature, embodied that essence of wisdom and truth which baffles the learned and great. Our Master always answered all questions, however trivial, with the utmost courtesy and responded genially to every subject of conversation; yet we noticed that He gave the most commonplace subject a higher significance, and transformed material things into spiritual realities. For instance, if anyone mentioned that the food was delicious, He smiled lovingly on the speaker and said:

That is because your heart is full of love; when the heart is filled with love everything seems beautiful and delightful to us.

Then He told us the story of the hermit; how once when the Blessed Perfection was travelling from one place to another with His followers He passed through a lonely country where, at some little distance from the highway, a hermit lived alone in a cave. He was a holy man, and having heard that Our Lord, Bahá'u'lláh, would pass that way, he watched eagerly for His approach. When the Manifestation arrived at that spot the hermit knelt down and kissed the dust before His feet, and said to Him: 'Oh, my Lord, I am a poor man living alone in a cave nearby; but henceforth I shall account myself the happiest of mortals if Thou wilt but come for a moment to my cave and bless it by Thy Presence.' Then Bahá'u'lláh told the man that he would come, not for a moment but for three days, and He bade His followers cast their tents, and await His return. The poor man was so overcome with joy and gratitude that he was speechless, and led the way in humble silence to his lowly dwelling in a rock. There the Glorious One sat with him, talking to him, and teaching him, and toward evening the man bethought himself that he had nothing to offer his great Guest but some dry meat and some dark bread, and water from a spring nearby. Not knowing what to do he threw himself at the feet of his Lord and confessed his dilemma. Bahá'u'lláh comforted him and by a word bade him fetch the meat and bread and water; then the Lord of the universe partook of this frugal repast with joy and fragrance as though it had been a banquet, and during the three days of His visit they ate only of this food which seemed to the poor hermit the most delicious he had ever eaten. Bahá'u'lláh declared that He had never been more nobly entertained nor received greater hospitality and love. 'This,' exclaimed the Master, when He had finished the story, 'shows us how little man requires when he is nourished by the sweetest of all foods – the love of God.' At the end of the dinner one of the Indian boys who served at table brought in a basket full of flowers sent by Abul-Qásim, the gardener of the Riḍván. The Master received them with pleasure, and held the fragrant bunches to His face, then gave one to each of the believers. Often He would hand to one of us, in passing, a bunch of blue hyacinths, these pure symbols of the hyacinths of wisdom and knowledge growing in the garden of El-'Abhá.[12]

Ella recounted another lunch with the Master during which He resumed some of the topics from their first meal together.

At the lunch table the talk was about Columbus discovering America, and the various expeditions to the North Pole. Our Lord said that it was amazing to think of the men who were willing to face the hardships of cold, ice and snow, privation, and almost certain death, in order to discover a piece of land that would perhaps benefit nobody after it was found; but that they never thought of stirring one step in order to try and find the Kingdom of God.[13] He said that Columbus had only worldly fame for discovering America. He received prison chains and finally death, and only after many years was he accorded any credit at all; and that even now his name would be remembered only a few years, as time is counted; whereas, if he had made a spiritual discovery he would be glorified forever in the Heavenly Realms as well as on earth.

The Master then began to speak of the ancient Greek philosophy and astrology. Of course they believed that the planets had great influence on the lives and destinies of men, and made sacrifices to Mars, Jupiter, Venus etc. But as a matter of fact, as man is the highest creation of God and therefore the planets are of a grosser material, it is impossible that they should have any effect whatever upon a superior being. Christ came and taught against their beliefs so they took up arms against Christianity, but in time they were obliged to accept it, for their old philosophies could not stand but Christianity still lives. None of their doctrines are ever talked of or taught nowadays, and even their names belong to an older time, but every single word that Christ uttered is prized and revered and believed in and lived up to when possible. His Name will last for all time. Greece had to be conquered by the Romans as a preparation for the coming of Christ, for at that time they were the most intellectual nation and would have been too strong an opposition, so their power had to be broken before He came. Just so it was ordained that Columbus should discover America as the place appointed for the greatest spreading of the Truth at this time, because it is the land of freedom, the land of growth, the land of plenty and promise, in fact, the blessed land.[14]

That same day, Ella shared the evening meal with the Master and again wrote about it in her journal. The conversation focused upon steadfastness in the face of tests, but with a touch of humour.

After returning [from a walk with ladies of the household] we went directly to the ladies' apartment and saw the Master there for about ten minutes. Then to dinner. He talked a little more about America and then told us a story of one of the believers in Persia. She had seen her husband killed for the Cause and then the judges brought her up before them and said, 'Now we have killed your husband, what shall we do with you? Shall we kill you or will you give up your faith?' She answered, 'You may kill me or not as you like, it makes no difference to me, but of course I shall not give up my faith.' They said, 'Do you believe then that your husband has gone to Heaven?'

'Indeed I do.'

'Well, how did he get there?'

'By the same stairs that Muhammad got there, by the same stairs that Moses got there, by the same stairs that Abraham, Elijah and Christ got there. O, there are plenty of stairs that lead up to Heaven, my lords, but so few people to climb them!'

They laughed and let her go. She was one of the most ignorant unlettered women in the land.[15]

The theme of the persecution of the believers in Iran, their steadfastness in the face of unendurable trials and the spiritual transformation through the Faith of the friends in Iran was expounded upon again during another evening meal.

The next day the Master said that even in this world there is happiness for the beloved of God. Sarah, the wife of Abraham, because through her

> faith she received such great spiritual blessings was given also the outward happiness of having a son in her old age and realizing that she was to be the earthly mother through whom the greatest blessings should descend to man. To Nell and me He said that the blessings that we had received in coming here we could not realize now. It was like a seed that would only show its fruit in the future.[16]

The Western pilgrims were, of course, circumscribed in their ability to communicate with the Master because of language. Kheiralla was the only person present whose English was adequate to the task of translating profound spiritual concepts. One of the Master's sons-in-law, Muḥsin Effendi,[17] spoke some English, but apparently not nearly as well as Kheiralla. Added to this dilemma was the fact that Persian was the primary tongue of 'Abdu'l-Bahá's household and most of the Persian believers knew little more than rudimentary Arabic. Kheiralla was a native Arabic speaker who knew little or no Persian. 'Abdu'l-Bahá was a master of both languages and on occasion spoke short phrases in English. Naturally then, the Master's conversations with the Americans were conducted in Arabic with Kheiralla as the translator, with the result that most other members of the household were unable to understand what was being said.

One way in which the Master sought to rectify the language problem was by arranging for Lua to begin learning Persian. She used her three months in the Holy Land to initiate her studies of the language and continued to work on it until, during later visits, she became fluent. The frustrations of not being able to converse directly with 'Abdu'l-Bahá or to read the largely untranslated body of Bahá'í scripture provoked Minnie Thornburgh-Cropper to begin the study of Arabic upon her return to London and for Helen to pursue it in Paris.

Kheiralla had quickly deduced that much of what he had taught the Americans about the Faith did not accord with the true teachings of the Faith expounded by 'Abdu'l-Bahá. In order to cover himself, he did not give proper renderings of the words of the Master to his American listeners, and most of the Persian friends had no way of catching this deception. The longer the Getsingers were in the Holy Land, the more they began to suspect that this was the case, and on one occasion they arranged a time to speak about their concerns with the Master through Muḥsin Effendi. Edward began to look for opportunities to expose Kheiralla's perfidiousness to the other Western pilgrims. There was one issue upon which Kheiralla's teachings in America were expressly contradicted by the Master: the matter of reincarnation. Kheiralla espoused reincarnation as a core Bahá'í belief when in fact the teachings of the Faith negate any idea of reincarnation of the soul after death. One day at lunch Edward asked a question to clear up this false teaching once and for all. Not surprisingly, it came in the midst of other questions regarding obscure passages of the Bible – a topic of great interest to the Americans raised as Christians. This particular conversation was so important to those present that Edward, Ella and Helen all wrote about it. The following is an excerpt from Ella's journal.

> At lunch time our Master sat with us and said to Mr. Getsinger, 'Why don't you talk doctor?' Doctor Getsinger therefore asked the interpretation of the 13th verse of the 12th Chapter of Daniel: 'But go thy way till the end be: for thou shalt rest, and stand in thy lot at the end of the days.' His question was[:] does it mean that Daniel will be reincarnated now in these latter days. Mussein Effendi interpreted for us. He does not speak very good English, but we managed to understand him. The answer was, 'There are two kinds of coming again, one is in the personality and the other is in the <u>spirit of</u> or <u>likeness of</u>. Daniel was promised that he should come again in his personality[;] that is, his soul would live at this time in another body; but in the case of most of the prophets it means simply that one shall come in the same spirit as the one before him, or shall be like him, teaching the same truth and showing the same spirit – like the lamp which has to be filled every day. The light is exactly the same, only the petroleum is different. In the instance mentioned in [the Book of] Revelations of the coming of the ten thousand saints or hosts, it means only that there shall be sent in this latter day ten thousand souls to do the same kind of work in the Cause of God as was done by the saints of the olden time. But in the case of John it is the same as with Daniel. He will come in his personality.'[18]

Nell's records of the same conversation noted that the Master spoke to Mírzá Muḥsin for a long time before the answer was conveyed to them in his broken English. Nell definitely felt that Muḥsin Effendi was not fluent enough in English to properly convey the Master's response. Edward was probably surprised by the answer because it did seem to confirm that the Faith accepted reincarnation in specific cases, thus substantiating one of Kheiralla's most important teachings. Unfortunately, when the Getsingers, Nell and Helen returned to Egypt, 'Abdu'l-Karím also explained reincarnation to them in such a way that they were left thinking that it was a teaching of the Faith. 'Abdu'l-Karím's understanding of the verities of the Faith proved over time to be deficient, so it is likely that this erroneous teaching was not born out of Kheiralla's fertile imagination or to please the Theosophists among his flock, but was something he was actually taught during his early days as a believer in Egypt. Only during the second pilgrimage of the Getsingers would it be properly explained to them by a more proficient translator that the teachings of the Faith do not include the return of any souls to earth a second time. Only the *qualities* of earlier souls are said to return.[19] This confusion would serve as a lesson to the Getsingers to trust only authoritative translations of the teachings or the direct words of the Master Himself.

'Abdu'l-Bahá returned again and again to Christ and Christian subjects. Until the Faith spread to America, the vast majority of its adherents had a Muslim heritage, with a minority coming from Jewish or Zoroastrian backgrounds. Even though the Haifa Bay region had almost as many Christians as Muslims, there were few Middle Eastern converts from Christianity. So the Western pilgrims were among the first of those to visit 'Abdu'l-Bahá who had a keen interest in the Bahá'í teachings regarding Christ. The Master sprinkled His talks with copious references to Jesus and the Bible, and His enraptured listeners were eager to hear more. One example was at a lunch, recounted by Ella, during which the Garden of Eden and Adam and Eve were among the topics.

> At lunch our Lord joined us at the table, and the question was asked about the meaning of the Garden of Eden. The Master said it only meant the space of time and also the part of the country covered by Adam in his teaching up to the time of Noah. When Noah came to carry on the work, he also had his Garden of Eden. Then, Abraham, Moses, and so on down to the time of Christ and Muhammad, and now the truth is extending over the whole world so that in this latter day the entire earth will be the Garden of Eden of this Manifestation.
>
> We also asked about the creation of Adam and Eve. We had a good deal of fun over this, the Master using Mr. and Mrs. Getsinger for illustration, saying that if she had been created out of one of his ribs, he could manage her very easily by simply picking her up and putting her in his pocket, she would have to be so small. Of course the story is an allegory, and means that Adam contained both the male and female principle – father and mother. As there is no female soul equal to God, He is father and mother in one. As He speaks through all His prophets and Adam was the first prophet, so in the spirit He was both (father and mother), as His God is. The same thing is true of all the prophets. The people were as Their spiritual children, the Father the spiritual guide, the mother the material expression of the love (of God).
>
> Someone asked the question as to the meaning of the story of Lot's wife turning to a pillar of salt. The Master explained that salt means death, and

> when Lot's wife insisted upon disobeying and looked back with longing upon the world, she died spiritually.[20]

Marian asked the Master a question which must have been on the minds of many of the early Western believers from Christian upbringings, that is, whether they should continue to study the Bible.

> I asked our dear Lord whether we were to use the Bible or not[;] he said, 'Yes, we ought to study and know the Bible, as the disciples knew the Old Testament at the time of Christ – with a spiritual understanding. At his time many of the Pharisees knew every word of the law, but only the letter, not the spirit and so were blind.[21]

Serious topics were often interspersed with humour. 'Abdu'l-Bahá had a keen wit and always delighted in the sound of laughter coming from the believers. May recounted one such moment during a lunch at the Master's home during February when Harriet told an amusing story.

> In a large hall where we dined,[22] were hanging two parrots in cages, and these, besides all the sparrows that flew in at the windows, twittering in the rafters overhead, made a great noise, so the Master bade one of the Indian boys remove the cages; and then the conversation turned on the treatment of animals. 'Abdu'l-Bahá said we should be kind and merciful to every creature; that cruelty was sin and that the human race should never injure any of God's creatures, but ought to be always careful to do nothing to diminish or exterminate any order of living thing; that human beings ought to use the animals, fishes and birds when necessary for food, or any just service, but never for pleasure or vanity and that it was most wrong and cruel to hunt. Then Mrs Thornburgh asked permission to tell a story of a little boy who had stolen a bird's nest full of eggs, and a lady meeting him on the road stopped him and rebuked him: 'Don't you know that it is very cruel to steal that nest? What will the poor mother bird do when she comes to the tree and finds her eggs all gone?' And the little boy looked up at the lady and said: 'Maybe that is the mother you have got on your hat.' How the Master laughed, and He said: 'That is a good story and a clever little boy.' The above incident is only one of many showing with what a universal spirit of joyousness, sweetness and sympathy the Master touches on all the concerns of our daily life, so that I have never seen such happiness nor heard such laughter as at 'Akká. The Master seems to sound all the chords of our human nature and set them vibrating to heavenly music.[23]

There were often small, informal moments with the Master. Nell remembered that several times the Master asked her and Ella to come and sit by Him. He would pat them lovingly on the back and say something pleasant to them in Persian – phrases they only understood in their hearts. They would be offered a cup of tea and then He would speak to them of the tasks ahead when they returned to America. He told them not to worry about their capacities to convey the message of the Faith to others because they would be inspired as they spoke.

> He also said we must all work in peace & sympathy in America, that there must be no divisions what so ever, as that would only weaken the Cause. Our greatest drawing card would lay in perfect union. If any one should do anything through weakness or ignorance, forgive him readily & work together in love & harmony for the good of the Cause. The one at fault must also be willing to take suggestions, as no one is perfect, no one knows it all.[24]

Toward the end of their pilgrimage, Ella and Nell were given the privilege of meeting privately with the Master – an unforgettable experience which would lead to another fascinating dinner discussion. Ella noted her special private conversation in her journal.

> . . . I was allowed to see the Master alone with Musein Effendi to interpret for me. Sitting on the floor at His feet I found it rather more difficult to begin than I expected, partly because I knew He was very tired and felt that I must not keep Him long. First I told Him about Mother, that she was a good believer, but that she was obliged to return to the family in California instead of coming to Acca with me as she would have liked to have done; that she was not very well and I wanted to beg for the blessing of health for her and also that our Lord would write her a Tablet. To all this He assented. Then I asked about the cultivation of talents and pursuit of art. If it was right to spend money on music lessons that might be given to the poor. He answered, 'Maloom (of course), study music for with your music you can teach even if not by your speech.' He said it was 'good, very good'. Then I asked if we were expected to marry. He answered yes, if we wished to marry. I questioned how can ones heart be cut from the world if one does marry? He answered, 'Because the occupation of man or woman should not interfere with the heart that is turned toward God. It makes no difference what we are doing, we can always work in the cause of God, and it is alright to marry' . . . I left Him feeling very thankful for His great kindness.
>
> At dinner time Dr. Khayru'llah was present and a number of our questions came up again, and were quite thoroughly discussed. It seemed to

> us a wonderful opportunity and the family told us they had never heard the Master talk so much upon these subjects which we were so anxious to understand in order to teach properly. The first question related to affinity . . . [that is, the achievement of perfect harmony between souls. He said that] The nearest we can come to it is to know the Truth and work in the Cause of God. Then nothing else matters to us and material things lose the power to affect our happiness one way or the other.
>
> The second question was whether or not we would know each other separately in the Kingdom, that is, would we all keep our individualities or would we be as one spirit. The Master said it was very difficult to speak of the spiritual Kingdom in any wa[y] to make our finite minds to understand, or even to grasp a faint conception of its mysteries and glories. When we speak of love – a thing we all know well, but cannot perceive with any of the senses – we are obliged to make a comparison and say it is like <u>fire</u> in order to convey the idea to the intellectual mind. So in order to give us any shadow of meaning of the infinite everlasting Kingdom, He compared it to this world as it might seem to a babe still in the womb of its mother. If it were possible to make the child in that condition [know] that there was such a spacious world that he would shortly be born into, could he have any conception of what it really was? Would he believe it at all? No. He thinks the whole world is just where he is, and that is our condition exactly. We try to believe, to have faith, but we cannot possibly understand. But this much is true and we can grasp it. The spiritual life is the real life, and when we reach that life this earthly existence will be to us as only a dream, and best of all, the ties and relationships of true love and affection, this is, the relationship of the soul – not of the flesh – will be intensified a thousand times. Just so much as we are capable of loving here that much more shall we be capable of loving there. For this is the sleeping time, the time of preparation. We are only dreaming now, and even the <u>real</u> things we only dimly realize; but those are the things that will shine out brilliantly when we reach the Kingdom, while the rest will all fade away. We will all keep our individuality according to the <u>heart</u>, and will not be swallowed up in one vast spirit like drops in the ocean.[25]

The next day at lunch, the Americans resumed asking questions along the lines of those Ella had asked during her private interview.

> During lunch we had one more important question, the same that I had asked in regard to education. The Master said that of two men, one ignorant and poor, the other a great scholar, if the ignorant one knew the Truth

> his station was much higher in the spiritual Kingdom tha[n] that of the other. But if they both knew the Truth, then the educated man had the higher place, because of the fact that he had used his God-given faculties, cultivated his talents and improved himself all he could, made him a greater power in this world so that in turn gave him so much greater opportunities for work in the Cause of God, that again earned for him his place in the Kingdom. It is the future we are working for, not worldly things, but if, by cultivating the intellect and gaining all the knowledge we can, we may have wider scope for spiritual work, surely we must do it. All knowledge comes from the Infinite in any case. Every material idea had to exist in the invisible first before it could be made manifest by man in the visible. So therefore if we neglect our opportunities here for education, we are just that much behind when we reach the other world and have it all to gain there.[26]

Nell Hillyer was fortunate to have two private meetings with 'Abdu'l-Bahá. During the first, He emphasized to her the importance of steadfastness in the Cause. The second interview came about through Nell's determination to ask a deep and personal question. Nell's daughter wrote years later that Nell, throughout her life, arranged everything so that she would never have to get out of bed before noon.[27] But during her time in the Master's household, she deliberately got herself up early one morning so that she could speak to 'Abdu'l-Bahá in private. Nell had lost her mother just as she was reaching puberty and was concerned about the spiritual condition of those who had passed to the next world without first hearing of the Manifestation of God for their time. He answered:

> The mysteries and glories of the Heavenly Kingdom are as much beyond our intellectual comprehension as the wonders of the world are beyond the comprehension of a babe in the mother's womb. When we reach there, this world will be as a dream. We will recognize and know each other and all this and connections between the souls will be intensified & increased. Just so great as they are in this world, will they be that much greater in the next. All will be for the best and for those who have gone beyond before hearing of this great Truth, we can pray & beg God to be merciful and their condition can be changed.[28]

When the Master expanded further on this theme at another time, Ella recorded that 'those who had gone before had every opportunity of being saved if they lead a life according to the revelation they had had in their generation.

Either to have followed Christ, Mohammed, Moses or any of the prophets and teachers sent to guide humanity & that we would also be able by our prayers to change their condition in the spiritual world . . .'[29] Before she left 'Akká, 'Abdu'l-Bahá wrote a prayer for Nell to say for her departed parents.

Since the Master was always occupied with tasks and cares, the time of the visits of most of the Hearst group was kept brief. He had very few opportunities to meet with them other than during meals. It appears, however, that He did take some time to meet with the February group and answer their questions apart from the conversations at the table. The session, which took place on 26 February, was recorded by Marian and for some years her typed notes were widely circulated among the early American Bahá'í community.[30] The notes indicate that, in addition to the Kheirallas, Julia Pearson, Anne Apperson, and May Bolles were present. It is likely that Robert Turner and Harriet Thornburgh were as well, Robert probably standing or sitting in the back and Harriet, who was becoming deaf, straining to hear during the session.

The pilgrim who began the conversation was Julia, who apparently had concerns about whether or not her family would ever embrace the Bahá'í Faith. Perhaps she is the nameless young lady mentioned by May in her journal, who was crying because her close family members were not believers. The Greatest Holy Leaf took the young woman in her arms and told her to consider the Holy Family to be her family. The Master told Julia that as she had accepted the Faith and been blessed by making a pilgrimage, this would cause her family to also be blessed and that they would come 'into the light' through her. He said that if her desire was to serve the Cause of God, a way would be made clear for her to do this. He then went on to explain that 'we can all serve in the Cause no matter what our occupation, no occupation can prevent the soul coming to God. Peter was a fisherman & yet he accomplished most wonderful things. But the heart must be turned always toward God, whatever our work is. This is the most important thing & then the power of God will work in us. We are like a piece of iron in the midst of fire & which becomes heated to such a degree that it partakes of the nature of the fire & gives out the same effects to all it touches. So is the soul that is always turned towards God & filled with the Spirit.'[31]

Julia then asked 'Abdu'l-Bahá if she would ever come again to 'Akká. He answered that she would and that when the time came, the way would be facilitated for her and she would have no difficulties.[32] The Master then went on to explain that there are two kinds of visits to the Holy Land.

> The first, the Visit of blessing, after the tidings & the Revelation [are] believed in & the seeker [is] received as a child of the Kingdom. But the

> second time is the Visit of the reward for work accomplished & victories gained. You are like soldiers sent out to fight. They depart in the midst of acclaims, of cheers, & music. But when they return after having fought their battles, done great deeds & conquered the enemies, then they come back to receive honours & rewards from their King. So it is with the children of the Kingdom.[33]

The Master continued to address this group of mostly young ladies by discussing a topic He would return to in his later correspondence with them following their return to America – the importance of women doing great deeds at this period in history.

> Many women in the past have made great names for themselves & been distinguished among the famous of the world in ways both spiritual & material. Remember that these women are of the same flesh and blood as yourselves, possessing the same faculties & powers, that which was open to them is open to you. And know that this is a far greater time than any preceding period in the whole history of the world, because God is pouring upon the earth of the highest of His gifts & blessings, upon the souls that are serving Him. Far higher is this time than the time of Christ, & yet see what wonderful things His disciples accomplished. You will be able to do more than they did, because the Holy Spirit of God is being poured out more abundantly on the earth.[34]

May then entered into the conversation and asked how one could cut one's heart from the world, that is, attain a degree of spiritual detachment. 'Abdu'l-Bahá answered, 'The hearts that are directed towards God, the love that burns in them, that love will separate them from all other things; that love will be the wall that will come between them & every other desire. The nearer to God, the farther from the world, the nearer to the fire, the farther from the cold, the nearer to heaven, the farther from earth, the nearer to life the farther from death. <u>This</u> is the balance, this is the balance!' He continued:

> One thing I ask of you for your own good & that you must do if you wish to gain the blessings. It is this. <u>To stand firm in the Faith</u> – without any wavering. Whatever troubles may come to you or to any of the believers, do not let your faith be affected in the slightest degree but stand as firm as a rock. Be like Mary Magdalene whose faith was so strong that it was never shaken even for a moment, when Christ was put to death, but with steadfast faith in Him she went to His discouraged disciples <u>at that time</u>

& renewed & re-kindled in their hearts the wavering light of their faith, by reminding them of the promise their Lord had made to them of His Constant Presence, & showing them that it was really of little consequence whether He were with them or not in the body. She so encouraged & strengthened them that their faith was confirmed, they became strong as lions & went out teaching in all directions, and, by the power of God working through them, the Knowledge of God spread over all the earth. Now in the eternal Kingdom their names shine as the most brilliant stars, & even here on this earth, their names are remembered with love & reverence by millions. So the best thing I can desire of you is to stand firm in the faith. Even if you hear of most great troubles & sorrows – even if you were to hear that I had been put to death or crucified as Christ was 1800 years ago, let not your faith be in anywise troubled or shaken. Arise for the work of God & His Cause, & you shall see His mighty Power working in you, & you will conquer all things. And remember, whether I am on earth or not, my Presence will be with you always.

But work as if you were all but one soul & one spirit living in different bodies. If you each work apart from the other with divided aims & interests, you would be like so many springlets that have neither volume nor power enough separately to accomplish any great work. But when these little springs are all joined together, they become a mighty force. So must you all be joined one to the other in heart & soul, & then you will all be prospered in the work & gain ever greater gifts, & the Cause of God will be spread through all countries by your means.[35]

Apparently the conversation meandered through a number of seemingly unrelated topics, most likely in response to questions. Below are a few examples of responses of the Master as recorded by Marian.

The Song of Solomon is a sacred poem representing Christ, the Bridegroom, & the Word of God, the Bride.

*****

There are three baptisms spoken of by the prophets. The baptism of water, of spirit, & of fire. The first signifies the condition when the soul receives the teaching of the Knowledge of God. The second, when the soul receives the Spirit. When the soul receives this baptism, the Spirit speaks through him, he has no need to be taught of men, or to ask questions, because the

Holy Spirit will enlighten & teach him. The third baptism is that of fire, when the soul becomes aflame with the love of God & insensible to any other attractions. This baptism Moses received when, as it is written, he saw God in the flame of fire & the same experience is recorded of many other prophets. In order to convey this spiritual condition to us, they used the illustration of the fire. For this reason, while the soul is on earth it receives sentional [sic] & intellectual perceptions. The first are those that come through the avenues of the five senses, the second are the abstract emotions, such as love, happiness, etc., & these cannot be perceived through or with any of the five senses. Now the things of the Kingdom cannot be perceived by the senses, & for this reason Christ taught the people always with parables & illustrations, because it is only through these outward signs & by comparisons, that the soul receives understanding. For this reason Moses & all the prophets gave their teaching in material objects, that through the outward forms the soul may receive the inward knowledge.

*****

There are three kinds of visions or dreams. The first are those that arise from over-excited nerves or disordered stomach, & are of no use whatever. The 2nd is when God sends a revelation to a soul that is not entirely pure from the world, to such He sends visions or symbols & signs; these experiences need the help of an interpreter. The 3rd kind is when a soul that is cut from the world receives a revelation from God – in such condition everything is clear & pure & needs no explanation.[36]

The Master, while allowing the questions to take Him away from his primary topic, nonetheless returned to it again – the spiritual life based upon faith.

Remember what Christ said 'You have taken the gifts of God without money & without price, so also you must freely give.' This command shows too, that all these gifts are sent to you by the free generosity of your God, not on account of any merit on your part, & you must rejoice greatly in the loving mercy of your God upon you & all. For all will taste of these free gifts before long – they will come from the East & the West to the Kingdom of God. And even as Christ foretold this also has come to pass, that the children of the Kingdom will be cut out, & so it is. Some of those who are nearest are cut off, while those from a far distance receive these great free gifts.

All the sufferings you pass through in gaining the Kingdom of God will be obliterated when you attain its perfect happiness. It is as a man who has been sick and helpless for two or three years, & afterwards becomes perfectly well & strong, then all he remembers of his pain & weakness vanishes. And more than this, happiness of the Kingdom is a perfect one, unlike the imperfection of our best earthly conditions, & are never to be clouded again with any vestige of sorrow. Whatever troubles we have on our way to the Kingdom is a rest [sic] to the soul. When the man enters this world it is in troubles & hardships, but he comes from the invisible to the visible to gain great things for himself. As the material birth is a time of trouble, so also is the spiritual. The way to God is impossible to be attained without troubles & difficulties. And remember what Christ said, that though the body is weak, the spirit is powerful.

Many great men & many great women have desired, century after century, to be in this great time in the Kingdom of God, & you ought to thank God with all your hearts that you have been chosen to be here at this time. Christ said 'The stone the builders rejected became the headstone of the corner.' This means that the spiritually great men & women of the world have been rejected & despised in all times by the builders of this world, but that now, in this the time of the Kingdom, these high spiritual ones will become the chief stones of the building.

Dr. Kheiralla was the first who took the Garment of Joseph – the fragrance of the Blessed Perfection – to America, & however grateful you feel to the one who brought this great mercy to you, you can never be grateful enough, & you ought to pray God day by day to bless him more & more, to give him more & more power & strength, & to add blessings upon blessings upon his head. If a teacher shows us how to read & write, we feel grateful to him, how much more you ought to be to the one who brings you into the living Light of the Kingdom of God.

Material relationship is nothing, it produces no eternal fruits. The spiritual relationship is the true & only one. Cain was the earthly brother of Abel, & yet he was not his real brother. Abraham was the son of Teerah, & yet not his son, for Teerah was an idol worshipper, while Abraham worshipped the True & Living God. Cainaan was the son of Noah & yet not his son. All these instances show us that earthly relationship is no tie.

The wise man works not for the present moment, but for the good results of the future. See in the winter time how bare & lifeless the trees & plants seem without leaves & without fruit. Suppose one passerby at this time who knew nothing of the condition of the earth & saw a man plowing it up & casting grain seeds in the furrows. Would he not say, 'how

> foolish this man is, he is troubling himself for no result, working for no purpose & wasting that which would give him food by throwing those good grains in the earth where they die and become rotten.' But in due time the showers of rain descend on the earth, the sun shines, the pure breezes blow, & we see the result in a great beauty & production. The seeds spring up & produce many fold, the trees that seemed so lifeless before are now laden with delicious fruits, & the shrubs and plants are covered with leaves & fragrant flowers. So is the work of the Holy Spirit of God in your hearts. The earthly sun is like the Sun of the Truth. The showers of rain as the showers of the mercy of God, the seeds as the Word of God, the air, the fragrant waves of His Holy Spirit, & the soil is the hearts of the people. Now the spiritual seeds are being scattered throughout the world & the heat of the Sun of Truth is interpenetrating through all souls, & the waves of the Spirit is blowing through the world & the showers of the mercy of God is pouring on the hearts of the people. The result will be a good & wonderful harvest, & every tree & flower & shrub will bear fruit, & you will see it.
>
> Suppose three or four Americans meet in a foreign country how pleased & delighted they are, how ready to serve or help in any way, how warm their feelings are one to the other. Yet this is only the result of a material condition, which lasts for a very few years, & will cease altogether at death. How much more should the children of the Kingdom, who are bound one to the other by eternal & supremely greater ties, be loving & good to each other, & ready always to serve & perform every good & loving action.[37]

This last lesson, to be 'loving and good to each other', was one 'Abdu'l-Bahá emphasized repeatedly, not only in His talks during the pilgrimage but in His later correspondence to the Western believers both collectively and to individuals. Unity was all. During the course of the pilgrimage incidents arose that provided opportunities to drive this lesson home. The particular Americans who made up the group of first Western pilgrims included in their number a handful of strong-willed individuals who did not always get along. Furthermore, Kheiralla's daughters did not contribute to the harmony of the group because those young ladies did not care for several of the Americans and therefore created difficulties as only adolescents can do.[38]

An added piece of baggage brought by the Americans was prejudice, the class and racial prejudices widely held in the United States. These two prejudices were tests during the pilgrimage, especially for May and Anne who, of the February group, were the ones born into privilege, and accustomed to servants. They had great difficulty accepting Robert Turner as an equal. The

Master, however, did treat him as one of the honoured pilgrims, not as a servant, and used several occasions during the pilgrimage to demonstrate the need to eliminate all forms of prejudice from their hearts. The first time he taught this lesson was the morning that the February group arrived in 'Akká. May set forth what happened.

> On the morning of our arrival, after we had refreshed ourselves, the Master summoned us all to Him in a long room overlooking the Mediterranean. He sat in silence gazing out of the window, then looking up He asked if all were present. Seeing that one of the believers was absent, He said, 'Where is Robert?' This was a coloured servant, whom one of the pilgrims in our party, in her generosity, had sent to 'Akká. In a moment Robert's radiant face appeared in the doorway and the Master rose to greet him, bidding him be seated, and said, 'Robert, your Lord loves you. God gave you a black skin, but a heart white as snow.' Then our Master spoke and said:
>
> 'We can all serve in the Cause of God no matter what our occupation is. No occupation can prevent the soul coming to God. Peter was a fisherman, yet he accomplished most wonderful things; but the heart must be turned always toward God, no matter what the work is; this is the important thing: and then the power of God will work in us. We are like a piece of iron in the midst of the fire which becomes heated to such a degree that it partakes of the nature of the fire and gives out the same effect to all it touches – so is the soul that is always turned toward God, and filled with the spirit.'[39]

The Master would teach servitude by insisting on serving the food to his guests himself, including Robert, despite their entreaties that Robert serve the meals. On one occasion, he relented and allowed Robert to *assist* him, which must have made that special pilgrim very happy.[40]

One afternoon during the visit of the February group, May and two other women were talking among themselves when May spoke negatively about 'a brother in the truth'. 'Abdu'l-Bahá was out tending to the poor and needy of 'Akká at the time and upon His return summoned Lua to Him. He informed her that something terrible had happened – one believer had spoken ill of an absent one. She was told to remain quiet about this and to pray about it. That evening at dinner, as May looked into the Master's eyes, such feelings of guilt and remorse overwhelmed her that she began to cry.

> A little later we all went to supper, and my hard heart was unconscious of its error, until, as my eyes sought the beloved face of my Master, I met His

> gaze, so full of gentleness and compassion that I was smitten to the heart. For in some marvellous way His eyes spoke to me; in that pure and perfect mirror I saw my wretched self and burst into tears. He took no notice of me for a while and everyone kindly continued with the supper while I sat in His dear Presence washing away some of my sins in tears. After a few moments He turned and smiled on me and spoke my name several times as though He were calling me to Him. In an instant such sweet happiness pervaded my soul, my heart was comforted with such infinite hope, that I knew He would cleanse me of all my sins.[41]

Some lessons did not require words.

CHAPTER 9

A Surprise Arrival amidst Farewells to 'Akká

It was the afternoon of 20 March, the eve of the Bahá'í New Year and the ancient Persian Festival of Naw-Rúz, both of which were set on the vernal equinox – the first day of spring. Lua Getsinger was once again making the now routine carriage ride along the beach to 'Akká where she alone among the remaining American pilgrims would be privileged to celebrate the start of the new year with 'Abdu'l-Bahá and His household.[1] Her husband, Edward, would join her the next day, but the Kheiralla family, Ella Goodall and Nell Hillyer would remain in Haifa to prepare to depart from the Holy Land. The beginning of the new year would mark the end of their pilgrimage.

Edward and Lua had inexplicably been given the gift of permission to remain in the Haifa Bay area throughout the period of this first Western pilgrimage, unlike their fellow American pilgrims whose visits could be counted only in days, much less months. Certainly Lua must have reviewed and relived her winter in the Holy Land as she watched the familiar landscape pass by during the drive north. Had it all been a dream? She and Edward had been in Palestine long enough to watch crocuses and wild narcissus give way to anemones and hillsides of pink cyclamen which in turn were transformed into yellow fields spread with wild mustard and royal crown daisies. Now, as the seasons changed, the Holy Land was fully arrayed in all its floral splendour with flowering red bud trees and a profusion of wild flowers more varied than back at the family farm in upstate New York. The cool rains of winter had produced a springtime, beautifully verdant beyond description, which should have boosted her spirits during the ride to 'Akká; but, as the carriage glided over the hard sand at the water's edge, the ever-present knowledge that this would be her last visit to her beloved Lord gnawed at her happiness.

A few hours earlier, just before Lua departed from Haifa, she had bade farewell to the Kheirallas, who would sail for Port Said the next day. The experiences the two families had shared together in the Holy Land had served to further fray their bonds of friendship, rather than strengthen them. Undoubtedly the parting was outwardly cordial, but nonetheless awkward for them all.

Ibrahim Kheiralla had arrived in triumph, but much had transpired since his arrival in November, and it seemed, as he packed to return to the United States, that worries and inner turmoil plagued him. His pilgrimage had shaken him to the very core of his being, and he would have much to ponder on the journey back to New York.

Kheiralla's great achievement, the establishment of the Faith in the West, had brought him many honours, but of them all, the most important, the greatest, had been one quietly bestowed upon him by the Master. It involved one of two significant historic events that took place during the period of the first visit of pilgrims from the continent of America, which would link the United States, and especially the Mother Temple of the West, in a mystical way with the Prophet-Herald of the Faith, the Báb. Ironically, the American pilgrims were unaware of the first of these two momentous events at the time.[2]

To appreciate the significance of these two historic events that were unfolding, we must return to that day almost a half century earlier when in 1850 the Báb was martyred in the marketplace of Tabriz. The Persian government officials decided to perpetrate one final humiliation upon that Messenger of God, even in death. His sacred remains were thrown outside of the walls of the city next to a moat, where it was hoped they would be desecrated by wild animals. Even though a guard was set over them, greed overpowered any sense of duty, making it possible for the heartbroken followers of that young Herald of the Cause of God to steal away His remains after paying bribes. From that time His coffin had been hidden, moved with great secrecy from place to place, often at the express direction of Bahá'u'lláh Himself and, later, of 'Abdu'l-Bahá. The dangers inherent in conserving such a precious Trust were enhanced tenfold with the defection of 'Abdu'l-Bahá's brothers following the passing of their Father. Spies in the employ of these disloyal members of Bahá'u'lláh's own family could be found in the telegraph offices and ports throughout the region.

Finally, during the winter of 1899, the blessed remains of the Báb (and His 18-year-old companion in martyrdom, Anís) arrived safely in 'Akká from Beirut. The final leg of their perilous wanderings had been arranged in great secrecy by 'Abdu'l-Bahá's brother-in-law, Mírzá Asadu'lláh, who had been given a code devised by the Master that would be used to convey His instructions. If told to send the sacred remains by land, they were to come by sea, and vice versa. The deception worked and the sacred cargo reached the port of 'Akká by sea some time during January or February while some of the American pilgrims were in the Holy Land, though neither they nor anyone else in the little community of believers knew of their arrival at the time, so confidential was this undertaking. The remains were hidden for a time in the chamber of Bahíyyih Khánum and apparently she was the only one in the household, apart from 'Abdu'l-Bahá, who was privy to the secret.

Related to the arrival of the holy remains of the Báb was a second historic event, though the details of this momentous occasion remain unattainable at the time of this writing. One day the Master asked Kheiralla to accompany Him to the site midway up the slope of Mount Carmel where in 1891 Bahá'u'lláh Himself had instructed that a befitting mausoleum for the remains of the Báb be erected. 'Abdu'l-Bahá directed Kheiralla to assist Him with laying the foundation stone of that sacred edifice – an inestimable honour bestowed upon Kheiralla because he was the founder of the Bahá'í community in the Great Republic of the West.[3] Of all the gifts given to Kheiralla during his time in the Holy Land, this was perhaps the one of highest worth.

Unfortunately, the great accolades and privileges heaped upon Kheiralla by both the Master and the Bahá'í community did not fortify his faith; instead, they swelled his ego and emboldened him. Indeed, he had accomplished much in America that was worthy of praise, but he had done so primarily for the wrong reasons and through deception. The carefully constructed American Bahá'í belief system encapsulated in his book began to collapse as his travelling companions came to recognize how shallow his knowledge of the Faith truly was. Even before the pilgrimage, Edward had begun to suspect that Kheiralla had deliberately altered the teachings of the Faith for his own purposes, or, more charitably, was not as learned as he appeared, and others among the pilgrims were starting to reach the same conclusion. Since his arrival in the Holy Land, Kheiralla had become increasingly obstinate and defensive in asserting his own teachings, even when they clearly contradicted those of 'Abdu'l-Bahá. The lack of deference shown to Kheiralla, which he felt was his due as the one who had first taught the Americans, both upset and frustrated him. As he prepared to leave Haifa, he was thus very conscious that his preeminence in the American Bahá'í community was in jeopardy.

Furthermore, the shiny veneer hiding Kheiralla's true character had melted in the bright light of the Holy Land, revealing a face beneath which showed one primary attribute – greed. His true purpose in teaching the Faith to the Americans had always been to make money, and his innate charm and intelligence could no longer mask his lack of sincere conviction and his dearth of insight into profound religious truths, despite his extensive knowledge of the Bible.

One day Kheiralla asked Edward to join him for a walk along the beach. As they watched the breakers roll in one after another, Kheiralla disclosed to Edward what was on his mind. He wanted Edward to use his influence with Phoebe Hearst to obtain a sum of money for him. Edward and Phoebe had already begun to discuss the requirements of the American Bahá'í community and the fact that there was a pressing need for someone to teach the American believers the verities of the Faith in more depth. As they strolled along the sand, Edward related to Kheiralla that he had already suggested a plan to Phoebe that would allow Kheiralla to devote himself full time to the Faith without worrying about making a living. Edward had proposed that Phoebe set up a trust fund, to be administered by a board of trustees, out of which Kheiralla would be paid a salary.[4] Phoebe was amenable to the idea. However, Kheiralla did not like that arrangement and instead insisted on receiving a substantial amount of cash paid as a lump sum. He had been quite impressed by how much money Mary Baker Eddy, the founder of the Christian Science denomination, had earned from the sale of her book – it had made her a wealthy woman. He anticipated that the same would happen from the sales of his book about the Bahá'í Faith. (Kheiralla was already agitated that 'Abdu'l-Bahá had made it clear that He would not accept the manuscript in its first draft form because of its discrepancies with the true teachings of the Faith and was insisting that he make corrections. But that issue was not the topic of the conversation on the beach.) Kheiralla pressed his case that if Phoebe would just buy the rights to the book from him and arrange for it to be published, he would be done with it and she could recoup her money through sales of the book. Edward was not happy with this proposal, but agreed to convey it to Phoebe.[5]

The Master was not deceived by Kheiralla and could see clearly what was really in his heart. Nonetheless He never spoke negatively about him to anyone but instead repeatedly emphasized to the American pilgrims that they should be eternally grateful to Ibrahim Kheiralla for giving them the message of the Faith. They were to pray for him, to hold him in esteem as their teacher, and to shower nothing but love upon him, just as He Himself did. And so they did. Their letters home to the American believers reflect this gratitude. But this did not allay their growing concerns about how the Faith could progress in America unless another, more reliable source of its teachings than Kheiralla could be found.

Phoebe, of course, was always a doer. She was not about to leave to chance the proper development of the Faith in the United States, especially once she was able to compare the sun of 'Abdu'l-Bahá to the dim glow of Kheiralla. Therefore, arrangements were made for Ella and Nell while they were still in the Holy Land to make a side trip on Phoebe's behalf to look over a man who might provide assistance to the American community. The two young women made a short visit to Nazareth, the boyhood home of Jesus nestled in a small valley in the Galilee hills about 20 miles east of 'Akká, in order to meet Dr Rafael Sadris, a pharmacist and medical doctor who was living and working in a Catholic convent hospital. Dr Sadris was a Bahá'í, but because of his employment by Christians, he had to be discreet about his religious allegiance. Dr Sadris spoke passable English and may well have been recommended to Phoebe by 'Abdu'l-Bahá. Phoebe hoped that he would prove to be a suitable candidate to move to the United States to serve as a translator, teacher of Persian and instructor in the Faith.

The young women spoke with Dr Sadris about California and what his life might be like if he went there. They found him to be affable and exceedingly hospitable. He professed a readiness to go to America if it was the wish of 'Abdu'l-Bahá.[6] As a result of this vetting by her young emissaries, Phoebe later arranged for Dr Sadris to come to California.

Having just said goodbye to the Kheiralla family that day, perhaps Lua meditated briefly about the dilemma of Kheiralla's future role in America as she rode back to 'Akká, but her thoughts were easily diverted to more pleasant topics. Her driver and only companion was the gardener, 'Abu'l-Qasím, and he helped make the time pass quickly by telling her stories of Bahá'u'lláh in simple Persian; he even recited from the Bahá'í Writings by heart. Lua was obviously becoming more and more fluent in that tongue because she could understand much of what he said, and cherished it all.

The carriage jostled over the sand dunes that separated the beach from the harder ground where they would make the last leg of their journey. The vehicle headed inland toward the rutted, unpaved road that wound along the edge of the bay to the land gate of the prison city. When they reached the gate they passed 'Abdu'l-Bahá, who was busy conversing with another person they recognized, but because many soldiers were also standing about, neither they nor the Master acknowledged each other.

The Master had worried from the beginning that the coming of the Americans would create fresh tensions and dangers with the enemies of the Faith. At the outset of their arrival, great care was taken to keep their visits secret or at least inconspicuous. But as the months passed, this prudence became less stringent; indeed, many of the local believers became accustomed to the presence of the Americans and stopped exercising caution. The consequences took some time to unfold but finally the hammer came down. A week earlier on Monday, 13 March, while Ella and Nell were in Haifa awaiting a summons to come again to the House of 'Abdu'lláh Pá<u>sh</u>á, the government officials of 'Akká had received word from Istanbul[7] that they were to prevent all foreigners from visiting 'Abdu'l-Bahá. A message reached Ella, Nell and Lua[8] that the local officials would disregard the order until the next day at sunset, so they were to leave for 'Akká with haste. Nell recorded that they did not leave for ʻAkká until after dinner and for the first time made the journey between the towns at night, this time with an air of danger and foreboding surrounding the trip.

> I think I shall never forget that drive by night along the sandy beach, with the slight bit of a moon, the lights of Haifa receding and those of Acca coming more into prominence; our entrance into the city wall and being stopped by the guard while our hearts were in our throats.[9]

When they arrived at the House of ʻAbdu'lláh Pá<u>sh</u>á about nine o'clock that evening, the Master was not at home but the ladies of the household affirmed that the rumours of the crackdown were true. Ella wrote that

> Trouble was brewing and our Lord wished us all to leave Haifa just as soon as possible. It made us very unhappy to think we were the means in a measure of creating trouble for Him. We were all quite agitated and anxious, and the poor members of the household looked utterly worn out for they had been bidding good-by to Oriental pilgrims who were obliged to leave immediately. One poor man from India who had arrived only that day was sent away the same night by steamer after having seen the Master for about five minutes. All the Persians who did not live in Acca had to go and it was truly pathetic, for they love Him so it seems as though they could not live to be sent away from the light of His face. He finally came in from outside looking very weary, but glad to see us as he always seemed. After a short talk we went to bed quite used up.[10]

But all was not lost. In an empire rife with injustice, the local officials of ʻAkká were often willing to ignore orders from above when it suited them and they decided to ignore this new command for at least another day. The Americans were granted a brief reprieve. Nonetheless, Nell wrote that the Master told them that 'it would be better for everyone, for them now, and for the Americans that would come in the future if we left as soon as possible'.[11]

Nothing is known for certain as to why the government chose 13 March to tightly enforce the restrictions promulgated long before (but since ignored) forbidding ʻAbdu'l-Bahá to receive foreign visitors. One possible trigger was the conspicuous arrival of two American women and their retinue. They may have tipped the balance. One of the two women, Margaret Bloodgood Peeke,[12] had altered their travel plans by adding ʻAkká so that she could meet ʻAbdu'l-Bahá. Was she the fifteenth pilgrim counted among the first Western pilgrims in the reckoning of the group by Shoghi Effendi?[13]

At age 60, Maggie, as her friends called her, was a most unusual woman for her time, or any time for that matter. Her husband of many decades, the Reverend George H. Peeke, was a well-educated[14] clergyman of the Reformed Dutch Church. She had been born in Schuylerville, New York,[15] but spent most of her childhood and youth in New York City. Her father died when she was 12, and consequently her illustrious uncle, Chancellor Erastus C. Benedict, who was not only a prominent academic but the author of the definitive book on admiralty law, took responsibility for her education and became her mentor and guide. At 16 she became a published author, successfully submitting many items to magazines. Maggie married at the age of 22 and from that point forward put aside her aspirations as a writer to devote her energies exclusively to her duties as the wife of a clergyman and to raising their six children.[16]

Maggie and her husband moved many times until finally settling in Sandusky, Ohio, in part because her husband's unconventional views got him into trouble with his congregations; for example, he was an outspoken proponent of the abolition of the sale of alcoholic beverages. After fifteen years of putting aside her pen, a period of ill health forced her to rest and gave her the unexpected gift of time to resume her writing. She composed songs, wrote magazine articles and published a novel about college life at the time her son was a student. Maggie also published poetry. In addition to her writing skills, she was a gifted public speaker who became a much-sought-after lecturer on the Bible.[17] As the years passed, her religious proclivities evolved and became more unconventional than her husband's. Perhaps the cause of Maggie's earnest search for answers to spiritual questions was the trauma of losing most of her children. All but two of her six children died young.[18] She penned a number of books about ancient mysticism, numerology and the occult that were written in the form of novels, making them quite popular in the 1890s.[19] At the time of her visit to 'Abdu'l-Bahá, she was doing well enough as a professional writer to employ a full-time typist.[20]

Maggie's relentless quest for spiritual knowledge had led her to 'Abdu'l-Bahá's book, *A Traveller's Narrative*, which Professor E. G. Browne had translated into English and published. Not surprisingly, she had also met some of the American believers – many of whom shared her interest in exotic religious teachings. She wasn't impressed. Her views of 'Abdu'l-Bahá's book, she confessed, were clouded by her dislike of the few Bahá'ís she knew. She had determined to make a journey to the Orient in order 'to learn some of the peculiar mystic phases of the East and the practical knowledge said to be understood and practiced there; also to become acquainted with the customs of those ancient sects which seem to have come down from remote ages'.[21]

When one of Maggie's Bahá'í friends heard about her upcoming spiritual pilgrimage, he suggested that she include a visit to 'Akká to meet 'Abdu'l-Bahá. Maggie returned her friend's suggestion with a smile that 'would have shown to the most casual observer that there was no thought or intention of doing anything of the kind'.[22] However, she couldn't remove the suggestion from her mind.

> . . . indifference gave place to curiosity; curiosity ended in interest; the impossible grew possible and possible became probable, until, by the time we reached Gibralter, I had made a change of route that took in Acca and Abbas-Effendi.[23]

Once in Cairo, Maggie wrote home to an American friend asking for a letter of introduction she could use to meet the Egyptian Bahá'ís who in turn would help her to meet the Master. She also found someone in Cairo who could give her information about the basics of the Faith. She then proceeded to Damascus and Beirut and from there to 'Akká. She wrote of musing over the turbulent and significant history of that ancient city as she approached it for the first time late in the afternoon. She passed Bahjí as she drew near to the prison city and intuitively sensed, as she surveyed the Mansion of Bahjí from a distance, that it must have been somehow associated with the life of Bahá'u'lláh. At four that afternoon of Sunday 12 March, she and her travelling companions pitched tents outside the walls of the city of 'Akká and sent a message to 'Abdu'l-Bahá asking if He would receive a non-believer. Within half an hour they had a reply inviting them to come at eight o'clock that very evening.

> The night was most dark; we were accompanied by our guide and interpreter, a soldier and a man carrying a lantern; and as we threaded our way along narrow streets, groups of men watching us were standing under arches that opened into a court-yard, where there were many other soldiers. All saluted us as we passed them to gain access to a long flight of stairs built on the outside of the house. We felt that this wonderful night would ever be a memorable one in our lives.
>
> 'You cannot enter,' said one of these soldiers to our faithful dragoman who had never yet left us since entering our service.
>
> 'Then I will stand by the door,' was his meek reply, as he followed us up the long flight of stairs to the door of the audience room.[24]

Upon entering the 'long bare room, scantily furnished' – the upstairs reception room of the House of 'Abdu'lláh Páshá – she immediately noticed the

Americans: Edward[25] and probably Kheiralla and Marian who were seated near the door. There were also a few local Christian Arabs, soldiers and women. Maggie recorded what happened next.

> From the other side of this long room, we saw a figure rise and advance to meet us.
>
> The motion was almost like gliding, so smooth was it, and as he drew nearer, we noticed the mouse-colored gown he wore with a turban to match, and there stood before us One who was the personification of all gentleness and meekness, and yet a sublime dignity rested upon him which we had never seen in others of the same faith, unusual in type as they were. He approached with extended hands, as if meeting friends and followers and then led us to seats at the upper end of the long room, motioning us to sit at his right hand. He ordered tea, which was served by a gentleman placing tiny round tables before each one and proceeded to give us the fragrant cup of tea. So far as we could notice not a glance had been directed toward us, though the visitors from America, knowing me to be a non-believer, watched with keen interest this kindly courtesy Abbas-Effendi extended me.[26]

One of the first things to impress Maggie was the manner in which the Master treated her dragoman, the same one who had been dealt with harshly by the soldiers outside of the house.

> Looking down the room while we were sipping our tea, what was our surprise to see our dragoman, Joseph, demurely sitting inside near the door with a countenance as unreadable as a sphinx. Abbas-Effendi also noticing him, motioned to him to come up nearer, and placed him at his left, saying in Arabic, that he would be glad to have him act as assistant interpreter. A cup of tea was also brought to Joseph.[27]

'Abdu'l-Bahá began to speak. Maggie had come expecting – hoping – that He would talk about the Báb and Bahá'u'lláh. She had anticipated stories of their suffering as martyrs for their Faith, indeed of His own suffering, of the history of the Faith and its fulfilment of prophecy. Surely He would use the opportunity to convert her. But, to her 'great astonishment', He instead talked about the 'Grand Architect of the Universe, about the Laws of Creation and Preservation' all the while not looking up to make eye contact with her. He finally did look up at her when she asked a question but then promptly resumed the theme He had begun. She wanted to ask Him a particular question but seemed to lose the ability to do so.

> I could find no question to ask on the most important subject of all: its [the Bahá'í Faith's] place in history and fulfillment of prophecy. Our knowledge was absolutely nothing; how we did ransack our memories for some hint from Prof. Browne's book[28] to help us out of our dilemma, but none came, and as if in response to this state of our minds, he avoided altogether any allusion to his own work or the significance of His Father's Manifestation.[29]

The words of the Master transcended mere allegiance to any one religion or philosophy, soaring on a higher, more all-embracing level.

> The conversation continued upon the plan of the Divine Being, who from the beginning, when the stars were sent forth into their places, till the present time, never changed a detail of what was in His plan. Worlds, empires, men and angels all had their station, which had been theirs from the ideal, first formed in the Mind of God. There had been no mistakes; there had been no retrogression. It was when ages had rolled by that man could see what had been accomplished and know that there was no possibility of frustrating even the smallest fraction of the Law. The great nations of the past had done the little part that was their work to do and the figure they completed in the tapestry of Life could never have been accomplished by any other peoples.
>
> So long as the world was under the Law of the Mineral, it could not know God except as it saw Him in the face of stone, but, as centuries and eons passed, there awoke in the creature, man, a feeling that he had some relation to this Being, who was holding in His hand the sun, moon and stars; nay even more than all, the thinking creature who was the king of His creatures. It was then that the first Manifestation of God (of record) was seen in the Moses of the mountain and the Law received from the Burning Bush. Then came the Prophets, with the inspiration of the Spirit, telling what was to come in the 'latter days'. There remained much that could not be explained even after Jesus the Christ had come, and had been the fulfillment of a great deal which was ended by His work. With every new Revelation there has come a clearer meaning of man's relation to the First Cause until the time grew near when the dark places would be made Light, and the unknown understood.
>
> When the rim of a new moon comes into view, if we had never seen it before, we would think it could be no greater, but night after night it grows from the crescent to the gibbous, and from that to the full moon, so also the Light of Truth had come by degrees, and when the fullness of the whole

> could be seen, it would be the same Light that had shown in the crescent, in the gibbous, and in the full moon, but differing only in degree.[30]

Two hours passed and it was time to depart. The evening had been fruitful beyond anything she had imagined. Maggie would always cherish the memory of it and hoped for nothing more from 'Abdu'l-Bahá, but He would surprise her.

> At ten o'clock we rose to take our leave, and while thanking our host for his kindness in granting us so lengthy an interview, he said in that soft, but commanding voice, which no one would think of resisting, 'I shall be glad to see you again tomorrow morning at nine o'clock.'[31]

Maggie was thunderstruck. The offer of a second interview had apparently never entered her mind and she could not believe her good fortune.

> Going forth into the darkness, to be escorted back to our tents, we felt a great interest awaken in this wonderful personality, so meek, yet so majestic; commanding, and yet so humble.
>
> When retracing our steps through the same arches and courts as before, we found the soldiers of the Sultan, sitting on the walls over-looking our tents, evidently watching our movements. They were playing on the instruments of their country, soft, sensuous, dreamy music, that seemed to belong to the lonely, lovely night, to the quaint place and our new experiences.[32]

Once the flaps of their tent were closed for the night and Maggie and her companion[33] were finally afforded a modicum of privacy, they sat on their beds and reviewed the evening's interview. Maggie was elated. The experience was not at all as she had expected. She could not believe that during the two hours 'Abdu'l-Bahá had never once talked about the Bahá'í Faith directly. He did not bring up the American Bahá'í community or point out Kheiralla to her as the teacher who first brought the message to her homeland. (Later, when she was writing her account and knew more about the Faith, she must have realized that Kheiralla was there, but he wasn't pointed out to her as anyone significant.) She was especially astounded that the Master in no way tried to tell them that the Bahá'í Faith was superior to other religions. He said nothing about either His Father, Bahá'u'lláh, or of His own role as Head of the Faith after His Father's passing. They marvelled at the 'greatness of his universal knowledge; the meekness of his character; the majesty of his humility'.[34] They had never encountered one like Him.

Studio photograph of the Greatest Holy Leaf, Bahíyyih Khánum, standing in front of a scenic backdrop with a vase of flowers beside her, c. 1895

Women of the Holy Family, with their children in the front row, and pilgrims standing in the back row. Middle row, left to right: Rúḥá Khánum, daughter of 'Abdu'l-Bahá; Ḍíyá'i'yyih Khánum, daughter of 'Abdu'l-Bahá and mother of Shoghi Effendi; Bahíyyih Khánum, Greatest Holy Leaf, sister of 'Abdu'l-Bahá; Munírih Khánum, wife of 'Abdu'l-Bahá; Túbá Khánum, daughter of 'Abdu'l-Bahá, Munavvár Khánum, daughter of 'Abdu'l-Bahá

The Hearst party in Egypt, January 1899. Back row, left to right: Julia Pearson, unidentified, unidentified, probably Agnes Lane, Anne Apperson. Front row, left to right: Robert Turner, probably Emily Bachrodt, probably Joe Clark, Phoebe Hearst, unidentified, Mary Virginia Thornburgh-Cropper, Orrin Peck, dragoman

The Hearst party visiting the Sphinx and the Pyramids, January 1899. Back row, on camels, left to right: Anne Apperson, Phoebe Hearst, unidentified, dragoman. Front row, on donkeys, left to right: Orrin Peck, Mary Virginia Thornburgh-Cropper, probably Joe Clark, Julia Pearson, probably Agnes lane, probably Emily Bachrodt, Robert Turner

The next morning, Maggie's companion decided to ride in the direction of Bahjí to get a better view of the Mansion, which the day before they had surmised was grander than any they had seen in Syria. She intended to rejoin Maggie later at the home of ʻAbdu'l-Bahá.

When Maggie arrived at the House of ʻAbdu'lláh Pá<u>sh</u>á the next morning, she saw some of the same ladies she had met the previous evening and was engaged in chatting with them and others when the Master approached.

> In a moment, every sound was hushed, as if in the presence of some divine person. He held in his hand three stalks of heliotrope-colored stockgilly flowers,[35] two of which he presented to me, keeping the third in his hand while he led me up to the same seat he had given me the previous evening.
>
> 'I should like to begin with the last question you asked me,' he said as soon as we were seated. 'I should have answered it a little more fully.' He began at that point, continuing as he had in our first conversation until it was twelve o'clock. Then my friend came in, and he handed her the other flower. He bade us adieu, and gave to each a precious message that must linger in our memory so long as life lasts.[36]

Both ladies felt blessed to have had the privilege of meeting ʻAbdu'l-Bahá, but they had other stops on their itinerary, especially the sites in the Holy Land associated with the life of Christ, therefore the Master left their thoughts until the voyage home. Maggie sent ʻAbdu'l-Bahá a note thanking Him for giving them so much of His time and was surprised when, some months later, a letter in Persian arrived for her at her home in the United States.

> One day, a most exquisite letter written in Persian, with a translation into English, came to me and I felt as never before when reading those words which vibrated through me as would music from the chords of a grand organ, nor could I understand the power that could cross the seas and oceans, and give me a sense of such nearness and spiritual longing. From that time to the present moment, Abbas-Effendi, or 'ʻAbdu'l-Bahá' has been to me an ever growing mystery, his letters have been filled with a spirit so great and holy that its equal cannot be found unless it be in the epistles of the New Testament. Only now can I analyze that feeling which has taken so deep a root in my heart and soul.[37]

By not trying overtly to convert her, ʻAbdu'l-Bahá won Margaret Peeke's heart. After some years of further study and correspondence with the Master, she became an avowed believer, as did her daughter-in-law, Dr Pauline Barton-

Peeke, who in 1911 arranged the publication of Maggie's account of her 1899 visit to 'Akká. The Master Himself had urged Maggie to write about it.

Edward must have reported these meetings with Maggie to Lua. The longer they were in the Holy Land, the more obvious it was that they had only begun to learn about their new Faith. Not only did they need to delve further into its verities; they had to become more proficient in presenting it to others. Surely Edward must have been impressed with the wisdom and love evident in 'Abdu'l-Bahá's approach to the two American women. Watching and listening when in His presence provided an unequalled education.

*****

It was nearly dark when Lua reached the home of the Master where she went straight to the room of Bahíyyih Khánum. She was served tea and then sat talking with members of the household while awaiting her Lord's return. When at last He appeared, she joined His daughters in their rush to welcome him. Lua had become an accepted member of 'Abdu'l-Bahá's private household during the course of the four months. As her Persian improved and the Master's daughters began to learn English, the barriers of language and culture started to melt away. She would join the family in their private quarters for meals, sitting on the floor on cushions around a low table Oriental-style, unlike the Western table arrangement provided for her fellow countrymen. The Master had clearly recognized her great capacity for service to the Cause and was training her. That March evening as she sat beside Him during the family's meal, He took a piece of bread and put some honey on it. He then handed it to Lua and told her to eat it, saying as He did so, 'Let all of your words be as sweetly flavoured by kindness to all people as this bread is flavoured by honey.' She wrote that at that moment she felt as she swallowed that bread as if she had received a great spiritual blessing.[38]

The next morning, the believers in 'Akká celebrated the beginning of a new calendar year, often called by its Persian name, Naw-Rúz. As was the custom in Iran, the date of the equinox was determined by more than just the calendar, the position of the sun and moon were also considered, and consequently in 1899 it fell on 21 March. For Bahá'ís, this joyous Bahá'í Holy Day is preceded by a nineteen-day period of fasting during which the believers between the ages of 15 and 70 refrain from eating or drinking between sunrise and sunset. Nonetheless, while the Master observed the Bahá'í fasting period, He did not encourage the other believers in the Haifa Bay area to do so at that time, most likely as a protection lest they antagonize the local population. He did encourage them to continue to fast during the Muslim period of Ramadan, and He observed that fast as well.[39] It is interesting to note that Ella and Nell's visit to the home of the Master fell during this period of fasting – both Bahá'í and Muslim[40] – yet no one told them that this was a teaching of the Bahá'í Faith. Ella noted in her journal that the Master was keeping a Muslim fast. He served them lunch but did not eat with them. As they would have had lunch apart from the rest of the household, they would have been unaware of other Bahá'ís who were fasting. Undoubtedly, the Master judged that their knowledge of the Faith was too limited and the concept of fasting was too foreign to Protestant Americans to introduce the nineteen-day fast to them at that time. It should be noted that most Protestant churches in the United States do not encourage fasting, and that fasting in the minds of many American Protestant Christians is associated with practices of Catholicism discarded through the Reformation.

Even though the pilgrims did not observe the Bahá'í nineteen-day fast, Lua recorded that just before their departure from the Holy Land, the Bahá'ís of Haifa and 'Akká were celebrating the New Year of the Bábí Calendar.[41] The observance of this happy occasion in the household of the Master was noteworthy for its simplicity.

> Next morning very early the Babis in Acca began to assemble at the home of our Lord, the ladies going to the room of the 'Holy Leaf", and the men remaining down stairs. The occasion of this gathering was on account of March 21st being New Year's day. Our Lord came into the room and gave to everybody some sweets from His hands, after which Rooha Khanam, one of his daughters, chanted a beautiful tablet. Then He arose, and saying a few words of welcome, went to the room occupied by the men. There He gathered all of the children together and gave each of them a few coins, – about ten or fifteen cents, – which made them all delighted and very happy, of course, because He gave it to them. After drinking tea and visiting a little while, they all went away. Then we had lunch and directly after prepared to make my last visit to the Tomb of the Manifestation.[42]

With the start of the new Bahá'í year, the historic first pilgrimage of Western believers was drawing to a close. As soon as Lua arrived back in 'Akká, the Master had reminded her that she was about to depart. He said, 'I am sending you back to America that you may work to gain a place beside Me in the Eternal Kingdom'.[43]

Those who had come and gone during the preceding months had been greatly moved by the final hours of their time in 'Akká as the Master prepared each group for its departure. The February group awoke for the last time in 'Akká as though engulfed in a black cloud, as thoughts of their impending separation from the one who had become the centre of their world filled their hearts with grief. But the Master would not allow them to leave in that state of mind. May recalled her last day.

> When we awoke on Saturday morning [25 February] it seemed that the full realization of this separation descended like a great darkness upon us, and we were utterly alone in the wide world, save only for Him. He called us to Him at an early hour, and as we gazed upon His merciful face we saw that He knew all and that He would uphold us and give us strength; that verily He was sufficient for the whole world. In the might and majesty of His presence our fear was turned to perfect faith, our weakness into strength, our sorrow into hope and ourselves forgotten in our love for Him. As we sat before Him waiting to hear His words, some of the believers wept bitterly. He asked them for His sake not to weep, nor would He talk to us or teach us until all tears were banished and we were quite calm. Then He said:
>
>> Pray that your hearts may be cut from yourselves and from the world, that you may be confirmed by the Holy Spirit and filled with the fire of the love of God. The nearer you are to the light, the further you are from the darkness; the nearer you are to heaven, the further you are from the earth; the nearer you are to God, the further you are from the world. You have come here among the first and your reward is great. There are two visits; the first is for a blessing; then ye come and are blest and are sent forth to work in God's vineyard; the second ye come with music and the banners flying, like soldiers, in gladness and triumph to receive your reward. If in times past those who have risen up and gone forth in the Cause of God have been helped and confirmed by His spirit, even to suffering death for Him, how much greater is the flood of life with which ye shall be flooded now! For this is the end and the full revelation, and I say unto you that anyone who will rise up in the Cause of God at this time shall be filled with the spirit of God, and that He will send His hosts from heaven to help you and that nothing shall be impossible to you if you have faith. And now I give you a commandment which shall be for a covenant between you and Me – that ye have faith; that your faith be steadfast as a rock that no storms can move, that nothing can disturb, and that it endure through all things even to the end; even should ye hear that your Lord has been crucified, be not shaken in your faith; for I am with you always, whether living or dead, I am with you to the end. As ye have faith so shall your powers and blessings be. This is the balance – this is the balance – this is the balance.[44]

One month later, as Ella and Nell prepared to depart, the Master also gave them a parting talk. Ella set down what happened on that memorable occasion.

> After lunch we went in to see the ladies for the last time. It was very hard to leave them for God knows when we will see them again. We were with them an hour or two, and then were summoned to the Master's presence for our last talk with Him. Only five of us were there, Mr. & Mrs. Getsinger, Nell and myself, and Dr. Khayru'llah to translate. The Master said that it had been a great pleasure to Him to have seen us and talk with us, and He hoped, as He would always remember our visit, that we would never never forget it. That we must let absolutely nothing shake our faith; that we might hear of dreadful happenings here where He was for [sic], as it is such a great Cause so will great events happen for and against it. But no matter what comes we must be as firm as mountains of iron. He then spoke of our work in America and told us that we must all pull together. If anyone did wrong through weakness we must forgive him and work in love and harmony together for the love and good of the Cause. He said many times that no matter if we did feel that we knew very little that when we went to America and began to teach all that was necessary for our success would be given to us, provided our desire was great enough and earnest enough. Also He said that we must strive to become confirmed by the Spirit. He illustrated by the simile of the tree which He likened to God. God is the trunk, on the tree are branches, twigs, leaves, blossoms and fruit. If we are content to remain leaves of the tree when the harsh winds blow we will fall to the ground so we must pray to become stronger as the twigs, and then finally, when we become branches, all the storms of Heaven cannot shake us, for we are close to the trunk then – part of it, in fact – like it – and that is what is meant by the confirmation of the Spirit for which we must constantly work.[45]

As the hour approached for each departing group to return to Haifa, the pilgrims were invited into the chamber of Bahíyyih Khánum for a wondrous, unforgettable experience – the viewing of the portraits of Bahá'u'lláh and the Báb. There were three, two of Bahá'u'lláh and one of the Báb. All three were housed in exquisite gold and silver frames with beautiful, fine filigree decorative details hand-wrought in China expressly for their precious contents. These frames were gifts from the family of the Báb – the Afnáns. The first portrait of Bahá'u'lláh was a photograph which His family claimed was a good likeness of Him. It was taken by order of the Ottoman government during His years in Adrianople, Turkey. The second was a series of three lovely paintings done by an Armenian Christian artist while Bahá'u'lláh was an exile in Baghdad. They showed Him on the left panel dressed as He would be in the public bath, on the right panel seated and clutching His prayer beads, and in the prominent centre panel was a head and shoulders portrait, posed as though He were giving a blessing – in the pose commonly used to portray Christian saints. These colourful paintings of Bahá'u'lláh included cherubs, a sunburst and other decorative edging common to Christian religious art. The colour portrait of the Báb was based upon a sketch for which He had posed while He was held as a prisoner in the town of Urúmíyyih in Iran during the last months of His life. In it, the Báb was presented seated on the ground but otherwise fully shown. The artist was not a follower of the Báb at the time he sketched the original pencil drawing, but years later he converted to the Faith and produced the colour version of the portrait at the express request of Bahá'u'lláh.

The Greatest Holy Leaf was the custodian for these sacred portraits as well as for the small collection of holy relics kept at the house of the Master. Ella recalled that before she, Nell and the other pilgrims entered the room, Bahíyyih Khánum herself first anointed their foreheads with attar of rose. The first items to catch their eyes when they crossed the threshold of the chamber were the portraits, which had been placed on the divan opposite the door. Each pilgrim in turn walked slowly up to the pictures, knelt before them and kissed them. They then rose and stood silently, all the while gazing at the portraits or praying and meditating. Ella found the photograph to be 'remarkable' and said, 'there the eyes seemed to hold one with unmistakable power, which gave a faint idea of what they must have been in life'.

May's tears had flowed as, on her knees, she viewed the portraits. She felt that she could stay that way always, but it was time to go and 'Abdu'l-Bahá Himself had summoned her from her trance.

> We could have remained thus for ever with our eyes fastened on that wonderful face, but the Master touched us on the shoulder, that we might see also the picture of His Highness the Báb. His was a beautiful young face, but I could not keep my eyes from the eyes of Bahá'u'lláh, until 'Abdu'l-Bahá turned suddenly to us, and raising His voice in a tone so poignant that it pierced every heart, He stretched His hands above us and said:
>
>> Now the time has come when we must part, but the separation is only of our bodies, in spirit we are united. Ye are the lights which shall be diffused; ye are the waves of that sea which shall spread and overflow the world. Each wave is precious to Me and My nostrils shall be gladdened by your fragrance. Another commandment I give unto you, that ye love one another even as I love you. Great mercy and blessings are

> promised to the people of your land, but on one condition: that their hearts are filled with the fire of love, that they live in perfect kindness and harmony like one soul in different bodies. If they fail in this condition the great blessings will be deferred. Never forget this; look at one another with the eye of perfection; look at Me, follow Me, be as I am; take no thought for yourselves or your lives, whether ye eat or whether ye sleep, whether ye are comfortable, whether ye are well or ill, whether ye are with friends or foes, whether ye receive praise or blame; for all of these things ye must care not at all. Look at Me and be as I am; ye must die to yourselves and to the world, so shall ye be born again and enter the Kingdom of Heaven. Behold a candle how it gives its light. It weeps its life away drop by drop in order to give forth its flame of light.

> When He had finished speaking we were led gently away by the members of the Holy Family, and for a moment it seemed that we were dying; but our Master never removed His compassionate gaze from our faces, until we could see Him no longer, for our tears. Then we were clasped one after the other in the arms of the Holy Family, and the hearts were wrung, and it seemed as if all the cords of life were breaking; until, as we drove away from the home of our Heavenly Father, suddenly His spirit came to us, a great strength and tranquillity filled our souls, the grief of the bodily separation was turned into the joy of spiritual union.[46]

Lua and Edward had observed each of their fellow pilgrims from America go through the stages of elation at meeting ʿAbdu'l-Bahá and deep grief as their time came to leave. They had been spared that heartache – until now. As they had been privileged to be the first to arrive, they would be the last to depart.

The day before the Getsingers sailed for Egypt, Edward rejoined Lua in ʿAkká.[47] The Master busily prepared Tablets for them to take back to specific friends in America and inquired about their journey home. He asked them to spend some time in Cairo where they could learn more of the Faith from the community there, but not too long because He wanted them to be back in the United States in six weeks time.

They arose early in the morning on Thursday 23 March in order to join the household in the room of Bahíyyih Khánum, where Lua sat at the feet of the Master as she drank her tea. As she gazed up at the face of ʿAbdu'l-Bahá her eyes filled with tears, though she did her best to conceal her feelings. He noticed and consoled her. 'Do not cry – be happy. I will go with you in spirit – the separation of the body is nothing. I will go with you.' She dried her eyes as best she could and followed Him to the room where He did His writing. He began to admire the photograph of Thornton Chase and others of Mr Clark and Mr Struven – believers in Ithaca, New York, taught by Lua. He kissed their photographs and asked her to tell those men that He had done so and that they were His sons whom He longed to meet in person and to kiss.

After a time, the Master called Edward into the room and presented him with a bottle of pomegranate juice. He then gave them each a little vial of attar of rose. As it became noon, 'Abdu'l-Bahá left to tend to other affairs and the Getsingers watched as He walked through the courtyard of the building, trying to emblazon in their memories an image of Him – of His gait, of His person. After a brief absence, He returned and joined them for one last luncheon, seating one of them on His right and the other on His left. The sorrow of parting took away their appetites and they hardly touched their food. As they were getting up from the table a servant announced that the carriage to take them to Haifa was ready.

Everyone in the household tried to put on a brave face as they bade the Getsingers farewell, but in the end they all cried. Lua felt faint and physically ill as she approached the Master one last time. He quickly came to her side and led her down the first flight of stairs toward the inner courtyard. She pressed His hand to her lips, and at that moment He turned away from her and silently kissed Edward on the cheek, then left the two in haste and returned upstairs. 'Abdu'l-Bahá, the centre of their world, was gone. They stumbled down the last stairs with leaden feet into the courtyard. Even though it was a beautiful spring afternoon, Lua felt that the sun had grown dark. They hastened to the great portal that was the entrance to the compound and stepped over the high threshold into the glare of the outer courtyard where their carriage was waiting, and reluctantly they climbed aboard.

The carriage rumbled through the gate of the outer wall of the compound and through the narrow, familiar streets. They passed once again through the land gate and onto the open dirt road, the ancient city at their backs. The carriage soon turned towards the beach and trekked along the sand, pointed towards Mount Carmel. The entire trip was made in silence; Edward and Lua were too overcome with emotion to utter a word. The carriage did not enter the gate of Haifa but instead went directly to the port where the ship that would take them to Port Said was riding at anchor, ready for them to board. Their movements were mechanical, automatic as in a daze they made their way to the ship. As the steamer set sail out of the bay into the open Mediterranean, they stood together on deck by a railing and stared at the distant city of 'Akká, never once removing their gaze until it vanished completely from view.[48]

CHAPTER 10

An Egyptian Education

No pilgrimage is complete until the pilgrim reaches home. The travel to and fro itself is integral to the spiritual experience. So it was for the first Western Bahá'í pilgrims as they left the Holy Land and made their way to their homes. All of them had other stops to make after leaving 'Akká. Phoebe Hearst and her grand party of relatives, friends and employees – including the majority of the American pilgrims – basked in the sights of the Greek Isles and rugged Turkish coastline as their cruise ship made its way north to Istanbul. These leisurely excursions provided those newly transformed souls with space and time to reflect upon all that they had felt, learned and observed during the magical sojourn in the Holy Land. Those who were privileged to remain there through the Bahá'í New Year – the Kheirallas, the Getsingers, Nell Hillyer and Ella Goodall – also made their way circuitously back to America. Ibrahim Kheiralla, alone among the travellers, was in a hurry because he was anxious to hasten to his flock in the United States after a brief stopover in Paris. He also had to finalize arrangements for his daughters to emigrate to America. Marian needed to take a detour in order to escort her aunt from Milan to London. And the Getsingers, Ella and Nell had been given a special charge to carry out before leaving the Middle East. 'Abdu'l-Bahá Himself requested that those four pilgrims tarry in Egypt, where they were to receive further instruction in the verities of the Faith, a coda to the pilgrimage.

Ella and Nell were in no hurry to return to Cairo after leaving Haifa. They had few constraints of time and funds and wanted to take advantage of the opportunity to tour more of the Levant, especially Syria. When they parted with the Getsingers on 23 March, they took a ship to the next major port to the north, Beirut. From there they travelled to Damascus and around that region sightseeing and enjoying the culture that was quite exotic to the two young Californians. The weather was still frigid, especially in the mountains, and they were not properly dressed for it, but the cold did not diminish their delight as they explored ancient ruins and shopped for bargains, such as oriental rugs and fabrics, at the local bazaars. Ella wrote to her family, 'You have no idea what fun it is to travel alone [that is, not in a tour group], for Nell and I have a very friendly atmosphere and these Orientals are so nice and cannot do enough for us.'[1] Their careful use of a few polite Arabic phrases, as well as the fact that they did not travel with the protection of a male escort, disarmed those they met. The local people assumed a protective posture toward the two innocent and kind, though naive, young strangers who were a long way from home. After their time basking in the glow of 'Akká, they were in love with everyone and people responded in kind.

The trip north into Lebanon and Syria was not totally devoted to pleasure; it included a visit to the wife and children of Anton Haddad, who had been away from his family for most of the last few years. Ella in particular was grateful to that devoted believer for sharing the teachings of the Faith with her and her mother during their stay in New York. Haddad's wife was thankful for the opportunity to meet them and to hear news of her husband. They found her to be highly intelligent, if not a beauty, and described her two young children, a boy of three and girl of seven, as much the same as their mother. Like her husband, she also spoke English well. Mrs Haddad travelled two hours from her village to rendezvous with them and it was immediately apparent to the Americans that the family was living in very straitened circumstances, so they insisted that Mrs Haddad accept money as a gift. Later they sent fabric to her from Paris to be made into clothes for the children.[2] These and other acts of kindness from the Goodall and Hillyer families would create over the years a special bond of love and friendship between them and the Haddads.

The two young ladies were also entertained by the tiny Bahá'í community in Beirut; the Baghdadi family was particularly hospitable. 'Of course they gave us tea and made us feel at home,' wrote Ella. After such warm treatment, she and Nell felt that 'we have been received into the fold . . .'.[3] With hearts full to overflowing, the Californians said a final goodbye to the Levant and headed south to Egypt to rejoin the Getsingers.[4]

When Nell and Ella landed again at Port Said on 5 April they were met by several Bahá'ís, among them Aḥmad Yazdí, the local Persian Consul and a prosperous Bahá'í merchant who spoke French beautifully. He and Nell were able to converse freely and the two women were charmed by his warmth and humour. They were especially touched when he presented them each with Bahá'í rings.[5] After their return to the United States, he would be a pivotal liaison, translating and transmitting their letters to the Master and then dispatching the answers, translated from Persian into French.[6]

Perhaps it was while they were passing through Port Said that Aḥmad Yazdí translated into French the Tablet 'Abdu'l-Bahá had written for Ella while she was in 'Akká. This short Tablet illustrates the Master's subtle humour and uncanny knowledge of English as he played with Ella's family name, Goodall.

He is El-Abhá!

> O my God! Thou seest Thy Servant who is believing in Thee, and supplicating through the door of Thy Oneness. Render her all good through Thy Bounty and Generosity. Thou art the Bestower, the Giver. [7]

Ella and Nell were reunited with Lua and Edward at the Hotel de Nil in Cairo where they all stayed for the week or so of their visit. The Master wanted them to receive further lessons about the Faith from Mírzá Abu'l-Faḍl and 'Abdu'l-Karím Ṭihrání (Kheiralla's first Bahá'í teacher). 'Abdu'l-Bahá undoubtedly perceived that the Americans had not been sufficiently instructed in the basics of the Faith during their limited time in the Holy Land. Extending their stay in the Haifa area was politically dangerous, so the option of being tutored in Egypt, a land under British oversight, was much less problematic. 'Abdu'l-Bahá facilitated the lessons by sending to Cairo a Persian believer who was fluent in English to serve as interpreter. This Bahá'í had arrived in 'Akká just as the last of the Western pilgrims departed, and so he had not been able to translate for them during the pilgrimage itself.[8]

It was already clear to Nell, Ella and the Getsingers that Kheiralla was an unreliable teacher and that somehow another means of educating the believers in the United States would have to be devised, so they were highly motivated to learn more, not only for themselves but to better serve the American community. Ella wrote to her mother that she should not expect Kheiralla's book to be published any time soon because it was full of inaccuracies, though she reassured her mother that the true teachings of the Faith were more wonderful than what Kheiralla had put forth. Ella also advised her mother not to speak of him as a preeminent Bahá'í teacher to other Americans and promised to explain later, but not in writing.[9]

The principal Bahá'í teacher in Cairo was the most distinguished of all Bahá'í scholars, Mírzá Abu'l-Faḍl. Like 'Abdu'l-Bahá, Mírzá Abu'l-Faḍl was born the year the Bahá'í Faith began, 1844, in the town of Gulpáygán, Iran. He came from a family of religious scholars and followed that family tradition, studying widely not only Islamic teachings, but many other areas of knowledge. He had an exceptionally keen mind that led many other scholars to revere him not only for his learning but also his wisdom. He became the head of a religious college in Iran and was ensconced in that position as perhaps the leading Persian religious scholar when he encountered the Bahá'í Faith for the first time in the 1870s. Ironically, it was questions put to him by an illiterate Bahá'í blacksmith that first opened his heart to the possibility that Bahá'u'lláh might indeed be a messenger sent by God. When he later announced his conversion to the new Cause, he was not only immediately dismissed from his position but imprisoned for five months – the first of several incarcerations for his faith – and most of his possessions were confiscated. He then began to travel throughout Iran and other Asian countries to spread the Cause and his prolific writings led to many conversions, especially among students of religion. Bahá'u'lláh himself wrote a prayer in which He supplicated that Mírzá Abu'l-Faḍl would be enabled to 'teach His truth, and to unveil that which is hidden and treasured in His Knowledge . . .'[10] In 1894, after spending most of a year in 'Akká, he was directed by 'Abdu'l-Bahá to take up residence in Cairo.[11] There he again became renowned as a preeminent scholar while teaching at the centre of Islamic learning at that time, al-Azhar University, until his allegiance to the Bahá'í Faith became known and he was dismissed for a second time from an academic post because of his beliefs.

'Abdu'l-Bahá recognized and extolled Mírzá Abu'l-Faḍl's vast knowledge which encompassed not only Bahá'í and Islamic teachings and history, but also the teachings and history of many other of the world's revealed religions. Mírzá Abu'l-Faḍl's writings expounded Christianity and Judaism as adeptly as they did the Islamic faith. But it was his sterling character that impressed the Master rather than his learning. Mírzá Abu'l-Faḍl did not simply study religion; he strove to manifest through his own life what he understood of religious truth. 'Abdu'l-Bahá praised his humility and meekness and commented that he never heard Mírzá Abu'l-Faḍl use the word 'I'. Nor did the great scholar make a show of his extensive knowledge. As 'Abdu'l-Bahá remarked, 'No one inhaled from him the odour of superiority.'[12] He lived simply and was always ready to put the happiness of others above his own ease and well-being. At the time of his passing in Cairo in 1914, 'Abdu'l-Bahá further remarked, 'It is a rare thing to find a person perfect from every direction, but he was such a person.'[13] In short, Mírzá Abu'l-Faḍl provided a very sharp contrast to Kheiralla for the American believers. One had both deep knowledge and sincere humility, the other possessed shallow knowledge and a strong ego.

The four Americans had their first session with Mírzá Abu'l-Faḍl at a favourite location for Bahá'í gatherings, a lovely garden owned by one of the Cairo believers just outside the city. Just as in 'Akká, the Americans asked Mírzá Abu'l-Faḍl to explain many obscure passages of the Bible, especially scriptural prophecies. He also spoke to them of themes such as the Day of Judgement and Islam's relationship to Christianity and the Bahá'í Faith. They apparently had only two or three interviews with him during their time in Cairo, but of all that they learned from the Egyptian believers during that week, his lessons were the ones they recorded most completely and remembered.

This was the first time that Mírzá Abu'l-Faḍl was called upon by the Master to instruct American believers, but it would not be the last. During the years ahead the great scholar would play a pivotal role in the development of the Faith in the West. And ironically, the destinies of Lua and this illustrious teacher would also intertwine in the future. Both would pass away in Cairo within two years of each other and be buried side by side, sharing one monument to their outstanding achievements in promoting the Cause of God.

The Americans apparently spent more time with 'Abdu'l-Karím than with Mírzá Abu'l-Faḍl. Kheiralla's elderly teacher took a special interest in Ella because he felt he had met her, at least in the mystical sense, five times before. 'Abdu'l-Karím promised, undoubtedly with a twinkle in his eye, to explain what he meant about 'meeting' her after she had been a devoted Bahá'í for many years and had taught the Faith to seven people. He also told her that he considered her to be his daughter and would always be with her in spirit. She was captivated by the youthfulness of this elderly man.[14] He visited the Americans daily, sometimes at their hotel and other times in his home, where he and his family extended warm Persian hospitality – which of course included tea. He was anxious to expound upon a variety of topics, including important events in Bahá'í history. His eager listeners were especially moved by the story of the death of the younger brother of 'Abdu'l-Bahá, Mírzá Mihdí – known as the Purest Branch – at the age of 22 while the family was incarcerated in the citadel of 'Akká. The version of the story that 'Abdu'l-Karím gave them did not relate all the facts accurately, but the essence of the story, the sacrifice made for the Faith by one so young, held great meaning for them.

By the time the four were concluding their lessons in Egypt, they had begun to comprehend how little they knew and how much more there was to know. Stretching before their minds and hearts was a vast ocean of spiritual knowledge. They had only begun to get their toes wet. Nell recorded what they had learned in Egypt, and wrote out more than two pages of questions in that last section of her pilgrimage journal. Many of them had not yet been answered. At the end of Nell's notes from Egypt was a list of books, perhaps further reading suggested to her by Mírzá Abu'l-Faḍl.[15] Their time in the Holy Land and with the Egyptian friends had given them many new ideas to ponder.

Even though it was only April, Cairo was unbearably hot. One day the group decided to relax rather than study, so Edward and Ella took a day-long Cook's excursion up the Nile to see Memphis and the Tombs of the Bulls, but it was too warm for Lua and Nell, who preferred to remain in Cairo. Finally, the heat got the best of all four, so they agreed it was time to conclude their visit to Egypt. Together they headed north for the sea breezes of Alexandria and then on to Port Said. They sailed for Naples and then proceeded overland to Paris, where the four stragglers were at last reunited with many of their fellow pilgrims.

Ella summed up the time in Cairo by writing that it was 'quite satisfactory' and that 'we got a lot that we needed in order to teach'. [16] She also had this to say about the believers she had met in the Holy Land, Lebanon, and Egypt:

> Always these wonderful people speak about God. It sounds strange to our matter-of-fact western ears, especially considering their frightfully difficult lives. But nevertheless the Love of God is the theme of most of their conversation.[17]

The group had much to relate to each other when they reconvened in Paris in late April or early May. In fact, it was the first opportunity Ella and Nell had to meet some of their fellow pilgrims, such as May Bolles. No two pilgrims' experiences had been exactly alike. Undoubtedly, those already in Paris were most interested to learn about the lessons from Cairo, while the Getsingers, Nell and Ella wanted to hear all about the cruise on the *S.S. Augusta Victoria* taken by the others.

During the cruise, May had used the lazy hours to get to know Julia Pearson better and the two had become friends. Julia must have poured out to May her concerns about how her family would react to her conversion to a new religion. because in a letter to Julia some months later May tried to reassure her, saying, 'I would be so glad to know how you found your family, if your Brothers find you greatly changed, and if their hearts seem drawn to the Truth, or if you must endure the long waiting for your dear ones that is my lot.'[18]

While the Getsingers were back in Paris, five of the young women posed for a group photograph, which they posted to 'Abdu'l-Bahá. May noted in that same letter to Julia that, 'indeed I remember that we all had a strange feeling that day in connection with that picture'.[19] In response, the Master sent the following prayer for the 'Five Leaves' by way of Aḥmad Yazdí in Egypt:[20]

> He is God!
>
> O my God! These are the five leaves of the tree of Thy clemency and the five servants of the sacred threshold of Thy oneness.
>
> O Lord, surround them with the angels of Thy holiness and enable them to serve Thy Cause.
>
> O my God! Make their faces to shine with the incomparable light of Thy Unity.

> O my God! Fill their hearts with a boundless joy that wafts like unto a breeze from the Abhá Kingdom, that they may be wondrous signs of Thine appearance above the all-highest Horizon.
>
> O my God! Confer upon them the gift of Thy words and praises, that they may become distinguished amongst all mankind.
>
> O my God, they are the signs of the fire of Thy love, wellsprings of the waters of Thy mercy, tokens of the light of Thy providence, and shining stars of Thy grace. Grant them such blessings as Thou hast showered upon the saintly heroines of past ages.
>
> Thou alone art He Who hath the power to choose![21]

In other group photographs of the younger members of the pilgrimage taken during that time in Paris, Lua holds a copy of the Greatest Name, a Bahá'í symbol and perhaps the most cherished item the group brought back for the Western communities. That rendition of the Greatest Name was set forth in the incomparable artistry of the master calligrapher and Apostle of Bahá'u'lláh, Mishkín-Qalam, whom they met while in the Holy Land. Copies would be made and widely circulated among the Western believers. Their luggage also contained other important items such as additional Bahá'í texts, photographs taken by Edward of the Holy Places[22] and a recording of the voice of 'Abdu'l-Bahá. Phoebe, of course, had supplied the camera and recording equipment.[23] There was also a small stack of Tablets from 'Abdu'l-Bahá addressed to specific believers back in the United States. With hindsight, it is difficult to fully appreciate how precious these items were until stock is taken of what was then available to believers in the West; as the Faith was still in its infancy, very little was available in English about the authoritative teachings of the Faith. The sacred texts and the tangible items they could look at and touch were confirming, awe-inspiring. Ella, for one, wrote about how thrilled she was that they were bringing back the Bahá'í symbol, the Greatest Name, and wrote also of how it was repeated 95 times a day by the believers – often with the aid of prayer beads.

> The Greatest Name brings you nearer than any thing else – here they say it three times a day 95 times, but another beautiful thing in the great book we are to have that contains all the commands of the Manifestation[24] is this. It says 'to work is to pray' and so whatever you are doing no matter how busy you are if it is with your heart turned toward God and God alone, it is accepted as prayer. To make it easy to say the Greatest Name they have a string of beads, 95, and I brought a string for you, that makes the counting mechanical and leaves your mind free to soar – see? [25]

Most of the returning pilgrims were bubbling over with desire to share the Faith with others. Harriet Thornburgh, old enough to be a grandmother to many in the group, taught 17-year-old Agnes Lane about Bahá'u'lláh, and she became a believer.[26] Agnes had been left behind in Egypt during the trip, so she did not meet 'Abdu'l-Bahá. Her conversion was the first tangible fruit of the pilgrimage.

The teaching work begun on the continent of Europe by May had also been taken up during the period of the pilgrimage by Emogene Hoagg in Milan, where she was tending to Marian Kheiralla's aunt, Marianne Brown. Most likely with the support of Miss Brown, Emogene had introduced the Faith to three people. Emogene wrote to Phoebe as the two Englishwomen were about to leave for London.

> Mrs Kheiralla and her Aunt expect to start away tomorrow for Paris,[27] and I shall feel quite deserted. I have so enjoyed the time with Mrs K. since her return which has been occupied with explanations of her glorious visit.
>
> One of the two I was teaching has accepted, that is my Maestro, who is really converted from non-belief, – the other, a lady, I hope may; but being advanced in years, and with her mind so clogged with Catholicism, it is difficult to turn the thoughts into a new channel, but if God is willing the light will be given her.[28]

Spiritual bounties bring with them tests of faith. How does one declare to old friends and relations that a new messenger has come from God, and that the old religion of the ancestors is no longer adequate for a new age? How does a believer face rejection and ridicule? How do they face pressure to recant and conform? The younger pilgrims especially, such as Julia, were undoubtedly apprehensive about facing those they loved when they returned home. May, whose new faith was rock-solid, offered these words of comfort to her friend Julia, as she called to mind their time together on the way home from 'Akká.

> We have both suffered since then dear, from those awful fires thro [sic] which we are passing on our way to the Kingdom. And I trust that in both of us much dross has been burned away. The process of dying to be born again of the Spirit, is long and too difficult to be described and we can only hold fast to The Master's words, 'The way to the Kingdom is strewn with difficulties, but they are all forgotten when we attain its perfect happiness.'[29]

There are tests that spring from within the body of believers as well and it was hardly surprising that it was Kheiralla who generated the first of many tests for his fellow believers while he was still in Paris in the April of 1899. Phoebe had become aware that he still owed money to the Egyptian believers, and she decided to furnish the funds to repay them. Kheiralla, however, took the bank draft intended for the Cairo friends and attempted to change the payee to himself, but the bank officials caught this forgery and notified Phoebe. Edward noted in his memoirs that when he and Lua arrived in Paris behind Kheiralla, he noticed a change in Phoebe.[30] She was beginning to wonder whom among the Bahá'ís she could truly trust. Kheiralla didn't dally long in Paris, for he was anxious to return to New York ahead of the Getsingers.

Back in the United States, the rapidly growing Bahá'í community eagerly awaited the return of their teacher as well as their fellow community members, little suspecting that a hurricane was beginning to form and would follow the pilgrims home across the Atlantic.

CHAPTER 11

Igniting Europe

Once home again in Paris, May Bolles wasted no time in teaching the Bahá'í Faith to others. She had already led one young American friend and artist, Brenetta Herrman, to accept the Faith in January of 1899 before leaving for 'Akká.[1] That spring, May soon attracted a number of people to the Cause, especially expatriate Americans. Most were friends of her brother, Randolph, especially his fellow students at École des Beaux-Arts. The second person to convert under her tutelage was Edith MacKay, a student of singing at the Paris Conservatoire, and a pupil of Massanet and Cavallo.[2] Many years later, Edith included a tribute to May in her description of how she became a Bahá'í at age 21.

> One evening (it was Christmas) I was invited to my godfather's home and on entering the salon I saw an angelic creature. It was May Bolles . . . A mysterious force drew me to her and I said: 'I believe that you have something to tell me'. 'Yes,' she said, 'I have a message for you.' She then disclosed to me this secret, which was the Bahá'í Faith.
>
> I saw her many times, and she taught me the marvelous story of the Faith . . . I always considered Mrs. Maxwell [May] as my spiritual mother.[3]

May wrote about her successful teaching work to Julia Pearson and hoped that Julia was also spreading the message.

> You will rejoice with me to know that all of my pupils are giving their hearts to God – all but one of whom I am not yet sure.
>
> Miss Herman [sic] has grown most beautifully, and she is filled with the fire of the love of God. My last pupil, Miss [?], who came all the way from America to learn of me, is about to become a teacher and has her first pupil.
>
> Our dear Master (blessed is He) sent me tablets for two of my pupils without any supplication, and I was bowed down with gratitude.[4] It seems wonderful to me to think that you are in God's vineyard amongst His chosen people where I so long to be to do His work.[5] But it shall be when He wills.[6]

One of the first persons to be strengthened in the Faith under May's enthusiastic guidance was Ethel Rosenberg, an accomplished painter of portraits and miniatures originally from Bath, England who often spent extended periods in Paris while maintaining her residence in England. Ethel came from a family that included not only artists, but also Sir William Jenner, known for his ground-breaking work on typhoid fever and the use of vaccinations. She never married. The circumstances of her introduction to the Faith during the summer of 1899 are unknown, though apparently she first heard of the Faith through Minnie Thornburgh-Cropper and her mother, Hattie Thornburgh.[7] Ethel quickly began to assist the two American women with spreading the Faith in England. This trio became the founding mothers of the British Bahá'í community: a hard-of-hearing widow, a childless divorcee, and a middle-aged spinster. Ironically, the eldest, Hattie, was the one with the fewest health problems – problems which impeded the service of the other two. All three struggled to get by financially and lacked the sort of spacious homes, such as those of several Paris believers, which could accommodate large gatherings. Despite these encumbrances, Minnie, Ethel and Hattie, like May, lost no time in their efforts to spread the Faith. Indeed, Minnie wrote to Phoebe about spending one morning 'teaching' and also visiting with Marian Kheiralla soon after both returned to the London area.[8] But the English group lacked a circle of young students such as May had access to in Paris, or a wide network of open-minded acquaintances; thus the fruits of their efforts unfolded very gradually. The slow growth of the Faith in England was exacerbated by the frequent absences from the country of one or more of the three ladies for extended periods. It seems that the longest stretch that the group was together consistently was the initial period of about a year and a half after the summer of 1899.

The London trio was split up for the first time during the winter of 1900–1901 when Harriet Thornburgh returned to 'Akká in the company of Ethel, who was making her first pilgrimage.[9] During the three months they were away, Minnie continued the teaching work in England by herself. Ethel did not linger long in London after she and Hattie returned, but within months was off to the United States for an extended period, including a visit to Phoebe during the summer of 1901 at her Pleasanton home, thereby strengthening the connection between the London and California believers. The mother and daughter team continued the work in England during Ethel's absence but by the end of that same year Minnie again was suffering from ill health to such a degree that her mother feared she was at death's door. Phoebe came to the rescue, as she had so many times before, by enabling Minnie to come for a long visit to California as her guest where the good weather could aid her recovery. While Minnie was away from England, departing during April of 1902, Harriet took up residence in a Paris boarding house whose guests came from a diverse group of nationalities, which pleased her.[10] Undoubtedly, Harriet was also happy to be able to be part of the more lively Paris Bahá'í community with its young people and growing number of attendees. It was Ethel's turn to shoulder the teaching work in London alone. Writing to Phoebe in 1903, Harriet expressed frustration with the teaching work in England, remarking that most of the people who came to the weekly Bahá'í meetings in London were not really sincere seekers of the truth. Nevertheless, a few people did respond positively and the little group grew, with Ethel, and to a lesser extent Minnie, informally carrying out the roles of organizer and leader. By the autumn of that year, Minnie was back in Europe, but staying in Paris with her mother while Ethel kept the teaching work in England alive. And so it went, with the three working like a relay team, carrying on the work alone for periods of time and at other times sharing in it together.

While Minnie and Harriet were absent from England, Ethel was able to participate in an opportunity to present information about the Báb to the general public. Though the three ladies in London did not have easy access to university students, unlike the Paris Bahá'í community, teaching opportunities among intellectuals did arise because of interest in the Faith generated by orientalists at British universities such as E. G. Browne. One such distinguished professor from Oxford University, J. Estlin Carpenter,[11] gave a public lecture on the Báb in London on 10 February 1903, and Ethel was invited to attend as the representative of the Bahá'í Faith.

> . . . Professor Estlin Carpenter of Oxford came to London at the request of his friend the Reverend Mr Corbet, who also resides at Oxford, to give an account of the Life and teachings of the Great Báb – and they requested me to be present at the meeting, and to speak. There were present about 120 to 150 of the most thoughtful & spiritually-minded men & women. Professor Carpenter gave the most beautiful lecture, which lasted just one hour, after which Mr Corbet, the clergyman, asked me to speak and answer questions, for the remaining half an hour, which I did. All the people were most kind and sympathetic, and at the end, I was told it was the best and most harmonious meeting ever held by the Christo-Theosophic Society, and that the people had gone away filled with enthusiasm and interest, and desiring to hear more of Thy Great Cause – for many of those present had never before heard so much as the name of the Báb.[12]

Like all the small stalwart groups of believers in the West, the London believers were hampered by the lack of published materials. This was remedied in part by Myron Phelps, an American lawyer from New York who, though never becoming a believer, visited 'Abdu'l-Bahá in December of 1902 and wrote an article about it for the British press. British believers found this publication to be especially helpful in answering the questions of those who became interested in the Faith as a result of talks by orientalists, such as Professor Carpenter.[13] Ethel in particular was hoping to make more inroads with 'these thoughtful and intelligent Western students and University men' such as the ones she met at Professor Carpenter's London talk.

> In our country of England it is these men who are the most thoughtful and wide-minded and developed – and it is these earnest and enlightened souls who will accept the Teachings if they are presented to them on a true and philosophical basis, and not in the utterly inadequate manner that has been heretofore the case.[14]

With Hattie and her daughter finally both back in England,[15] Ethel was able to return for a period of months to 'Akká in 1904, where she continued to improve her knowledge of the Persian language in order to assist with translations into English. At the beginning of 1905 Ethel went away yet again, this time to Paris, leaving the London work to Minnie and Hattie. While there, Ethel gave talks on the Faith and met with individual believers, especially American expatriates, in order to deepen their understanding of the verities of the Faith by drawing upon what she had gained during two visits to the Holy Land.[16] With these comings and goings, the London group was in many respects a satellite of the more rapidly expanding Paris Bahá'í community and would not begin to grow at a similar pace until after 1907, when Lady Blomfield[17] and her daughters heard of the Faith while visiting Paris. The teaching work in England finally quickened when that outstanding British woman applied her great capacities to promoting the Faith, becoming Minnie's friend and ally. Nevertheless, bolstered continuously by the unfailing prayers, guidance and encouragement of 'Abdu'l-Bahá, the devoted, tireless efforts of Harriet, Minnie and Ethel[18] during those first years scattered the requisite sparks that enkindled England.

In October of 1905 Helen Goodall received a letter, not from Minnie but from Ethel Rosenberg, reporting that Harriet Thornburgh had become the first of that special group of Western pilgrims to pass to the next world.[19] Her death had been quick and unexpected – what Harriet had always said she wanted rather than to go after a long illness in bed. Ethel had joined Hattie and Minnie for Sunday lunch in London and the mother and daughter had both seemed 'very bright and happy'. But on the afternoon of the following day Hattie suffered a stroke which left her severely paralysed on one side. She passed away on Wednesday 19 October on her 67th birthday. Ethel reported, 'For minutes after her death the most wonderful look of peace and happiness transfigured her face.'[20]

Minnie was devastated and too overcome with grief to convey the news herself, even to Phoebe.[21] She received a letter of condolence from 'Abdu'l-Bahá in which He said that He shared her grief at the loss of her honoured mother and described in joyous words the limitless realm to which her soul had flown. He encouraged Minnie to once again resume her spiritual responsibilities to carry forward the Faith despite her grief.[22]

Harriet did not figure much in the correspondence and journals of the Hearst pilgrims, perhaps because her increasing deafness precluded easily joining in conversations. She always pushed her daughter to the forefront anyway. Nonetheless, the absence of many accounts of her does not accurately reflect the depths of her devotion. She spent at least three months in 'Akká in 1901, during which time she taught English to about 12 or 14 members of the household.[23] Ali-Kuli Khan related that he became much attached to her during that second pilgrimage, in part because she nursed him back to good health during a period when he was ill while serving in the Master's household.[24] In 1903 in a letter to Phoebe, Harriet proposed that she, Minnie and Phoebe return to 'Akká, promising it would be better than the first visit because Minnie had been trying to learn Persian and members of the household were learning English under Harriet's own tutelage.[25] Phoebe did not take her up on the suggestion but commented in a letter to her old friend Clara Anthony that she thought it would be a good idea if it was arranged for Harriet to live in 'Akká to the end of her life.[26]

It would have been easy to all but overlook Harriet Thornburgh, because she only lived seven years after embracing the Faith and because her daughter Mary Virginia Thornburgh-Cropper overshadows her in the annals of the Cause since Minnie is considered to have been the first active believer in England and lived long enough to serve on its first National Spiritual Assembly as well as to carry out many services during the Master's visit to England and Scotland. Nevertheless, Shoghi Effendi ensured that this devoted, steadfast mother, who was one of the three founders of the British Bahá'í community, was never forgotten. He posthumously named Harriet one of the Disciples of 'Abdu'l-Bahá, a very high honour.[27] Quiet forms of service – even if that service is simply being wholeheartedly supportive of the actions of others – as well as unfailing constancy in faith; those virtues were Harriet's hallmarks. And Harriet was able to make 'Abdu'l-Bahá laugh!

Minnie, on the other hand, has come to be regarded as the Mother of the British Bahá'í community. She served the Faith in many capacities until old age and ill health no longer allowed her to do so. She would be especially instrumental in assisting the Master during his visits to those shores in 1911 and 1913. After she passed away in London on 17 March 1938,[28] Shoghi Effendi expressed his thoughts in a letter to Lady Blomfield.

> What has profoundly grieved the Guardian, however, is the very sad, and indeed distressing, news of the passing away of Mrs. Thornburgh-Cropper. Her departure must have surely been deeply felt by the believers, and especially by the older ones who knew her well and intimately. You will all miss her lovely presence, and the love and affection which she cherished for the friends. Shoghi Effendi will specially pray at the Holy Shrines for the soul of our departed sister that in the Realms Above it may progress and attain the highest state of spirituality and peace.
>
> *[Postscript in the handwriting of Shoghi Effendi:]*
> I will continue to pray for you, as well as for the soul of our dear, distinguished and departed Bahá'í sister and co-worker, whose passing I truly deplore.[29]

In June of 1899 Phoebe Hearst let go her Paris apartment, and so the Bolles family were forced to secure other accommodations. May's mother, Mary Bolles, (and Nell Hillyer) assisted Phoebe with the disposition of her Paris furnishings. The Bolles family moved to 100 Rue du Bac, not far from the renowned Bon Marché department store. It was to that apartment that one of Randolph Bolles's fellow architectural students, a young man from Washington, D.C., came calling in the autumn of 1899. Charles Mason Remey, who went by the name Mason, was the son of an admiral in the United States navy stationed in Washington, D.C., thus Mason was accustomed to moving in socially prominent circles and knew Phoebe, Anne Apperson and Agnes Lane from his Washington connections. As an eligible young bachelor from a good family, he had been invited to some of the Hearst parties held in Paris. Through those occasions he had come to know May's mother in her role of chaperone of the young ladies and he had become exceedingly fond of that good-hearted matron. May, however, was only a passing acquaintance from those social affairs. Mason was sincerely interested in spiritual truths; therefore when he heard about May's religious pilgrimage to the Holy Land, he was eager to learn about the new religion to which she had become fervently dedicated, even though he was devoted to Christ. Spurred on by this desire to know more, he called on May one evening in order to make enquiries, but found only her mother at home. He recounted that Mary Bolles 'told me that she could give me no information, as practically no information had been given her (in those days the Teachings were given only in secret), but she assured me it was very fine and knew it was just what I needed'.[30]

May taught the Faith to Mason as she herself had been taught, using the thirteen lessons developed by Kheiralla, despite having gained many insights about the Faith while sitting at the feet of 'Abdu'l-Bahá herself and being aware of the growing scepticism about Kheiralla. She continued the secrecy imposed by Kheiralla, only getting to the heart, the 'pith', of the lessons after a long build-up. Mason arranged to meet with May over a series of weeks to receive the lessons one at a time. Writing later of this course of study, he recounted that, 'They were short lessons, as I remember, and I was anxious to learn more rapidly, but she stuck to her system and would only give me one lesson at a time. These lessons were interspersed with prayer, and I joined with her in this spiritual exercise with great anticipation of what was to follow.'[31] He was especially relieved and pleased that what he learned did not undermine his love for Christ, but rather enhanced his understanding of Christianity.[32] What he did not fully understand was that May expected him to keep the lessons confidential. He had an American friend, another architectural student, who hailed from Omaha, Nebraska, 25-year-old Herbert W. Hopper.[33] Herbert was also seeking spiritually and was anxious to find out what Mason was learning from May.

> Each lesson that I received I went immediately to Herbert Hopper and shared it with him. When, through some remark that I made, May discovered that I was passing each lesson on to Herbert she immediately stopped that – told me that I must not say anything until I had arrived myself and then I would really have something to tell him. Herbert was impatient when I told him I wouldn't be able to tell him anything more until the end of the course.[34]

Finally, on New Year's Eve of 1899 as the calendar was about to turn to a new century, May gave Mason 'The Message'. He was so ecstatic that he spent most of the day in a daze.[35] Shortly thereafter, Herbert also completed the lessons and became a believer. With the addition of those two gentlemen, the number of believers in Paris rose to four – all Americans – May, Edith, Mason and Herbert.[36] The group grew in the coming months with the arrival of a believer from New York City, and the conversion of two other Americans who were in Paris for a few months, including May's cousin, Helen Ellis Cole, widow of a prominent New York lawyer and daughter of a wealthy financier. The first meeting of the Bahá'ís of Paris as a group occurred in Mason's small apartment, accessible only by climbing a multitude of stairs, on a Sunday morning in 1900. Unfortunately, the 'spiritual mother' of them all, May, was ill that day and unable to attend. It was, nonetheless, memorable as Mason remembered it.

> Herbert Hopper, Edith MacKaye [sic], Mrs. Conner[37] and Marie Squires[38] and myself made up the group. We read the few prayers and Tablets that we had, and we talked of the Cause, but . . . in those days we had very little real information about the Teachings. We depended mostly upon our faith and on our feelings rather than actual information. It was a time however of great Spiritual romance and adventure. The great religious fire of the Cause was uppermost in our minds; we all sang as it were a lyric Spiritual Song, and like all youth the adventure and the new outlook created a tremendous enthusiasm in our hearts.[39]

The Faith in Paris continued to revolve around the American expatriate community, and especially the American students at the École des Beaux-Arts. Mason wrote of the first time that the little group of believers decided to work as a group to spread the Cause; they chose the annual ball for the American architectural students for the occasion. The eight Bahá'ís assembled at ten o'clock that evening in the large hall of a public building in the Faubourg Saint Germain area. Despite their small number, they were aware that the Faith had already generated a buzz among their close friends and acquaintances and that evening they were determined to make the most of it. Before entering the ballroom, they said prayers together and prepared themselves to teach the Faith. During the course of the party, those who showed an interest in the Faith were guided off the dance floor to one of the alcoves along the side for more in-depth conversations about the Cause. (Those seating spaces were draped with tapestries that muffled noise, so they were quite private.) As Mason recalled, 'It was the first time in Paris that we had *en masse* invaded a group of people with the intention of teaching.'[40]

Mason used the occasion of a 'fancy dress'[41] dance, this one held at a boarding house for young ladies, to teach the Faith to Marion Jack, a round-faced, 34-year-old artist from St John, New Brunswick, Canada, who was residing in the Latin Quarter of Paris to study painting. She must have been quite a sight that evening dressed in her own creation, a fiery red costume made of crinkled paper and topped with a huge hat decorated with yellow flowers. He was not put off by her attire and she became attracted to his religion – after some initial hesitation.

> When I first heard of the Cause in Paris, I heard of it as something 'queer'. This thought made me curious & fortunately I was led to someone, Mr Charles Remey, who explained things so beautifully & reverently, that I found the 'queer' was something great & precious.[42]

The year 1900 saw more declarations in Paris and, even better, visits from American pilgrims as they travelled to and from the Holy Land. The Getsingers made a second visit to the Master in September and visited Paris en route. The Arthur Pillsbury Dodge family from the New York Bahá'í community passed through. 'Abdu'l-Bahá, ever concerned about the spiritual development of these tender new believers, not only encouraged the Paris community through correspondence, usually channelled through May, but also by sending 'Abdu'l-Karím and Mírzá Abu'l-Faḍl to meet with and teach the believers in France. Both spent time in Paris in 1900 on their way to New York, with Anton Haddad then accompanying Mírzá Abu'l-Faḍl as his interpreter.

Before Mírzá Abu'l-Faḍl's departure for the West, 'Abdu'l-Bahá had given him many instructions, including some regarding his time in Paris.

> According to both spoken and written reports there is in Paris a new-found receptivity . . . The divinely enkindled flame of guidance must now be quickly fanned into a blaze so that, by the heavenly brilliance of its light, it may dispel these gloomy shadows, and allow the Day-Star of the World to shine forth in all its splendour.[43]

During his stopover in Paris, Mírzá Abu'l-Faḍl's talks with the believers and friends centred around what interested the Western believers the most, that is, the Bible and the fulfilment of Biblical prophecy.[44]

Among those who accepted the Faith in Paris during the year of the great scholar's visit was another young lady from a wealthy, socially prominent family, Laura Clifford Barney.[45] Twenty-one-year-old Laura, called 'Elsa' by her friends, had first heard about the Faith in Washington, D.C., but it was May who confirmed her. Aided by her dogged determination to learn Persian and Arabic, this scholarly young American's serious inquiry into the teachings of the Faith would result in the creation of one of the most significant Bahá'í texts. All Bahá'ís of the future would be indebted to Laura for *Some Answered Questions*, a major work of Bahá'í scripture based upon questions she systematically put to 'Abdu'l-Bahá over an extended period of time during repeated visits to 'Akká. It was for many years the primary book expounding topics of interest to those of Christian backgrounds.

Laura's future husband, and the first Frenchman to become a Bahá'í,

Hippolyte Dreyfus, was also introduced to the Faith during 1900 and taught by May. He was a lawyer from a Jewish background, and most of his family also embraced the Cause. He would write one of the first introductory books about the Faith in French and for many years provided translations of the Bahá'í Writings into French. He also travelled widely in Asia in order to spread the Cause. He was especially appreciated by Shoghi Effendi for the assistance he provided to the Guardian in the period following the passing of 'Abdu'l-Bahá.[46]

During January of 1901, a small group from Paris and London went on pilgrimage to 'Akká. Charles Mason Remey, Laura Clifford Barney, Helen Ellis Cole, Edith Tewksbury Jackson, and Sigurd Russell[47] joined Ethel Rosenberg, the Getsingers and Harriet Thornburgh – all Americans except for Ethel.[48] By then, the Getsingers were becoming part of the Master's household, though during most of the time the London/Paris group was in 'Akká, Lua and Edward were in Egypt again receiving additional instruction from Mírzá Abu'l-Faḍl. The Getsingers returned to 'Akká from Cairo in March of 1901, toward the end of the stay of the believers who came from Europe.

The growing number of Westerners making the pilgrimage to 'Akká led to the conversion of another important believer who would for a time contribute to the development of the Faith in Paris. In 1900, a young American lady from a distinguished family of Christian missionaries, who had grown up at the family mission post in Hawaii, was touring Europe. While staying at a *pensione* in Rome, Agnes B. Alexander was introduced to the Bahá'í Faith by Charlotte Brittingham Dixon[49] and her two daughters, who were on their way home to the United States after visiting 'Abdu'l-Bahá in 'Akká. Mrs Dixon gave Agnes May's Paris address and at the end of January 1901 May responded to her first inquiry with a warm letter addressed to 'My precious Sister!' in which she wrote, 'Please God we may soon welcome you in our midst in Paris and that you may then receive the full Revelation, and much help and instruction.' By then, there were a few pamphlets and prayers in English and these were enclosed with the letter. She also warned Agnes that, despite her enthusiasm as a new believer, she should be cautious in telling others of the Faith 'for every soul is not ripe'.

Agnes arrived in Paris during the spring of 1901 where May quickly became her 'spiritual mother' – in fact she had become the 'spiritual mother' to a growing 'spiritual family' of believers, still primarily Americans. Weekly meetings continued to be held at Mason's student apartment. Agnes never forgot the first one she attended or the atmosphere that pervaded that small spiritually-intoxicated group at that time:

> The first meeting I attended there, someone asked as I entered the room with May, 'Is she a believer?' The reply was, 'Look at her face!' As I looked around the room, I saw the same look of peace and light on the faces. They had found their Lord and were at rest . . . Such an atmosphere of pure light pervaded the Paris meetings that one was transported, as it were, from the world of man to that of God. In the spiritual light of those meetings all questions vanished. One of the Paris believers, Berthalin Lexow,[50] wrote of that time: 'We were a little group of about twenty in Paris but there was such a strong feeling of unity among us, we had so much love for one another, which made us as one.'[51]

As May worked to spread the Faith, she of course wrote to 'Abdu'l-Bahá, beseeching that she should receive divine confirmations and assistance in serving the Cause.[52] In response, the Master wrote: 'Verily, I remember thee in my prayer and supplication to God, and implore my Lord to make thee a flame of the Fire of the Love of God.'[53]

The Bolles family was accustomed to spending the months of July and August at a resort town along the French coast of Brittany and usually let go their rented Paris apartment during that time. But May refused to leave Paris during the summer of 1901 despite her family's insistence. 'Abdu'l-Bahá had expressly asked her to stay in Paris until further notice and she would do nothing contrary to his wishes even if her obedience resulted in a fuss with her mother. May moved into a small apartment connected to the spacious home of a new believer – a wealthy, elderly American widow, Edith Tewksbury Jackson, while her family was away from Paris. 'Madame Jackson', as she is usually remembered in Bahá'í literature, was a soft-hearted Bostonian from a prominent Massachusetts family[54] who had married a wealthy Frenchman. The couple apparently had no children, thus she inherited most, if not all, of her husband's fortune, including a luxurious Paris apartment. She was part of Phoebe's social circle, both in Paris and the United States. Edith Jackson became a devoted believer through May and frequently opened her home for Bahá'í gatherings.

One day that late summer of 1901, a 29-year-old Englishman found his way to the Jackson apartment looking for May. Thomas Breakwell was an idealistic, capable young man who had emigrated to the United States in 1887 just shy of his seventeenth birthday. He came from the small market town of Woking in Surrey. He first lived in Chicago and then moved to New Orleans, Louisiana where he was employed as a manager in cotton mills.[55] The port city of New Orleans that he knew at the end of the nineteenth century was one where the wealth of the few was gained by the sweat of the many. It had a polyglot people, including many of African heritage who were still recovering from the terrible effects of slavery. Child workers of all races were exploited in the mills and factories. Even though Thomas's job paid well, his conscience tormented him because his employment afforded numerous opportunities to witness at first hand abuse of workers – especially the child labourers, many of whom were probably descendants of slaves. Troubled, he had taken a leave of absence from his work and headed for Europe hoping to forget the injustices that gnawed at him, by visiting his British family and touring that continent. Perhaps another more ominous reason for the journey was to seek treatment for his recurring tuberculosis.

Thomas had been raised in an evangelical Christian family that belonged to the Primitive Methodist Church. But as an adult, he had started on his own spiritual quest and had become drawn to the Theosophical Society, which had been founded in the United States in 1875. This group was mystical and promoted exotic oriental religious teachings. En route to Liverpool, one of his fellow passengers on board the steamer happened to be a friend of May Bolles. This lady, a Mrs Milner, quickly sized Thomas up as a seeker of religious truth who might well be interested in the new religion May had espoused. So when he arrived in Paris several months later,[56] Mrs Milner took him to meet May.[57]

May later recalled the lovely summer day that she first encountered Thomas and her lady friend standing on her doorstep. He impressed her immediately. She later remembered him as being of 'medium height, slender, erect and graceful, with intense eyes and an indescribable charm'.[58] The conversation that day centred on the Theosophical Society – at the time a very fashionable group – as well as on his background and projected summer travels. But May could not keep her eyes away from Thomas because she 'discerned a very rare person of high standing and culture, simple, natural, intensely real in his attitude toward life and his fellowmen'.[59] He likewise studied her with 'a searching gaze'[60] and at the end of the first meeting asked if he could call upon her again the next day.

When Thomas arrived the following morning, he was in an indescribably radiant mood. May recounted that his eyes were burning with 'a hidden fire'. He asked her with great earnestness if she noticed anything different about him from the day before. She said he appeared to be happy. He related to her what had come over him during the interim.

> When I was here yesterday . . . I felt a power, an influence that I had felt once before in my life, when for a period of three months I was continually in communion with God. I felt during that time like one moving in a rarefied atmosphere of light and beauty. My heart was afire with love

> for the supreme Beloved, I felt at peace, at one with all my fellow-men. Yesterday when I left you I went alone down the Champs Élysées, the air was warm and heavy, not a leaf was stirring, when suddenly a wind struck me and whirled around me, and in that wind a voice said, with an indescribable sweetness and penetration, 'Christ has come again! Christ has come again!'[61]

Thomas asked if she thought him crazy. 'No,' May replied, 'you are just becoming sane.'[62] May began to tell him all about the Faith, apparently no longer using the lessons of Kheiralla, but from her heart. He took it all in and longed for more. His strongest desire became to visit 'Abdu'l-Bahá. He cancelled his earlier travel plans and decided to accompany Herbert Hopper, who had already received permission to make a pilgrimage to 'Akká. Thomas shot off a supplication to the Master which said, simply,

> My Lord, I believe, forgive me, Thy servant Thomas Breakwell.

May sent his declaration of faith off to 'Akká with a request that he be allowed to join Herbert Hopper.

The very evening after May mailed this request to the Master, she found a little blue cablegram waiting for her at her apartment. It was from 'Abdu'l-Bahá and said, 'You may leave Paris at any time!' Through her obedience, she had fulfilled the will of the Master and led an angelic soul to his Lord. With 'winged feet' she began to immediately prepare to join her family in Brittany. When her mother, who had greatly resented May's unwavering devotion and service to the Cause after her pilgrimage, heard the full story, she began to cry and said, 'you have, indeed, a wonderful Master'.[63]

When Thomas returned to Paris in the autumn from his pilgrimage, he began to transform the growing group of twenty-five or thirty believers. May said that he became

> . . . the guiding star of our group, his calmness and strength, his intense fervor, his immediate and all penetrating grasp of the vast import to mankind in this age of the Revelation of Bahá'u'lláh, released among us forces which constituted a new Epoch in the Cause in France. In the meetings he spoke with a simplicity and eloquence which won the hearts and quickened the souls, and the secret of his potent influence lay in his supreme recognition of the Manifestation of God in the Báb and in Bahá'u'lláh, and of the sublime Center of the Covenant, 'Abdu'l-Bahá. Not by reason but by faith did he triumph.[64]

Alas, the time given to Thomas to serve the Faith, and especially the Paris Bahá'í community, was short. Tuberculosis finally claimed him and he passed away in June 1902 at the age of 30.[65]

That same year the Paris Bahá'í community also had to endure the loss of its 'spiritual mother', but for a happy reason. One day in 1899, May's brother Randolph brought home another architectural student to join the family for lunch. When he left, May demanded that her brother never bring home 'that big Canadian' again. Taken aback by his sister's reaction to his friend, Randolph demanded to know why. 'Because he stared at me all the time!' But that young Canadian was determined to return because during the course of that lunch he had decided to marry May. William Sutherland Maxwell was tall and broad-shouldered with bright blue eyes, chestnut hair and rosy cheeks that gave away his Scottish ancestry. He was also an exceptionally gifted artist who did well at the École des Beaux-Arts school of architecture. This 'big Canadian' was so overawed by the frail young lady some four years his senior that he could barely get the words out of his mouth when he proposed marriage to her.[66] May, as always, would not do anything without the blessing of 'Abdu'l-Bahá, who consented to her departure from Paris and told her, 'With the strength of thy heart promote the word of God . . . in that remote region [Canada].' The wedding took place in 1902 in London, after which the newlyweds set up residence in Montreal from where May turned her energies to establishing the Bahá'í community in Canada. After some years, she led her devoted husband to the Bahá'í Faith as well. During that first year in Montreal, May supplicated the Master that she might be 'as a mountain of Faith and strength in Thy Cause, to withstand every test and calamity, which God may cause to descend, and the violence of storms.'[67] Indeed she did endure every test and calamity as a mountain of faith, for to her last breath May got up from her couch and soldiered on to serve the Cause of God despite the relentless toll it took on her chronically weak body. Her poor health was such that throughout her adult life she was little better than an invalid. She passed away quickly of a heart attack while in Argentina in 1940 during a teaching trip which she undertook in response to a call for Bahá'ís to travel to South America to open that vast continent to the Faith. Prudence would have dictated that she remain at home in Canada and not embark upon such an arduous journey because of her infirmities, but as always, she forged ahead because it was in service to her Lord. She was posthumously named a 'martyr' by Shoghi Effendi.

May's record of accomplishments during those three short years following her pilgrimage was remarkable. In essence, she single-handedly established the Faith on a firm footing on the continent of Europe. It is a tribute to her as a teacher that the Paris community continued on – different because of her absence, but still vibrant for years to come. Those she led into its fold went on to provide invaluable services to the Faith. The most noteworthy are as follows:

- Agnes Alexander carried the Faith not only to her native Hawaii but also to Japan. She was named a Hand of the Cause of God by Shoghi Effendi.

- May's husband, William Sutherland Maxwell, joined his brother's architectural firm in Montreal which became the foremost architectural firm of Canada for the time, designing many Canadian landmarks. But his most famous accomplishment as an architect was the design of the superstructure for the Shrine of the Báb in Haifa which dominates the city skyline. He was named a Hand of the Cause of God by Shoghi Effendi.

- Charles Mason Remey as a young man travelled extensively in both the United States, Europe and Asia to spread the Faith. In 1909, in the company of Howard Struven, he circled the globe, especially assisting with the work of the Faith in Hawaii, Japan, Burma and India. He was the architect for the International Bahá'í Archives Building, the Western Haifa Pilgrim House,[68] and the first Houses of Worship for Africa and Australia as well as those planned for Iran and Mount Carmel. He was appointed to the International Bahá'í Council by Shoghi Effendi and served as its president. He was also named a Hand of the Cause of God by Shoghi Effendi.[69]

- Hippolyte Dreyfus and his wife, Laura Clifford Barney, gave great service to the Faith, especially by translating the Bahá'í Writings into French and English. Hippolyte Dreyfus was named a Disciple of 'Abdu'l-Bahá by Shoghi Effendi.

- Thomas Breakwell, despite his brief time as a believer, was named by Shoghi Effendi as one of three luminaries shedding lustre on the annals of the Irish, English and Scottish communities.[70]

- Marion Jack was given the nickname 'General Jack' by 'Abdu'l-Bahá because of her firm and determined service to the Cause. She pioneered to Bulgaria and refused to leave her 'spiritual children' after that

Part of the group in Paris, May 1899, shortly after returning from their pilgrimage. Back row, left to right: Julia Pearson, Lua Getsinger, Brenetta Herrman, Edward Getsinger. Front row, left to right: May Bolles, Anne Apperson. In response to this photograph, 'Abdu'l-Bahá sent a Tablet addressed to the 'Five Holy Leaves' (see pp.171-2), that is, the five young ladies (all wearing oriental headscarves)

Laura Clifford Barney

Agnes Alexander

Hippolyte Dreyfus

Marion Jack

Ethel Rosenberg

country was invaded by Nazi Germany even though she understood the danger that remaining there as a Canadian citizen posed to her personally. She endured severe hardships during the Second World War in order to stay at her pioneer post and continued to withstand even more troubles during the takeover of the country by the Communists at the end of the war. She is remembered as one of the greatest of the intrepid Bahá'í pioneers who spread the Faith across the globe. She was certainly among the most heroic. Her landscape paintings of the sites in the Holy Land associated with the Faith continue to grace a number of Bahá'í Holy Places.

- Edith MacKay de Bons took the Faith to Switzerland during a visit there in 1902. She married a Swiss dentist, who became a devoted believer. She and her husband visited the Master in 'Akká in 1906.[71]

- Herbert and Marie (Squires) Hopper were firm believers to the end of their lives. Tragically, Herbert died in 1908 at the age of 34 from tuberculosis. His family concluded that he contracted that disease through nursing Thomas Breakwell. While on pilgrimage with Thomas, he had asked to give his life for the Faith as a martyr. When 'Abdu'l-Bahá sent Marie Hopper a loving Tablet following the passing of Herbert, He affirmed that Herbert's wish had been granted. Their daughter and her descendants have served the Bahá'í Faith tirelessly in El Salvador.[72]

- Helen Ellis Cole left a substantial sum of money for the establishment of the meeting building at the Green Acre Bahá'í School in Maine when she passed away in 1906. She was also the one who asked and received from the Master the first English translation of the Kitáb-i-Íqán, translated for her by Ali-Kuli Khan.

- Edith Tewksbury Jackson remained a steadfast believer and played a role in the construction of the House of the Master in Haifa in addition to opening her Paris home to Bahá'í gatherings for many years. She made several pilgrimages to Haifa and 'Abdu'l-Bahá himself made a special point of visiting her when she was elderly and infirm during His visit to Paris in 1911.

- Sydney Sprague was the first Western believer to visit the Bahá'ís in Iran, the cradle of the Faith; and he was the second Western believer to strengthen the bonds between East and West through marriage to an Iranian Bahá'í. As a young believer, he travelled extensively, including a journey with Mason Remey to Odessa, Baku and 'Ishqábád to bolster those Bahá'í communities.[73]

- Edith Sanderson, a Californian and daughter of the Chief Justice of the California Supreme Court, Silas Sanderson, served the Faith tirelessly in Europe, rendering especially noteworthy service during the First and Second World Wars.[74]

The rise of the Paris community with its illustrious early members was one of the first tangible results of the pilgrimage. That special community would be sore tried in the years ahead, as well as incomparably blessed by the visit of 'Abdu'l-Bahá in 1911. Nonetheless, that brief period of less than four years when May served as its spiritual mother would forever be remembered as halcyon days when the spiritual vibrancy of the Paris Bahá'í community sent forth rays of light to many corners of the world.

CHAPTER 12

Kheiralla's Downfall

The letters penned by the pilgrims while in the Holy Land for the believers in the United States were tantalizing; they confirmed that the new Faith was wondrous indeed, that 'Abdu'l-Bahá was more than anyone could have imagined and they invariably included expressions of exasperation – that it was impossible to put into words what they were experiencing and feeling. This correspondence must have generated much longing anticipation and heightened expectations among the American believers as the travellers began to return home from the fountainhead of knowledge and inspiration. Certainly they must have been especially pleased that the first to return to New York after the stopover in Paris was none other than their beloved teacher, Ibrahim Kheiralla.

Kheiralla, however, boarded the ship at Cherbourg a troubled man. Nothing during his seven months away from his flock had transpired as he had hoped. His life had begun to unravel during that brief period and he was determined to stem the disintegration, to turn his fortunes around, to regain the ascendancy he had achieved earlier through his development of the Bahá'í Faith in America. Unlike his fellow pilgrims, he had not gone to 'Akká as a suppliant seeking guidance but as one seeking affirmation. He had expected to be rewarded for taking the Faith to America. 'Abdu'l-Bahá owed him! And he had been rewarded with praise and showered with loving kindness, but it was not enough. Accolades and honours were not what he wanted most. He had expected to be given a title that would solidify his position as head of the Faith in the West. He had anticipated as well that there would be material compensation for his long hours and extraordinary efforts to take the Faith to new communities. Instead he was returning empty-handed, with neither a title nor even hope of funds. He had ruined his relationship with Phoebe during the return visit to Paris by attempting to subvert the funds meant for the Egyptian friends, so he could no longer count upon her largesse for more than the price of his ticket to New York. Even his marriage had fallen apart during his time in 'Akká. Marian had left him for good once they departed from Haifa, and had remained in Europe.

What thoughts must have swirled through his head as he paced the ship's decks during his Atlantic crossing! Accompanying him to New York were his daughters, Nabitha and Labitha. The eldest wanted to marry a man from Lebanon and, of course, Kheiralla had to provide her with a dowry, yet he had no means of livelihood. He had counted upon making his fortune from the sale of his introductory book about the Faith. Anton Haddad was still translating the manuscript from English into Arabic when Kheiralla had hurriedly left for his pilgrimage the previous September. Kheiralla had anticipated when embarking for the Holy Land that the Master would endorse the book, it would be speedily published, and his financial worries would be over. But it became clear to Kheiralla after spending some time in the presence of the Master that he could not submit the manuscript in its original form, so he had written to Haddad asking that he not forward it to 'Akká. Unfortunately, that letter did not arrive in time; Haddad had already sent it on with Nell Hillyer and Ella Goodall in February. The Master praised the effort but said that changes would have to be made, and this was unacceptable to Kheiralla.

In fact, Kheiralla saw no reason why his own interpretations of the Faith shouldn't be the accepted ones for the North American community, even if they were not in accord with those of the Head of the Faith. During their time together in the Holy Land, Kheiralla and Edward Getsinger began to spar with each other over Kheiralla's teachings about the Faith – did they in fact represent the true Bahá'í interpretations of Biblical scripture. The Master was called upon to intervene and refused to take sides. He patiently explained that Biblical verses lent themselves to a plethora of meanings; therefore, even though Kheiralla's interpretations of certain Biblical passages were valid, they were not the only way in which the verses could be understood. This reasonable and kind approach only inflamed Kheiralla.[1] His thirteen lessons were primarily based upon his interpretations of Biblical prophecies, and by opening up to other understandings his authority as the preeminent Bahá'í teacher in America would be undermined.[2]

Kheiralla also argued about Bahá'í doctrine with no less a person than Ḥájí Mírzá Muḥammad Taqíy-i-Abharí (known as Ibn-i-Abhar), one of the four believers named a Hand of the Cause of God by Bahá'u'lláh Himself, who was visiting the Holy Land while Kheiralla was there. Ibn-i-Abhar was one of the few believers in the Holy Land who had correctly perceived Kheiralla's lack of true understanding of the verities of the Faith. One open discussion between the two became so rancorous that 'Abdu'l-Bahá Himself was called upon to mediate. He diplomatically suggested that the origin of the disagreement lay in semantics but went on to warn Kheiralla to desist from advocating some of his ideas that ran counter to the true teachings of the Faith.[3]

In essence, Kheiralla's hopes collided with the fundamental verities of the Faith. The Bahá'í Faith upholds the principle that everyone has the right –

indeed the duty – to freely seek out truth for himself or herself, and all are urged not to permit themselves to follow blindly the traditions of the past or whatever may now be presented to them by others. The Faith also teaches that, to preserve the unity of the Faith and the purity of its teachings, Bahá'u'lláh established, in writing, a Covenant by which, after His passing, all should turn to 'Abdu'l-Bahá, who is the Centre of that Covenant, whom Bahá'u'lláh appointed as the authoritative Interpreter of His Teachings.[4] Thus, Ibrahim Kheiralla, by challenging 'Abdu'l-Bahá and propounding interpretations at variance with those of the Master, was being disloyal to the Covenant.

Furthermore, to protect the Faith against distortion by the unwisdom and ignorance of its own members at a time when they are still few and the Faith is relatively unknown, 'Abdu'l-Bahá had laid down the temporary policy that any book about the Faith authored by a Bahá'í was not to be published without receiving the prior approval of a Spiritual Assembly. In order to reinforce this policy, the Master had, on one occasion, instructed that a translation was to be submitted to a Local Spiritual Assembly in Egypt for approval even though He Himself had already approved it. In due course, the Universal House of Justice will decide when the time has come for the relaxing and eventual abolition of this requirement.

Thus, there was no latitude in the Faith for Kheiralla to come up with his own doctrines and call them 'Bahá'í' if they did not in fact accord with the authorized teachings, and he knew it. How could he tell his students in America that he had been wrong about many aspects of the Faith? They were eagerly expecting his masterwork, indeed giving him advance payments for his book on the Faith. How could he disappoint them? And if he could not publish it, how would he support himself?

Then there was the issue of the Getsingers – especially Edward. Kheiralla had never liked Edward and the antipathy had only strengthened during the time shared as fellow pilgrims, despite the Master's clarion calls to show forth love and unity bolstered by the very example of His own forbearance and limitless patience toward His sworn enemies. Kheiralla believed that Edward meant to usurp him as head of the Faith in America. This had to be prevented. Even though the Getsingers had been in the Holy Land almost as long as Kheiralla, they had not had the advantage of language, of understanding everything the Master said. Kheiralla, acting as their interpreter, had been able to deliberately keep some of what was said by 'Abdu'l-Bahá from them. But he knew, nonetheless, that Edward was keen to expose the ways in which Kheiralla's teachings differed from 'Abdu'l-Bahá's. The Getsingers' more than four months in the Holy Land would give them credibility, would attract people to them. Furthermore, prior to the pilgrimage, 'Abdu'l-Bahá had sent less than a handful of letters to the United States. If that changed, the friends would no longer need to turn to Kheiralla for guidance.

Finally, Kheiralla held one very personal grudge against the Master – the failure of his marriage to Marian. The believers in New York and Chicago had noted prior to the pilgrimage that the Kheirallas did not always seem happy together and Kheiralla had not really wanted his wife to accompany him to 'Akká, despite outward appearances to the contrary. He had tried to have her remain in England, but the Getsingers intervened and assisted her to come to the Holy Land. Consequently Kheiralla's closest relations experienced a number of unpleasant surprises during his return to the Middle East. His third wife in Cairo was surprised to find out he had divorced her and remarried. His daughters were surprised to learn that they had a new stepmother when Marian unexpectedly arrived at the Master's home. And Marian was surprised that her husband was not merely a widower but also divorced; he had apparently never told her that she was wife number four, not number two. (It has been surmised that the unpleasant details about wives two and three were conveyed to Marian by Nabitha and Labitha.) During the pilgrimage, the long-simmering problems within the Kheiralla family erupted and the other pilgrims could not help but be aware of the tension. Ella wrote to her mother that the Master was attempting to counsel both Ibrahim and Marian Kheiralla to reconcile the marriage, but in the end those efforts were fruitless and 'Abdu'l-Bahá affirmed that Marian need no longer tolerate her husband's abusive behaviour and could separate from him.[5]

Thinking about all of this, a plan hatched in Kheiralla's mind. He would use his advantage of being the first to return to the United States to prepare the friends for the arrival of the Getsingers, to undermine their credibility so that no one would believe their reports of their time in 'Akká. Furthermore, he resolved to ask some of the leaders among the Bahá'í community to write to 'Abdu'l-Bahá on his behalf, supplicating that the Master instruct the wealthier American believers to provide him with money. He would even insist that all correspondence between the Bahá'ís in America and 'Abdu'l-Bahá be channelled through him; no direct correspondence between individual believers and the Master could be tolerated. Finally, as to the question of his position as head of the Faith in America, he had one secret card to play if the Master refused to acknowledge his well-earned standing. During his time in the Holy Land, he had surreptitiously made contact with 'Abdu'l-Bahá's most vicious enemy, his half-brother Muḥammad-'Alí.[6] This arch-enemy was smarting from the successes of the Faith in the West and especially from the arrival of the first Western believers to see 'Abdu'l-Bahá, so he was undoubtedly delighted to discover that Kheiralla might be interested in joining forces with him against the Master. Kheiralla was intelligent and perceptive enough to know from numerous credible accounts that Muḥammad-'Alí was darkness to 'Abdu'l-Bahá's light, unworthy to be a lowly servant in the household of the Master, much less Head of the Faith. Yet, if 'Abdu'l-Bahá became an impediment to his own ambitions, Kheiralla was resolved to turn sides and back the Master's would-be usurper.

The New York Bahá'í community joyfully welcomed their teacher home during the first days of May 1899 and feted him at a number of meetings. He was effusive in describing the bounties he had received in the Holy Land and his words had the effect of solidifying the Faith of his audiences.[7] He openly extolled 'Abdu'l-Bahá while at the same time quietly spreading rumours about the Getsingers, especially Edward. Everyone seemed happy, that is, everyone except Anton Haddad.

Kheiralla had assumed that his old friend, business partner and confidant was loyal first and foremost to him, as he had been during their early days in the United States, but he underestimated how much Haddad's own pilgrimage to 'Akká in 1897 had affected him. Haddad had become a true believer whose motives for embracing the Faith no longer left room for hopes of material gain. He loved 'Abdu'l-Bahá with all his heart and his first loyalty was to Him. When, shortly after his return to New York, Kheiralla confided to Haddad what was on his mind and in his plans, Haddad was horrified. He tried to reason with Kheiralla – to dissuade him – but his arguments had no effect. Haddad decided that the best course of action would be to confide his alarming conversation with Kheiralla to the Getsingers.

By May of 1899, Lua and Edward were not the same people who had left for 'Akká the previous September. Their eight months away had not only opened new vistas for them as they became acquainted with the world outside their homeland, but their four-and-a-half months in the Holy Land had wrought a profound inner transformation and raised their vision of what it meant to be a spiritual being. Writing to Thornton Chase after three months in the shadow of the Master, Lua said:

> When I left America I thought I knew a good deal, and felt that I was quite near the door of His bounty, but after seeing the Master (and other members of the household[)], I am sure I know nothing, and as yet the sprinkles of His gifts have not descended! But I am praying for mercy, and hope I will succeed in becoming one of the chosen! Everything depends on one's own efforts, we must work our own way into the Kingdom, and 'tis no easy thing to do, while the world and its allurements surround us! But by the help of God, the Most Merciful it can be done![8]

The Getsingers landed in New York between the 20th and 22nd of May.[9] One must surmise that their mood crossing the Atlantic must have been one of jubilant anticipation. They had wondrous experiences and new ideas to share; their hearts were full to overflowing with joy and new spiritual insights that would undoubtedly thrill their fellow believers. They were also bringing back with them a number of items that they knew would also be gratefully received by the American Bahá'í community, including a copy in Arabic of the Kitáb-i-Aqdas – the Most Holy Book – and other prayers, communes and passages from the Holy Writings. That they were bringing these invaluable items rather than Kheiralla speaks volumes as to Kheiralla's desires, or rather lack thereof, to promote the betterment of his flock while in the Holy Land. So we may imagine the Getsingers' hurt when they received an icy welcome. The rumours spread by Kheiralla had had their intended effect.

But Lua and Edward were not completely unprepared for this challenge because they had discussed their concerns regarding Kheiralla with 'Abdu'l-Bahá prior to leaving 'Akká, even though Lua felt that Kheiralla had changed for the better while in the Holy Land and had become 'less aggressive'.[10] The Master had emphasized to them that they must show Kheiralla only love and gratitude for bringing them into the Faith that had so enriched their lives. Therefore, as they spent their first two weeks back in the United States in New York City visiting the friends, they praised Kheiralla whenever possible. This must have required a supreme exertion of willpower on Edward's part and generated surprise in their listeners. They were determined to be obedient to the Master and did genuinely feel grateful to Kheiralla for being their first Bahá'í teacher. Edward later wrote:

> We were told by the Master before we left Acca that we must not have any quarrel or dissension with Dr. Kh. in America about what he told or taught but must leave him entirely in the hand of God. This we endeavored to do as far as it was possible. We did our best to unite with him and did everything we could excepting to deny Abdul-Baha, in order that we might pacify him, but it was of no use.[11]

In the long run, by returning good for evil, praise for slander, the Getsingers restored and enhanced their standing among the other believers. Needless to say, those who had heard the rumours began to think less of Kheiralla. He had already left for Chicago by the time Edward and Lua arrived in New York, so they did not have an opportunity to confront him in person. Instead they tried through correspondence with him to eliminate the tensions that had begun to permeate the Bahá'í community.[12]

In the time since the pilgrims had sailed from New York in September of 1898, the number of Bahá'ís registered on the list of believers had grown by about 500. By the early summer of 1899 there were about a thousand Bahá'ís in the United States[13] in widely scattered communities – a remarkable achievement. The largest concentrations were in Chicago and New York, but the teaching successes of Kheiralla's lieutenants had spread the Faith to many other areas as well, such as Washington, D.C., Philadelphia, Boston, Kenosha (Wisconsin), Ithaca, and Baltimore. Kheiralla was undoubtedly pleased with the state in which he found the American Bahá'í community when he returned.

It is worth noting that membership in the Bahá'í community in the West during the first few decades was fluid. Those who registered did not necessarily think that they had joined a religion in the same sense that one joined a church through the sacraments of baptism and confirmation. Instead, they thought of themselves as members of a movement or association much as one might join the Masons or the Theosophical Society, not at all incompatible with continued membership in a church. Indeed, until 1935 many active Bahá'ís in the West maintained active church memberships. Since the commitment was slight, it was easy to gain adherents, but it was also just as easy to lose them. Writing from 'Akká, Lua had explained to Thornton Chase that the process of becoming a believer, as it was normally carried out in the United States, was not sufficient:

> we must all throw away our desires and weed out our imperfections then we will receive the full confirmation and in reality become children of God – simply taking the lessons and receiving the 'Greatest Name' does not mean that we are confirmed. We must work for that great blessing, and without work we shall <u>never receive it</u>. And oh, it is worth all the effort we can make![14]

Lua and Edward spent only about two weeks in New York and then on 2 June travelled to Ithaca[15] to the Moore family farm where they undoubtedly received a much warmer welcome. But the hurt of their New York reception still lingered, compounded by worries that the Faith they loved more than life itself was in jeopardy. They knew that Kheiralla intended to undermine 'Abdu'l-Bahá, at least in America. The best thing to do was to await the return of Phoebe Hearst and seek her advice and assistance.

The Master always could perceive what was hidden in the innermost chambers of people's hearts, and He knew Kheiralla well. He did not wait for Kheiralla to write to Him from America but wrote to him first with loving words of encouragement and promises of the bounties that come from steadfastness, in an attempt to direct him to the straight path, the path of obedience to the Centre of the Covenant. 'Abdu'l-Bahá offered him a high spiritual station but not an earthly one.

> To the Presence of Ibrahim Effendi Kheiralla:
> Upon him is Beha Ullah, El Beha
>
> O Thou who hast spread the fragrance of God: May God confirm thee!
>
> Since thou hast reached America, we have not received any message announcing to us thy safe and sound arrival there, but Mr. Anton, in a letter to us, has endeavored to explain in detail that thy return was like showers of rain to that country, and like the attack of a lion upon those valleys and mountains. He also informed us that thou hadst been received there with honors by the best men; by those whose chests were expanded by the gentle breeze coming from the gardens of the Kingdom of God.
>
> And oh, thou who warmest thyself by the fire of the love of God, spreading from the Tree of [the] Covenant, let thy soul be at ease, and thy heart in peace, concerning the perfect success and progress which the pen is not able to express, for in a short time thou shalt see the flag of the Kingdom waving in those far and wide regions, and the lights of the Truth shining brilliantly in its dawn above those horizons, and thou shalt know that thou art the centre of the circle of the love of God, the axis around which souls revolve in their way and supplication to God. Therefore thou must widen thy heart, expand thy chest, have patience in plenty, calmness of soul, and cut thyself from everything but God.
>
> By God, the truth is that if thou goest according to the teachings of El-Abd ['Abdu'l-Bahá], and followest the steps of him who is annihilated in God, thou shalt see that the cohorts of the Kingdom of God will come to thy help, one after another, and that the hosts of the might of God will be in thy presence in steady succession, the gates of the great victory opened, and the rays of the brilliant morning diffused. By thy life, oh my beloved, if thou didst know what God had ordained for thee, thou wouldst fly with delight, and thy happiness, gladness and joy would increase every hour. El Beha be upon thee!
>
> Present to the beloved people of God, there, my longings for them. Preach to them the glad tidings of God. Give my greetings to Sitt [sister] Nabiha and Sitt Labiha, and also to the honorable maidens of the Merciful God. El Beha is upon them all.

P.S. Present my best greetings to the honorable and spiritual women; to those who are very much attracted toward God, and particularly to that one who has proved that it is possible for a camel to pass through a needle's eye. May God keep them in joy and happiness, and burning with His love.

[signed 'Abdu'l-Bahá Abbas][16]

The effect of this Tablet upon the intended recipient is unknown.

This Tablet of 'Abdu'l-Bahá is also interesting in that it provides insight into the Master's evaluation of Phoebe, to whom He is unquestionably referring in the postscript as 'that one who has proved that it is possible for a camel to pass through a needle's eye'. Christians would immediately recognize this as a reference to the saying of Christ, mentioned in three of the Gospels, that it is easier for a camel to pass through the eye of a needle than for a rich man to enter the kingdom of God.[17]

When Phoebe returned to New York in mid- to late June, Haddad and the Getsingers wasted no time in filling her in on what was happening with Kheiralla. He had already angered her, thus his behaviour after returning was hardly a surprise.[18] What especially incensed her, however, was not his lack of honesty but the interviews he had given to a New York newspaper shortly before her return. It was bad enough that he told the reporter that he was the head of the Bahá'í Faith in North America, a title never bestowed upon him by anyone but himself, but that he had broken the secrecy of the movement by divulging its most intimate teachings – the essence referred to as 'the pith'. She met with the New York believers and through recounting her own time in 'Akká with the Master did much to strengthen their faith and their devotion to 'Abdu'l-Bahá, and consequently eliminated many seeds of doubt planted by Kheiralla.[19] She also offered her home in Washington, D.C. to the Getsingers as a temporary refuge while they restored their spirits and contemplated their next steps.

As for Kheiralla, the solution was to seek the help of the Master. Phoebe dispatched Anton Haddad with all possible haste to 'Akká and, to prevent Kheiralla from knowing what was afoot, word was spread that she had sent him to California. Phoebe wrote to let Nell Hillyer in on what was happening once she got to her Washington home.

I came here Sunday, & leave for N.Y. today, and start west Thursday. I will write as soon as I reach home and tell you <u>many</u> things. Dr. Kheiralla has taken a strange course since his return to N.Y. and things look so serious. I have asked Mr. Haddad to go to Cairo & A__ and fully explain matters.

> He expects to sail a week from today and will go to Paris for a day or two. I hope he can see you . . .
>
> No one will know where he has gone. I mean only two or three people. Kheiralla is to be told that Haddad has gone west.
>
> Kheiralla has given the material for two articles in the N.Y. Herald, giving almost the entire Pith, etc. He is an awful old beast.[20]

Lua also wrote a veiled letter to Nell, who was still travelling in Europe with Ella Goodall, about what was going on. The undated letter was probably written in late June or early July during the Getsingers' time in the Hearst New Hampshire Avenue home in Washington, D.C. Undoubtedly, Nell could read between the lines.

> . . . You will see dear Anton Haddad very soon – so I will not tell you, anything that is going on here – as I do not want to write any bad things. Dear Mrs. Hearst – came home when we were in great trouble indeed, and bestowed upon [us] her love in great abundance – and stood by us – like the true loyal soul she is. I am glad now the trouble came – in one sense – for it gained for us a manifestation of her love – which we have always wanted – that and nothing more! She invited us to go down to Washington and went with us and – we were alone with her from Sunday until Wednesday. I could hardly believe it for she is so busy – and has so many always around her – but now she has gone – and left us here to rest up a bit – but we leave Wednesday next for Detroit! I love her today as I have never loved her before – because she has shown us her love – and called us both, her children – I have written a letter to the Master – begging a great blessing for her. It is when one stands for us – when others upon whom we have relied turn against us – that we appreciate that one's friendship – and for such a friendship – I would lay down my life! . . . Oh Helen dear, I love so much – but I am afraid you do not realize – it for you do not understand how much Edward and I are one – consequently you do not know my pain when he is attacked in any way![21]

In the meantime, Anton Haddad left New York for France in early July. Kheiralla apparently believed the cover story that he had been sent to California by Phoebe, until chance revealed the true destination. In the Marseilles railway station Haddad ran into relatives of Kheiralla headed for New York. Kheiralla was no longer fooled as to his former friend's intentions or reasons for going east. While he was away, Kheiralla would have to work diligently to cement his own plans. He hurried off a letter to 'Akká asking the Master to grant his wishes and placing his case before Him in an effort to counteract Haddad.

Faced with the very real prospect that Kheiralla would shatter the Cause of God in America, the Getsingers set out for Edward's home in Detroit where they met with the Bahá'í community. While there, they wrote to Kheiralla, who was in Chicago at the time, pleading with him to remain loyal to the Master. His replies to their letters were characterized by Edward as 'of a very severe and insulting nature'.[22] At this point in time, many of the believers saw the tensions between the Getsingers and Kheiralla as no more than a conflict of strong-willed, ambitious personalities. James Hooe, one of Phoebe's managers, was monitoring the situation on her behalf in an effort to look out for her interests and to prevent her name from becoming embroiled in any unpleasant business. He characterized the situation simply as a conflict between Kheiralla and Edward.[23] But in reality, it was not Edward whom Kheiralla was seeking to undermine, it was 'Abdu'l-Bahá. From the beginning, Kheiralla had taught the Americans that Bahá'u'lláh was the one mentioned in the New Testament as 'the Father' and that 'Abdu'l-Bahá was the return of Christ. The Master never claimed to be the return of Christ; in fact, the Bahá'í teaching is that the Father and the return of Christ are both among the stations of Bahá'u'lláh. Nonetheless, Kheiralla was now attempting a difficult balancing act. In order to retain his own position as leader of the American Bahá'í community, he had to subvert 'Abdu'l-Bahá's position as Head of the Faith. Yet he had lavishly praised 'Abdu'l-Bahá to his congregants and taught them to believe that 'Abdu'l-Bahá was indeed the return of the Messiah.[24] Now, to reverse course, he wanted to undermine the Master in their eyes and he began to do so with whispers. The Getsingers were determined to stop him.

The first showdown took place in the birthplace of the Faith in America, Chicago, in August of 1899. A large hall was rented for the Getsingers to talk about their time in the Holy Land and hundreds of people attended. The Getsingers had conferred with Kheiralla before the meeting and had offered that Lua should take on all the blame for the tension between them so that Kheiralla could save face. Kheiralla, in turn, would cease sabotaging or criticizing 'Abdu'l-Bahá and would help to restore harmony among the believers. According to Edward, this was the agreement reached by the three. Edward later recounted what happened that evening.

> When the time of meeting arrived he [Kheiralla] was in the rear of the hall and I could see from the way he was moving about that he had decided that night to make a coup d'état, and that he would turn this meeting to his own advantage by denouncing the Center of the Covenant and telling the people not to believe what he had taught them before but to accept

> what he was teaching them now, since he had been to Acca and had learned more of the matter. Loua [sic] came to the platform and talked with the people and laid the foundation for Dr. Kh. to appear and join with us in harmony and unite. Instead of that he refused to do this but spoke about his own ideas and about his book which would give the true teachings of Bahaism and that he would have henceforth his own followers come to him and in another hall where he would teach them the Truth free from all previous errors . . .[25]

Just as in New York, Kheiralla had paved the way for the Getsingers' return to Chicago by spreading rumours and making derogatory statements about them, so their initial welcome was tepid; in fact, a few of Kheiralla's most virulent followers had even tried to prevent their coming. But at that large August gathering, Lua consistently praised Kheiralla with no hint of criticism. Even in their private conversations, the Getsingers spoke only positively of him. Again, their returning good for evil had its effect and, though the majority of believers in the Chicago area had at first sided with their old teacher, most took note of the more conciliatory attitude of the Getsingers and were won over to their side.[26] Licking his wounds, Kheiralla retired to finish writing his book.

The Getsingers returned to Detroit after their brief stay in Chicago. For the first time since their marriage, they could make an attempt to settle down and begin to build a more normal domestic life together. Detroit was familiar territory to Edward and near to the majority of his relatives. His medical licence had been issued in Michigan. It was time for him to return to earning a livelihood, and it can be imagined that even wanderlust as strong as Edward's had been sated by the journeys of the past two years. There is no record of where they lived or their activities during this brief interlude, but in short order the foul winds blowing over the American Bahá'í community began to gather speed and intensity and they were again called to serve.

The Getsingers had returned home from Chicago emotionally drained and worried and they immediately dispatched a full report to 'Abdu'l-Bahá. Edward, in particular, asked the Master to pray for Kheiralla at the Shrine of Bahá'u'lláh.[27] The matter was out of their hands and in those of the One they trusted the most to resolve it lovingly and appropriately. Then something happened, another mystical, unexplainable event, which made them feel that they were indeed being divinely assisted, giving them renewed strength to carry on the work of the Faith. It happened one evening in mid-August. Lua described what happened in a letter to a believer in Chicago, Mrs Bartlett.

. . . night before last, at about 9 P.M. we were sitting together in the twilight when suddenly we felt a powerful Presence in the room, which made me tremble and cry; though Mr. Getsinger was very white and calm, he was greatly affected.

We did not move for some time, then I became so weak I could not sit up and Mr. Getsinger helped me to the bed and we both lay down and the Blessed Presence still remained, though we did not see anything, and at the time I was very thank[ful] for I know I could not have lived, my breath almost left me as it was and the tears were streaming over our faces.

It remained for about a half hour and we could not move or speak, then left us, but we did not sleep all night and we both felt our utter unworthiness to a degree that was painful.[28]

Mrs Bartlett had written to Lua asking her to explain the discrepancies between her explanations of the Bible and those of Kheiralla, and Lua replied:

I told you what the Master told us. If Dr. K. says differently don't dispute with him or anybody, but pray. The Holy Spirit will answer your questions, then none can dispute you. If he has disputed what I told you, which came from the sacred lips of our Lord, I have nothing more to say and you must excuse me for not answering you, for I must not put myself in the attitude that would proclaim me 'a stirrer of strife' for the Master commanded me to be a 'Peace maker' and when I was troubled about some of the very questions, He read to me the 3rd chap. of 1st Cor. and I likewise tell you to read it and let it answer for the present. In time all will be known for the fire will reveal each man's work of what sort it is. Thus it will be with Dr. K's book. Wait. If it is the Truth it will stand, if not it will fall of itself. I would advise all of you now who are so hungry to stop all questions, all reading of books, except the words of Christ (Praise be to His every utterance) and pray without ceasing for the baptism of the Spirit: that is the most important thing, for then as the Master said 'You will not need to ask questions of any man for the spirit will teach you.'[29]

The reference to the 3rd chapter of St Paul's First Epistle to the Corinthians, cited by 'Abdu'l-Bahá in order to instruct Lua, was one in which St Paul discussed infighting within the early Christian community with factions siding with different teachers.

Finally, Lua in that period following the August meeting with Kheiralla had this advice for the Chicago friends.

> I beg of you all each day to pray for Dr. Kheiralla and be generous with his mistakes. He has done much for us and for this alone we should ever be grateful and pray God to fully open his eyes.[30]

In the meantime, Anton Haddad had reached Beirut, a necessary first stop to reunite with his family and attend to personal affairs. His departure from New York had been so hasty that he had not had time to write to 'Abdu'l-Bahá for the necessary permission to visit Him in 'Akká. Miraculously, when he reached Beirut, he found a telegram from the Master awaiting him saying 'Let Haddad come without permission.' The situation of the Master had remained as dangerous as it was when the last of the pilgrims departed in March. The Master Himself was restricting the number of pilgrims from the East in order to demonstrate to the Ottoman government that His interests were entirely religious and not political. After being updated by the Baghdadi family in Beirut on the hazards then surrounding 'Abdu'l-Bahá, Haddad was doubly thankful for the blessing of being allowed to travel again to 'Akká and left for the prison city forthwith.

Haddad told 'Abdu'l-Bahá everything he knew of what was happening in America. The report 'made Him very sad and He said that it caused Him more sorrow than all the persecutions and oppressions combined'.[31] Despite the report of Kheiralla's perfidy and machinations against the Master, 'Abdu'l-Bahá was not angry, but expressed with great loving compassion his pity for one who could have risen very high in the spiritual realm but was instead plunging himself into the depths of perdition. Haddad reported that the Master said:

> I am very sorry for Kheiralla, a most precious crown was prepared for his head in the spiritual kingdom, but now he has covered himself with a great stain and much mud. However, I supplicated God, the Almighty Father, to have mercy on him and to forgive him his sins and to protect him from the vanity of the world and that he will illumine his heart, purify and sanctify his mind, bless his soul, guide him in the right path, and be with him and his children and bring them back into the fold of His sheep. Verily, He is the Merciful, Generous and Clement![32]

'Abdu'l-Bahá then proceeded to instruct Haddad over the period of two weeks he was in 'Akká. Haddad took careful notes, undoubtedly in Arabic, and these in turn were corrected by the Master in His own hand. Haddad then translated the guidance into English. When he returned to the United States in November after a more than a four-month absence, he used these notes to deliver talks and as the basis for a pamphlet entitled *Message from Acca*, which was printed most likely at the beginning of 1900 and then circulated among the American believers, beginning in the New York community. Haddad put the following admonition at the beginning of the publication:

> Keep its contents ever before you as a guide to the path of Righteousness. This is not intended as a tract, and should be known only to those who have received and respect the message. Consider yourselves the guardian of it.

This pamphlet would be eagerly received, not only as a balm to the growing rift within the community but because it contained teachings of the Master at a time when the friends in America still had very little of those directly from the source. They were thirsty for spiritual guidance.

In addition to these notes prepared for the generality of believers, the Master wrote a Tablet for Kheiralla himself while Haddad was in 'Akká in 1899. The gist of the Tablet was that no one, including Kheiralla, should expect to be appointed a leader in the Faith. Leadership comes instead through good deeds and through attaining true spirituality and leaders must be servants who act with honesty and sincerity.[33] This was not what Kheiralla wanted to hear.

The messages Haddad brought back from 'Akká in late December or early January[34] only served to inflame Kheiralla further. No longer exercising either discretion or the slightest semblance of loyalty to 'Abdu'l-Bahá, he began to make statements like the following to Haddad and others:

> If there can be no chief of the Behaists in America, then there will be no chief of the Behaists in Acca, and I will show Abbas Effendi that I mean what I say and He shall see [t]hat I am able to prove it.[35]

The disunity was beginning to takes its toll as hundreds of members of the American Bahá'í community began to slip away, especially in Chicago and New York, the two communities most affected by the growing crisis. By the end of 1899, both communities had divided into two factions with separate meetings and governing bodies.[36]

Haddad and the Getsingers once again took to the road, visiting a number of Bahá'í communities and sharing the message from 'Abdu'l-Bahá. The three jointly addressed the Chicago community on 11 February 1900 with Kheiralla present. Kheiralla was offered an opportunity to speak at that gathering, but declined. Edward made a point of embracing Kheiralla in front of the audience to signal that reconciliation between the two had been achieved.[37] One of the trio's other stops was Kenosha, which had a large Bahá'í community loyal to Kheiralla. The Kenosha friends had apparently been unaware of what was happening among many of the other communities until the three told them of Kheiralla's doubts about the station of 'Abdu'l-Bahá. Not knowing whom to believe, the Kenosha friends invited Kheiralla to come and explain his views about the Master and his place in the Faith.

Kheiralla's visit to Kenosha on 8 March 1900, less than a year after the completion of his pilgrimage, was the decisive turning point because during that trip he openly repudiated 'Abdu'l-Bahá. This immediately caused a schism among the friends in that locality. Confusion and dismay spread.

In late April help arrived from the East. 'Abdu'l-Karím-i-Ṭihrání, Kheiralla's old teacher and friend to the Western pilgrims, arrived in New York from Egypt accompanied by Dr Rafael Sadris and another Persian translator. 'Abdu'l-Karím must have heard about the situation from Anton Haddad when he passed through Port Said in July the previous summer, because by August Lua had already received a letter from him expressing his concern.[38] It is easy to imagine his dismay when he learned what his star pupil was plotting following his return to America. 'Abdu'l-Karím had begged 'Abdu'l-Bahá to allow him to go to Kheiralla to straighten him out and the Master had agreed. At first glance, 'Abdu'l-Karím would have seemed the best person to deal with Kheiralla given their history as teacher and student, but he was not the right person to strengthen the American believers. His English was barely passable and, as a former Muslim, he never really understood the spiritual needs and longings of the American Bahá'ís. They were searching for spiritual truths, he was focused upon saving them from Kheiralla. Furthermore, in order to elevate his own background, Kheiralla had for years bragged to the Americans about his old teacher's wisdom, superior knowledge and intelligence. In fact, he had told his students that 'Abdu'l-Karím was second only to 'Abdu'l-Bahá. 'Abdu'l-Karím was a devoted and deepened believer but he was not of the calibre of Mírzá Abu'l-Faḍl or others among the more illustrious Persian teachers of the Faith. It was impossible for 'Abdu'l-Karím to live up to the expectations Kheiralla had sown in the minds of the Americans.[39]

Surprised by the arrival of his old teacher, Kheiralla hurried from Chicago to New York to meet him. What happened next is anyone's guess. The two holed up in the home of Howard MacNutt and seldom left that house for almost two weeks. When they ended their seclusion, 'Abdu'l-Karím had obtained from his pupil a pledge of loyalty to 'Abdu'l-Bahá. A meeting was held on 8 May with about 200 members of the New York community in attendance at which Kheiralla made the following statement from the podium:

> Dear Friends, there were many rumors about me, that I have denounced the Master; and in reality these rumors, as I heard them, are falsehoods, and I never denounced Him . . .
>
> . . . I had strong doubts [about Him] . . .
>
> . . . Praise to God, these doubts are annulled, finished, and I declare to you now that they are finished and to every American Believer that I believe that Abdel Baha, Abbas Effendi, is the Greatest Branch from the ancient Truth[,] as the Blessed Perfection, the Ancient of Days [Bahá'u'lláh], said . . . and His command is to follow the one who He appointed . . .[40]

At the end of the meeting, Edward again publicly embraced Kheiralla. It seemed that the crisis was over, solved by the sage from Egypt.

The next day 'Abdu'l-Karím sent forth a circular letter to all the American believers announcing Kheiralla's pledge of loyalty. Apparently this was more than had been agreed to in private, so Kheiralla fumed. He had asked to be allowed to first meet with his flock in Chicago to prepare them before any such statement was issued. The situation began to rapidly deteriorate again. When Kheiralla returned to his home in Chicago he met enraged believers who felt betrayed after following him rather than 'Abdu'l-Bahá. With the financial assistance of some of the American friends, having arrived in the New York with only fifty-four dollars in his pocket, 'Abdu'l-Karím followed Kheiralla to Chicago and there tried for weeks to renegotiate a statement of loyalty. On 2 June 'Abdu'l-Karím sent him one last draft of a loyalty statement and demanded that he sign it no later than 4:15 p.m. the following afternoon. Kheiralla refused. The battle of wills was over. Kheiralla and his followers would go one way and those loyal to the Master would go another.[41]

CHAPTER 13

The Sun Comes Out after the Storm

Edward, Lua, Thornton Chase, and Anton Haddad travelled to community after community to strengthen the believers and minimize the damage from Kheiralla's defection. This was a particular sacrifice for the Getsingers who were of limited means. As the summer drew to a close, they must have felt that they were survivors surveying the damage caused by a hurricane. A few big trees had fallen: William James, the first person to register as a Bahá'í in the United States; Maude Lamson, Kheiralla's secretary and the keeper of the membership registry; and the women who had taken the Faith to Cincinnati and Philadelphia. But most of the tall oaks were still standing. The community had shrunk considerably during the year of turmoil, losing by one estimate half of its membership. But those who remained had proven themselves to be steadfast and devoted. In truth, the storm bypassed some communities, especially those which Kheiralla had never visited.[1]

The decisive factor which most likely saved the majority of believers from falling away was the little pamphlet, *Message from Acca*. The power generated by the words of Bahá'u'lláh and 'Abdu'l-Bahá pulsating throughout that historic publication not only inspired the friends, it gave them a first real glimpse of the majesty, of the profound depth of the teachings of their Faith. Many of the American believers took that message into their hearts and with new-found resolve, set about the work of repairing the rift left in Kheiralla's wake. They also resumed the task of spreading the Faith to new people and localities. 'Abdu'l-Bahá knew well the fierce storm they were passing through and had sent them the life-line they needed to weather it.

In his introduction to the pamphlet, Haddad begins by reminding the reader in his own words of the great station of 'Abdu'l-Bahá.

> . . . These words are sent to you by the Greatest Branch, Abbas Effendi, the one whom God has chosen and desired, the one who is branched from the Ancient of Days . . . It is sent by Abdul-Beha [sic], the servant of God, who has clad Himself with the mantle of servitude and devotion for the beloved of God, and who is the Eldest Son . . . by the One whose Supreme and Exalted position is acknowledged by everyone, and even by his most

> bitter enemies. By the One to whom the Manifestation referred to [sic] in the Tablet to the Czar of Russia, saying: 'The Father has come, and also the Son in the Holy Valley, who cries out, "Labeick, O God, Labeick." Meaning, 'I am ready, O God, I am ready.' By the One whose Love is incomparable, whose character is unquestionable. By the One who sends to you His great Love, salutations and blessings.[2]

Haddad then goes on to explain to the American believers who they really are – the ones who have attained the unique privilege of carrying forward God's work in the Day of God. He elevates their vision by giving them the long perspective that they are pioneers who will be remembered down through the ages and that they must become worthy of so august a station.

> The Message is sent to the American believers, to the beloved of God, to the honest, sincere and faithful servants of God. To you who are pioneers, and whose actions and like will linger in the memories of those who will come after you. To those upon whose character, uprightness and energy the success of the Cause depends. To those who are requested to lay a solid and valid foundation for the Kingdom of God on Earth; a foundation which will not be affected by storm or wind. To those who will be called upon to oppose, with the sword of wisdom and truth, the armies of error with whom you are surrounded, and not to oppose each other. To you whose duty it is to ignore everything for the sake of union and agreement. To you who are now laboring under trying circumstances – tested as to your firmness and faith – and who must pass through the fire of purification. To you who are not to allow any seditious rumors to prevent you from coming into the Kingdom. To the Beloved Children whose hearts have been Kindled with the love of God. To those who are commanded to live as one soul dwelling in different bodies, to live as brethren of one family, and who are expected to make this vivifying truth the basis of their practical life. To those who are commanded to spare no means within their power to promote the cause of God and exalt His word. To those on whom rests the responsibility of creating and maintaining peace and harmony. To those whom God has chosen to become the vivifiers of the world . . .[3]

The seventeen-page publication contained many direct quotations from the Master's words. The themes were repeated many times over. Summarized, they were that 'now is *the time to unite with each other*, and live in *perfect agreement* . . .'[4] Given the importance of this first lengthy message to the American community from 'Abdu'l-Bahá, substantial excerpts from that historic document are given here. The reader should keep in mind that the translation from the Arabic does not meet the rigorous standards for translation later introduced by Shoghi Effendi; nonetheless, the essence of these excerpts is still of great value. Haddad was given excerpts of the Writings of Bahá'u'lláh to transcribe, translate and include in the *Message from Acca,* some of which are now available in authorized translations, and references to these are given in the notes. Furthermore, the reader should ever keep in mind that many of the following passages are categorized as 'pilgrim's notes'.

Haddad divided *Message from Acca* into sections. In addition to an introduction, there is a first section titled, 'A Message from Acca'. Next follows, 'The Words of Our Lord Relating to Disagreement Among the Believers', 'A Tablet to the Guides', 'Tablet: Directions for Guides', 'Instructions to Guides and Believers', and finally another short section also titled, 'Instructions to Guides and Believers'.

It will be readily clear to the reader that 'Abdu'l-Bahá had in mind Kheiralla's desire for a special status within the community as he dictated to Haddad, and that this sort of ambition was the antithesis of the true teachings of the Faith. In the first section, Haddad reports that the Master said to him:

> The field in America is now likened unto a field of land in which are planted small trees having not the powers within themselves to stand any assault or attacks from outside, or to repel the powers of storm and wind. Therefore, it is very necessary at first to treat such trees very mildly and take much care of them until they become very strong, solid and firm.
>
> Consequently the guides and teachers who are in charge of this field must first deny themselves and practice chastity, purity, and love all sincerely, [cut] out of their hearts from the world and not care for the comforts of their bodies or for any other worldly thing. And they must also abolish from their minds the word 'Ego' or 'I', and be servants unto all, faithful and honest shepherds, watching very strictly day and night, putting all their efforts to the care of their sheep and secure them inside the fold. If any of the sheep go astray, they must do their best and not rest until they find it. They have to *serve* the worshippers of God, for He (praise to Him) is not in need of our service, our submissiveness or prayers, our kindness or assistance, etc., but those who are in need of such things are the worshippers of God, and by this they will please God the Almighty. Jesus said, And whosoever shall give to drink unto these little ones a cup of cold water, only in the name of a disciple, it is as though he had given it to me, Verily, I say unto you, he shall in no wise lose his reward.
>
> Everyone of us, and especially the guides or the deliverers of the truth

> must know that what he does or acts, he does only to himself and none will profit but himself, and in giving the truth none will enjoy but himself.
>
> The singer who has a sweet, soft and gentle voice, will, when he sings, please himself far better than he pleases his audience, and therefore his pleasure and delight is confined to himself. It is so in the case of the artist, the photographer and the inventor. Each one of them has a special delight in himself – in the thing he does – more than others have in their works. The same is true with the deliverer of the Truth. There is nothing in these days more important than the delivery of the Truth. It is the best thing and the greatest, because the future happiness of man and his comfort, the highness of his position and exaltation, depends on his delivering the Truth to the worshippers of God.
>
> The guide will not be confirmed by God unless he is a sincere and faithful servant to God. It might be that sometimes it happens that the guide will be successful, but it is only for a short time, but at last he will fall down if he is not thoroughly sincere, even if he is the greatest philosopher and the most learned man. It happens sometimes that the simple surpass and excel the intelligent and bright.[5]

After this discussion of the qualities of a teacher of the Faith, 'Abdu'l-Bahá continued with an exposition on the importance of eliminating contentions within the community through ignoring the faults in others.

> We are requested by Our Lord 'to live in peace, love, union and agreement, and overlook the faults and defects of others and to see only their good actions and not their bad ones. These are things that will lead to perfect success and thorough happiness.'
>
> To illustrate this more fully, Our Lord, Abdel Beha [sic], told the following story: 'Once on a certain time when Christ and his disciples were travelling from one place to another, they came near a dead dog. One of the disciples said: "How ugly this dog is;" another said, "How offensive and putrid he is," another, "How bad;" and another, "Fie on him, how abominable." On this Christ was anxious to show to them something that was good in that dog, thus to teach them that first they should look for the good things without caring in the least for the bad, and in some manner, he made the dog's teeth appear, saying to his disciples, "How white and beautiful are his teeth." This made the disciples ashamed, realizing at the same time that they were mistaken and that what they said was wrong. This lesson teaches us how to behave toward each other and how to view and treat each other, i.e. to look for the good things in each other, caring

> not for the bad.[6] He ['Abdu'l-Bahá] said also, 'Tell the believers, if they hear some day that something has happened to their Chief, Abdel Beha [sic], whether killed or crucified, they must not fear or feel broken-hearted, sad, or afflicted, but on the contrary should strengthen and comfort each other, stand firm and continue working in the field of God, teaching and delivering the truth to all the people. Tell El-Ahbab [sic] in America, that it is very necessary in these days that they should not notice the bad things of others, nor mind the small, trifling, worldly things, but seek the spiritual, which tends to their strengthening and confirmation, for these days are the days of persecutions, dangers and perils, and accordingly they ought to unite with each other, for union is power, and let them take as their example in everything, Abdel-Beha [sic], The Master.'[7]

'Abdu'l-Bahá reminded the American believers of the importance of attaining a strong measure of faith that could not be shaken, and of striving for spiritual transformation. He urges them to assist each other with their spiritual growth.

> The Master also said, 'Perhaps you have heard some thing about Ibn-Abhar.[8] He is a Persian teacher and one of the greatest in knowledge and spirituality and holds a very high position among the believers; still, when asked by anyone about any other certain believer he generally says, "I am not worthy to unloose the latchet of his shoes." This teaches us humility and that we ought to speak very well of others, even to prefer them to ourselves, that we should not boast by saying, – "I am *the* man and nobody else." The believers should be thankful to the guide or teacher, and faithful to him for what he has done for them, in giving them that treasured thing which could not be estimated or re-compensated. 'What use will it be to you if you are an extinguished lamp and the other lamps are so bright and brilliant, or what harm will it do you if you are bright and the others dark? What profit will you get if you are poor and the others rich, or what harm will it do you if you are rich and the others are in need of you? And so on in all cases. Under these circumstances, everyone should at first reform himself and better his condition; when this is settled with him he will do [a] great deal of good to others and be competent to fulfill many very important duties, then his words will have a great effect on the hearts of others. I love everyone [sic] of you and therefore I wish you to love each other sincerely.'
>
> He also said, 'Tell the believers that I want the strong ones among them to strengthen the weak, just as Mary Magdalen did after the death of Christ. On that famous event the disciples of Christ became very weak

and disappointed, and some of them were full of doubts, and were likely to disbelieve in him. At last they went to Mary and said to her, "Do you not know He is dead." She replied, "Well it does not matter; Was the soul killed or the body?" They answered "The body"; Then she said to them, "Do not fear, he is still alive and will be with us always, and is ready at all times to help us. Go, be firm and strong, and do not let small things trouble you or fill you with doubts. Go and preach the word of God to everyone with sincere faith and you will be confirmed by the Holy Spirit." So they were encouraged by her and went on preaching and teaching, thus she was the cause of strengthening them and promoting the truth among all the people.'

Abdel Beha [sic] wants you to follow the steps of that great woman, especially if you come under similar [circumstances]. He wants you to take no thought for any other thing but the cause of God, and to be as St. Paul when he said, 'I once had knowledge, wisdom and philosophy, but after I knew Christ I forgot everything, and now I do not know but Christ.' If believers or guides fall into temptations, or commit any wrong, the others ought [to] reform such infirmities with the spirit of sincere love for his edification, that you may with one mind and one mouth glorify God. Whosoever of you, if he had a certain beautiful tree in his garden for a long time, during which long time it was giving good fruits, would cut it down if, for one year he seeks fruit on this tree and find none; will he not be sad and have pity? Will he not wait another year and take much care of it, until he removes all cause which stood against that tree and injured it: this must be the case with the believers, especially with the teachers and guides. Whosoever, if he had all his clothes saturated with water, would care in the least if some small drops of water were thrown on him by another? Of course he would not care, for such drops will not affect him at all. Thus we should not notice the small faults committed against us by others. To speak evil against the believers, the guides or the teachers, will hurt but yourselves. Everyone is liable to mistakes and to fall into temptations; therefore we ought not to expect perfection in anybody. Jesus said, 'There is none good, but One, and He is God.' No one can claim the Behaist [sic] religion unless very sincere and honest 'and born of water and the Spirit', as Jesus said. Therefore, he who comes to this religion with perfect and pure sincerity will prosper and succeed thoroughly; otherwise, success will be only for a short time and then will fail.[9]

In the second section, which contained many quotations from Bahá'u'lláh, the believers were admonished not to allow disagreements to arise that would drive a wedge among them. The Cause of God can survive disunity, but that strife can delay its victories. Disagreements among the believers were likened to clouds which hide the radiance of the sun. While these clouds do not have the power to extinguish the sun's rays, they can prevent the world from attaining their benefit for a time. The coming of spring is also considered. Cold and desolation may reign for a time during winter, but could all the powers of the world, even if united, stop the coming of the springtime? So, likewise, the flowering of the spiritual springtime can be delayed but not stopped.

The passages then cited go on to speak of the smallness of the army of God in the early days, thus it is important that dissensions – differing opinions as to which arms to deploy – not lead to defeat. For in truth the armies of the world stand ready to stop the army of God. Unity alone will bring forth victory.

Haddad then provides a translation of an extract from Bahá'u'lláh's Súriy-i-Haykal in which he addresses the Emperor of France, Napoleon III. The extract is produced below in its authorized translation, not as it was rendered by Haddad.

> God hath prescribed unto everyone the duty of teaching His Cause. Whoever ariseth to discharge this duty, must needs, ere he proclaimeth His Message, adorn himself with the ornament of an upright and praiseworthy character, so that his words may attract the hearts of such as are receptive to his call. Without it, he can never hope to influence his hearers. Thus doth God instruct you. He, verily, is the Ever-Forgiving, the Most Compassionate.
>
> They who exhort others unto justice, while themselves committing iniquity, stand accused of falsehood by the inmates of the Kingdom and by those who circle round the throne of their Lord, the Almighty, the Beneficent, for that which their tongues have uttered. Commit not, O people, that which dishonoureth your name and the fair name of the Cause of God amongst men. Beware lest ye approach that which your minds abhor. Fear God and follow not in the footsteps of them that are gone astray. Deal not treacherously with the substance of your neighbour. Be ye trustworthy on earth, and withhold not from the poor the things given unto you by God through His grace. He, verily, will bestow upon you the double of what ye possess. He, in truth, is the All-Bounteous, the Most Generous.[10]

Bahá'u'lláh, as the address to Napoleon III continued, included instructions as to how to convey the Faith to others, and admonished the believers to not be dismayed by rejection.

> Say: We have ordained that our Cause be taught through the power of utterance. Beware lest ye dispute idly with anyone. Whoso ariseth wholly for the sake of his Lord to teach His Cause, the Holy Spirit shall strengthen him and inspire him with that which will illumine the heart of the world, how much more the hearts of those who seek Him. O people of Bahá! Subdue the citadels of men's hearts with the swords of wisdom and of utterance. They that dispute, as prompted by their desires, are indeed wrapped in a palpable veil. Say: The sword of wisdom is hotter than summer heat, and sharper than blades of steel, if ye do but understand. Draw it forth in My name and through the power of My might, and conquer then with it the cities of the hearts of them that have secluded themselves in the stronghold of their corrupt desires. Thus biddeth you the Pen of the All-Glorious, whilst seated beneath the swords of the wayward.
>
> If ye become aware of a sin committed by another, conceal it, that God may conceal your own sin. He, verily, is the Concealer, the Lord of grace abounding. O ye rich ones on earth! If ye encounter one who is poor, treat him not disdainfully. Reflect upon that whereof ye were created. Every one of you was created of a sorry germ. It behoveth you to observe truthfulness, whereby your temples shall be adorned, your names uplifted, your stations exalted amidst men, and a mighty recompense assured for you before God.[11]

The text in the section 'A Tablet to the Guides' then reminds the fledgling believers in North America that the Faith calls them to rectitude of conduct. They must demonstrate their faith through integrity that includes not only trustworthiness, but forgiveness of the wrong-doings of others. They are admonished to always speak truthfully. The believers, while commanded to deliver the Word of God to others through explanations and arguments, are warned that, while delivering the divine message, they are not to dispute with anyone nor to feel themselves in any way superior to another soul.

The Master emphasized that the believers were living in a very special time – the earliest days of a new Dispensation sent from God – by reminding them of the first days of Christianity and speaking to the Americans in a manner reminiscent of Christ's words in the New Testament.

> Let no seditious rumors prevent you from coming into the Kingdom of God and receiving the Spirit of Confirmation. Take for example Jesus Christ, when He was here on earth 1900 years ago, how He was despised by the people to an extent unimaginable. How the Jews and even the Romans refused to have Him buried in their cemeteries, and at last He was interred in a dung-hill which they call now Golgotha. How in the

second century after Christ some of the so-called learned people sprang up and wrote many books in which they denied Christ and His appearance among the people – that there was no person such as Christ, and, in fact, there was no one by this name, that it was only the invention of Peter and Paul, and so many other things besides. But look at the result now, and see! Consider how powerful is the cause of God! Be firm in the faith and let no doubts come to your mind, for THIS CENTURY IS THE MOST IMPORTANT OF ALL. He who pronounces one word of truth now, that word will continue to wave and vibrate without end and will never be annihilated; but not so the contrary. The same result follows those who commit good deeds and bad deeds. Think of the actions and deeds done in the time of the prophets and apostles, and consider – what were they? They were nothing but trifling things in comparison with those done after their times; but we know very well that these small things became known to everybody and will be forever and ever; while the great things done after the times of the apostles were known for a short time only and then were forgotten. What was done by some of the women and men mentioned in the Scriptures, in the time of the apostles? They did nothing of great importance. Some of them received the apostles in their houses, others rendered them service, while others gave them protection and assistance. But after the time of the apostles many built churches, others spent all their money in a charitable way, but nothing is now known about them. What a great difference there is between their works.

Look at the time of Christ! What of the two thieves crucified with him? Each pronounced but one word, and these two words became known for many generations up to the present time, and will still linger in the memories of those who will come after us, although a great many people did greater things after the time of Christ, they were not to be compared with the words of the thieves.[12] Why is this? It is because what took place in the time of Christ and apostles was done in the time of their appearance, the time of distress and persecution. This is the case at present. He who does a very small thing now, that thing will be remembered forever by everyone, but the things done after this time, however great they may be, will never have the same effect, but will be remembered by some and last only for a short time. To do now is of greater preference and importance than hereafter, owing to the paucity of the number of the believers and the circumstances they are surrounded with; for after this time the believers will number millions and millions and they will be the majority everywhere. You are the pioneers and have to work very hard.

You have to be firm and solid. If success in the worldly things (which are nothing in comparison with spiritual) depends on firmness, how much more is the spiritual? He who stands firm will succeed, but the cowards who draw back will never see success. Disagreement is just like poison – whenever the poison enters the body it will kill it all at once, notwithstanding its vitality and strength. So beware not to let this kind of poison enter your heart.[13]

'Abdu'l-Bahá uses other language drawn from the New Testament to instruct the Americans. He elevates their sight, calling them to think about the meaning of the term 'Kingdom of God', a phrase used repeatedly by Christ, and how their actions will bring it about on earth or undermine its coming.

The Kingdom of God is also likened unto the temple of man. We know very well that such temple is composed of many members which differ greatly in shape, form, action and office, and when these different members act in harmony with each other and have the real perfect affinity and attraction among them, they form together that temple which will be thoroughly ready to receive the Spirit – although so various and different. We cannot say that one member is preferred to another, or is of greater importance in the formation of the temple. No, we cannot say that, for each member has its own office and by the action of all in harmony and unison, a perfect result is produced. So is the case with the Kingdom of God, which Kingdom is composed of different members, and if these members, although differing in quality, form, shapes and characters, act in harmony with each other and in perfect agreement, they will form the Kingdom of God and will be ready to receive the confirmation of His Spirit. But if disagreement falls among them and EACH ONE WANTS TO MAKE HIMSELF GREATER THAN THE OTHER, THINKING OF HIS HIGH OFFICE AND IMPORTANCE, the Kingdom of God will not be formed of such members and they will NEVER BE READY OR WORTHY to receive the confirmation of His Spirit.

The Kingdom of God is also likened unto a garden of trees. We all know that a garden in order to be beautiful must contain a good number of trees, various in size and different in colors, flowers and fruits. Some of the trees are tall and some short, some bear good and sweet fruits, some sour and some bitter, but all these trees are necessary to form a garden. No tree can say to the other, 'I am the most important organ of the lot,' or 'I am more profitable than you.' Not so whatever. Because all the trees in that garden are watered by the same Hand, having the same sun and the same breeze passing on them. If any distinction is to be made among

> them, such distinction must belong to the owner of the garden and not to the trees themselves.
>
> So is the Kingdom of God. He is the owner and Lord of the Kingdom, and everything relating to the members of the Kingdom is in His Hands and belongs to Him only, although two members are not equal in everything, but different in size, disposition, quality, character, conduct, color and fruit. Yet, all of them are necessary to form the Kingdom, but they cannot make any distinction among themselves. High distinction belongs only to the Lord of the Kingdom. No one can prefer himself to others, because all are watered by the same Hand, having the same sun, the same breeze of air passing over them; therefore, they should be as one, loving and respecting each other and considering themselves as brothers and sisters and even more, for in spirituality, kinship is not to be considered whatever. Jesus Christ said, 'He who hears my word is my brother, sister and mother.'[14]
>
> Agreement, union, affinity and attraction have a great effect on the universe. Take our globe, for instance. I[t] became so large through the great and perfect union, cohesion, affinity and attraction among the different ingredients and particles of which it is composed, but the small things which we see could not be any larger, owing to the lack of affinity between their and other substance. Thus affinity has a great effect in the enlargement of anything. So also among the believers. It should be the most important factor and the basis of their growth, otherwise they will go asunder if they ever meet with collision or difficulty.[15]

Finally, the Master apparently repeated over and over to Haddad the gist of the following words of Bahá'u'lláh:

> My captivity cannot harm Me. That which can harm Me is the conduct of those who love Me, who claim to be related to Me, and yet perpetrate what causeth My heart and My pen to groan.[16]

In the end, only a handful of people followed Kheiralla other than his own relatives – though in the first months after his defection several hundred adhered to him. He did publish his long-awaited book on the Faith, *Behá'U'lláh,* around the time that the crisis came to a head in 1900, but it did not sell well and was poorly received. A review of it in the *American Journal of Theology* described it as 'a well-meaning production which, however, is so lamentably weak in scientific character as to be practically worthless except as a religious curiosity'.[17] From that point on, Ibrahim Kheiralla rapidly faded from view, exerting no further influence upon the American Bahá'í community. Edward noted in his memoirs that as Kheiralla had begun as a peddler of oriental trinkets, so he returned to that position.[18] In time his only son, George, reverted to Christianity and then converted to Islam. Only his daughters and a small number of others remained loyal to him. He died in obscurity in Beirut on 8 March 1929, as a result of burns received when the boiler on the ship on which he had travelled to Lebanon exploded.[19] Ironically, it was the same day of the year as the one when he had first publicly denounced 'Abdu'l-Bahá in Wisconsin.

Looking back some years later on this unpleasant turning point in the development of the Faith in the United States, Edward wrote:

> . . . the American believers are people who are absolutely sincere seekers of the Light and who are with their heart beats panting at the door which was promised would be opened unto them. When they accept a truth it is at once a part of their life and it matters not who is the person who delivers this truth, when that person loses their confidence he simply places himself outside of their society, and the truth which he taught and which their heart accepts is not sent with him. They retain what they believe to be true, although they may thereafter reject the teacher who taught them. It was this character which Dr. Kh. did not understand. It was this character which made him entirely fail in his plan and which kept the Cause from disruption. It was this character which made the people believe, although they did not have [but] only a few scraps of paper from the Divine Plan upon which to found their faith outside of the prophecies in the Holy Books. It was this character which made it possible for the Holy Spirit and the Divine Mercy of God to so confirm the people who heard the Message and make them strong and sta[u]nch believers without having more than a few words which were uttered by the Manifestation and by Abdul Baha. It was this character which made it possible for them to hear the voice [of the] Shepherd and to flee to the One who utters the Word. It was not the wisdom, the logic, the knowledge nor the cleverness of Dr. Kh. which made a thousand or more intelligent Americans believe in this Revelation, but it was the Spirit which was ever present when he was teaching the people which confirmed them and made them believe . . .[20]

In spite of the damage to the Cause in the West, the Master continued to keep the door open for Kheiralla to return to the fold. Edward must have been dumbstruck and humbled when he read the following words in a letter he received from 'Abdu'l-Bahá in September 1901 in response to Edward's report of his old teacher's defection.

> The person of whom thou didst complain, it behooveth thee to praise him for he was to thee a guide in this Path, and a remedy to thy sick heart, and he was the cup from which thou didst drink the wine of knowledge and the water of faith. If thou receivest a letter containing the news of thy beloved, wouldst thou not kiss it many a time at every moment? And is this not a sign of devotion to thy adored one? And an attraction to the Beauty of thy desire? And if a messenger or a herald comes to thee bringing the news of the arrival of thy loved one, wouldst thou not kiss his hands and feet for the sake of love to thy beloved?[21]

With Kheiralla gone, the remaining steadfast friends set about rebuilding the Faith in America, but this time based upon a much firmer footing. Edward, with the help of others, was able to begin publishing snippets of the Bahá'í Writings. Among the items brought back to America by Kheiralla was a copy of the Hidden Words, one of Bahá'u'lláh's most profound books, even though it is very short. This was translated and printed in March 1900, as were other extracts from Bahá'u'lláh's Writings and Tablets of 'Abdu'l-Bahá. Translating became Haddad's primary occupation. A more formal publishing committee was established in Chicago in 1908. Furthermore, the friends finally began to read the writings and translations of E. G. Browne. The importance of these early publications is self-evident – of course the believers longed for their holy scriptures to be in their own language. But they also filled another void. Until Kheiralla's defection, the friends had relied upon his series of lessons to initiate new believers. Now those lessons were discredited along with their author. Without new, authoritative publications, what could replace them?[22]

'Abdu'l-Karím-i-Ṭihrání returned to Cairo in August after staying only three-and-a-half months in America. Other than forcing Kheiralla to show his true intentions, his primary impact on the American community was encouraging the establishment of Houses of Spirituality, that is, governing councils, in the major communities.[23] Otherwise, his lectures provided little advancement in the knowledge of the true teachings of the Faith and even less inspiration to his American audiences.

By late summer of 1900, the Getsingers were again crossing the Atlantic in the company of a few other Americans on their way to 'Akká to undertake a second pilgrimage. The Dodge and Hoar families arrived in Haifa with them in September. Over the course of the next decade, a number of other American believers would also make pilgrimages to the Holy Land, strengthening not only the connection of their community to 'Abdu'l-Bahá but also to the budding Bahá'í communities in other parts of the world. The Americans began to see themselves as part of something much larger – a world religion.

In the year-and-a-half interim between the first and second pilgrimages of the Getsingers, steps had been taken to solve the language barrier. The daughters of 'Abdu'l-Bahá undertook the earnest study of English, and the Master brought several young reliable believers from Iran who were proficient in English to serve in his household. Lua reported to the believers in Chicago how changed the situation was from before.

> We have found since we are here this time that our dear Master (May my life be a ransom to the dust of His feet!) explained many things to Dr. K. during our first visit, which he (Dr. K) never translated to us, as the teachings of our Lord conflicted with his own ideas – thus he translated, if at all, everything that would substantiate his book. But, thank God, now everything will be made clear, for the Truth is like the light of the sun, – nothing can hide it.[24]

'Abdu'l-Bahá also sent Marian Kheiralla back to New York in October 1900 in the company of Mírzá Asadu'lláh-i-Iṣfahání, in order to deepen the believers. Marian had been privileged to visit the Master a second time following her separation from her husband. Lua vouched for them both in her letter to the Chicago friends.

> This teacher [Asadu'lláh] is one of the best and most trusted servants of our dear Lord, so you can rely upon his every utterance, and Mrs. Kheiralla is born of the Spirit and can show you the right way.[25]

Marian did not follow her former husband, but remained firm in her loyalty to the Faith and to 'Abdu'l-Bahá at least during the first crucial years immediately after Kheiralla's defection.[26] During her second period in 'Akká, Marian wrote to one of the American believers:

> Forget everything you have been taught except that Bahá'u'lláh came and has passed away. 'Abdu'l-Bahá, Center of the Covenant is here, but He is not the re-incarnation of Jesus Christ.[27]

She wrote to Ella about the situation in New York and how it was beginning to recover from the recent crisis. The letter does not give the year, but most likely it was written in May of 1901 or 1902.

> Thank God in New York the believers are becoming a beautifully united body, & so are being more and more moulded into a spiritual understand-

> ing of the blessed Light. Of course one cannot expect a sudden change in the soul's conditions and qualities, but where there is growth, there is life, & this life is very visible in the New Y[ork] Assembly, by the bounty & mercy of God.
>
> But we all need more – oh so much more –of the spirit of the Kingdom of El-Beha [sic], & the fulfillment in our souls & the realisation of His wonderful promises, which will surely appear through some channels sooner or later. God grant through us! I have been here a week. Came with dear Miss Farmer who had been staying in New York for some little time strengthening the believers by the power of her faith & love, & by her soul's pure ideals & understanding. Many have come back who had wandered away, not finding in the presentment hitherto given the Bread of Life for which their souls were seeking – this was especially the case with some who had come to the Faith before a wider understanding & knowledge had come & who had kept-off since then . . . [28]

Lua's October 1900 letter from Haifa, mentioned previously, also contained the good news that 'Abdu'l-Bahá was about to send the great Bahá'í teacher and scholar, Mírzá Abu'l-Faḍl, to the West. While the Getsingers were again in the Holy Land, Mírzá Asadu'lláh, Ḥájí Mírzá Ḥasan-i-Khurásání and Ḥusayn Rúhí arrived in the United States. Mírzá Asadu'lláh is best remembered for his role in bringing the sacred remains of the Báb to the Holy Land from Iran, an heroic undertaking requiring stealth, courage and judgement. He was married to the sister of 'Abdu'l-Bahá's wife, Múnirih Khánum and was very knowledgeable about many aspects of the Bahá'í teachings but, unfortunately, was mainly interested in the mystical aspects of the Faith. Mysticism was a key element of Kheiralla's lessons, and consequently many of the American Bahá'ís found Mírzá Asadu'lláh's classes to be very appealing, especially those interested in dreams, miracles, spiritualism, faith healing and other exotic but perhaps less important religious topics. Women in particular flocked to him, as they had to Kheiralla, to have him interpret their dreams and visions.[29]

Despite his emphasis on mystical subjects, Mírzá Asadu'lláh was able to impart critical information to the Americans about many basic Bahá'í teachings through weekly talks given in Chicago, including some of the religious laws of the Faith such as daily obligatory prayer, fasting for nineteen days once a year, and laws regarding marriage and divorce. The Americans were also eager to learn more about Biblical prophecy, and Mírzá Asadu'lláh was very happy to expound upon that topic as well. But unlike Kheiralla, he was able to support what he said with quotations from the Bahá'í Writings, especially the Kitáb-i-Íqán, Bahá'u'lláh's masterful explanation about the Messengers of

God and their relationship to the Almighty.[30] After Mírzá Asadu'lláh had been in the United States for four months, Thornton Chase extolled him, stating:

> . . . we are beginning to understand what in reality was taught by the Manifestation [Bahá'u'lláh] and explained to us by Abdel Baha; these [lectures by Mírzá Asadu'lláh] are being printed from time to time . . . you, no doubt, will find them as we have found them, so powerful, so direct, so simple, that there will be no question as to what we will teach.[31]

While the Getsingers were on their second pilgrimage they had become acquainted with a bright Persian believer in his early twenties who knew passable English, Is͟hti'ál-ibn-i-Kalántar, better known as Ali-Kuli Khan. Khan would come to play an important role in the development of the Faith in the United States and was unknowingly being prepared for it by 'Abdu'l-Bahá, who was employing Khan's services in His own household as a translator and secretary. 'Abdu'l-Bahá directed him to go to the United States in 1901 ahead of Mírzá Abu'l-Faḍl in order to serve as the translator for the great scholar. The Master understood all too well the crying need for authoritative Bahá'í literature in the fledgling Western communities. He wished not only for Mírzá Abu'l-Faḍl to give lectures, but also that he should write a general book about the Faith. Khan met up with Mírzá Abu'l-Faḍl in Paris, where he was already being assisted by Anton Haddad, and then preceded him to New York in June.[32] Khan gave a number of talks in New York, to mixed reviews. Like most of the Persians sent to instruct the Americans, it took time and experience for him to understand his audience.[33]

Finally, in September of 1901, the preeminent scholar himself arrived in the United States to much greater fanfare than had greeted the earlier Persian Bahá'í teachers. Mírzá Abu'l-Faḍl's reputation as a renowned academic at the centre of Islamic scholarship, Cairo, attracted attention from the press and others in addition to the Bahá'í community. He spent brief periods in New York and Chicago before taking up residence at a boarding house in a fashionable section of Washington, D.C. where he was the guest of the Barney family. Alice Barney, the mother of Laura Clifford Barney, had returned from Paris and she, as well as Laura, took responsibility for providing comfortable surroundings for the great man as he began his most pressing task, the writing of a general book about the Faith for Western readers.

Mírzá Abu'l-Faḍl met with many believers and others, patiently answering their questions. He was the ideal person to instruct the Americans because he was a student of religion in general and not just the Bahá'í Faith. He had already penned a book for Jewish readers and another for Zoroastrians. His erudition included detailed knowledge of Christianity, a topic of much interest to the Americans. He lived in the United States much as he had in Cairo, as an ascetic. He ate mainly crackers and drank copious amounts of tea. In fact, he strictly denied himself basic necessities, such as food, to such an extent that one day he collapsed from lack of nourishment and had to be persuaded by his hostess to begin eating the food readily available to him (and already paid for) at the boarding house. Between his meetings with inquirers and his public lectures, he cloistered himself in his room and slowly wrote. Years later Ali-Kuli Khan confided to his family that he had had to 'pull' the book out of the author.[34] The unsurpassed scholar felt unworthy to undertake such an assignment but carried it out as an act of obedience to 'Abdu'l-Bahá.

In his introduction to his book Mírzá Abu'l-Faḍl wrote of why the work was necessary – alluding to the many incorrect accounts of the Faith abroad in both the East and the West.

> It is known to men of learning, that down to the present year, this new Movement, the light of which has penetrated most of the eastern and western countries; – this religious belief upon which depends the reformation of the world and the unification of nations; – according to the testimony of the Holy Scriptures, has been founded and upheld by three holy persons. As those who have attempted to write of this Movement, particularly the writers of newspapers and magazines, have mixed up true and false statements, and have colored historical facts with personal prejudices, it is therefore impossible for readers and students to rely upon and profit by their accounts. Even the very sources of their records and the obvious contrast between them, bear testimony of their unreliability. It has therefore been deemed necessary to depict in these pages a true, substantial and succinct account concerning the birth, fountain-source and circumstances of these 'Three Lights', which cannot be disputed or doubted. With regard to misrepresentations made by prejudiced people concerning certain facts, we leave the exposure of these to the natural and inevitable laws of development and progression; for time and circumstances do not permit the writer to enter into details of proofs and arguments upon all these points. God the Exalted will enable us to accomplish our undertaking.[35]

When the book, *The Bahäi Proofs: also A Short Sketch of the History and Lives of the Leaders of This Religion,* was published in 1902, for the first time the believers in the West (both in Europe and North America) had an accurate and comprehensive text about the history and teachings of their Faith. It was a momentous achievement and another turning point.

The correspondence between the Master and the Western believers beginning in 1900 had accelerated. Almost every week, Ali-Kuli Khan, who had taken over the role of translator after Haddad returned to Lebanon in 1902, would receive a large packet of responses to correspondence from the American believers in the mail from 'Akká. He would then spend countless hours – often beginning at six in the morning – translating 'Abdu'l-Bahá's messages before posting them with cover notes to the recipients.[36] Khan raised the level of translation, not only because of his growing command of English but because he had spent time working directly with the Master. This issue of translation would remain a problem for the believers who did not speak Arabic or Persian for many decades and would ameliorate during the time of Shoghi Effendi's ministry when the Guardian laid down guidelines for transliteration and would himself provide the templates for future translators through his exquisite renditions of many passages of the Writings into English. But in 1901, Ali-Kuli Khan at age 22 was breaking new ground.

By 1903, Thornton Chase was able to write the following optimistic description about the health of the mother community of the United States, Chicago – the one most damaged by Kheiralla.

> Chicago is prospering. The group meetings are doing noble work. The Sunday evening meetings are blessed by the Spirit of God. They are well attended, and strangers are attracted to them. They are peaceful, dignified and spiritual. The test of time and patient waiting has sifted out the manifestations of self-desires, and those who have stood have gained in strength and understanding. Praise be unto God for His Mercies to each of us.[37]

In the end, the misrepresentations of the Bahá'í Faith during its infancy in the West did not matter. Distortions of doctrine, false teachings, and fanciful additions were ultimately corrected. Time was the great healer when love and patience were amply applied. The Master showered the Western friends with love and encouragement, first through His correspondence and their pilgrimages and then by His own visit to the West between 1911 and 1913. That historic journey provided the remaining necessary adjustments to the change of course set in motion by the first Western pilgrimage. Finally, the sails were unfurled and the ship was under way, its course true.

CHAPTER 14

Keeping the Candles Ablaze

Nell Hillyer and Ella Goodall had no occasion to notice the storm clouds gathering over most of the Bahá'í communities in the United States. They were floating through Europe, enjoying themselves as only single young people who need not worry about money can do. Ella, less travelled than her companion, probably considered the experience to be a once-in-a-lifetime opportunity to taste first hand all the culture, history and adventure Europe had to offer.

Back at home in Oakland, California, Ella's mother was keenly following their journey through her daughter's correspondence. Helen Goodall was so energized by the teachings of the Faith imparted to her by Haddad in New York, even though that knowledge was very limited, that she wasted no time in sharing the Faith with her friends. It didn't take long before several ladies showed at least polite interest. Helen would share Ella's letters with them and Ella would do her best to assist with the teaching work by adding messages to them in her notes home. She even wrote directly, while still in Europe, to one of those her mother was teaching about the Faith.[1] Even in those early experiences of sharing their new-found beliefs, there was recognition of the need for wisdom and prudence. For example, in one letter Ella instructed her mother to share her letter with one of the interested ladies, but after consulting with Nell, added a postscript that perhaps it would be better not to do so. Through her correspondence, Ella certainly increased her mother's longing to know more, and, despite her detailed descriptions of her time in 'Akká, assured her mother that a letter could never do the visit justice; only coming home and telling her about it face to face would suffice. Ella had hardly left Haifa for the last time before she was full of ideas of what they should do to promote the Faith in California, bolstered by a restored sense of hope for the future. Apparently, prior to the pilgrimage, she and her mother had ascribed to Millennialism – a belief widely held in late nineteenth-century America that the Biblical Day of Reckoning was at hand and the end of the world was nigh. They needn't worry, wrote Ella, that their work to spread the Cause would end suddenly in the Apocalypse:

> ...I must tell you that the Millennium is not so near as we thought it was so that things are not going to bust up all at once, but the world will go on for many thousands of years yet and we have to live this life in a way to best prepare us for the next one. You know how absolutely we all lost interest in everything as nothing seemed worth while if everything was going to smash in a few years.[2]

When Nell and Ella arrived in Paris[3] after their sojourn in Egypt, perhaps they noticed the same thing that Edward did – that their benefactress was no longer in as good a mood as when they had last seen her on their arrival in the Holy Land.[4] Edward surmised that Phoebe Hearst was upset because of Kheiralla's behaviour, especially his attempt to cheat her and the Egyptian friends out of money. Undoubtedly that incident didn't help, but other matters were occupying her mind. The weighty responsibilities and cares of her life tracked her down in Paris, punctured the joys she had found in 'Akká and undermined the restorative effects of her holiday cruise. As always, the largest problem occupying her thoughts was her son. William Randolph Hearst wanted more than anything to become President of the United States, and his role in bringing about the Spanish–American War had stoked the flames of his political ambitions. He had become a national player on the American political stage and was calculating his next move in his pursuit of the country's highest office. The Hearst newspapers provided Will with a powerful means of influencing voters on the East Coast and the West Coast, but he had come to recognize that his ambitions were handicapped by not having a voice in the Mid-West, the heartland of America. The obvious solution was to buy or start a newspaper in Chicago as soon as possible, before the fame he had won through the recent war waned. Phoebe, however, controlled the family treasury, Will's easiest source of capital. Will wrote to her in Europe in the spring of 1899, as she was returning from her travels in the Middle East, demanding that she provide the funds for him to start a Chicago newspaper. She was resolved to deny him because she believed that the two newspapers he already owned only drained the Hearst estate.[5] She knew that establishing a newspaper was as costly as opening a new mine, and that in the end it would likely prove to be a hole in which to bury money, not make it; and she was already feeling financially stretched. Will, as usual, would not take 'no' for an answer and threatened to come to Paris to argue his case. She was not unsympathetic to his claims that, by right, he should have half of his father's estate, but she was only too conscious of her son's spendthrift tendencies. This battle of wills drained her. In the end, she won the round but paid a heavy price emotionally. Her son would not get a Chicago paper, at least, not yet.[6]

Phoebe had one other matter to attend to upon her return to Paris: Anne Apperson's presentation at the Court of St James in London which had been arranged by Phoebe's friend, the United States ambassador to England. Presentation at the English court was the apex of being a debutante and would also save Phoebe the bother and expense of a lavish ball in Washington, D.C. or New York in order to present Anne to society.[7] Always the good foster mother, Phoebe offered Nell the same opportunity to be presented to the English court or, alternatively, the funds it would cost. Nell wisely took the money.[8]

Ella and Nell enjoyed watching Anne go through the flurry of dress fittings in Paris and always remembered how lovely she looked in her ceremonial robes with three feathers in her carefully arranged hair.[9] Though the gown was custom-made in Paris, the last touches – feathers for Anne's hair and the length of the train – were finalized in London because the court apparently had rules about such things, lest any young debutante overstep the bounds of good taste. On 8 June, Nell and Phoebe escorted Anne in the carriage to where she was dropped off for her presentation and by the time the carriage had circled the nearby park and returned, Anne was already at the curb waiting for them, the entire event over in a matter of minutes. Nell summed it up years later: 'Dear me, dear me, such fol-da-rol. I was glad I had not weakened and gone to all the fuss and bother.'[10]

With Anne 'brought out' and the vacating of Phoebe's Paris residence well under way, Phoebe, Anne and her remaining entourage sailed for New York leaving Nell and Ella behind to continue their extended holiday.[11] Ella had relations and an old friend to visit in England. Phoebe assigned Nell tasks to carry out in Paris and London, such as dealing with government offices on her behalf. The young ladies made new friends while in London, including two young bachelors who were already or would later become popular writers: Frank Gelett Burgess[12] and Oliver Onions.[13] Oliver was also a violinist and Nell recounted how the four of them went to a performance together one evening.

> Once there was a very special performance on at Covent Garden and we could get no seats, so we proposed buying sandwiches for dinner and standing in line for gallery seats. No quicker said than done. We were able to get apple boxes to sit on so we did not have to stand too long, and reinforced by our sandwiches and milk we got along quite nicely . . . Ella was specially musical, of course Oliver was and felt the full gamut of emotions. Once during the performance he asked Ella for the opera glasses and when he put them to his eyes he found the rims all wet. He turned to Ella

and said, 'Why, you have been crying. I never thought anybody did that but me.'[14]

As the summer of 1899 wore on London became intolerably warm, and so the young ladies headed for the cooler countryside of France where they hired bicycles and 'had great fun gliding over the wonderful country lanes'.[15]

Several of the returning pilgrims took time while in England to contact E. G. Browne, whose writings on the Faith Kheiralla had asked the American believers to eschew. Perhaps 'Abdu'l-Bahá suggested that they make contact as He Himself was corresponding with that eminent orientalist during that period. Mrs Thornburgh-Cropper recounted that Browne stated to her that the Bahá'ís he encountered in Iran were 'the most truly religious people he had ever met'.[16] Browne also gave Nell the name of someone in Paris who could teach her Arabic and she did make the attempt to pursue learning that language upon returning to Paris by contacting the recommended teacher.[17] It does not appear that this initial contact with the only Western scholar to ever meet Bahá'u'lláh was pursued further by any of the believers in Europe, at least for some years.

That June of 1899, Nell wrote to 'Abdu'l-Bahá and told Him of her intention to remain in Europe during that summer to pursue the study of Arabic so that she could become proficient enough to read the Bahá'í Holy Writings in their original language. She told Him how much her time with Him and the members of His household had deeply touched her, that she reflected daily upon that visit and on every word He had uttered to her. She was still trying to truly realize the blessings she had received.

> The wonderful atmosphere of love and kindness that surrounds the entire Household, is also most dear to my memory, and I only hope that a little of it has clung to me and with God's help I may be able to diffuse the same spirit in many quarters of the world.[18]

However, Nell went on to tell 'Abdu'l-Bahá that she was not yet teaching others about the Faith because she did not feel that she had enough knowledge to give proofs. She wanted to be thorough enough in her rendering of the Truth so that 'no doubts could enter any one's mind'.[19]

Ella and Nell purchased and dispatched gifts to 'Abdu'l-Bahá with their correspondence as small tokens of their love, gratitude and esteem. Nell sent Him a silver spoon and Ella a snuff box, the latter being a very odd choice as the Master did not use tobacco products, but instead discouraged their use, though a small box could be employed in other ways. They had surely observed that the Master had no interest in material possessions and so it must have been difficult to decide what to buy for Him. The Master sent a reply to Ella later that year in which He had this to say about her gift to Him:

> As to the snuff box which thou hast sent, We are using it and thinking of thee, and We will call upon God for thee at all times. And as the snuff box doeth away with a cold in the head and doth perfume the channel of breathing, I shall ask God that through thee He will even so clear away the stoppage (or cold) of the spirit out of men and women, and make them to breathe in the sweet savors of the gardens of the love of God, which doth quicken the souls and maketh the hearts of the people of salvation to live.[20]

By November they were finally on their way back across the Atlantic on a big freighter where they enjoyed 'excellent big staterooms and the run of the boat'.[21] Upon reaching New York, the two companions finally went their separate ways, Nell going first to Washington, D.C. to see Phoebe before leaving for California and Ella speeding west, bound for home and her eagerly waiting family. Nell had more to occupy her thoughts than just her pilgrimage when she finally departed the East Coast.

> There was someone in San Francisco I was most anxious to see. Of course, I wired Sister when I was arriving and knew she would notify a number of my enquiring friends, but there was one that I knew would do no communicating so I sent a special wire.
>
> Some of my friends and the family came over to the pier to meet me and others were at the ferry, among them dear Edward Sheldon, who said, 'Do come downtown for dinner with us all and we'll give you a jolly welcome.' I had hopes for another plan for the evening so I said, 'Not tonight, make it tomorrow.' Of course, that was all right and I went home to my sister and the children. They were all sitting around me in an admiring circle listening to me chatter when at about six p.m. the telephone rang and it was the voice I had hoped to hear. It said, 'What are you doing this evening?' My reply was, 'Spending it anywhere with you.' Whereupon, he said, 'I will be out about eight.' The voice was that of Philip King Brown, the man that became my beloved husband.[22]

Six months after her return to California, Nell became the first of the pilgrims to marry. The small wedding ceremony, on 7 March 1900, was held at the Hearst penthouse in downtown San Francisco; that same Hearst residence which only eighteen months earlier had been the scene of the first Bahá'í classes in the western United States. Phoebe carried out the role of mother for the orphaned bride. No-fuss Nell kept it simple, though she did wear a gown of satin and rare lace. A judge rather than a clergyman officiated at the ceremony, which was witnessed mainly by close relatives.[23] It would be a long and happy union which produced three sons and a daughter named Phoebe – making Nell the only one of the pilgrims to have a large family.

The bridegroom, Dr Brown, was an outstanding member of the medical profession. His mother had been a prominent physician, the founder of a hospital for children and a friend of Phoebe.[24] He was a graduate of both Harvard University and its medical school and had continued his studies with postgraduate work in Germany. He was an early advocate of health insurance, a member of the medical faculty at Stanford University and the founder of a notable sanatorium for women suffering from tuberculosis. Nell shared his interest in helping the patients at the sanatorium for many years, though her primary occupation remained the well-being of her children and household.[25]

Next to marry was Julia Pearson who, no longer employed as a teacher for Agnes, married in 1901. Her husband, William Hunt, was a fellow graduate of Cornell University and worked as an engineer. They lived primarily in the greater New York City area and Connecticut. Their only child, Pearson Hunt, continued the Pearson family trait of excelling in the academic world by serving for many years as a distinguished professor at the Harvard University School of Business. Julia apparently worked solely as a housewife after her marriage.

Anne Apperson had 'as elaborate and beautiful a wedding as ever took place in California'[26] when she married Dr Joseph Marshall Flint in a Parisian gown of white satin at the Hacienda – Phoebe presiding, of course. The Episcopal ceremony, held on 15 September 1903, was conducted in the cavernous music room which had been transformed into a chapel complete with an altar, great vases of pink and white tiger lilies and baskets of pink and white flowers, which were hung from the rafters. Flowers were everywhere. An enormous tent was erected over a patio for the wedding breakfast. The guests not only included her illustrious first cousin, Will, then the only declared candidate for President and a first-term Congressman, but the highest academic officials in California and other distinguished friends of her aunt.

Dr Flint, originally from Chicago and a Princeton graduate, was, like Dr Brown, a medical researcher connected with Stanford University at the time. He later became the first full-time professor of surgery at Yale University Medical School and is best remembered for organizing and leading the Yale mobile surgical hospital during World War I. His time spent near the front lines of that conflict cost him his health and required his early retirement from teaching medicine. The Flints had no children, perhaps because Anne often suffered from health problems throughout her life. Anne was widowed in 1945 and would be one of the last of the first Western pilgrims to pass away. She died on 13 July 1970 at the age of 92,[27] just a few weeks before Julia Pearson Hunt passed away at the age of 93.[28] Despite the advantages of wealth and prominent connections, Anne's life was full of tests and difficulties. At the time of her marriage, 'Abdu'l-Bahá sent a message to her through Ella reminding her of the bounty of being a Bahá'í:

> Verily thy Lord has chosen thee for His service, and elected thee for His Knowledge, that thou mayest receive the Fire of His Love, and be attracted by His breeze! And the kingdoms of the earth, or the treasures of the whole world are not to be compared to this Gift. Therefore know its value and appreciate its worth![29]

In other Tablets written after her marriage, 'Abdu'l-Bahá called Anne to firmness and steadfastness in the face of severe trials and encouraged her to lead her husband to the Faith.[30]

The Master had tried to subtly warn the young ladies among the pilgrims of the danger of being pulled away from the Faith through the pressures exerted upon them by their families. The world of women during the late nineteenth century, despite reforms brought about by the women's suffrage movement,[31] continued to revolve around the home. Most women were powerless to make the important decisions of their own lives, and were controlled because of economic dependence first by their fathers and then by their husbands. During Nell and Ella's time in 'Akká, the Master told Nell the story of St Barbara, an early Christian born into wealth and privilege who was persecuted by her own family because of her acceptance of the Faith of Jesus. Despite the severe trials brought upon St Barbara by her own father and relatives, her faith never wavered. (The Master did not go so far as to relate the end of the story of St Barbara. According to Christian tradition, she was martyred at the insistence of her father for her refusal to recant her faith.)[32] Nonetheless, 'Abdu'l-Bahá, Who knew the human heart better than any mortal, proved correct. As the young ladies married, they began to drift away from the Bahá'í Faith. Julia apparently completely lost touch with the Bahá'í community and her fellow pilgrims after her marriage. Anne continued to cherish the Faith in her heart, but as the elderly widow of a strong-willed husband, she related to Ella that her ability to participate actively in the Faith had been severely circumscribed for many years by those close to her.[33] From the earliest years of her marriage, her husband opposed her connections to the Faith and urged her to give it up.[34] Anne had continued to attend Bahá'í gatherings at the Goodall home for several years after her marriage.[35]

On the other hand, Nell Hillyer Brown and her husband invited the Master to visit them at their San Francisco home during His visit to the United States in 1912, though it happened that when He did finally come to California, the Brown family was travelling at the time. Nell wrote to 'Abdu'l-Bahá of her 'deepest regret and disappointment' that she did not get even a glimpse of Him and that she had missed the opportunity to entertain Him in her home and to introduce her husband and children to Him. Nonetheless, she expressed the hope that they would meet before He departed from America.[36] Apparently, she finally did see Him while He was in Washington, D.C.[37] Even though Nell seldom if ever participated in the gatherings of the Bahá'í Faith after her marriage, she wrote warmly of it in her memoirs, which were penned during her final illness. None of her children became believers.

So it was when Ella, the last to marry, wrote to the Master in 1902 to announce her engagement to Dr Charles Miner Cooper, that 'Abdu'l-Bahá made the following reply.

> Thou announceth thy marriage to a servant of God to occur in the near future, asking divine blessing on this union, so that God grant thee children which may be reared in the Bosom of the Love of God, and to receive the Bounty of the Kingdom of God. Blessed is this good intention. But it is incumbent on thee to strive greatly and to exert ample endeavour to guide thy revered husband, because some of the maidservants of God have been in a state of the greatest longing and attraction for the Kingdom of God, and when they married the husbands overcame them and they became lukewarm in the Love of God and forgot 'Abdu'l-Bahá. But some remained firm as mighty mountains in the Cause of God and led their husbands to the Kingdom of God.
>
> Make thou thy feet firm in this great Cause and guide thy revered husband into the Kingdom of the great Lord, so that the Divine blessing comprehend both of thee and ye become confirmed in a Cause whereby those horizons become radiant by the light of a sun in the day of the Covenant.[38]

Ella's engagement to Dr Cooper, a younger distant relative and native of England, was prolonged for more than a year, so that he could get his medical practice in California on a firmer footing.[39] The wedding took place on 11 May 1904, at her parents' Jackson Street home which was abundantly decked with flowers for the occasion. Like Nell, she invited only close relatives and friends to the evening affair. Despite the small guest list, Ella, in keeping with her social standing, wore a costly white chiffon gown trimmed in Irish lace, and carried a bouquet of white orchids and lilies of the valley.[40] She sent 'Abdu'l-Bahá a photograph, most likely her wedding portrait, and received the following note of congratulations:

> Though happiness and joy have taken place through earthly marriage still I hope bounty and heavenly blessing will surround you and that your honorable husband by associating with (you who are) the servant of God will be attracted towards the Greatest Name so that you both will dwell like two doves in the nest of the love of God, and at last you will soar upwards to the height of the Supreme Concourse. That happiness will be perpetual and everlasting throughout the centuries of eternity, and that joy will be the cause of felicity in all the worlds of God, and spiritual feelings will surround (you) from every direction. O servant of God, truly until now you have moved and walked in the path of the Everlasting Light with firmness and steadfastness and if God wishes now, more than heretofore, you will be assisted to be firm in the Covenant and you will be the cause of the guidance of others.
>
> O God, make this marriage the cause of heavenly blessings, the cause of enkindling (hearts) by the fire of Thy love in the everlasting Kingdom. Grant (Thy) favour that both may become near to Thy Holy Threshold, and firm in Thy love, and day by day may progress in spiritual conditions, and may become two manifest signs amongst the people of faith and assurance.[41]

Ella took this message from 'Abdu'l-Bahá to heart and began to teach her husband the Faith. Dr Cooper did ask questions and attended occasional lectures by visiting Bahá'í teachers, such as one given by the accomplished speaker, Isabella Brittingham,[42] but he never became formally enrolled in the Bahá'í Faith and his thoughts on religion remain unknown. Nonetheless Ella's marriage did not curtail her service to the Cause, perhaps because she had a firm and strong ally in her mother and the young couple lived most of their first years as husband and wife with Ella's parents, first in Oakland and then across the bay in San Francisco. Dr Cooper, like Dr Brown and Dr Flint, was also a medical researcher and professor associated with Stanford University. He became a distinguished cardiologist of such renown that when President Warren Harding suffered a heart attack (that would prove fatal) while visiting California, Dr Cooper was called upon to attend to the President during his final days. Dr Cooper also wrote articles for popular magazines and published some poetry. The marriage did not produce any children. The couple remained devoted to each other to the end of their lives; in fact, Ella suddenly passed away while in the process of arranging her husband's funeral in 1951.

In the end, the only husband of any of the young ladies who were unmarried at the time of the pilgrimage to become a Bahá'í was William Sutherland Maxwell, who married May Bolles. Even though May had an extraordinary ability to attract hearts to the Cause, he did not formally enter the Faith until 1909, seven years after their marriage. The Maxwells would have only one child: a daughter Mary who married Shoghi Effendi in 1937 and is better known to history as Amatu'l-Bahá Rúḥíyyih Khánum – certainly one of the greatest believers produced by the Faith. Both May's husband and daughter would be named Hands of the Cause of God.

When the pilgrims departed from the Holy Land in 1899, 'Abdu'l-Bahá was well aware that some left as bright torches but others were only flickering small flames whose new-born faith would not easily withstand the tests they would face in the greater world. He did his best, given the limitations of correspondence, to strengthen them, to admonish them to be firm. For example, He addressed Ella in 1903:

> O thou maidservant of God: Verily the Cause is great, great, and the tests and trials severe, severe. The winds of trials shall uproot great trees and this was witnessed in the time of Christ, for Peter, the disciple, although addressed by Jesus thus: 'Thou art the Rock and upon this Rock I shall build my church'; nevertheless, when trials appeared, he denied Christ thrice. Therefore know thou the power of trials and grieve not at anything. Let thy bosom expand with the fragrances of God. Verily God will confirm thee in all conditions and circumstances . . .
>
> The Pharisees cast suspicion [doubts] at all times among the hearers, saying: these are facts garnered from the contents of the Torat, or the intellectual proofs known to the public and to the chosen. With these doubts they aim to shake the footing of the weak, but to those who are firm in knowledge, these doubts were more flimsy than a spider's web. Nay, rather, a mirage but no water. I ask God to make the hearts as firm as mountains, unshaken by the strongest winds, or the storms of doubt.[43]

After the return of the pilgrims, it quickly evolved that May was the conduit of correspondence between most of the believers in Europe and 'Abdu'l-Bahá; Ella (and sometimes her mother) served the same role for the believers in the western United States, with Lua and, to a lesser extent, Edward running in between. The Paris/London and California communities had not been affected by the troubles brought about by Kheiralla and provided a balance to the Chicago and New York communities which took some years to recover from the severe tests that had almost destroyed them. May's move to Canada ended her role as liaison for Europe, but Ella's continued on for many years. In fact, after several years of not being able to post letters, the first message the Master sent to the American believers following the cessation of hostilities in Palestine at the end of World War I was conveyed through Ella.[44] She proved to be a trustworthy and competent correspondent, and her social position made it possible for her to discreetly pass on messages to those for whom the arrival at their home of a letter from 'Akká could prove awkward. Her role as primary correspondent for the West Coast only ended with the development of the Bahá'í Administrative Order in the United States and the first election of Assemblies and their officers. Not surprisingly, she was among the nine members elected to the first National Spiritual Assembly of the United States and Canada in 1922.[45] (Likewise, Mary Virginia Thornburgh-Cropper would be elected to the first Spiritual Assembly for England in 1922, and its first meeting would be held in her home.[46])

The first letters sent to Ella from the Master demonstrated the dangers that perpetually dogged Him, dangers enhanced by the visit of the first Western pilgrims. Messages were dispatched from Haifa to Port Said where Aḥmad Yazdí would translate them into French and then forward them to Ella. The language was guarded, with never a direct mention of 'Abdu'l-Bahá, 'Akká or the Faith. Instead the vague letters referred to the 'Beloved' and 'Holy Spot', for example, rather than using direct names and places. The recipient was assumed to be able to read between the lines, and it was obviously hoped that government censors or spies in the post office could not.

After the visit of the Hearst party set off alarms in Istanbul, 'Abdu'l-Bahá was again severely restricted, but in a few months the edicts from the Ottoman capital began to be forgotten or ignored and He enjoyed some freedom to move about the area and to welcome the second wave of American pilgrims between September of 1900 and the spring of 1901, during which time the Getsingers and Harriet Thornburgh made their second visits. The construction of the Shrine of the Báb was also progressing during this brief respite, and the two achievements – the construction of the mausoleum and the visits of more American Bahá'ís – provided new excuses for the enemies of 'Abdu'l-Bahá to complain to the government. The Americans were reported to be foreign agents sent to help Him overthrow the Turks, and the building on Mount Carmel was alleged to be a fortress. Taking no chances, in 1901 an order was issued from the Sublime Porte at the express direction of the Sultan himself, demanding that 'Abdu'l-Bahá be kept within the confines of the walls of 'Akká. He was not even allowed to visit His Father's resting

Anton Haddad (left against fence) and 'Abdu'l-Karím-i-Ṭihrání at a picnic with the Chicago believers at the Thacher farm in 1900, where Edward Getsinger had his series of visions several years earlier

The Chicago friends with Mírzá Asadu'lláh-i-Isfahání and other Persian teachers and interpreters, c. 1900

Mary Virginia Thornburgh-Cropper ('Minnie'), called 'Maryam Khánum' by 'Abdu'l-Bahá

Earliest known portrait of Ella Goodall Cooper, taken in 1917

May Maxwell

Ella Goodall Cooper (left) and Helen Goodall (centre) with an unidentified friend

place within sight of the prison city. Again, pilgrimage for both Western and Eastern believers was curtailed.

After the first pilgrimage of the Western believers, during which the need for a competent, unbiased translator was painfully apparent, 'Abdu'l-Bahá brought to 'Akká not only Ali-Kuli Khan, mentioned previously, but also another young Persian believer who knew English, Youness Afroukhteh (Yúnis Kh<u>h</u>án), who served as translator and secretary. Both recounted in their memoirs how the barrage of letters from America and Europe kept them busy for long hours each day. In the midst of the dangers and hardships surrounding the household of the Master, the reports from the West of the growth of the Faith brought joy and served as a counterweight to the sorrows from renewed persecutions in Iran and machinations of the enemies of the Faith in the Holy Land.[47] Not only would 'Abdu'l-Bahá make the letters from the Western friends available to visitors from the East to peruse, He would often direct that some of them be translated and sent to Iran where they gave heart to that sore-tried community.

Typical of the letters sent to the American pilgrims after their return was the following sent to Nell via Ella in 1902 or thereabouts. 'Abdu'l-Bahá did not wait for those He was concerned about to write to Him first. He called them back to God, to the life of the spirit, when the world pulled them in the opposite direction.

He is God!

O thou who art inclining thine ear to the words of Abdu'l-Baha! Months and years have passed and no news of thee came to this Consecrated Spot, until thy affectionate sister, thy very dear friend, the handmaid of God, Goodall, spoke of thee. Her mention of thee before Me moved the sea of my yearning for thee, and stirred My love for thee. Wherefore I desired to make mention of thee in words that would dilate thy breast with heavenly gladness, and spiritual joy, and celestial glad-tidings, and holy fragrances.

O thou handmaid of God! Call thou to mind the nights and days when thou wert one of a company in the Holy Shrines, and 'Abdu'l-Bahá addressed thee with words which cheered the heart and delighted the hearing, and gladdened the breast, and rejoiced the souls.

O handmaid of God! Know thou, every comfort passeth away, and every joy and pleasure fadeth, and every ease and bounty perisheth, and only that which belongeth to the Abhá Realm abideth forever. Consider past ages: they came, they passed. And thousands of queens have vanished away, like scattered dust, and no name or word or trace of them remaineth.

> They became as if they had never been. Their crowns were shattered, their realms divided, their hosts dispersed, their assemblages broken up, their covenants made void, their gladness changed to mourning.
>
> But consider the handmaids of the All-Merciful: these are as pearls attracted by the sweet fragrances of God in ages past, and their stars will gleam on the horizon of sanctity for evermore, and the luminous jewels of their crowns shine down on the passage of aeons and cycles. Truly in this is an admonition to men of insight.
>
> O handmaid of God! My spiritual love for thee is ardent, and I desire that thou become distinguished by heavenly attributes in this glorious age, this wondrous day. And upon thee be greeting and praise![48]

Though separated by great distances, 'Abdu'l-Bahá showered his love upon these fledgling believers through his letters. These precious epistles, though often brief, reminded them to be steadfast, to teach the Faith to others. Often He emphasized the spiritual virtues that were theirs, or could be with effort. Occasionally he answered a specific question. Above all, his Tablets provided encouragement. He always assured them of His prayers on their behalf. Ella wrote about how the receipt of a letter from 'Abdu'l-Bahá was an event to be celebrated among the small handful of believers in the Oakland area.

> There being no Baha'i books available in English . . . the believers were dependent for their teaching upon some of the communes and an occasional tablet from 'Abdu'l-Bahá. The receipt of a tablet caused the greatest joy and the friends would be called together at Mrs. Goodall's home and many hours would be spent in making long-hand copies to share with one another.[49]

The pilgrims also corresponded with several of the Egyptian believers and with a few of the ladies of the Master's family, especially those of his daughters who were learning English. Often they asked questions, such as the meaning of Biblical passages, in their letters to 'Abdu'l-Karím and the other Persians sent to the United States to deepen their knowledge, rather than bother 'Abdu'l-Bahá with their enquiries. They also wrote to each other. May, Ella, and Minnie in particular cemented the friendships established during the period of the pilgrimage by maintaining a correspondence that continued intermittently to the end of their lives. They reported to each other how the teaching work was progressing in their own communities, passed on news, sometimes elicited help from their sisters in the Cause of God, and generally encouraged each other. One can only imagine in those early years, when even London,

Paris and San Francisco boasted no more than a handful of believers, how much it must have been appreciated to know that they did not labour alone.

As those of the first pilgrims who became brightly burning candles took what they had gained from their experiences at the feet of 'Abdu'l-Bahá and began to apply those lessons to their lives, especially through acts of service, they began to reflect on the pilgrimage and the progress they had made in their personal development because of that transforming journey. Ella wrote to 'Abdu'l-Bahá in 1905:

> . . . I know that in many ways I have grown since that first Visit, it seems as if I could appreciate the meeting so deeply now, and 'emptying my cup' would come away from Thy Holy Presence so filled with the Water and Fire of God's love, that people would only need to look at my face to become believers! Alas! Why did I not know all this upon that first happy occasion when I was like a child just beginning to learn to talk, who, charmed with its own performance, neglects to listen enough to the Source of Wisdom? However it is not to be that I shall have that blessing again now, and so I crave the happiness of a Letter . . .[50]

Margaret Peeke, who also busied herself with teaching the Faith to others and then in strengthening those new believers in her small Ohio community, wrote to the Master in 1904:

> It will soon be five years since I was led by the Spirit to Acca, and as the years and months have passed, the love for the Lord has increased, until it seems as if I could write volumes on his goodness and his wonderful works to his children. That evening when you met me so graciously, and then received your kindness next morning and gave me the beautiful flowers is as vivid to me as if it were yesterday; and when I realize that at that time, (through prejudice that had entered my mind by a false teacher,) I really had no interest in all that Acca represented, I see clearly your marvellous insight into my heart, that enabled you to look through the prejudice, and see my earnest desire for Truth. Sometime when we meet I know you will tell me why I have been so greatly blessed with your loving kindness.[51]

And in a subsequent letter written during the twilight of her life, she expressed her gratitude for the time in 'Akká.

> In my heart birds are singing, and the Spirit of God fills it with joy that in that year of 1899 I visited Acca, though at that time I went blindly. Never

> shall I forget the first time I saw you raise your eyes and look upon me. It was after we had taken our cup of tea together. You looked through me and knew me, and I, who did not know myself, have never ceased to feel those eyes still reading my soul.[52]

Margaret repeatedly remarked to 'Abdu'l-Bahá in her letters that she felt His presence, that she had come to understand that physical proximity was not important when hearts were joined, and she took much comfort in this insight. There is no doubt that she, among those privileged to travel to 'Akká that fateful winter of 1898–1899, was not alone in keenly sensing that 'Abdu'l-Bahá was always by her side, encouraging and assisting her. As she said to Him, 'You know my heart – I do not need to tell you anything and I know you see all my shortcomings – but you also feel my love.'[53]

Speaking of her spiritual growth after her visit to Him, 'Abdu'l-Bahá wrote:

> When thou wert at Acca, the seeds of the love of God were sown in thy heart, through the power of the Spirit. At that time they were not so much manifest. Now that pure seed is growing more verdant and refreshed, day by day, and becometh more manifest. This is why thou findest thyself possessing more and more spiritual sentiments.[54]

In that same Tablet, the Master also gave her the mission of travelling around the United States in order to spread the Faith.[55]

As Margaret lay dying in Pomona, Tennessee on 2 November 1908, she asked those attending to write to 'Abdu'l-Bahá on her behalf to tell Him that she loved Him very much. Her last words were these, which were directed to her son and only surviving child, 'and you, too, Benedict, must love 'Abdu'l-Bahá'.[56] When the Master was informed of her death, he revealed a Tablet in her memory that included within it an invocation that her wish that her descendants would remain steadfast in the Faith would be fulfilled.

> He is God!
>
> O thou daughter of the Kingdom; O thou esteemed maidservant of God!
>
> O thou Mrs. Peeke, pure and sanctified is the Lord of the Kingdom who released thee from this earthly world and led thee unto the Divine World, who took thee into the pure world out of this world of dust, delivered thee from separation, longing and yearning, and caused thee to soar up into the rose-garden of vision and meeting.
>
> O thou who art attracted unto God, happy is thy condition, for in

> this mortal world thou didst devote thy life to spiritual pursuits, didst call people to the Kingdom, with inner attractions night and day, and didst partake of Eternal Life, and of the Meeting of the Lord of the Kingdom.
>
> Before long the Queens of the world will be nameless and forgotten, but thou art shining and luminous like unto a star on the eternal horizon; during future centuries thy name will be on all tongues and thy eternal glory shall be clear and manifest, though this bounty is not at present clear and manifest, but in the future it will before long become visible and evident.
>
> Happy, happy is thy condition, for thou hast become a recipient of the favors of His Highness, the Merciful One, and hastened unto the assemblage of the Beauty of Abha.
>
> O thou Creator! Glorify this esteemed daughter of the Kingdom in the Divine World, and cause this longing one to attain unto the honor of Thy union. Give this thirsty one to drink of the Fountain of Life and cause this enraptured one to seek rest and peace in thy shelter.
>
> Grant the wishes of her heart and soul and make her survivors firm and steadfast in the right way and in the Path of the Kingdom, so that they may light the lamp of that attracted one, and walk in her footsteps. May her descendants be related to Thy threshold in this world and may they be known in the Name.
>
> Thou art the Clement, the Gracious, the Forgiving, the Powerful.
>
> [Sig.] E.E. 'Abdu'l-Bahá 'Abbás[57]

Margaret had longed to return to 'Akká, to the presence of 'Abdu'l-Bahá. But it was not to be. The Master comforted her with words that could be applied to all who participated in the historic visits to the Holy Land during the winter of 1898–1899.

> Although thy visit to Acca in the year 1899 was short, yet it was the breath of life. Later on its traces will become manifest.[58]

Even the two members of the pilgrimage who did not or could not remain active in the Faith were nevertheless profoundly affected by that brief time in the Holy Land during their youth. When in her eighties and losing her eyesight, Julia Pearson Hunt was visited by a Bahá'í neighbour, May Bolles's sister-in-law, Jeanne Ruhangiz Bolles, who spoke with her about what had happened to the Cause in the years since her visit to the Master, and showed her a brief film of 'Abdu'l-Bahá taken during His visit to the United States and photographs of the Bahá'í gardens in Haifa and 'Akká developed by Shoghi Effendi. Julia wept.[59]

As an elderly widow, Anne Apperson Flint wrote to Ella about how her Faith had not wavered but that she had been prevented from taking active part in it. A letter written years earlier to Emogene Hoagg expresses the balancing act she had to perform in deference to her husband, who agreed with Bahá'í principles but otherwise opposed the Faith. She had received a Bahá'í booklet from Emogene and had put it out on her tables where others would see and comment upon it, affording her opportunities to tell them about Bahá'u'lláh and His Faith.[60] In another letter she speaks of how much her own faith was centred on the person of 'Abdu'l-Bahá Himself and was tested by His passing in 1921.

> Since Abdul Beha [sic] left us, I can't think of Haifa. I must say frankly the reality has gone and it remains a beautiful ideal, the essence of which I hold dear despite the opposition my husband has energetically waged for over 20 years!
>
> And Shoghi Effendi wasn't even born when I was there![61]
>
> But the beauty is all locked up in an inner shrine of my being and I try to live the life of a true Christian trusting God will understand.[62]

With neither encumbered by small children, the opposition of husbands, ill health or the infirmities of age, the close collaboration in spreading the Faith which developed between Helen Goodall and her daughter Ella Goodall Cooper in California would be even stronger than that of Harriet Thornburgh and Mary Virginia Thornburgh-Cropper in London, and would last right up until Helen's death in 1922. The spacious Goodall home at 1317 Jackson Street in Oakland quickly became the unofficial headquarters of the Bahá'í Faith for the West Coast of North America for almost two decades. There they would host many notable Bahá'í teachers, including Lua Getsinger. The Master Himself stayed there overnight during His visit to California in 1912. It seems that for the first few years after Ella's return, the Goodalls did not hold Bahá'í meetings for any except avowed believers, because they thought they had to be cautious in spreading the Faith lest it be classified among the 'isms' by the misinformed. They taught their friends one by one. But after about 1903, that wealthy family's grand home became the scene of more and more memorable Bahá'í gatherings open to believers and seekers alike, such as one Ella described to 'Abdu'l-Bahá which reunited her with Robert Turner.[63] Most of those who attended the Bahá'í gatherings were women, but on that occasion in 1906, men were present in greater numbers than usual.

> Thou wilt remember Robert the servant of Mrs. Hearst who made the Visit to Thy Holy Household among the first Americans – He came to

> the meeting and with him another colored man who used to serve Mrs. Hearst and is a most sincere and devout believer, Charles Tinsley – with our Japanese boy Moto it made a most wonderful mingling of races and religions – and to see all those happy faces gave my mother and me such pure joy to think we are blessed with the privilege of gathering the people together under her roof. The spirit of peace and harmony was so strong and comforting that it seemed to us all that Thy Spirit was indeed with us, according to Thy promise in the Tablets . . .[64]

Emogene Hoagg described the meetings she attended at the Goodall's Oakland home during those early days and the difficulties the small stalwart group of believers in California faced.

> These meetings were a great blessing, as perfect harmony always existed. However much general interest was not awakened because of the very quiet way in which the Teachings were given. And we had only the Hidden Words and the Surat ul Hykle [Súriy-i-Haykal] translated into English. So while we were isolated and had none of the Persian Teachers to instruct us, we were obliged to depend upon the teaching of the Spirit. We grew in knowledge and strength slowly, but surely. Very few have ever fallen away from our number.[65]

Ella and her mother Helen would even water the spiritual seeds sown by Agnes Alexander in Hawaii, while visiting those Pacific islands. They confirmed several people who had been introduced to the Faith there by Agnes. Their years of efforts to lead others to the Faith resulted in unanticipated achievements. For example, the first of her friends that Ella taught, Edith Coxhead Fraser, moved to Johannesburg, South Africa and became the first believer there.[66] The seeds for this successful teaching work were sown in the fertile soil of California by Ella's indefatigable mother even before her return from her pilgrimage and were fertilized and watered even more vigorously after Helen's 1908 pilgrimage. When 'Abdu'l-Bahá was no longer a political prisoner and could openly receive visitors, Helen Goodall was finally able to make her own pilgrimage, accompanied by her daughter. Together this mother and daughter team penned an enduring work, *Daily Lessons Received at 'Akká, January 1908*, which has inspired generations of believers with its detailed account of that two-week sojourn in the Holy Land.

During the last months of His life, 'Abdu'l-Bahá would recognize their tireless service and the bonds of affection that had developed between Him and Ella from the time of her first pilgrimage.

He is God!

O my dear and affectionate daughter!

I am the servant of the Beauty of Abha, and thou art a dear maidservant at that threshold. The affection, therefore, which exists between us is a thousand times greater than the affection existing between a father and his daughter. Know with absolute assurance that not a single day passes in which I do not think of my sister, Mrs. Goodall, and my daughter, Mrs. Cooper. This is because I have great confidence in you. Ye have verily given up everything and have completely attached your hearts to the Kingdom of God. Ye are striving day and night in order that ye may render some service to the realm of the Kingdom. This is your aspiration. I know it. Offer thanks unto God that ye have abandoned everything, rent asunder this worn-out garment of the world of nature, put on the robe of sanctity, obtained heavenly spirit, and attained to divine happiness. How nice would it be, if some more people could, like you, be confirmed to arise with heart attracted to the Kingdom of Abha, with soul rejoiced with the glad tidings of God, with mind concentrated in the service of His Cause, and with body occupied in bearing calamities in His path! Know ye with absolute assurance that ye will progress more and more day by day! What bounty is greater than this? . . .[67]

After her mother's passing, Ella continued her exemplary services to the Cause, primarily across the bay in San Francisco, where she and her husband had moved from Oakland. She was entrusted by both 'Abdu'l-Bahá and Shoghi Effendi to carry out sensitive undertakings on their behalf. She was the primary organizer of the first International Bahá'í Congress, held in conjunction with the Panama-Pacific International Exposition in 1915 in San Francisco. Among those to whom she taught the Faith were a group of young women she referred to as her 'Peaches' and they called her 'Mother Peach'. A number of those who participated in her study class, called the 'Peach Tree', went on to offer many services to the Faith.[68]

As old age and ill health sapped Ella's energy and curtailed her participation in the Bahá'í community, she received these comforting words written on behalf of Shoghi Effendi, which also stand as a testament to her fellow early believers in the West.

You should never feel discouraged. Your great love for the Faith, your unswerving loyalty and devotion, are in themselves a form of service and

> an example to others. Indeed 'Abdu'l-Bahá may well feel proud of His earliest followers in the west, for they have shown a tireless activity and steadfastness which neither age, tests, nor illness have obscured!
>
> He will pray that your health may improve and enable you to fulfil your heart's desire in the service of the Faith.
>
> He will also pray that your dear husband and brother may embrace the Cause and give you this great happiness.[69]

Posthumously, Ella, like Lua, was honoured with the title 'herald of the Covenant' by Shoghi Effendi, who also called her a 'dearly loved handmaid of 'Abdu'l-Bahá, greatly trusted by Him'. He also went on to say in his cable at the time of her passing that, 'Her devoted services during concluding years of Heroic Age and also Formative Age of Faith unforgettable'.[70]

CHAPTER 15

Lives of Service Together and Apart: The Getsingers

Even though all those who visited 'Akká during the winter of 1898–99 returned home changed in profound ways, most settled back into the same lives they had had before. The Getsingers, however, had not only given their hearts to the Faith, both wanted to consecrate themselves completely to its service. Like moths to a candle, they would return again and again to the Blessed Spot to bask in the radiance of 'Abdu'l-Bahá and to breathe deep the sweet scents of the Holy Places. Mundane, worldly pursuits had lost their appeal and instead Lua and Edward longed to devote all their time to carrying forward the work of the Cause. Edward well expressed what was in his heart in a poem he penned in honour of 'Abdu'l-Bahá early in 1900, the last stanza of which reads as follows:

> I am standing on the mountain crest,
> Watching for Thy beckoning hand,
> That will bid me in Thy arms to rest –
> And tread the shores of Acca's strand.
> O bid me come – stay not the wing
> That would fly me where my Father lives,
> There at His feet as an offering
> My heart I'll lay – my life I'll give.[1]

So it was that when the Getsingers completed their second lengthy sojourn in the Holy Land and Egypt in 1901, they headed for California, where with the support of Phoebe Hearst they would resume their earlier work of spreading the Faith in those far climes. Given all that had transpired since Edward's arrival in the San Francisco Bay area in the spring of 1898, it must have seemed to them as if a lifetime had passed. This time, they would approach the work of spreading the Faith in California with greater vigour and determination, bolstered by the prayers and encouragement of 'Abdu'l-Bahá. They had much more true knowledge to impart to their eager listeners than before.

Phoebe, who had wasted no time in carrying out her own undertakings for the Faith after her return to the United States, had been given a title by 'Abdu'l-Bahá Himself, one unique to her. He called her the 'Mother of the Faithful',[2] an apt description of her role in the years immediately following the pilgrimage. Her hand guided much of what was happening to promote the Faith in the West during the first days of the twentieth century. Her ability to provide funds was especially useful when Edward, with the help of a few others, worked to publish the first English collection of Bahá'í scripture, which was printed in the early months of 1901. She paid many of the expenses of the Persians sent to the United States to deepen the believers. She sent £500, a substantial sum at the time, to 'Abdu'l-Bahá for the repair of the access road to the Shrine of the Báb.[3] She invited a group of prominent African–American educators to her home in Washington, D.C. and not only entertained them sumptuously – it would be impossible to overestimate how socially courageous that was at the time – she spoke to them of the Bahá'í Faith.[4] Many of the early American Bahá'ís looked to her for advice and assistance and she truly served them as a mother.[5]

Both Phoebe and 'Abdu'l-Bahá must have recognized the dangers inherent in her involvement with the Faith. She and her two companions were the only ones of that first group of Western pilgrims deliberately brought to 'Akká from Haifa under the cover of darkness. Her visit to the Master's household was possibly the cause of the restrictions imposed on Him in March 1899 just as the remaining Americans of the group were about to depart. And the perils went both ways. Phoebe's involvement with the Faith could be misconstrued and used against her and her son. William Randolph Hearst had a growing list of detractors, having offended many people with his brazen journalism. His special targets were the 'trusts', that is, the large corporations that had developed monopolies of vital industries. He was not alone in wanting to 'bust the trusts' and in a few years legislation would be passed to make the competition of the marketplace less rigged toward only a few players, but his strident public advocacy of their demise had made him many well-connected enemies even as he became a hero to the working class. His newspapers vilified President McKinley, a strong supporter of the business community, with a few of his writers even proposing in print that the President's death would be a welcome event. Even though Will was not personally responsible for those reprehensible statements, they were run in publications he owned, thus when McKinley was assassinated, he found himself in ill repute with even more people. His ambition for elected office was also at its peak during the years immediately after his mother's pilgrimage, and, after losing other elections, he would finally be elected to the United States House of Representatives in

1902. (He only served two terms in Congress and would never hold another elected office.)

Phoebe had to be careful lest her association with the Faith harm either 'Abdu'l-Bahá or her son. She was discretion personified,[6] but, unfortunately, other Bahá'ís were not. All believers are tested as to the sincerity of their beliefs and Phoebe was no exception. Just as her role in promoting the Faith was writ large, so too would be her tests and difficulties. It is a sad tale with a happy ending.

After Phoebe's return from her pilgrimage to 'Akká, two letters allegedly written by her were distributed to a select few friends. These spoke glowingly of her time in 'Akká and of 'Abdu'l-Bahá. The problem was that she had not written them herself.[7] The truth regarding these two letters will probably never be known, but it seems from what is known that Phoebe may have asked Lua to assist her by answering some correspondence enquiring about her trip to the Holy Land and Lua responded, as if she were Phoebe, by writing in the first person. It is also probable that the letters reflected statements that Phoebe had made in private about her visit and that the actual author of the letters thought they accurately reflected her impressions and feelings. Even if Phoebe did authorize the drafting of the letters, she did not authorize their publication, thus she was understandably upset when they appeared in a book and a newspaper without her prior consent. Whether or not Lua was in fact to blame, Phoebe thought she was and so angrily dismissed the Getsingers from her home. This was in 1901.

As if that rift with the Getsingers was not enough of a test, at about the same time two men from the Middle East, who were ill-disposed towards the Faith, arrived in San Francisco. They had heard about Phoebe's connection to 'Abdu'l-Bahá while in the Levant and decided to create some mischief. They told several newspaper reporters from papers that were rivals to the Hearst newspapers that the prominent philanthropist and *grande dame* of West Coast society, the mother of William Randolph Hearst, was a member of an obscure Persian cult. Reporters started snooping around, even making a visit to Edward.[8] Phoebe's son could not suffer this accusation, not when he was preparing to run for Congress. A statement appeared in his paper, the *San Francisco Examiner*, in early March of 1901, purportedly quoting Phoebe herself, renouncing the authorship of the two letters after they had been printed in another local rival newspaper, *The Bulletin*. It included a telegram sent from Washington to the Managing Editor of *The Examiner*:

> The article printed in the Bulletin concerning letters purported to have been written by me is absolutely false. I did not write nor dictate nor

> have knowledge of the letters until long after they were received by a Mr. Bradford, whom I do not know. When extracts were published I took no notice of them. Now I wish to deny the authorship of the letters.
>
> P. A. Hearst[9]

It is unlikely that Phoebe had any more control over the publication of that statement and the article distancing her from the Faith than she did the publication of the two letters. If she did draft it, it should be noted that she did not claim that her association with the Faith was false, only her authorship of the two letters.

No longer sponsored in their work by Phoebe, Edward and Lua spent much of the next year roaming from community to community to assist the small but growing number of American believers in the establishment of their Bahá'í groups. In the process they ran through their savings and went into debt. Finally, Edward had to cease travelling in order to concentrate on making a living.[10] He tried his hand at making medicines and also at carrying out research into a cure for tuberculosis. In 1902 Lua returned to 'Akká without Edward, this time for a full year. She became a member of the Master's household, teaching English and helping with translations. During that extended stay she made an extraordinary attempt to develop her spiritual side, and spoke often of her longing to prove her devotion by sacrificing her very life for the Faith, as had a number of persecuted believers in Iran. The Master told her not to seek martyrdom – that living for the Cause was just as important. By the time she embarked for the United States to rejoin her husband, she was truly transformed. Her state, even her appearance, made an indelible impression on Yúnis Khán, the Master's young English translator and secretary.

> One of the most astonishing things that I have ever witnessed in my service to the Cause was Lua's state when she came to say goodbye. It can never fade from my memory, nor can I find adequate words to describe it. Her face was so utterly luminous and spiritual, and her bearing so transformed, that it seemed as though an angel had been incarnated in the body of a human being. I was never more deeply moved than when I witnessed her tender and kindly disposition as we said our farewells. Never before had I beheld so wonderful and heavenly a countenance; I gazed at her in utter amazement.
>
> Next day the Master asked, 'Did you see Lua when she left? Did you notice her face and her demeanour?'
>
> I responded that I had, and that I had been astonished by her state of spirituality.

> The Master replied, 'It is a pity, but she won't be able to maintain that spirit. It is impossible to remain in that state. Now consider where we find these wandering souls and how we educate them!'[11]

Lua's only desire was to spread the Faith far and wide. She became one of the Faith's boldest teachers, earning the title 'Mother Teacher of the West' from the Master. She gave public lectures on the Faith and conducted study classes from California to New York with many stops in between. Years later, John Bosch of California was asked about his memories of her:

> 'Lua was a good speaker. Impressive. Spiritual.'
> 'Who do you know now like that?'
> 'No comparison.'[12]

Lua also courageously upheld the station of 'Abdu'l-Bahá by unabashedly confronting his enemies while in the Holy Land. Together with several of the believers in Paris, she twice presented a petition to the Shah of Persia during his visit to that city and, had the Master not intervened, would have done the same with the Sultan of Turkey.[13] The petitions implored the Shah to extend his protection to the persecuted believers in the Cradle of the Faith and to alleviate the restrictions placed upon 'Abdu'l-Bahá. In recognition of her courageous defence of the Cause, 'Abdu'l-Bahá gave her the name 'Livá', meaning 'banner', and also called her a 'Herald of the Covenant'.

Edward shared his wife's longing to devote all of his time to the Faith, but as the Faith had no clergy, he had no choice but to settle down in order to earn a living, and so he lived for a time in the New York City area and then established a home in Washington, D.C. He also defined service to the Cause differently than did Lua. From the time he was a small boy he had been interested in how the world worked, including the origins of the universe. During his lifetime, major breakthroughs in the fields of physics and astronomy were radically transforming mankind's conceptions of the universe. Edward keenly followed much of the work of the scientific giants of his age, such as Einstein, and yearned to play a part in carrying knowledge forward. The clash between the explanations of the origins of creation as told in the Book of Genesis and the findings of leading astronomers fascinated Edward. The period encompassing the closing years of the nineteenth and the beginning decades of the twentieth centuries was one of obsession within the intellectual community, with the war between the scientific and religious establishments in large measure because of the repercussions from the publication of Charles Darwin's *Origin of Species*.

Edward showed his astronomical charts to Ella while they were in the Holy Land in 1899. She reported to her mother, 'He has a most wonderful new system of astronomy that the Master approves of and you must get him to show you his charts. Any child could understand it and it certainly does seem most reasonable. Of course he expects that the world will accept it someday. It knocks the present system sky-high and the queerest part of it is that it all came by inspiration for when his head was filled to bursting with these ideas he knew absolutely nothing about astronomy at all.'[14]

One day during either his first or second pilgrimage to 'Akká, Edward was using his free time to continue his study and research into the creation of the universe, when he was interrupted in his work by 'Abdu'l-Bahá Who told him that it was not yet the time for him to worry about such things, so Edward put his personal research aside.[15] The Master was probably not intending to say that all scientific exploration of the origins of the universe was not timely, but most likely meant that Edward's services were needed desperately to get the Faith established at that moment in history. The exact conversation is not recorded, thus one can only go by Edward's impressions of it. At a later time, during another conversation with 'Abdu'l-Bahá, Edward thought that he had been given a specific directive by the Master to reconcile science and religion. The Bahá'í Faith teaches that science and religion must agree because there is only one truth, so if Holy Scripture seems incompatible with a proven fact, it is probably because the scripture is symbolic rather than literal. Edward made this charge to reconcile the scientific and religious teachings about the origins of the universe his life's work; and, given the milieu in which he revolved, he may have felt that there was a genuine need for the Faith to speak out on that controversial topic. When 'Abdu'l-Bahá addressed three successive Tablets to Edward calling upon him to learn and attain the spiritual quality of detachment from the world of being, Edward took this to mean that he should stop pursuing his medical work and should instead devote his time to the reconciliation of science and religion.[16] (The Tablets are very general in their wording; Edward perhaps read into them what he wanted.) Clearly, he could never achieve this towering objective if he was preoccupied with running from place to place helping Lua with her teaching work;[17] but he missed his wife and wanted her to come home.

For her part, Lua had no desire to be a *hausfrau* stuck in even as big a city as Washington, D.C., despite 'Abdu'l-Bahá's explicit instructions to her to obey her husband's wishes. Possessed of a strong will and independent spirit, she was driven to spread the Faith far and wide, often without considering Edward. Service to the Cause had once united the Getsingers, but now it began to take them on divergent paths. The periods apart lengthened and became more frequent. These separations were exacerbated by Lua's innate naiveté and habit of only looking for the good in others. She began to travel in the company of some of the young Persian men without a chaperone. Even if there was nothing improper in this behaviour, at the time it looked scandalous. Rumours reached Edward, which strained the marriage further.

Finally, perhaps in part to help the Getsingers rekindle the bonds of affection which once had been so strong, 'Abdu'l-Bahá asked them to go together to India to assist with the establishment of the Bahá'í community in that vast subcontinent where they could also hopefully revive their marriage away from the distractions and gossip of America.[18] They arrived in Bombay in late December 1913 after a visit to the Master while He was sojourning in Egypt. Edward went willingly to India in the beginning – even enthusiastically – but he was soon miserable. Unbearable, unremitting heat, lack of money or means of earning any, barriers of language and customs, and frequent bouts of ill health, especially for the frailer Lua, finally overwhelmed him. He gave up and decided to return to the United States,[19] even if Lua was not yet ready to leave. Edward's departure marked the end of the marriage.[20]

They had each learned through trials and difficulties that the Faith would only be spread by hardship and sacrifice, but sometimes the tests seemed too much to bear. Shortly before leaving for India in 1913, Lua had written to a friend back in the United States.

> Since I first entered the Cause sixteen years ago – my instructions from the Master have ever been the same. 'Go and teach: Speak the glad tidings – and be <u>severed</u> <u>from</u> <u>all</u> <u>save</u> <u>God</u>.' How I have suffered to learn that these <u>words</u> are the <u>real</u> and <u>only</u> <u>measure</u> <u>of</u> <u>my</u> <u>capacity</u> <u>as</u> <u>a</u> <u>Servant</u> <u>in</u> <u>His</u> <u>Vineyard</u>. God in His Mercy has denied me everything on a material plane until at last, I have learned the lesson.[21]

At such times of trial, Lua must have employed a prayer revealed for her by the Master many years earlier.

> Thou knowest, O God, and art my witness that I have no desire in my heart save to attain Thy good pleasure, to be confirmed in servitude unto Thee, to consecrate myself in Thy service, to labour in Thy great vineyard and to sacrifice all in Thy path. Thou are the All-Knowing and the All-Seeing. I have no wish save to turn my steps, in my love for Thee, towards the mountains and the deserts to loudly proclaim the advent of Thy Kingdom, and to raise Thy call amidst all men. O God! Open Thou the way for this helpless one, grant Thou the remedy to this ailing one and

bestow Thy healing upon this afflicted one. With burning heart and tearful eyes I supplicate Thee at Thy Threshold.

O God! I am prepared to endure any ordeal in Thy path and desire with all my heart and soul to meet any hardship.

O God! Protect me from tests. Thou knowest full well that I have turned away from all things and freed myself of all thoughts. I have no occupation save mention of Thee and no aspiration save serving Thee.[22]

Both Edward and Lua visited 'Akká again as they headed west, where one last attempt at reconciliation failed. After Edward departed, Lua lingered in the Holy Land for eight months despite the hardships and dangers of World War I. The Holy Land once again became a theatre of war, as the Turks entered the conflict on the side of Germany and placed the Levant under martial law. Lua witnessed the bombing of Haifa and 'Akká and the widespread suffering of the civilian population. At the end of August 1915 she had to be sent away by 'Abdu'l-Bahá Himself for what would prove to be the last time. It would be too risky for an American to remain in Turkish-held territory if the United States entered the war. She was evacuated to Crete on a United States naval cruiser along with the last group of foreign nationals in the region, and from there she made her way to her Bahá'í friends in Egypt. She carried with her messages from the Master for the friends in Egypt, Europe and America, whose mail to and from the Holy Land had been cut off since the hostilities began.

It is impossible to know what thoughts occupied Lua's mind as she found herself again in Cairo for months on end with no money, far from her native land, and with Edward back in the United States bringing divorce proceedings against her. Undoubtedly, the worst oppression for her was the one inflicted by the war – being entirely cut off from the greatest joy of her life, 'Abdu'l-Bahá. Like all the believers throughout the world, she must have worried incessantly about His safety. The years of travelling, of enduring harsh physical conditions in order to spread the Cause, and the heartbreak of the failure of her marriage had begun to take their toll. Lua was ill most of that winter of 1915–1916, but she rallied herself enough to carry on the teaching work in Cairo while enjoying the kindness and hospitality of the local believers. On the evening of 2 May 1916, she died unexpectedly at the young age of 43, and, with much love and respect, was buried beside her old teacher, Mírzá Abu'l-Faḍl. The Master was visiting the Sea of Galilee when He heard the news, and was deeply affected. Many times afterwards He would repeat in a moving voice, 'What a loss! What a loss! What a loss!'[23]

'Abdu'l-Bahá conveyed his heartfelt condolences to Edward after Lua's passing – a letter which could only be dispatched more than a year later, after the conclusion of the war. It reads in part:

> The enkindled maid-servant of God, with the fire of his love, Lua, has passed away. In the latter days of her life, the heart disease with which she had been afflicted had greatly aggravated.
>
> From the Bounties of God I hope that she may in the Eternal Realm attain unto everlasting comfort and happiness.
>
> Verily she was endowed with an eloquent tongue and had a heart overflowing with the Love of God. I hope that in the immortal world thou shalt find her in the utmost joy and gladness.[24]

Unfortunately, the marital problems of the Getsingers had been the object of whisperings among the American believers for some time and, as with most such cases, people took sides. Both Edward and Lua tried to present themselves in the best possible light, while subtly putting down the other in their correspondence and comments to third parties – they were only too human, like most people in such hurtful circumstances. Lua's early death at age 43 sealed her canonization in the minds of many, while Edward's initiation of the divorce proceedings tarnished his myriad contributions to the Faith for those who sided with Lua, especially after her untimely passing.

Indeed, Lua's contributions to the establishment of the Faith cannot be measured. True, she was impulsive and mischievous, and she never let her head overrule her heart; but her passion and unwavering love for the Faith, coupled with her relentless desire to serve her Lord, overshadowed her more earthly failings. Many were the believers who called her their 'spiritual mother'. One of those spiritual children, May Bolles Maxwell, wrote a prescient tribute to her dear friend after learning of Lua's unexpected death.

> As Kurat-ul-Ayn was the Trumpet of the Dawn in the Orient in the Day of Bahá'u'lláh, so Lua Aurora shall wave forever and ever the Banner of the Dawn of the Day of the Covenant. Even as her age and generation knew her not, seeing only her mortal frailties – so future ages and cycles will love her – adore her – venerate her blessed name – and strive to walk in the path of her utter servitude, severance, and sacrifice. The passion of Divine love that consumed her heart shall light the hearts of mankind forever and forever.[25]

Edward continued to work to advance the Faith, but the roaring flame had reduced to a low-glowing ember after years of being smothered by controversy and ridicule. To the end of his life he loved 'Abdu'l-Bahá intensely and was proud that the Master had called him His son. He was loyal and faithfully obedient to the Master's successor, Shoghi Effendi. But Edward had always been his own person, not one for the group. When the National Spiritual Assembly and a growing number of local Spiritual Assemblies were established in the United States, Edward's strong, nay eccentric, personality sometimes ran afoul of those nascent bodies.[26] This was especially ironic because he was the one who had urged the Master to allow the National Spiritual Assembly for the United States to be formed, but 'Abdu'l-Bahá had replied that it wasn't yet time.[27] He also assisted a community in New Jersey with forming one of the first administrative committees in the United States, a precursor of a local Spiritual Assembly. Over time, his participation on the national scene of the American Bahá'í community dwindled. He increasingly turned inward and focused his time on his research on the oneness of science and religion – carrying forward the charge he thought the Master had given him. He moved to California where he remained active in Bahá'í community life, but primarily in the Los Angeles area where his home was in Hollywood. Edward continued to teach the Faith, especially to his students of science. But his passion, his *raison d'être*, was his research which took him increasingly further from hard science into the study of ancient religious texts. He became an expert in ancient languages such as Biblical Hebrew, while supporting himself as a laboratory technician, tutoring, and through occasional translation work. He lived modestly and eventually remarried. As he approached his last days, he considered his greatest achievement to be the multi-volume manuscript he produced outlining his findings about the origins of creation and reconciling them with the Book of Genesis, which he determined had been written in a sophisticated code.[28] He never realized that what he would be most remembered for by posterity were his invaluable contributions to the establishment of the Faith during those first two crucial decades of the Bahá'í Faith in America. His steadfastness in the face of Kheiralla's rebellion, his contributions to the publishing of the Holy Writings in English, his unwavering support of the Master, and his travels and talks to spread the Faith surely earned him the gratitude of generations of Bahá'ís who would follow him. Of course, his greatest contribution was introducing the Faith to Phoebe Hearst, even if their relationship was strained during later years.

He passed away in Hollywood on 12 March 1935, at the age of 69.[29]

CHAPTER 16

Mother of the Faithful

Because of the turbulence of the years immediately following the return of the first Western pilgrims, Phoebe became very cautious in her association with her fellow Bahá'ís. Kheiralla had tried to cheat her out of money and Lua had broken her heart. Others saw her as only a checkbook. Edward wrote to the Master about the mess following the publication of the two letters, and 'Abdu'l-Bahá advised him to try to smooth things out with Phoebe, if possible, but added that He doubted she was in a mood to hear what he had to say in his own defence at that time, and so suggested that he not seek to rectify the situation.[1] Phoebe's secretaries began to restrict the access of most Bahá'ís to their employer, something they probably had wanted to do earlier.

It is a testimony to Phoebe's devotion to the Faith that, despite these personal tests, she never gave up her beliefs. Although she withdrew from active involvement in the affairs of the Bahá'í community, she always stayed abreast of what was going on. In 1902, the year following the blow-up with the Getsingers, she wrote of her concerns with the lack of progress in getting accurate information about the teachings in a letter to Helen Goodall:

> My dear Mrs. Goodall,
>
> It gave me much pleasure to receive your kind note and enclosures. I gave to each one the Tablets intended for them.
>
> I received a letter from Anton Haddad in which he told me, he had asked and received permission to go to his home . . . It will be as well and perhaps better for him to be there. He will be helpful to the Master, having lived in America and understanding the conditions. He will also be of help to those permitted to visit the Holy Household in the future, and he can continue his translating and writings.
>
> I am pleased to hear that Mr. Harris has decided to go[2] . . . He is a very intelligent and able man and will probably study the language. We have been sadly in need of such an arrangement. It will be much better, than their sending over people who are not very capable, & so unlike ourselves in every way, & make so many mistakes. I must say I felt very much discouraged and depressed for two years now, and felt no great advance could

> be made until some trustworthy man, in whom we had confidence, could go over and stay and study most carefully to gain accurate information, concerning things that we wish to know & should know.
>
> I hope I may have the pleasure of seeing you, when you return from the country. I would be most happy if you and Ella could come up and stay a day or two with us. There are so many things I would like to talk to you about . . .
>
> Pardon this long letter & accept for yourself and Ella, much love,
>
> Very Sincerely
> P. A. Hearst[3]

Phoebe also wrote to her friend Clara Anthony about who was on pilgrimage to 'Akká in 1903. She kept Bahá'í literature in her bedroom until the end of her life[4] and she always maintained her friendships with Ella and her mother and a few other Bahá'ís. Phoebe even employed Ali-Kuli Khan and used her connections to gain him appointment as Persian consul to Washington. For many years, Ali-Kuli Khan facilitated her correspondence with the Master, which apparently continued long after she backed away from active participation in the American Bahá'í community.[5]

Robert Turner remarked about his mistress's estrangement from most of the other believers, that dust had been thrown in her eyes. Her feelings did not affect his or those of her maid, Amalia (Emily) Bachrodt. Both continued to be steadfast believers to the end of their lives. Because they were servants, it is difficult to trace much about their lives, but Emily did write to Phoebe in the coded language used by the early Western believers commenting that she was pleased that a lady was showing interest in the 'Truth', the term usually used to refer to the Faith.

> Miss . . . came on the 1st of Feb. to the Hacienda to stay one month with Mrs ____, she is a very nice girl. I like her so much, she is no trouble what ever, just think Mrs Hearst she is ready and up to the Truth . . . So many people tell me, that there was a great change in me, that I was now full of sunshine, (I hope that it is so,) and I will strive even harder each day to be more sure of it, and thank you for it in every one of my prayers, as you Mrs Hearst are the Course [Cause][6] of my happiness.[7]

Ella recorded that Emily attended the Bahá'í gatherings at the Goodall home in Oakland until her passing on 19 February 1926.[8] Emily never married and served the Hearst family until her retirement, after which she lived out the rest of her days at the home of her sister-in-law and niece in Fruitvale, California.

Some years after Robert's passing on 15 June 1909, Louis Gregory, the only person of African–American descent to be named a Hand of the Cause of God, took a special interest in his life and made attempts to learn more about him. Among the few tidbits he was able to uncover was an account of Robert's death after a lingering illness. Inasmuch as Robert's wife and only child died before him, his last days were spent at the home of friends. His attendants remembered that even during the delirium of his final illness he kept repeating a strange expression in another language over and over – Alláh-u-Abhá, the Greatest Name. The Master promised Robert that if he remained steadfast to the end, he would be a door through which his whole race would enter the Kingdom of God.[9]

Phoebe's intimate friend Clara Anthony consoled her in a letter written after Robert's passing, saying, 'It saddened me to hear . . . that you had lost your faithful and devoted [?] Robert, whose affection and fidelity were boundless. I can scarcely picture the home without him. Can you ever replace him? Such faithfulness is a plant of slow growth.'[10]

Robert was able to convey through Ali-Kuli Khan one last message to the Master from his deathbed in which he assured 'Abdu'l-Bahá of his love and asked for His prayers.[11] Robert did not live to receive the last Tablet the Master sent to him (care of Helen Goodall).

He is God!

O thou servant of God!

Thank thou God that from the day of the meeting until now 'Abdu'l-Bahá has not forgotten thee. He remembers thee always. I ask of the Lord of the Kingdom that He may make thee dear in this world and the world to come; crown thee with the love of God and make thee an ignited and enkindled candle among the colored race.

Upon thee be Bahá el ABHÁ!

(signed) 'Abdu'l-Bahá 'Abbás[12]

By all accounts, Robert was a warm-hearted, amiable man around whom people, including children, felt at ease.[13] Ella recorded that during the 1898–99 Hearst pilgrimage he acted as 'major-domo' and courier. 'He became an indispensable member of the party.'[14] He and fellow pilgrim Harriet Thornburgh must have shared a sense of humour. Robert had told her that second only to Phoebe, her daughter Minnie was the 'loveliest lady that he had ever seen'. Harriet replied that that 'showed his good taste'.[15] Robert, like Harriet, would also be given the honour of being named a Disciple of 'Abdu'l-Bahá by Shoghi Effendi.

Ali-Kuli Khan informed 'Abdu'l-Bahá of the circumstances of Robert's passing and that he had placed a Bahá'í ring on Robert's finger at the time of his burial. (He had been instructed by his then employer, Phoebe, to attend to one to whom she was strongly attached. She was away from California at the time.) In response the Master penned the following tribute.

> As to Mr. Robert (Turner), the news of his ascension saddened the hearts. He was in reality in the utmost sincerity. Glory be to God! What a shining candle was aflame in that black-colored lamp. Praise be to God that that lighted candle ascended from the earthly lamp to the Kingdom of Eternity and gleamed and became aflame in the Heavenly Assemblage. Praise be to God that you adorned his blessed finger with the ring bearing the inscription: 'Verily I originated from God and returned unto Him' . . . this too is a proof of his sincerity and that in his last breath, he breathed the Alláh-u-Abhá, whereby the hearts of those present were impressed.
>
> O Thou Creator! O Thou Forgiver! Glorify the precious Robert in Thy Kingdom and in the garden of the Paradise of Abhá. Bring him in[to] intimate association with the birds of the celestial meadow. O Thou Knowing God! Although that sinless one was black in color, like unto the pupil of the eye, he was a source of shining light.
>
> O Thou forgiving Lord! Cause that longing one to attain Thy meeting and cause that thirsty one to drink the water of life in abundance. Thou art the Forgiver, the Pardoner, the Compassionate.[16]

Though Robert did not live to see the Master's historic trip to the United States, his mistress did. Nell and her husband sent an invitation to 'Abdu'l-Bahá asking Him to visit them in California, as did the Goodall-Cooper family. At first it did not appear that His journey through the United States would take Him west of Chicago, but in the end He did cross the remainder of the continent and spent a little less than a month in California, arriving in San Francisco on the evening of 1 March 1912. Phoebe could not let His time in her area pass without inviting Him to the Hacienda after first going to see Him in Oakland at the Goodall home. On Sunday the 13th, Helen Goodall sent Him to Phoebe in her own automobile driven by her Bahá'í chauffeur.[17] He spent three days and two nights at the pink Hearst mansion, perhaps the most comfortable place He ever stayed.

By 1912, the passage of time and events had thwarted if not cooled Will's political ambitions and the Master was no longer a prisoner of conscience of the vanquished Ottoman Empire, so Phoebe had no inhibitions about introducing her Guest to her relatives and friends, including her growing brood of grandsons. He spoke to them about the Faith, both its history and its teachings. He walked her luxuriant gardens and admired her extensive greenhouses, even requesting that seeds of particular flowers be sent to Haifa for planting in the gardens surrounding the Holy Shrines. He entertained her other guests with his banter and words of wisdom – the latter given in talks which were deliberately brief, given the diversity of his audience. He answered many questions. He said prayers for the assembled group before each meal. All in all, His hostess must have been supremely happy.

During His visit, Phoebe specifically asked that He chant a particular Tablet in Arabic, one which He had chanted during her visit to the House of 'Abdu'lláh Pá<u>sh</u>á that had touched her deeply even though she had not understood the words. He obliged, of course. 'Abdu'l-Bahá also gave a talk during the visit about aspiring to become President of the United States and said that no one should actively seek such an office, that the office should in effect seek the right person.

> The president must be a man who does not insistently seek the presidency. He should be a person free from all thoughts of name and rank; rather, he should say, 'I am unworthy and incapable of this position and cannot bear this great burden.' Such persons deserve the presidency. If the object is to promote the public good, then the president must be a well-wisher of all and not a self-seeking person. If the object, however, is to promote personal interests, then such a position will be injurious to humanity and not beneficial to the public.[18]

Phoebe told her guests the story of her own pilgrimage to 'Akká, of the joy that it had brought her. After several days with the Master, her own faith was revived, and several of her guests wished to become Bahá'ís.

'Abdu'l-Bahá not only showered his love upon Phoebe's friends and relatives, He did not forget her servants. He made a particular point of visiting the other African–American Hearst employee, Charles Tinsley, who was laid up with a broken leg. This man was already a believer, most likely through his earlier friendship with Robert Turner, and he never forgot that visit of the Master.[19] As 'Abdu'l-Bahá prepared to depart that idyllic home, he asked that all of the employees – cooks, maids, butlers, and other attendants – be gathered together. As they stood in a line before Him, 'Abdu'l-Bahá called upon them to carry out their assigned tasks with devotion, truthfulness and honesty. He said, 'As I am like a father to you, I wish to leave a memento with you.' He then pressed into the hand of each two guineas – a handsome sum that was about as much as, if not more than, their full wages for the days of his visit. The assembled guests of high social rank were astounded by such a show of generosity from a man of such material modesty who had refused all offers of monetary assistance from Americans throughout His visit. He was willing to accept only their sincere hospitality and their love.

Phoebe implored the Master to allow her to accompany Him on the long drive back to San Francisco. During that trip He tried to counteract the harm that had been inflicted upon her by those who claimed to be believers, who nonetheless wished to get their hands on her money or to otherwise embarrass her. He told her:

> The Cause of God is sanctified from all political power and worldly affairs. Among the divine teachings are trustworthiness, detachment and sanctity. So if you should see a man coveting property and evincing greed toward the wealth of others, know that he is not of the people of Bahá. The people of Bahá are they who, should they happen to come upon a valley of gold and silver, would pass by it like lightning in utter disregard.[20]

Alas, even the benefits of this heavenly visit were tarnished by the actions of one member of 'Abdu'l-Bahá's entourage. While most of the Persian believers who accompanied the Master were, by all accounts, upright – even angelic – believers, there was one spoiler, the nephew of 'Abdu'l-Bahá's wife, Dr Ameen Fareed, who had received his university education in the United States, thereby attaining a high proficiency in English. However, Fareed would never have been allowed on Phoebe's property had he not been accompanying the Master because she had had difficulties with him and his father years before. Fareed took advantage of the Master's visit to the Hacienda to forge a letter, purportedly from 'Abdu'l-Bahá Himself, asking her for funds. Phoebe was all too familiar with people trying to get her money and did not take the bait. It further confirmed that her wariness in associating with many in the Bahá'í community was justified. She undoubtedly was, however, clear in her mind about the distinction between the teachings of the Faith demonstrated through the upright character of 'Abdu'l-Bahá and those who simply wished to use something that was pure in its essence to further their own unscrupulous designs.

Phoebe's coolness toward Bahá'í activities may have led some to think that she did not approve of the Faith. One example is a letter from a New England socialite and friend who had been assisting Sarah Farmer for years with the summer programmes held at Green Acre. She wrote to Phoebe in horror when it became clear that Sarah intended to turn over that conference centre to the Bahá'í community following the Master's visit to it. She was convinced that the Bahá'ís had used some underhanded means of wresting the property from that mutual friend and was certain that Phoebe would be equally alarmed and would intervene. Phoebe, who had supported the Green Acre conference centre since its inception, responded by providing more funds. She clearly approved of the transfer.[21]

The severing of formal church membership was not required of Western believers until 1935, and even then, they were welcome, as they still are, to visit and associate with churches and synagogues.[22] Consequently, many early Bahá'ís in the United States had multiple religious memberships. They freely believed in Bahá'u'lláh as the Manifestation of God for this day but did not consider their association with the Bahá'í community to preclude membership in any other religious organization. Phoebe was one such believer who never wished to be tied to any one religion in a formal way. Yet her love for the Faith was never extinguished, despite the tests and challenges it posed for her, and she felt a need to reaffirm her devotion to it at the end of her life.

During the closing days of World War I, a great epidemic caused more deaths throughout the world than had the fighting. Influenza decimated populations on many continents bringing death in a most horrible fashion, especially among young adults who happened to be the group most vulnerable to that particularly virulent virus. Phoebe contracted that strain of influenza while visiting Will and his family in New York City during the Christmas holidays of 1918. Phoebe must have had a premonition that her days on this earthly plane were drawing to a close before she became ill, because she rearranged financial details in her will and made her son promise to build a museum at the University of California with part of his inheritance. She recovered enough to make her way home to Pleasanton, but the effects of the illness had weakened her to the point where it was apparent she could not linger for long. She knew that there was still one bit of unfinished business to attend to before the end came.

Phoebe requested that Ella pay her a visit. Ella's husband was one of Phoebe's attending physicians, but when Phoebe first requested that Ella come, Ella herself was ill and in a hospital. As soon as she was able, Ella accompanied her husband on the long journey out into the countryside to the Hacienda. Ella knew that Phoebe's favourite colour was violet; in fact, she teasingly referred to Phoebe as 'Violet Lady'. So that day she brought a large bunch of violets as a small token of her affection for her old friend. She found Phoebe resting on the sun porch wearing a violet bed jacket.[23] Ella's intention had been to share with Phoebe the Bahá'í teaching on life after death, but she quickly surmised that that might not be the appropriate time to do so, that a more light-hearted conversation was in order. She found that although Phoebe was 'quite weak bodily, her mind was as clear and awake as ever'.[24] Ella reported to 'Abdu'l-Bahá that the following conversation took place during that visit.

[Mrs. H:] Oh my dear, I have so longed to see you. It was good of you to come. You have not been well. Are you much better?"

Ella: Indeed it is a great joy to come. Yes I am better and I just had to come and smile at you and tell you how much I love you!

Mrs. H: And I love you!

E [Ella]: Here are a few violets for you. It seems like 'carrying coals to Newcastle' to bring flowers to The Hacienda, but you always loved violets.

Mrs. H: Yes indeed – You remembered my favorite color – how sweet!

E [Ella]: I always used to call you 'the Violet Lady' – do you remember?

Mrs. H: Yes. I loved that, as the violets are so fragrant. Thank you, dear. I have longed to see you to thank you for sending me word about the health and safety of 'Abdu'l-Bahá. The copy of the cable reached me when I was in New York visiting my son, and Anne was with me. I was too miserable to write, but oh, how I did appreciate receiving that good news! All these awful four years I have wondered how he was faring, and fearful of what those terrible Turks might do to him.

E [Ella]: But 'Abdu'l-Bahá is always under the protection of God. We must remember that.

Mrs. H: To be sure that is true. How wonderful that is – how wonderful that is!!

E [Ella]: In a few days I shall write to Him. What message will you send, dear?

Mrs. H: Oh, give him my love and tell him that I have thought about him a thousand times and I am thankful that that country is safe and all is well with him.

E [Ella]: Indeed I shall be happy to send this word.

The conversation then turned to Dr Cooper and how much Mrs Hearst liked him. Ella told her one of 'Abdu'l-Bahá's Persian stories and made her laugh. Mrs Hearst then spoke most lovingly of Anne (Mrs Flint) and of her pleasure on receiving news that Anne was en route to California, despite the illness of her husband. She hoped that while Anne was there it might be possible for Ella to pay them a visit. Ella then spoke again of 'Abdu'l-Bahá. She asked about Mrs Hearst's grandchildren, especially John, the little boy the Master particularly loved and had blessed. She 'seemed so joyful in recalling that fact' and that John was there with her, along with other members of her family.

Ella continued in her letter to the Master to describe the most important moment of her last visit with Phoebe:

> In another minute I said: 'Suppose we say the Greatest Name together. Wouldn't you like to do that?'
>
> She assented at once with a smile. I held her frail hand to my lips and we repeated the Blessed Name nine times. Then she lay back on her pillows with such a contented peaceful sigh, and murmured: 'Oh – what a comfort that is – <u>what a comfort that is</u>!'
>
> "Abdu'l-Bahá's Presence seems right here with us – doesn't it, dear,' said I.
>
> 'Yes', she softly answered, 'How beautiful, how beautiful!'
>
> Then I left her. As I stood at the door she smiled again and said: 'I like to see you in blue' and, I gayly answered: 'I like you in violet.'
>
> *Mrs. H:* We go together very harmoniously.
>
> *E [Ella]:* Yes indeed – and we always did. Although we have not seen each other often during these years yet in our hearts we have always understood, haven't we?
>
> *Mrs. H:* Ah, yes – we have always understood! Thank you for coming – goodbye dear!
>
> *E [Ella]:* Lets say 'au revoir', shall we? Au revoir, dear!
>
> So we parted, both supremely happy for those few brief moments. I did not see her again for she soon failed rapidly and finally went to sleep – but that night, after our little talk, she was quite a good deal better.[25]

Ella then addresses the following words to 'Abdu'l-Bahá:

> Oh Beloved – how well I know that Thou didst plan and arrange all this so that she – that really great soul – should turn to Thee and Thy friends in her last hours. How can I ever be thankful enough to have been the humble link over which her thoughts flew to Thee, and her heart was comforted by the Name of the Blessed Beauty!
>
> Thou hast taught us that there are no accidental happenings, and I feel sure that it was part of the divine plan that Dr. Cooper should have been called in to the case. He was absolutely surprised, for he did not know Mrs. Hearst except very casually, but he did know her attending physician very well. As Thou canst imagine, it has all made a profound impression upon him; and I pray and supplicate that it may help in his ultimate confirmation in the Cause of God . . . Soon I hope to see dear Anne Apperson Flint and tell her of this beautiful incident over which we will rejoice together! Mrs. Hearst told Dr. Cooper that she loved her like a daughter. How wonderful it was that Anne could be with her at the last! That too was a matter guided by 'Abdu'l-Bahá![26]

That was the last time Ella saw her old friend, for Phoebe passed away two weeks later on 13 April 1919.[27] Ella informed the Master about Phoebe's death and of her last visit with Phoebe. In response 'Abdu'l-Bahá wrote:

> Thou hast written concerning the death of the believing and assured maid-servant of God, Mrs. Hearst. This news grieved me deeply but my consolation lies in the fact that that respected soul has been freed from the prison of this earthly abode and has hastened to the Divine Court. She was a drop that attained the ocean and was a ray that returned to the sun. She was a bird that flew to the Divine rose-garden and was a star that gained admittance into the solar system. A prayer, supplicating forgiveness for that respected one, has been written and is herewith enclosed. Publish it among the firm friends that it may perpetuate her memory. Although at present it is not known, yet in future her name shall be uplifted and her fame shall spread abroad. Mary Magdalene was during her lifetime destitute of every fame and position, she was a peasant but now consider what has happened! . . .
>
> Praise be to God in the last hours of the life of the respected maid-servant of God, Mrs. Hearst, thou has been enabled to meet her and hast been the cause that she uttered nine times the Greatest Name and turned her face to the Abhá Kingdom and in the utmost faith and assurance hastened from this mortal world to the Immortal Realm. Her face therefore like unto a star shall shine at the horizon of the Kingdom of God and her

spirit shall fly in the Limitless Realm and her memory shall live throughout cycles and generations. It was highly favorable and fitting that thou hast met her; it was indeed providential. [28]

Enclosed with the letter to Ella was the following Tablet.

A prayer in supplication for forgiveness for:–
The dear maid-servant of God, the respected Mrs. Hearst;
Upon her be Bahá'u'lláh il Abha

HE IS GOD

O Divine Providence, O Forgiving Lord!

Mrs. Hearst has hastened from this dark and dreary world to the realm of Light; and has become detached from this nether world and has flown unto the realm on High.

O my God! Endowed with a seeing eye, she beheld the rays of the Sun of Truth and endowed with a hearing ear, she hearkened to the call of the Kingdom. Possessing a keen sense of smell, she inhaled the fragrant scent of the Paradise of Abha, and gifted with a pure heart she overflowed with Thy love.

From the Far West, she journeyed to the Holy Land, attained the privilege of visiting the Sacred Spot and served Thy Kingdom.

O thou Pardoning God! Ignite her candle and cause her star to become resplendent in the Immortal Realm. Let her memory be spread abroad over all regions and her name, like unto that of Mary Magdalene, be ever illustrious among the denizens of the Kingdom. Cause her fame to be world-wide and her voice to reach the ears of the Supreme Concourse.

Exalt the members of her family and place upon their heads the diadem of everlasting glory; that they may appreciate the value of that honourable soul and may realize what a magnificent edifice she has erected for them and what a standard of everlasting glory she has hoisted, so that of her, her family and kindred may be eternally proud.

O Compassionate Lord! Although at present Thy favour on her behalf is unknown, yet in future, like unto the sun, it shall be made manifest.

Verily thou art the Forgiver, the Bestower and the Compassionate.

[Signed] 'Abdu'l-Bahá 'Abbás[29]

Ella told the Master that several memorial services had been held for Mrs

Hearst 'as she was a widely known public woman, loved and respected for her long life of good works'. The family held a private service at the Hacienda, another for her friends and family was conducted in her old neighbourhood, Nob Hill, at the Episcopal Grace Cathedral in San Francisco with a bishop presiding, and finally a large service for the general public was held at the San Francisco Civic Center Auditorium. Ella stated that 'many places were closed on that day out of respect for her and really the whole country and especially the state of California mourned her loss'.[30]

May Bolles Maxwell remembered Mrs Hearst as

> a woman who loved to do good more than all else in life – she liked to help others, and many times I have seen her face which was full of strength & sweetness illumined with the light of happiness when she had transformed some young life from dull hopeless monotony into a new world of power & possibility, of education and attainment, not alone by the power of her money, but by the deeper magic of her love, her sympathy, and her deep insight into the needs & aspirations of her fellow beings.[31]

Her close relationship with Mrs Hearst during the early years of her life afforded her opportunities to hear directly from her about her visit with 'Abdu'l-Bahá.

> Mrs. Hearst was profoundly impressed, deeply touched and subsequently, when she was with us in Paris, told me of a number of remarkable experiences, of direct guidance and unique inspiration she had received from the Beloved Master.[32]

From the great lady herself, May learned of one promise of the Master that undoubtedly cheered Phoebe's heart.

> He told her that all her philanthropies and good deeds had been accepted at the Threshold of God, but that even these were as nothing in his sight compared with the fact that she had been the means of bringing the first group of people from the western world to the prison of Akka and that for this act she would obtain an eternal reward.[33]

One final quiet but profound honour was bestowed upon Mrs Hearst posthumously. When Shoghi Effendi was able to secure possession of the Mansion of Bahjí in 1929 and to restore it, he transformed it into a museum showcasing the achievements of the Faith for both Bahá'í visitors and the general public. There, in a room overlooking the Shrine of Bahá'u'lláh not far from the chamber where Bahá'u'lláh passed away, he very purposefully placed three portraits on an interior wall in a vertical line. The top portrait was of Thornton Chase, the first steadfast believer from the West. The bottom portrait was of Anton Haddad, the first believer to travel to the western hemisphere and who faithfully upheld and promoted the Faith in those far regions during a time of severe testing. Finally, in the centre, he placed the portrait of the 'Mother of the Faithful', the one who made possible the flourishing of the Cause of God in the West, Phoebe Apperson Hearst.

©Bahá'í World Centre

'Abdu'l-Bahá at the Goodall home in Oakland, California, 1912, with some of his entourage

©Bahá'í World Centre

Ella Goodall Cooper in later years when she wrote her memoirs of the first Western pilgrimage

Courtesy of James Brown and Anthony Brown

Helen Hillyer Brown with her husband Dr Philip King Brown and children, California, c. 1912

Phoebe Hearst at work. Her grandson remembered her often working late into the night to manage the Hearst business empire

ANNEX I

Members of the First Western Pilgrimage

December 1898 to March 1899

Mrs Phoebe Apperson Hearst
Travelling companion for Mrs Hearst: Mrs Mary Virginia Thornburgh-Cropper (Minnie)

Mrs Hearst's Bahá'í teachers:
Dr Edward Christopher Getsinger
Mrs Lucinda Louisa Aurora Moore Getsinger (Lua)

Translator and teacher: Mr Ibrahim George Kheiralla
Spouse: Mrs Marian Augusta Miller Kheiralla

Mrs Hearst's family:
Niece: Miss Anne Drucilla Apperson
Foster child: Miss Helen Adelaide Hillyer (Nell)
Travelling companion for Miss Hillyer: Miss Ella Frances Goodall

Mrs Hearst's staff:
Butler: Mr Robert Turner
Ladies' maid: Miss Amalie Bachrodt (Emily)
Tutor to Mrs Hearst's teenage ward (and cousin) Agnes Lane: Miss Julia Pearson

Invited friends of Mrs Hearst
Miss May Ellis Bolles
Mrs Harriet Burtis Thornburgh (Hattie) *(mother of Mary Virginia Thornburgh-Cropper)*

* * *

Unexpected American visitor to 'Abdu'l-Bahá during the First Western Pilgrimage:
Mrs Margaret Bloodgood Peeke

The First Western Pilgrimage: A Timeline
1898 to 1899

November	*December*	*January*	*February*	*March*
				3rd: Nell and Ella meet Mrs Hearst in Jaffa on their way to Haifa
		Hearst party begins cruise down the Nile		5th: Nell and Ella arrive in 'Akká
11th: Kheiralla arrives in 'Akká	8th: Getsingers arrive in Haifa 10th: Getsingers arrive in 'Akká			12/13th: Margaret Barton-Peake granted two meetings with 'Abdu'l-Bahá
			16th: May & Harriet arrive in Haifa	
	About 20th: Mrs Hearst arrives in Haifa with her maid and Minnie		20th: Robert, Anne and Julia arrive	21st: Kheirallas leave Haifa
	These three return to Egypt before the 25th			23rd: Getsingers leave 'Akká
	At some point in December Mrs Kheiralla arrives		25th: all five leave Haifa. They rejoin the Hearst party in Jaffa, early March	Nell and Ella leave Haifa

ANNEX 2

Tablet of 'Abdu'l-Bahá to Sarah Farmer

O thou who art attracted to the Fragrances of God!

I am already informed of the import of thy wonderful letter and the meanings of thine excellent words. I was rejoiced to find how it expressed that thou art devoted to God, turning unto the Supreme Horizon, enkindled with the fire of the love of God and attracted to the fragrances of God.

I beg of God to increase thy separation from the world, thy supplication before the Kingdom of God and thy yearning for the Beauty of God.

What thou hast said (in thy letter) concerning the servant of Bahá, the 'Mother of the Faithful,' is but true. Verily she is purified in soul, enkindled by the fire of the love of God, hath sincerely turned unto her Master, hath completely faced toward the Kingdom of God and hath arisen to diffuse His fragrances in all parts and serve His friends with a sincerity and joy unto which the Supreme Concourse beareth witness. She shall surely have a firm and steady footing in the Cause of God, her face shall shine forth from the Horizon of Loftiness, her fame shall be spread in the Kingdom of God, and [she] shall have a ringing voice throughout regions, and the lights of her glorious deeds shall beam forth during cycles and ages.

As to [Robert, Alice] and [Louise], verily the faces of these are as the pupil of the eye; although the pupil is created black, yet it is the source of light. I hope God will make these black ones the glory of the white ones and as the depositing of the lights of love of God. And I ask God to assist them in all circumstances, that they may be encompassed with the favors of their Loving Lord throughout centuries and ages.

As to [Apperson], verily God hath ordained for her a noble station. The lights of knowledge shall surely shine forth from her face upon the world. Verily she is attracted to the word of her Lord, was dilated by hearing the speech of Abdu'l-Bahá at the time of meeting and her eyes became consoled by witnessing the signs of her Mighty Lord.

As to the maid-servant of God [Cropper]: God hath indeed favored her with an excellent disposition which is like fragrance from a garden of the Merciful and she passeth her days in serving the Cause of God. I beg of God to confirm and assist her under all aspects and circumstances.

As to the son of the 'Mother of the Faithful': I beg of God to make his ears attentive, his eyes observing, his heart abounding with the lights of guidance and to make his soul as one of the signs of his Mighty Lord. Pray ye in his behalf night and day that God may strengthen him in a matter which may shine, beam and glow in the niche of the Kingdom of God and that He may cause him to arise and assist the pious ones, to seek bounty from the signs, to gain illumination from the lights, deliver the necks of all men from the chains of superstition, to feed the needy ones upon the food of the Kingdom of God and support the weak ones with a penetrative power from the Word of God. Verily thy Lord is the Confirmer![1]

ANNEX 3

The San Francisco Examiner: An Interview with 'Abdu'l-Bahá

Notes by Ahmad Sohrab

I would now like to translate from my Persian notes a most interesting interview between a correspondent of the Examiner and the Master in San Francisco. The date is October 3rd, 1912. The hour is about eight P.M. This fine interview appeared the next day in a most crude form, almost unrecognizable:—

Correspondent: Are you pleased with the United States?

Abdul Baha: The Continent of America is most progressive. The means of instruction are prepared; the educational institutions are thoroughly equipped and the pupils are being systematically trained and educated. Its wealth is on an upward tendency. Its government is democratic. Its advancement unceasing. Its nation hospitable. Its people loyal, energetic and noble. Its inhabitants free and lovers of liberty. Its men civilized and its women cultured, refined and idealistic. On the other hand, all these advantages are on the objective plane and I observe that the majority of the people are submerged in a sea of materialism and agnosticism. Its material civilization is well nigh perfect, but it is in need of the civilization of heaven – divine civilization.

Correspondent: What do you mean by divine civilization?

Abdul Baha: Divine Civilization is the light. Material civilization is the lamp. Material civilization is the body; in itself it is not sufficient, and humanity, from every point of view, stands in need of divine civilization. Natural civilization produces material welfare and prosperity; divine civilization develops man's ideal virtues. Natural civilization serves the physical world; Divine Civilization serves the world of morality. Divine Civilization is a symposium of the perfections of the world of humanity. Divine Civilization is the improvement of the ethical life of a nation. Divine Civilization is the discovery of the Reality of phenomena. Divine Civilization is spiritual philosophy. Divine Civilization is Knowledge of God with rational and intellectual evidences. Divine Civilization is Eternal Life. Divine Civilization is the immortality of the soul. Divine Civilization is the breath of the Holy Spirit. Divine Civilization is heavenly wisdom. Divine Civilization is the Reality of the Teachings of all the ancient prophets. Divine Civilization is Universal Peace and the Oneness of the world of humanity. The Holy Manifestations of God have been the founders of Divine Civilization, the first teachers of mankind and the spreaders of the fragrances of holiness and sanctity amongst the children of men.

Correspondent: Are you satisfied with the American people?

Abdul Baha: The Americans are a kind, and affectionate people. All nations are welcomed in their midst. They give to every one the right of living and allow each to seek happiness in his own way. Here no one feels a foreigner. I am most pleased with them.

Correspondent: I have heard that you advocate the complete equality of men and women. This radical teaching coming from an Oriental thinker, is of great interest and supreme significance. Just at this juncture the Californian women are clamoring for the right to vote for all the National and State officials, and your opinion on this important question would be greatly appreciated by the people.

Abdul Baha: The question of equality between men and women has made greater advancement in America than anywhere else, and day by day it is assuming more importance and coming nearer to its full realization. However, so long as complete equality does not exist between men and women, the world of humanity will not make extraordinary progress. The woman is an essential column, while the man is also an essential column. If we aim to have a lasting building, the foundations of both columns must be laid very deep. Women are the first teachers of the children. They instruct them and inculcate morality in their minds and hearts. Later these children attend schools and universities for higher education and specialization. Now if the teacher or instructor is deficient, how can the scholar be properly trained? Therefore, it is proven that the culture and development of men will be intensified and will attain perfect fruition when women have equal opportunities with them. Consequently, the women must enjoy all the learning they are able to assimilate, so that they may reach to the level of men. The same privileges and opportunities must be conferred upon both; so that, just as they share life and its responsibilities, they may also share the same virtues of the world of humanity. Undoubtedly partnership in education and culture presupposes equality in rights. The world of humanity has two wings, one the male, the other the female. Both wings have to become strong so that mankind may soar to the empyrean of its destined perfection; for if one wing is left weak, the upward flight must from necessity be slow. God has created both human. They enjoy in common all the faculties. No one is endowed with special privileges. How can we make a distinction which is unknown in the sight of God? We must follow the policy of God. Moreover, there are male and female in the vegetable kingdom. They are on equal footing. Inherently they enjoy suffrage and there is no distinction between them. Likewise in the animal kingdom, the right of suffrage and equality is enjoyed without any feeling of superiority or privilege. Therefore it is admitted that there is no distinction of gender in the vegetable and animal kingdoms, although they are deprived of reasonableness and have not the distinguishing faculties. But we, who are confirmed with the bestowal of reason, and who enjoy all the characteristics which distinguish man from the animal, how can we act in this manner, and build these false barriers? Many women have appeared who have won for themselves fame and name by the versatility of their thoughts. Amongst the Bahai women a number have shown remarkable talent for literature, science and art, and have rendered distinct services in all the departments of life.

In history many capable women have displayed special genius for government and political administration, like Semiramis; Zenobia, Queen of Palmyra; and Queen Victoria of England. In the religious world the Israelites wandered for forty years in the wilderness and could not conquer the Holy Land. Finally a woman achieved this signal victory. In the dispensation of Christ, the apostles became confused; even Peter denied Him thrice, but Mary of Magdala became the cause of their firmness and steadfastness. In the religion of Baha-Ullah, Kurrat-Ul-Ayne, and many other Persian women, demonstrated their knowledge and wisdom to such an extent that even the men were astonished and listened with deference to their advice and counsel.

Correspondent: What is your object in coming to America?

Abdul Baha: I have come to America to promote the ideal of Universal Peace and the solidarity of the human race. I have not come for pleasure, or as a tourist.

Correspondent: What do you think about woman's fashions?

Abdul Baha: We do not look upon the dresses of women, whether they are of the latest mode. We are not the judge of fashion. We consider rather the wearer of the dress. If she is chaste, if she is pure, if she is cultured, if she is characterized with heavenly morality and if she is favored at the Threshold of God, she is honored and respected by us, no matter what manner of dress she wears. We have nothing to do with the ever-changing world of mode and picture hats.

Correspondent: 'What is the greatest thing you have seen in America?'

Abdul Baha: The greatest thing I have seen in America is its Freedom. In reality this is a free nation and a democratic government.

Correspondent: What is your opinion about Turkey and the Balkan war?

Abdul Baha: We have nothing to do with war. We are advocates of Peace. Speak to us about the conditions of Peace. Go to the diplomatists and militarists and ask their opinions about this war. But as regards Peace: In the world of humanity there is no more important affair, no weightier cause. It is conducive to the well-being of the world of creation; the means of the prosperity of nations, the reason of eternal friendship between peoples, the cause of solidarity between the East and the West, the promoter of real freedom and the most eminent Favor of His Highness the Almighty. We must all strive to upraise the Flag of International Peace, the Oneness of the world of humanity, and the spiritual brotherhood of mankind.

The correspondent tried to ask a few more questions, but Abdul Baha interrupted him by this final statement, while putting his hand on his shoulder and kissing his face:—

Consider how much I love thee and to what extent I respect Mr. Hearst that, notwithstanding the fatigue coming over me as the result of a very busy day, I have answered all thy questions.

Thus the young man left the presence of Abdul Baha with a sense of awe and respect that one feels only when one is saturated with the holy atmosphere which is created wherever he is – the Center of Spirituality and heavenliness.

PORT SAID, EGYPT,
JULY 24, 1913

Bibliography

Books and Printed Articles

'Abdu'l-Bahá. *Memorials of the Faithful.* Wilmette, IL: Bahá'í Publishing Trust, 1971.

— *Selections from the Writings of 'Abdu'l-Bahá.* Haifa: Bahá'í World Centre, 1978.

— *The Secret of Divine Civilization.* Trans. Marzieh Gail. Wilmette, IL: Bahá'í Publishing Trust, 1957.

— *Tablets of Abdul-Baha Abbas.* Chicago: Bahá'í Publishing Society; vol. 1, 1909; vol. 2, 1915; vol. 3, 1916. Available online at http://reference.bahai.org

— *A Traveller's Narrative Written to Illustrate the Episode of the Báb.* Trans. E. G. Browne. Cambridge: Cambridge University Press, 1891. New edition: Wilmette, IL: Bahá'í Publishing Trust, 1980.

Abu'l-Faḍl, Mírzá. *The Bahá'í Proofs and a Short Sketch of the History and Lives of the Leaders of this Religion.* Trans. Ali-Kuli Khan. Wilmette, IL: Bahá'í Publishing Trust, 1983.

Adiprasetya, Joas. 'The 1893 World Parliament of Religions', in W. Wildman (ed.): *The Boston Collaborative Encyclopedia of Modern Western Theology.* Boston, 2004. Available at http://people.bu.edu/wwildman/WeirdWildWeb/course/mwt/dictionary/mwt_themes_

Afroukhteh, Dr Youness. *Memories of Nine Years in 'Akká.* Trans. Riaz Masrour. Oxford: George Ronald, 2003.

Armstrong, Karen. *A History of God: The 4,000-Year Quest of Judaism, Christianity and Islam.* New York: Ballantine Books, 1993.

Atkinson, Anne Gordon et al. *Green Acre on the Piscatuaqua.* Eliot, MA: Green Acre Bahá'í School Council, 1991.

Bahá'í Community of Switzerland. 'Swiss Bahá'ís Celebrate 100 Years of Contribution to World Civilisation'. Available at http://www.bahai.ch/english/centenary_interlaken.html (accessed September 2008).

The Bahá'í World. Wilmette, IL: Bahá'í Publishing Trust: vol. 3 (1928–1930); vol. 4 (1930–1932); vol. 6 (1934–1936); vol. 8 (1938–1940); vol. 12 (1950–1954); Haifa: The Universal House of Justice: vol. 13 (1954–1963).

Bahá'u'lláh. *The Kitáb-i-Aqdas: The Most Holy Book.* Haifa: Bahá'í World Centre, 1992.

— *The Summons of the Lord of Hosts: Tablets of Bahá'u'lláh.* Haifa: Bahá'í World Centre, 2002.

— *Tablets of Bahá'u'lláh Revealed after the Kitáb-i-Aqdas*. Hafia: Bahá'í World Centre, 1978.

Balyuzi, H. M. *'Abdu'l-Bahá: The Centre of the Covenant of Bahá'u'lláh*. Oxford: George Ronald, 1971.
— *Bahá'u'lláh: The King of Glory*. Oxford: George Ronald, 1980.
— *Edward Granville Browne and the Bahá'í Faith*. Oxford: George Ronald, 1970.
— *Eminent Bahá'ís in the Time of Bahá'u'lláh*. Oxford: George Ronald, 1985.

Beeley, Brian W. 'The Turkish Village Coffeehouse as a Social Institution', in *Geographical Review*, vol. 60, no. 4 (Oct. 1970).

Bible. *Holy Bible*. Revised Standard Version. New York, Oxford: Oxford University Press, 1973.

Blauvelt, W. H. 'Banking', in Sam P. Davis (ed.): *The History of Nevada*, vol. 1 (1913), pp. 624-5. Available online at www.nevadaobserver.com (accessed October 2008).

Blomfield, Lady. *The Chosen Highway*. London: Bahá'í Publishing Trust, 1940. RP Oxford: George Ronald, 2007.

Bonfils, Winifred Black. *The Life and Personality of Phoebe Apperson Hearst*. San Francisco: printed for W. R. Hearst by J. S. Nash, 1928. Photographic reproduction, Friends of Hearst Castle, 1991.

de Bons, Mona Haenni. 'Edith de Bons and Joseph de Bons', in *The Bahá'í World*, vol. 13 (1954–1963). Haifa: The Universal House of Justice, 1970, pp. 878-81.

Brown, Helen Hillyer. *For My Children and Grandchildren*. San Francisco, CA: Hillside Press, 1986.

Brown, Ramona Allen. *Memories of 'Abdu'l-Bahá: Recollections of the Early Days of the Bahá'í Faith in California*. Wilmette, IL: Bahá'í Publishing Trust, 1980.

Cameron, Glenn; Momen, Wendi. *A Basic Bahá'í Chronology*. Oxford: George Ronald, 1996.

Campbell, Thomas H. 'A New Church is Born', ch. 4 of *Good News on the Frontier: A History of the Cumberland Presbyterian Church*. Memphis: Frontier Press, 1965. Available online at the official Cumberland Presbyterian Church website, http://members.aol.com/mleslie598/ (accessed August 2008).

Carmel, Alex. *Die Siedlungen der württembergischen Templer in Palästina 1868–1918*. Stuttgart: W. Kohlhammer, 1973.
— *Palästina – Chronik 1883–bis 1914: Deutsche Zeitungsberichte von der ersten jüdischen Einwanderungswelle bis zum ersten Weltkrieg*. Langenau-Ulm: Armin Vaas Verlag, 1983.

Davis, Richard W. ' "We are All Americans Now!" Anglo-American Marriages in the Late Nineteenth Century' in *Proceedings of the American Philosophical Society*, vol. 135, no. 2 (June 1999).

Dichter, Bernard. *Akko: Sites from the Turkish Period*. Ed. Alex Carmel and Zalman

Baumwoll. Haifa: Gottlieb Schumacher Institute for Research of the Christian Activities in 19th-Century Palestine, University of Haifa, 2000.

Dodge, Bayard. 'American Educational and Missionary Efforts in the Nineteenth and Early Twentieth Centuries', in *Annals of the American Academy of Political and Social Science*. Pennsylvania, PA: Sage Publications, Inc; vol. 401, *America and the Middle East* (May 1972), pp. 15-22.

Ferguson, Niall. *Empire: The Rise and Demise of the British World Order and the Lessons for Global Power*. London: Basic Books, 2003.

Foote, H. S. (ed.). *Pen Pictures from the Garden of the World or Santa Clara County, California, Illustrated*. Chicago: The Lewis Publishing Company, 1888, pp. 443-4. Available online at www.santaclararesearch.net (accessed August 2008).

Gail, Marzieh. *Arches of the Years*. Oxford: George Ronald, 1991.
— *Other People, Other Places*. Oxford: George Ronald, 1982.
— *Summon up Remembrance*. Oxford: George Ronald, 1987.

Garnett, Porter. *Stately Homes of California*. Boston: Little, Brown, and Co., 1915.

Gelernter, David. *Americanism: The Fourth Great Western Religion*. New York: Doubleday, 2007.

Getsinger, Edward. Memoirs written about May 1909 in Washington, D.C. Unpublished. Getsinger papers, USBNA.

Goodall, Helen S.; Cooper, Ella Goodall. *Daily Lessons Received at 'Akká: January 1908*. Wilmette, IL: Bahá'í Publishing Trust, 1979.

Gregory, Louis G. 'Robert Turner', in *World Order: The Bahá'í Magazine,* vol. 12, no. 1(April 1946), pp. 28-9.

Haddad, Anton F. *An Outline of the Bahai Movement in the United States: A Sketch of its Promulgator and Why Afterwards Denied His Master, Abbas Effendi*. Unpublished paper, New York, 1902. PAH papers, held by the University of California at Berkeley Bancroft Library. Available online at www.bahai-library.org
— *Message from Acca* (c. 1900). Available online at www. bahai-library.org

Haifa City Museum. *Ottoman Haifa: Aspects of the City, 1516–1918.* Exhibition catalogue (Curator: Ron Hillel). Haifa: Haifa Museums, 2009.

Harper, Barron J. *Lights of Fortitude*. Oxford: George Ronald, rev. ed. 2007.

Hatch, Willard P. 'Edward Christopher Getsinger', in *The Bahá'í World,* vol. 6 (1934–1936). Wilmette, IL: Bahá'í Publishing Trust, pp. 493-6.

Ḥaydar-'Alí, Ḥájí Mírzá. *Stories from the Delight of Hearts*. Trans. and abridged by A. Q. Faizi. Los Angeles: Kalimát Press, 1980.

Hearst, Kathryn P. *Phoebe Apperson Hearst: The Making of an Upper-Class Woman, 1842–1919.* Unpublished doctoral dissertation, Columbia University, New York, 2005.

Hearst, William Randolph, Jr. *The Hearsts: Father and Son.* Niwot, Colorado: Roberts Rinehart, 1991.

Hobsbawm, Eric. *The Age of Empire: 1875–1914.* New York: Vintage Books, 1989.

Hollinger, Richard (ed.). *Community Histories.* Los Angeles: Kalimát Press, 1992.
— 'Ibrahim George Kheiralla and the Bahá'í Faith in America', in J. R. Cole and M. Momen (eds): *From Iran East and West. Studies in Bábí and Bahá'í History,* vol. 2. Los Angeles: Kalimát Press, 1984.

Honnold, Anna Marie. *Why They Became Bahá'ís: First Generation Bahá'ís by 1963.* New Delhi, India: Bahá'í Publishing Trust, 1994.

Jasion, Jan Teofil. *Never Be Afraid to Dare: The Story of 'General Jack'.* Oxford: George Ronald, 2001.

Johnson, Paul. *A History of the American People.* New York: Harper Perennial, 1999.

Jones, William Carey. 'The First Benefactors', in *The University of California Magazine,* vol. 5, no. 3 (April 1899), available at http://sunsite.berkeley.edu/uchistory/archives (accessed August 2008).

Kark, Ruth. 'From Pilgrimage to Budding Tourism: The Role of Thomas Cook in the Rediscovery of the Holy Land in the Nineteenth Century', in Sarah Searight (ed.): *Travelers in the Levant: Voyagers and Visionaries.* Durham: Astene, 2001. Available online at http://sachlav.huji.ac.il/courses/40939_2002/upload/texts/cookredis1.rtf (accessed 2007).

Khan, Janet A. *Prophet's Daughter: The Life and Legacy of Bahíyyih Khánum, Outstanding Heroine of the Bahá'í Faith.* Wilmette, IL: Bahá'í Publishing Trust, 2005.

Kheiralla, Ibrahim G. *Beha 'U'lláh.* Chicago: I. G. Kheiralla, 1900.

Lakshman-Lepain, Rajwantee. *The Life of Thomas Breakwell.* Trans. Olive McKinley. London: Bahá'í Publishing Trust, 1998. English translation of *La vie de Thomas Breakwell* (Paris: Librairie Bahá'í, 1997).

Levenstein, Harvey. *Seductive Journey: American Tourists in France from Jefferson to the Jazz Age.* Chicago: University of Chicago Press, 1998.

Ma'ani, Baharieh Rouhani. *Leaves of the Twin Divine Trees: An In-depth Study of the Lives of Women Closely Related to the Báb and Bahá'u'lláh.* Oxford: George Ronald, 2008.

Maḥmúd's Diary: The Diary of Mírzá Maḥmúd-i-Zarqání Chronicling 'Abdu'l-Bahá's Journey to America. Trans. Mohi Sobhani with the assistance of Shirley Macias. Oxford: George Ronald, 1998.

Maxwell, May. 'A Brief Account of Thomas Breakwell', in *The Bahá'í World,* vol. 7 (1936–1938). Wilmette, IL: Bahá'í Publishing Trust, pp. 707-11.
— *An Early Pilgrimage.* Haverhill, Suffolk: Lowe & Brydone, 1917. Rev. ed. Oxford: George Ronald, 1969.

McDougall, Walter A. *Freedom Just Around the Corner: A New American History 1585–1828*. New York: HarperCollins, 2004; Perennial, 2005.

— *Throes of Democracy: The American Civil War Era 1829–1877*. New York: HarperCollins, 2008.

Meacham, Jon. *American Gospel: God, the Founding Fathers, and the Making of a Nation*. New York: Random House, 2006.

Menand, Louis. *The Metaphysical Club: A Story of Ideas in America*. New York: Farrar, Straus and Giroux, 2001.

Metelmann, Velda Piff. *Lua Getsinger: Herald of the Covenant*. Oxford: George Ronald, 1997.

Miller, A. L. 'Wind from the West', in *Saudi Aramco World*, vol. 20, no. 6 (Nov./ Dec. 1969), pp. 4-7. Available online at http://www.saudiaramcoworld.com/ issue/196906/wind.from.the.west.htm (accessed August 2008).

Minard, John S. *Allegany County and its People: A Centennial Memorial History of Allegany County, New York*. Alfred, NY: W.A. Fergusson & Co., 1892. Available online at www.ancestry.com (accessed August 2008).

Mitchell, Sarah E. 'A Late Victorian California Interior with Mexican Influences: Interior of Phoebe Hearst's Home, Hacienda del Pozo de Verona, Pleasanton, California.' Available online at http://www.vintagedesigns.com/id/latevic/ca/ index.htm (accessed August 2008).

Momen, Moojan (ed.). *Selections from the Writings of E. G. Browne on the Bábí and Bahá'í Religions*. Oxford: George Ronald, 1987.

'Morgan Kroesen Thornburgh', in *The Bay of San Francisco*, vol. 2, pp. 569-70 (Lewis Publishing Co, 1892). Available online at www.ancestry.com

Munírih Khánum. *Munírih Khánum: Memoirs and Letters*. Trans. Sammireh Anwar Smith. Los Angeles: Kalimát Press, 1986.

Nakhjavani, Violette. *The Maxwells of Montreal*. 2 vols. Oxford: George Ronald, forthcoming.

Nasaw, David. *The Chief: The Life of William Randolph Hearst*. New York: Houghton Mifflin, 2000.

Nickliss, Alexandra M. 'Phoebe Apperson Hearst's "Gospel of Wealth", 1883–1901', in *The Pacific Historical Review*, vol. 71, no. 4 (Nov. 2002), pp. 575-605.

Oliphant, Laurence. *Haifa, Or Life in Modern Palestine*. Edinburgh and London: William Blackwood and Sons, 1887. Modern facsimile edition, Elibron Classics, 2005.

An Outline of American History. Ed. Howard Cincotta. United States Information Agency (ISIA), 1994. Chapter 4: 'The Second Great Awakening'. Available online at http://www.let.rug.nl/

Parsons, Agnes. *'Abdu'l-Bahá in America: Agnes Parsons' Diary*. Los Angeles: Kalimát Press, 1996.

Peeke, Hewson L. *A Standard History of Erie County, Ohio*. Vol. 1. Chicago and New York: The Lewis Publishing Company, 1916.

Peeke, Margaret B. *My Visit to Abbas-Effendi in 1899*. Cleveland, Ohio: Dr Pauline Barton-Peeke, 1911.

Perkins, Mary. *Servant of the Glory: The Life of 'Abdu'l-Bahá*. Oxford: George Ronald, 1999.

Phelps, Myron H. *The Master in 'Akká*. Los Angeles: Kalimát Press, 1985. Reprinted from *Life and Teachings of Abbas Effendi: A Study of the Religion of the Babis, or Beha'is, Founded by the Persian Báb and by His Successors, Beha Ullah and Abbas Effendi*, Second Revised Edition, New York and London: G. P. Putnam's Sons, 1912.

Proctor, Ben. *William Randolph Hearst: The Early Years, 1863–1910*. New York: Oxford University Press, 1998.

Prothero, Stephen. *Religious Literacy: What Every American Needs to Know – and Doesn't*. New York: Harper One, 2007.

Rabbani, Ahang (trans.). 'Khátirát-i-Hayát by Mírzá Habíbu'lláh Afnán', in *Online Journal of Bahá'í Studies* (OJBS), vol. 1 (2007), pp. 298-400. Available at www.ojbs.org

Rabbaní, Rúḥíyyih. *The Priceless Pearl*. London: Bahá'í Publishing Trust, 1969.

Randall-Winckler, Bahiyyih. *William Henry Randall: Disciple of 'Abdu'l-Bahá*. Oxford: Oneworld, 1996.

Remey, Charles Mason. *Reminiscences and Letters*. Typed multi-volume autobiography, Copy 8, USBNA.

Robinson, Judith. *The Hearsts: An American Dynasty*. Newark: University of Delaware Press, 1991.

Rose, Julie K. *The World's Colombian Exposition: Idea, Experience, Aftermath*. Dissertation, University of Virginia, published 1 August 1996. Available online at http://xroads.virginia.edu/~MA96/WCE/title.html

Ruby, Robert. *Jericho: Dreams, Ruins, Phantoms*. New York: Henry Holt, 1995.

Ruhe, David S. *Door of Hope: The Bahá'í Faith in the Holy Land*. Oxford: George Ronald, 2nd rev.ed. 2001.

Ruhe-Schoen, Janet. *A Love Which Does Not Wait: The Stories of Lua Getsinger, May Maxwell, Martha Root, Keith Ransom-Kehler, Hyde Dunn, Susan Moody, Dorothy Baker, Ella Bailey and Marion Jack*. Riviera Beach, Florida: Palabra Publications, 1998.

Scott, Donald. 'Evangelicalism, Revivalism, and the Second Great Awakening'. Available online at http://www.nhc.rtp.nc.us/tserve/nineteen/nkeyinfo/nevarnrev.htm

Sears, William; Quigley, Robert. *The Flame: The Story of Lua*. Oxford: George Ronald, 1973.

Seikaly, May. *Haifa: Transformation of an Arab Society 1918–1939*. London and New York: I. B. Tauris, 2000.

Shoghi Effendi. *Citadel of Faith: Messages to America 1947–1957*. Wilmette, IL: Bahá'í Publishing Trust, 1965.
— *The Dispensation of Bahá'u'lláh* (1934): Wilmette, IL: Bahá'í Publishing Trust, 1970. Also included in Shoghi Effendi, *The World Order of Bahá'u'lláh.*
— *God Passes By*. Wilmette, IL: Bahá'í Publishing Trust, 1944.
— *Messages to the Bahá'í World: 1950–1957*. Wilmette, IL: Bahá'í Publishing Trust, 1958.
— *Unfolding Destiny: The Messages from the Guardian of the Bahá'í Faith to the Bahá'í Community of the British Isles*. London: Bahá'í Publishing Trust, 1981.
— *The World Order of Baha'u'llah*. Wilmette, IL: Bahá'í Publishing Trust, 1938.

Smith, Peter. 'The American Bahá'í Community, 1894–1917: A Preliminary Survey', in J. R. Cole and M. Momen (eds): *Studies in Bábí and Bahá'í History*, vol. 1. Los Angeles: Kalimát Press, 1982.
— *A Concise Encyclopedia of the Bahá'í Faith*. Oxford: Oneworld, 2000.

Sohrab, Ahmad. *Abdul Baha in Egypt*. New York: J. H: Sears an Co. for the New History Foundation, 1929. Available online at http://bahai-library.com

Star of the West. RP Oxford: George Ronald, 1978.

Stockman, Robert H. *The Bahá'í Faith in America*. Vol. 1: *Origins 1892–1900*. Wilmette, IL: Bahá'í Publishing Trust, 1985; vol. 2: *Early Expansion, 1900–1912*. Oxford: George Ronald, 1995.
— 'Robert Turner: A Door to the Kingdom', in *The American Bahá'í*, vol. 36, no. 8 (23 Nov. 2005), p. 3.
— *Thornton Chase: First American Bahá'í*. Wilmette, IL: Bahá'í Publishing Trust, 2002.

Swanberg, W. A. *Citizen Hearst: A Biography of William Randolph Hearst*. New York: Charles Scribner's, 1961.

Taherzadeh, Adib. *The Child of the Covenant: A Study Guide to the Will and Testament of 'Abdu'l-Bahá*. Oxford: George Ronald, 2000.
— *The Covenant of Bahá'u'lláh*. Oxford: George Ronald, 1995.
— *The Revelation of Bahá'u'lláh*. Oxford: George Ronald, 1974–1987; vol. 1: *Baghdad 1853–1863*; vol. 2: *Adrianople 1863–1868*; vol. 3: *'Akká, The Early Years 1868–1877*; vol. 4: *Mazra'ih & Bahjí 1877–92.*

Thomas, Richard. 'The "Pupil of the Eye": African–Americans and the Making of the American Bahá'í Community', in Gwendolyn Etter-Lewis and Richard Thomas (eds): *Lights of the Spirit*. Wilmette, IL: Bahá'í Publishing Trust, 2006.

Thompson, Juliet. *The Diary of Juliet Thompson* (1947). Los Angeles: Kalimát Press, 1983.

Townshend, George. *'Abdu'l-Bahá, The Master*. Comp. David Hofman. Oxford: George Ronald, 1987.

Traxel, David. *1898: The Birth of the American Century*. New York: Vintage Books, 1998.

Tuchman, Barbara W. *The Proud Tower: The World before the War, 1890–1914*. New York: Random House, 1962; New York: Ballantine Books, 1996.

The Universal House of Justice. *Messages from the Universal House of Justice 1963–1986: The Third Epoch of the Formative Age*. Comp. Geoffry W. Marks. Wilmette, IL: Bahá'í Publishing Trust, 1996.

Weinberg, Robert. *Ethel Jenner Rosenberg: The Life and Times of England's Outstanding Bahá'í Pioneer Worker*. Oxford: George Ronald, 1995.

Whitehead, O. Z. *Portraits of Some Bahá'í Women*. Oxford: George Ronald, 1996.
— *Some Bahá'ís to Remember*. Oxford: George Ronald, 1983.
— *Some Early Bahá'ís of the West*. Oxford: George Ronald, 1976.

Whitmore, Bruce W. *The Dawning Place: The Building of a Temple, the Forging of the North American Bahá'í Community*. Wilmette, IL: Bahá'í Publishing Trust, 1984.

Whyte, Kenneth. *The Uncrowned King: The Sensational Rise of William Randolph Hearst*. Berkeley, CA: Counterpoint, 2009.

Willard, Frances Elizabeth; Livermore, Mary A. *Great American Women of the 19th Century: A Biographical Encyclopedia*. Amherst, NY: Humanity Books, 2005. A reprint of *American Women*. New York: Mast, Crowell & Kirkpatrick, c. 1897.

Winchester, Simon. *A Crack in the Edge of the World: America and the Great California Earthquake of 1906*. New York: HarperCollins, 2005.

Yazbak, Mahmoud. *Haifa in the Late Ottoman Period, 1864–1914: A Muslim Town in Transition*. The Netherlands: Brill, 1998.

— 'Templars as Proto-Zionist? The "German Colony" in Late Ottoman Haifa', in *Journal of Palestine Studies*, vol. 28, no. 4 (Summer 1999), pp. 40-54.

Zachs, Fruma. 'Toward a Proto-Nationalist Concept of Syria? Revisiting the American Presbyterian Missionaries in the Nineteenth-Century Levant', in *Die Welt des Islams*, New Series, vol. 41, issue 2, (Jul. 2001), pp. 145-173.

Archival Collections

Phoebe Apperson Hearst Papers (PAH), Bancroft Library, University of California at Berkeley

United States Bahá'í National Archives (USNBA):
Helen Hillyer Brown papers
Ella Goodall Cooper papers

Edward and Lua Getsinger papers
Helen Goodall papers
Henrietta Emogene Hoagg papers
May Bolles Maxwell papers
Charles Mason Remey papers
Mary Virginia Thornburgh-Cropper papers
Albert Windust papers

University of Delaware Library, Special Collections

The papers of the estate of Amatu'l-Bahá Rúḥíyyih Khánum

Orrin Peck Collection, Huntington Library

Henry Munroe Rogers Memorial Collection, Houghton Library, Harvard University (Apperson–Flint wedding photographs)

Frequently Used Websites

www.ancestry.com (for the US and UK Censuses, ship passenger logs, US passport applications, histories of counties, death records, immigration and naturalization records)

http://bahai-library.com

Newspapers

The American Bahá'í
The Times (London)
New York Times
The Fresno Bee
Oakland Tribune
Sacramento Bee
San Francisco Examiner
San Francisco Bulletin

Notes and References

Foreword

1 Shoghi Effendi, *God Passes By*, pp. 257-60.

Chapter 1 Expectations

1 Public schools in the United States included stories from the Bible as part of the curriculum during the nineteenth century. In addition, during that period, Protestant churches began the widespread practice of holding structured classes for children on Sunday mornings in addition to the weekly worship service. 'Sunday School' became a major influence on the lives of a substantial portion of the American population by the end of the nineteenth century. Lua Getsinger in particular, raised in a church-going family in a town dominated by Baptists and Methodists, would very likely have attended a Sunday School. For a discussion of religious education and the Sunday School movement which undoubtedly affected not only the Getsingers but the other American pilgrims in this book, see Prothero, *Religious Literacy*, pp. 69-83.

2 On 8 December 1898 Jupiter's luminosity was a magnitude of –1.8. See http://www.calsky.com.

3 Edward C. Getsinger, US passport application, no. 5206, issued 19 September 1898 in Washington, D.C. Until photographs were required for passports in the mid-1910s, the applications included physical descriptions that provide details not discernible from black and white photographs.

4 Hatch, 'Edward Christopher Getsinger', pp. 493-6.

5 Mrs Edward C. Getsinger, US passport application, no. 59880, issued 5 July 1902 in New York, New York.

6 The rock under the 'Noble Sanctuary' (The Dome of the Rock) is reputed to be the spot from which the Prophet Muhammad ascended to heaven during his Night Journey accompanied by the Angel Gabriel.

7 Kark, 'From Pilgrimage to Budding Tourism'.

8 The account of the Getsinger's first 24 hours in the Holy Land is based upon Lua's handwritten letter to the Chicago believers (USBNA; also published in Metelmann, *Lua Getsinger*, p. 15); and also from ch. 3 of Edward Getsinger's unpublished typed memoirs written approximately in May of 1909 in Washington, D.C. (Getsinger papers, USBNA). Some details about Haifa and 'Akká are derived from the author's many years as a resident of Haifa as well as from the accounts of the other pilgrims about their arrival by ship. It seems from the accounts of the Hearst pilgrims that the steamers coming from Port Said were on a regular schedule, usually arriving at Haifa late on Thursday evenings.

9 Carmel, *Palästin–Chronik 1883–bis 1914*, pp. 200-04.
10 Ruby, *Jericho: Dreams, Ruins, Phantoms*, p. 15.
11 Afroukhteh, *Memories of Nine Years in 'Akká*, pp. 31-2.
12 It is estimated that by 1900 the population of Haifa was about 45% Muslim and 45% Christian. The Christians were the most educated segment of the population. See Seikaly, *Haifa*, pp. 21-2.
13 Beeley, 'The Turkish Village Coffeehouse as a Social Institution'.
14 Afroukhteh, *Memories of Nine Years in 'Akká*, pp. 150-51.
15 'Abdu'l-Bahá, *Memorials of the Faithful*, pp. 70-71.
16 'Akká has been called a number of names throughout its 5,500 years as a town. In this book the name 'Akká is used rather than the more modern Akko or Acre, because it was the name during the Ottoman period and because it is the one used in most Bahá'í literature. In the New Testament it is called Ptolemais and during the Crusades it was St Jean d'Acre.
17 Yazbak, *Haifa in the Late Ottoman Period, 1864–1914*, passim, provides an excellent overview of the history of Haifa in the nineteenth century. See also Oliphant, *Haifa, Or Life in Modern Palestine*, pp. 22-33; Ruhe, *Door of Hope*, pp. 129-31; Artzy, *Ottoman Haifa: Aspects of the City, 1516–1918*.
18 For general information on the Templers and their settlements in the Holy Land, see Carmel, *Die Siedlungen der Wurttembergischen Templer in Palästina 1868–1918*; Ruhe, *Door of Hope*, pp. 191-5; Yazbak, 'Templars as Proto-Zionist? The "German Colony" in Late Ottoman Haifa', pp. 40-54.
19 Oliphant, *Haifa*, p. 22.
20 Carmel, *Palästin –Chronik 1883–bis 1914*. See a photo of the Kaiser's arrival at the new dock at the German Colony on page 203. The street is now called Ben Gurion Avenue. It runs from the access road of the new port to the entrance plaza at the foot of the Terraces of the Shrine of the Báb. The modern port, built during the British Mandate period, reclaimed much land, altering the shoreline of Haifa beyond recognition and depriving the German colony of direct access to the sea. The Kaiser's visit was the apex of the history of the little colony and would be commemorated with a stone marker that today sits just above the entrance at the top of the Terraces of the Shrine of the Báb.
21 It is likely that the Getsingers were staying at the new Carmel Hotel located on the main street of the German Colony, because it was near where the Cook Travel Agency would have its Haifa office a few years later in 1903. The Getsingers did not record the name of their hotel in their written accounts. The Cook Agency closely supervised those hotels in the Holy Land which served its clients, to ensure that the standards of comfort expected by Western travellers were met. See Kark, 'From Pilgrimage to Budding Tourism', p. 9 (online Nov. 2006).
22 Ruhe, *Door of Hope*, p. 187.
23 It is quite probable that the reason they were not summoned to 'Akká on that first day was because it was the Muslim Sabbath and a very busy day for 'Abdu'l-Bahá. Friday mornings were usually spent ministering to the poor of 'Akká, and the Master routinely attended Friday noon services at the central mosques of 'Akká or Haifa to the end of his life. (It was Shoghi Effendi who ended the practice of Bahá'ís in the Holy Land regularly attending Muslim services on Friday.) This probably also explains why the Getsingers were not invited to be guests for

a midday meal on 9 December, since lunch was normally the main meal of the day in the region, and because of attending the noon services the local Bahá'ís would have been unable to prepare a repast worthy of special guests.

24 See the summary of his life given by 'Abdu'l-Bahá in *Memorials of the Faithful*, pp. 118-19: '. . . he faithfully waited upon the believers, and his home was a way station for Bahá'í travelers. He had an excellent disposition, a wonderful character, and high, spiritual aims. He was friendly with friend and stranger alike; he was kind to people of every nation and wished them well' (p. 119).

Chapter 2 A Seed Sprouts in America

1 Throughout this book Haddad's name is spelled as it was in the 1890s by the Americans, not as it was more correctly transliterated from Arabic by Shoghi Effendi.

2 At the time his homeland was part of the Ottoman province of Syria, which included the future countries of Israel, Jordan, Lebanon and Syria.

3 Anton Haddad remained constant after Kheiralla's defection. He wrote *Divine Revelation: The Basis of Civilization* and *Message from Acca*, as well as his unpublished paper *An Outline of the Bahai Movement in the United States.*

4 This college would later be renamed the American University of Beirut and would become widely acclaimed as the foremost university of the region, sending forth many graduates who became renowned and accomplished, including Shoghi Effendi.

5 See, for example, the following summaries of the history of the American University of Beirut and its impact upon the region: Dodge, 'American Educational and Missionary Efforts in the Nineteenth and Early Twentieth Centuries', pp. 15-22; Miller, 'Wind from the West', pp. 4-7; Zachs, 'Toward a Proto-Nationalist Concept of Syria? Revisiting the American Presbyterian Missionaries in the Nineteenth-Century Levant', pp. 145-73.

6 The most thorough account of Ibrahim Kheiralla's early life is to be found in Hollinger, 'Ibrahim George Kheiralla and the Bahá'í Faith in America'. See also Haddad, *An Outline of the Bahai Movement in the United States*; Stockman, *The Bahá'í Faith in America*, vol. 1, pp. 13-15.

7 For a discussion of British control over Egypt from 1882 to 1922 see Ferguson, *Empire: The Rise and Demise of the British World Order and the Lessons for Global Power*, pp. 230-35. See also Hobsbawm, *The Age of Empire: 1875–1914*. pp. 68, 287.

8 It is unclear when this third marriage occurred. It is possible that it took place after Kheiralla began to investigate the Bahá'í Faith, because his third wife was the sister of a Bahá'í. See Hollinger, p. 98.

9 The Bahá'í Faith discourages its adherents from involvement with the occult or 'black magic' and teaches that even though there are many unexplained forces in the universe, most of the practice of magic, astrology and spiritualism is based upon superstition and retards rather than promotes spiritual development.

10 For information about this period, see Haddad, *An Outline of the Bahai Movement in the United States.*

11 See Helen Hillyer's handwritten notes from her sessions with 'Abdu'l-Karím in Cairo in 1899. Brown papers, USBNA.

12 Stockman, *The Bahá'í Faith in America: Origins 1892–1900* (vol. 1), pp. 17-19.
13 Kheiralla, *Behá 'U'lláh*, pp. vi-viii, quoted in Stockman, op. cit. p. 19.
14 Stockman, ibid. pp. 22-3. Emphasis mine.
15 Haddad, p. 4.
16 ibid. pp. 6-7.
17 ibid. pp. 4, 7.
18 The Exposition was meant to open in 1892, but as a government-planned event it opened a year late.
19 Libraries in the United States held books that mentioned the Faith, and there had been brief mentions of it in newspapers, but never before in the United States had it been mentioned in a public talk.
20 From the poem 'Chicago' by the American poet Carl Sandburg.
21 Menand, *The Metaphysical Club*, p. 318. Dewey taught at the University of Chicago and is regarded as one of the greatest minds and social reformers ever produced by the United States, especially in the field of education.
22 Rose, 'The World's Colombian Exposition'.
23 Adiprasetya, 'The 1893 World Parliament of Religions'.
24 Cameron and Momen, *A Basic Bahá'í Chronology*, p. 117.
25 It seems likely that Kheiralla and Jessup must have at least met, since Kheiralla was among the original students of the college that Jessup helped to establish.
26 Stockman, *Thornton Chase*, pp. 116-17.
27 The designation 'Disciple of 'Abdu'l-Bahá' was an honour bestowed posthumously (and without explanation) upon nineteen Western believers by Shoghi Effendi in 1930; see *The Bahá'í World*, vol. 3 (1928–1930), pp. 84-5. Later, he bestowed the title on several others following their passing.
28 Metelmann, *Lua Getsinger*, p. 3.
29 Burton's English translation of Middle Eastern folk tales, entitled *The Book of a Thousand Nights and a Night*, (often referred to colloquially as 'The Arabian Nights') was published in 1885 and became an immediate bestseller.
30 Menand, *The Metaphysical Club*, pp. 291-2.
31 In 1894 this was the equivalent of six weeks wages for a working man.
32 Haddad, pp. 8-9.
33 See McDougall, *Freedom Just Around the Corner: A New American History 1585–1828*, a general history of the United States based upon the proposition that America is a nation of hustlers.
34 Edward Getsinger, unpublished memoirs, ch. 1, p. 24.
35 See application for regaining her British citizenship for her full name, Certificate 2,544 issued 5 March 1917. Most basic information on Marian Miller, comes from her Certificate of Re-naturalization (into British Citizenship). Application for Nationality and Naturalisation: Kheiralla, Marion, 27 November 1916, The National Archives (United Kingdom). She was born on 25 February 1861 in Kirkwhelpington, Northumberland.
36 Stockman, *Thornton Chase*, pp. 117, 121.
37 Marian Miller's father, Reverend Thomas Elton Miller, was the son and grandson of clergymen, and her mother, Agnes Margaret Brown Miller, was the daughter of a clergyman. Her parents' brothers were also clergymen. Both sides of her family came from northern England. Her mother's side of the family apparently

had inherited wealth. This information is derived from both Marian Miller's Certificate of Re-naturalization, and information from the 1851, 1861, 1871 and 1881 England Censuses.

38 The following discussion on religion in America is based primarily upon Armstrong, *The History of God*; Gelernter, *Americanism: The Fourth Great Western Religion*; Johnson, *A History of the American People*; Meacham, *American Gospel: God, the Founding Fathers, and the Making of a Nation*; McDougall, *Freedom Just Around the Corner: A New American History 1585–1828*; McDougall, *Throes of Democracy: The American Civil War Era 1829–1877*.

39 Johnson, *A History of the American People*, p. 112.

40 ibid. p. 116. For an excellent general summary of the first Great Awakening, see McDougall, *Freedom Just Around the Corner*, pp. 131-5.

41 Meacham, *American Gospel*, p. 78.

42 The actual wording of the First Amendment is: 'Congress shall make no law respecting an establishment of religion, nor prohibiting the free exercise thereof.'

43 Quoted in Meacham, *American Gospel*, pp. 134-5.

44 The British academic, writer on religion and former Roman Catholic nun Karen Armstrong found the First and Second Great Awakenings of America to be too emotionally charged, even violent, for her taste. Armstrong, *A History of God*, p. 323.

45 McDougall, *Throes of Democracy*, p. 172.

46 ibid.

47 ibid. p. 174.

48 Another irony was the association of the first Bahá'í community in the United States with Freemasonry, a secret social society with religious overtones. A number of the first recruits to the Faith were involved with Freemasonry. For many years after the Faith became established in Chicago, the Bahá'ís rented a meeting hall at the Masonic Lodge for large gatherings. At that time the American believers were unaware of the teachings of their Faith which forbid membership in secretive, exclusive societies such as the Masons. This restriction is based upon a primary emphasis of the Faith – the promotion of unity among the peoples of the world – which is undermined when organizations are built upon secrecy and exclusivity.

Nonetheless, it is interesting that the roots of the Faith in the United States briefly intertwined with the Masons because the Freemasons played a pivotal role in the birth of the United States and its early years of independence. Walter McDougall, in *Freedom Just Around the Corner*, credits the Masons with the creation of what is often referred to as the American 'civic religion'. That is, Americans have an intense form of nationalism that permeates its society and takes on some of the trappings normally associated with religion. He argues that this 'civic religion', born during the early days following the American Revolution, was only challenged during the 1960s and 1970s when the very underpinnings of American society and culture came under attack (pp. 328-33).

49 During the nineteenth century homeopathy was a very common and popular form of medical treatment in the United States and there were a number of schools teaching it. This changed in the 1930s when the American Medical Association began to attack this form of medicine as quackery. States tightened their regulations and homeopathy moved out of the mainstream of medical practice to

become an unregulated 'alternative' medicine, where it remains despite renewed popular interest in it during the last decades of the twentieth century. Acceptance of homeopathy is more widespread outside the United States.

50 Dr Thacher would become a devoted believer who made important contributions to the establishment and promotion of the Faith in the Chicago area during the first decade of the Faith in America. His sudden death in 1907 diminished the memory of his achievements, especially his participation in the early committees of the American Bahá'í community. He was named a Disciple of 'Abdu'l-Bahá by Shoghi Effendi.

51 Her first name is given as Lucinda in the 1880 US Census.

52 1880 US Census. According to that census, she was born in 1870, but according to her US passport application, her birth year was 1872. For the purposes of this book, the year of birth she herself used, 1872, is accepted because census takers were not always reliable, especially when recording information about children.

53 Minard, *Allegany County and its People*, p. 772 (available on www.ancestry.com, August, 2008).

54 ibid.

55 The Millerites evolved to become the Seventh Day Adventist Church. The Jehovah's Witnesses in turn became an offshoot of that church.

56 The Church of Jesus Christ of the Latter-day Saints, the formal name of the Mormon Church, was begun in Palmyra, New York.

57 The first organizing meeting of the Women's Rights movement was held at Seneca Falls, New York in 1848.

58 Sears and Quigley, *The Flame*, p. 17.

59 Factual details about the Moore family come from the 1880 US Census and Minard, *Allegany County and its People*.

60 This summary of her early life is drawn from Sears and Quigley, *The Flame*, pp. 10-18. Even though the authors are vague about their sources, they state that some of the material about Lua and the Moore family came from the recollections of one of her sisters.

61 Metelmann, *Lua Getsinger*, pp. 1-3.

62 Stockman, *The Bahá'í Faith in America: Origins 1892–1900*, pp. 35-40.

63 For a fuller summary of Kheiralla's lessons, see Stockman, *The Bahá'í Faith in America: Origins 1892–1900*, pp. 60-84. See also Smith, 'The American Bahá'í Community, 1894–1917: A Preliminary Survey', pp. 87-92.

64 Stockman, *The Bahá'í Faith in America: Origins 1892–1900*, p. 48.

65 He was born with the last name Göetzinger on 8/9 January 1866, but by the time he was an adult most of his family had anglicized their names (1870 and 1880 US Censuses). Several of his older brothers worked as butchers, including his brother William (Wilhelm), who resided with him in Detroit in the early 1890s. See *Detroit City Directories*, 1893 and 1894. In those directories, both brothers spelled their last name 'Getzinger'.

66 Getsinger, unpublished memoirs, ch. 1, pp. 10-12.

67 This town was established by German Lutherans about twenty years before Edward was born. During his childhood, its adult population was overwhelmingly native German. It is not far from the larger city of Saginaw, thus Edward often gave that city as his hometown; Frankenmuth is located in Saginaw

County (1870 and 1880 US Census). Edward's parents lived first in Detroit before moving to Frankenmuth (1860 US Census).

68 Getsinger, unpublished memoirs, ch. 4, p. 6.

69 1870 and 1880 US Censuses.

70 Hatch, 'Edward Christopher Getsinger', pp. 493-6.

71 Getsinger, unpublished memoirs, ch. 1, p. 3.

72 The US Census of 1880 lists the 16-year-old Edward as a 'clerk' rather than as a 'student', so presumably his formal schooling had stopped by that time.

73 If, as stated by the Hatch article (see above), he finished his training as a homeopathic doctor by age 22, then most likely he did his required internship at the homeopathic hospital in Detroit. At the time, Michigan was one of only a few states that granted licences to homeopathic physicians. For some years the University of Michigan offered a homeopathic track at its medical college, but Edward did not study in that program (email on behalf of the University of Michigan, 29 July 2008 to the author). The other option for training in homeopathy in Michigan was a residency at the homeopathic hospital in Detroit, apparently the means by which he gained his licence.

74 In his unpublished memoirs (ch. 1, p. 5) Edward says that more than once, people who attended his classes would come up to him afterwards and ask if he knew Kheiralla, who had also given lectures while in Kalamazoo. While Kheiralla was in Kalamazoo, he resided at the home of an elderly couple named Roddeman. Mrs Roddeman in particular became very interested in Kheiralla's ideas. It is possible that she was in fact the first American believer, though it seems that Kheiralla may not have begun speaking about the Faith directly until after reaching Chicago. Mrs Roddeman provided Kheiralla with financial assistance to help him reach Chicago. Later she travelled to Chicago herself where she wholeheartedly accepted the Faith and remained a faithful believer. In 1899 she went to considerable trouble to travel to Detroit to see the Getsingers to hear about their first pilgrimage (ibid. pp. 7-8).

75 Menand, *The Metaphysical Club*, p. 121.

76 For an excellent and lengthy discussion of these nineteenth-century academic debates see Menand, *The Metaphysical Club*, passim.

77 Getsinger, unpublished memoirs, ch. 1, p. 4.

78 The following account of Edward's unusual experience comes from his memoirs, ch. 1, pp. 12-19.

79 A 'tel' is an artificial hill created by earth and debris covering over many centuries the remnants of a town or city. The Tel of 'Akká was used by Napoleon Bonaparte to mount his cannons during his 1799 siege of the city.

80 Getsinger, unpublished memoirs, ch. 12, p. 15.

81 ibid. pp. 15-19.

82 ibid. pp. 22-3.

83 Quite probably the friends in Egypt had impressed upon Kheiralla the need for caution in teaching the Faith. The religious freedom of the United States would have been incomprehensible to anyone reared in the Persian or Ottoman Empires at that time; consequently Kheiralla needed to get to know his students before he trusted them with information about the Faith.

84 Metelmann, *Lua Getsinger*, p. 4; Getsinger, unpublished memoirs, ch. 1, pp. 28-9.

85 Stockman, *The Bahá'í Faith in America*: Origins 1892–1900, p. 37.
86 Getsinger, unpublished memoirs, ch. 1, p. 31.
87 ibid. pp. 31-2.

Chapter 3 The Good Fairy

1 Her parents spelled her name 'Phebe', but most of the time, as an adult, she used the more conventional spelling 'Phoebe'.
2 Other important characters in this book – May Bolles, Harriet Thornburgh and Mary Virginia Thornburgh-Cropper – all called Phoebe 'Fairy' in their letters to her. PAH papers, Bancroft Library.
3 Biographical information on Phoebe Hearst comes from hundreds of letters from her personal correspondence in the Phoebe Apperson Hearst (PAH) collection held by the Bancroft Library at the University of California at Berkeley, and from the following publications and dissertation, all of which repeat the basic details: Winifred Black Bonfils, *The Life and Personality of Phoebe Apperson Hearst*; Kathryn P. Hearst, *Phoebe Apperson Hearst: The Making of an Upper-Class Woman, 1842–1919* (doctoral dissertation); William Randolph Hearst, Jr., *The Hearsts: Father and Son*; David Nasaw, *The Chief: The Life of William Randolph Hearst*; Ben Proctor, *William Randolph Hearst: The Early Years, 1863–1910*; Judith Robinson, *The Hearsts: An American Dynasty*; W. A. Swanberg, *Citizen Hearst: A Biography of William Randolph Hearst*; O. Z. Whitehead, *Some Early Bahá'ís of the West*. With numerous award-winning biographies of William Randolph Hearst already in print, one would think that there would be little to add. However, the most recent work on this towering figure by the Canadian journalist Kenneth Whyte proves that old material can be reinterpreted from a closer examination. His biography seeks to remove much of the mire that has stuck to the reputation of William Randolph Hearst, often thrown at him undeservingly by his enemies, Hollywood, and business rivals. See Whyte, *The Uncrowned King: The Sensational Rise of William Randolph Hearst*.
4 Prior to the Civil War, the southern region of the United States was known for its political conservatism, warm hospitality, and genteel manners.
5 They were 'land poor', that is, never lacking in basic necessities but frequently short on hard cash. In addition to storekeeping and farming, Phoebe's father occasionally had to hire himself out as a labourer. Randolph Apperson's talents didn't include making money. William Randolph Hearst was apparently embarrassed by his mother's family's poverty during the Missouri years. Thus, from the beginning when biographers began to examine his mother's background, her family was touted by Hearst sources as being more prosperous than they were. The family of George Hearst, on the other hand, was the wealthiest in Franklin County; in fact, Randolph Apperson worked for them occasionally when he needed money. There is no doubt that Phoebe would have grown up expected to do her share of the relentless, back-breaking work of farm life on the American frontier. However, the Appersons would not have thought of themselves as 'poor' because their lot would have been little different from that of most of their friends.
6 Kathryn Hearst, *Phoebe Apperson Hearst*, pp. 23-7.
7 ibid. p. 31.

8 Jones, 'The First Benefactors', in *The University of California Magazine*, vol. 5, no. 3 (Apr.1899), pp. 101-17.
9 Robinson, *The Hearsts*, p. 17.
10 Nickliss, 'Phoebe Apperson Hearst's "Gospel of Wealth", 1883–1901', in *The Pacific Historical Review*, vol. 71, no. 4 (Nov. 2002), pp. 575-605.
11 Foote (ed.), *Pen Pictures from the Garden of the World*, pp. 443-4.
12 This church began the formal ordination of women in 1889.
13 See Campbell, 'A New Church is Born'.
14 The Appersons were apparently known for their attention to their neighbours during times of need. See Bonfils, *The Life and Personality of Phoebe Apperson Hearst*, p. 4.
15 Kathryn Hearst, *Phoebe Apperson Hearst*, pp. 31-4.
16 For a lively discussion of the geology of the western United States as well as a brief history of the 1849 California gold rush, see Winchester, *A Crack in the Edge of the World: America and the Great California Earthquake of 1906*, pp. 112-30, 137-8.
17 One of his contemporaries said, 'There are no differing thoughts among his friends, who were numbered by thousands from the humblest to the highest, as to the intrinsic worth of Senator Hearst's character. In private and in public life he was a man of scrupulous integrity. He was a faithful friend. He was without pretense or presumption of any kind'. (Jones, 'The First Benefactors').
18 George, who had served only briefly in the Confederate army, had to take Phoebe on a dangerous and circuitous route to get out of Missouri and away from the fighting and had to enlist the aid of friends to obtain a pass to leave the territory (Robinson, *The Hearsts*, p. 54).
19 My primary source for this description of San Francisco in the nineteenth century is Winchester, *A Crack in the Edge of the World: America and the Great California Earthquake of 1906*. Simon Winchester provides a vivid history of the rise of San Francisco from a small Spanish settlement to a bustling city. His book of course leads up to the story of the earthquake and fire of 1906 which directly affected Helen Hillyer, discussed later in this chapter, who wrote a first-hand account of that calamity that was published posthumously by her daughter years after the event. Other Californians who appear in the present book were less affected. 'Abdu'l-Bahá, in a Tablet to a Californian believer written several years before the earthquake, predicted that San Francisco was soon to face a catastrophe.
20 Winchester, ibid. p. 209.
21 Kathryn Hearst, *Phoebe Apperson Hearst*, pp. 67-70.
22 Apparently Phoebe had a difficult delivery with her son and problems with becoming pregnant again after that first birth, consequently she visited a number of places that claimed to help infertile women, including such facilities in Europe. Kathryn Hearst, ibid. p. 61.
23 Whyte, *The Uncrowned King*, p. 11.
24 Letter from Phoebe Apperson Hearst to Orrin Peck, 22 December 1886. Peck papers, quoted in Robinson, *The Hearsts*, p. 206.
25 Anne (Annie) Apperson was born on 20 April 1878 in San Luis Obispo, California, the daughter of Elbert C. Apperson and Elizabeth Sutherland Apperson.

Elbert Apperson was a farmer. Anne's maternal grandparents were from England. US Emergency Passport Application, 10 June 1895, US Embassy London, no. 340. 1880 US Census.

26 Robinson, ibid. p. 73.

27 ibid. p. 204.

28 Undated newspaper clipping, PAH collection, Bancroft Library

29 Phoebe's interest in assisting African Americans to advance is especially noteworthy because apparently her husband did not share her sentiments. Her efforts to establish free kindergartens for black children did not begin until after she was widowed and had full control of the estate (Nickliss, 'Phoebe Apperson Hearst's "Gospel of Wealth", 1883–1901', p. 584).

30 Phoebe also gave money to the University of Pennsylvania.

31 It is interesting to note her broadmindedness in this regard. Another contemporary philanthropist of the time, Andrew Carnegie, established hundreds of free libraries throughout the United States. One of his intentions was to force immigrants to improve their English by only providing books in that language. For this reason, his libraries did not contain materials in other languages. Phoebe's libraries, however, included materials, especially periodicals, in the native languages of the members of the communities that they served (Nickliss, op.cit. pp. 585-7).

32 ibid. p. 589; Kathryn Hearst, *Phoebe Apperson Hearst*, pp. 276, 314-16.

33 Phoebe underwrote George A. Reisner, who pioneered scientific archaeology; Max Uhle, the 'Father of South American Arcaheology'; and Rufus B. Richardson's dig at Corinth, among others. She also corresponded with Sir Flinders Petrie.

34 Anne Gordon Atkinson et al, *Green Acre on the Piscatuaqua*, pp. 25, 61. See also the Sarah Farmer correspondence in the PAH papers at the Bancroft Library.

35 There are a number of examples of this throughout the Phoebe Apperson Hearst papers held by the Bancroft Library.

36 William Randolph Hearst is a study in contradictions. He flouted conventional middle-class sexual morality with his open affairs, most notably his long-standing one with actress Marion Davies. Yet he gave up drinking alcoholic beverages and was responsible for purging San Francisco's infamous Barbary Coast of its brothels.

37 The newspaper was the voice of the Democratic Party in California and for that reason George had been propping it up financially. Finally, he acquired it outright.

38 *The Harvard Lampoon* is a student-run humorous publication, famous for its biting satire.

39 Whyte, *The Uncrowned King*, p. 34-5.

40 The will stipulated that the estate would revert to William if Phoebe remarried. George Hearst had deeded the *San Francisco Examiner* newspaper to William prior to his death. By that time the newspaper was earning a profit, thanks to William's efforts. Will also received the million-acre Hearst ranch in Mexico, so his father did not leave him destitute (ibid. p. 17).

41 Phoebe herself was uncomfortable with the twitter surrounding the estate and did feel that her son was due part of the fortune. She was advised, however, not to turn over part of the estate outright to Will because his newspapers attracted

lawsuits and her lawyers and business managers feared that the fortune would be jeopardized if too closely connected to the Hearst newspaper business. She sold her interest in the Anaconda mine and gave part of the proceeds to Will as a down-payment on his future inheritance.

42 William Randolph Hearst, Jr., *The Hearsts: Father and Son*, p. 18.

43 Phoebe worked hard to keep what she had but did not seek to expand the empire. She was a hard-headed businesswoman who did not allow sentimentality to control her financial decisions. For example, her first order of business following her husband's death was to sell all her husband's thorough-bred horses, even though George had been very attached to them.

44 Will supported Bryan out of loyalty to the Democratic Party and his desire to further his own political ambitions. He actually disliked Bryan in the beginning.

45 Joseph Pulitzer, owner of a rival New York newspaper, is also given partial credit for whipping up war fever against Spain.

46 William Randolph Hearst has attained almost mythic status in the United States in large measure because of the famous Orson Welles film, *Citizen Kane*, which was loosely based upon his life. He is also remembered because of his palatial home, San Simeon (often called 'Hearst Castle'), which he gave to the State of California. The legacy of Hearst influencing the public affairs of the day was continued by his sons and grandchildren after they assumed the reins of his publishing empire. None, however, would equal Will.

47 Lua Getsinger, letter to Mrs Lawson, written in Ithaca, New York, 3 February 1898. Getsinger papers, USBNA.

48 This estate is not to be confused with the Hearst property along the Pacific shoreline where William Hearst would build the San Simeon mansion after his mother's passing.

49 Robinson, *The Hearsts*, p. 258. See pp. 258-9 for a more detailed description of the Hacienda. See also Garnett, *Stately Homes of California*, ch. 3, available online; Mitchell, 'A Late Victorian California Interior with Mexican Influences: Interior of Phoebe Hearst's Home, Hacienda del Pozo de Verona, Pleasanton, California'. Following his mother's death, Will sold the estate and it became a country club, with outer parcels sold for homes. In 1969 the main building burned and a new one, in the style of the Hacienda, was built on the site.

50 Robinson, The Hearsts, p. 259.

51 Notes of Ella Goodall Cooper based upon the recollections of Anne Apperson Flint, Cooper papers, USBNA.

52 Edward Getsinger, unpublished memoirs, ch. 1, pp. 33-4.

53 Kathryn Hearst, *Phoebe Apperson Hearst*, p. 162.

54 ibid. p. 94.

55 Swanberg, *Citizen Hearst*, pp. 9-10.

56 Kathryn Hearst, *Phoebe Apperson Hearst*, p. 94.

57 Robert C. Turner US passport application, issued 8 October 1892, no. 39 by the US embassy in Paris. I am indebted to Roger Dahl for sharing his research into Robert Turner's background.

58 Robinson, *The Hearsts*, p. 63.

59 PAH papers, Bancroft library, reel 121, Mrs Hearst writing from Sonoma County Camp House about 1891.

60 Response to questionnaire from Ella Goodall Cooper submitted to Anne Apperson Flint some time in 1944. Cooper papers, USBNA.

61 The Leland Stanford family, friends of George and Phoebe Hearst for many years, made a fortune in railroads and established Stanford University. 'Abdu'l-Bahá gave a talk at that university during his visit to the San Francisco area.

62 Mark Twain, the pen name of author Samuel Clemens, was a long-time friend of George Hearst. Helen Hillyer recounts in her autobiography the memorable evening when she had dinner with Twain, the Hearsts, and her father while visiting New York City as a young adolescent.

63 Helen made two applications for US passports, one in 1896 and the other in 1899. The 1896 application, which appears to be in her own hand, lists 1872 as her year of birth. The 1899 application lists it as 1871 (Helen Adelaide Hillyer US passport application dated 22 January, 1896, no. 6665, issued 23 January 1896; Helen Adelaide Hillyer US passport application dated 25 February 1899, issued 25 February 1899 at the US consulate in Cairo).

64 Helen, in her published memoir, *For My Children and Grandchildren*, does not state the nature of her mother's illness or when she died.

65 The information about Helen Hillyer Brown and her early years comes from her autobiography, *For My Children and Grandchildren*; and also from the US Census of 1880.

66 Gail, *Arches of the Years*, p. 53.

67 Whitehead, *Portraits of Some Bahá'í Women*, p. 2.

68 Even though Ella was born in California, her parents chose to give her British citizenship through her father. At the time, British citizenship was more advantageous than American because of the expanse of the British Empire. Ironically, she had to go through the naturalization process in the 1920s to become an American citizen legally despite her lifelong residence in California. With both an English father and husband, she must have imbibed many English cultural attributes.

69 Captain Edwin Goodall and his brother Charles were the principal partners of the Goodall, Nelson & Perkins Shipping Company which later became the Pacific Coast Steamship Company. They were innovators at using steamships to ply the coast of California and both were experienced, expert seamen.

70 See for example, *Oakland Daily Evening Tribune*, 19 January 1889, p. 9: 'The evening also marked the first production of a new work written by Miss Ella Goodall, a young lady of considerable ability and musical talent. The work was orchestrated especially for the evening, but will be published in a few days.'

71 Ramona Allen Brown, *Memories of 'Abdu'l-Bahá*, p. 4.

72 At the time, the American Bahá'ís did not know that among the teachings of the Faith was a prohibition against consuming alcohol unless prescribed by a medical doctor.

73 Helen Sturtevant Arey Goodall, who was often called 'Nellie', was born in Winterport, Maine, on 13 March 1847. She would be honoured posthumously with the title 'Disciple of 'Abdu'l-Bahá'. Information about her comes from US Censuses and her July 1920 US passport application, no. 74440. Her maiden name, Arey, comes from US Census information and Ella's death certificate. Her maiden name is sometimes mentioned as Mirrell. The reason for this discrepancy is unknown.

74 Gail, *Arches of the Years*, p. 53.
75 Robinson, *The Hearsts*, pp. 305-6.
76 Phoebe Apperson Hearst, letter to Mrs Anthony, 22 August 1898. PAH collection, Bancroft Library.
77 Kathryn Hearst, *Phoebe Apperson Hearst*, passim.
78 ibid.
79 Quoted in Stockman, *The Bahá'í Faith in America*, vol. 1, p. 136.
80 ibid. p. 137.
81 ibid. p. 140.
82 Agnes Lane would become a believer toward the end of the trip during the return to Paris. She was only 17 at the time and perhaps was considered too fragile or too young to go to 'Akká, so she stayed behind in Egypt. She was born and raised in Missouri and may have been living with her cousin Phoebe because her parents were living apart. Phoebe took over her care so completely that she even assumed the role of parent at Agnes' wedding a few years after the pilgrimage. It is not surprising that many books incorrectly state that she was a niece. Agnes' grandmother, Phoebe Whitmore Clark, was the sister of Phoebe Hearst's mother, making Agnes a first cousin once removed of Phoebe Hearst (http://virts.rootsweb.com/~pinnell/html/fam/fam05887.htm visited August 2008).
83 Passenger log for 11 November 1895, *Etruria*, arriving in New York City from Liverpool, England. Also, Phoebe Hearst included Amalia Bachrodt in her own US passport application of 19 September 1898 issued in Washington, D.C. (no. 5208). On it, Amalia's date of birth is listed as 22 August 1851.
84 Orrin Peck met Phoebe when he was two years old and for the remainder of her life she took a motherly interest in him, promoting his career as an artist and providing him with partial support. She also confided in him. In 1898 he and his sister, Janet, were residing in Munich, Germany where he made a living painting portraits and landscapes. It is unclear at what point he joined the group during that winter trip. He was with the group in Egypt. (His sister Janet was a close personal friend of Mary Virginia Thornburgh-Cropper, who will be introduced in the next chapter.)
85 Clark and Peck did not sail with Phoebe from New York. Clark most likely came later and Peck would have probably joined the group in Egypt from his home in Germany.
86 For more on the life of Emogene Hoagg and her important contributions to the development of the Faith see Whitehead, *Portraits of Some Bahá'í Women*, pp. 1-27.
87 See letters of Phoebe Hearst to Clara Anthony dated 22 August and 19 September 1898, PAH collection, Bancroft Library.
88 In a letter to Ella Goodall Cooper years later, Anne Apperson Flint recalled that the group did not all travel east together from California. She travelled with Lua and Emogene. Sometimes Phoebe put up members of her group in other accommodations than her own. Cooper papers, USBNA.
89 Those who did not have passports applied for them while in Washington.
90 Phoebe Hearst, letter to Clara Anthony dated 19 September 1898. PAH collection, Bancroft Library.
91 Dr Alonzo E. Taylor was a medical researcher whose work Phoebe supported and whom she assisted to gain a position at Stanford University Medical School

(letters from Alonzo Taylor to Phoebe Hearst, PAH papers, Bancroft Library). There are hints in his correspondence that Phoebe may have received a recommendation for Julia through a second source as well.

92 US passport application of Julia L. Pearson, issued 18 November 1898, no. 314, at the US embassy in Paris. Note her Social Security Death Index lists the year as 1878.

93 Julia's son, Pearson Hunt, talked about what a remarkable teacher his grandmother was. See Pearson Hunt on the official website of Harvard University.

94 At the time, Julia was probably living with her brother, Dr Leonard Pearson, in Philadelphia where he was teaching at the University of Pennsylvania and serving as the State Veterinarian for the State of Pennsylvania. Another of Julia's brothers would become the President of first the University of Iowa and later the University of Maryland.

95 Stockman, *Thornton Chase*, p. 142.

96 Stockman, *The Bahá'í Faith in America*, vol. 1, p.140.

97 'Printed Passenger List of the *S. S. Fürst Bismarck* voyage departing New York on 22 September 1898', Hoagg papers, USBNA. *The Fürst Bismarck* was owned by the Hamburg-American Line. The ultimate destination of that voyage was Hamburg, Germany, with stops in Southampton and Cherbourg. In addition to the pilgrims, Mr Jacob B. Reinstein, a young San Francisco lawyer and another member of the Board of Regents of the University of California at Berkeley, and a friend of Phoebe's, was also a passenger. Mr Reinstein had been instrumental in persuading Phoebe to sponsor an architectural competition for the makeover of the campus of the University of California at Berkeley and he served as chairman of the board overseeing it. Most likely, he was on his way to Antwerp (probably at Phoebe's expense) where the first round of judging entries was about to begin. He must have spent some time on board ship with the Bahá'í group. He was from a prominent Jewish family. Emogene Hoagg wrote a brief note about him beside his name on her copy of the ship's passenger list.

Chapter 4 Paris and the Dawning of the Faith in Europe

1 'Amatu'l-Bahá Rúḥíyyih Khánum (Rúḥíyyih Rabbání), Mary Bolles's granddaughter, usually recounted that her family's connection with Phoebe Hearst came from her great-grandmother Martin. It was said that they were school friends. For Rúḥíyyih Rabbání's account of this, and this period of the Martin/Bolles family, see Ruhe-Schoen, *A Love Which Does Not Wait*, p. 35. See also the 1860, 1870 and 1880 US Census information on the Martin and Bolles families. Nevertheless, the connection through Mrs David Martin seems unlikely because Mrs Martin was at least ten years older than Phoebe and her childhood home in Ohio was far from Missouri. The more probable connection to the Hearst family is Mary's older brother, Dr Benjamin Ellis Martin, who served as the port surgeon for a shipping company in San Francisco and was a good friend of Mrs Hearst for many years.

2 I am indebted to Nell Golden for information about the Martin and Bolles families, and especially about John Harris Bolles and Mary Martin Bolles. Their granddaughter, 'Amatu'l-Bahá Rúḥíyyih Khánum, often remarked that Nell, her assistant for many decades, knew more about her family than she did.

3 See the many *New York Times* articles about this in the *New York Times* archives available online.
4 Charles Mason Remey, unpublished memoirs, USBNA, p. 46.
5 *New York Times* notice of the marriage of Mary Ellis Martin and John Harris Bolles, 9 October 1868.
6 From the *Dictionary of Literary Biography* article on Octavius Brooks Frothingham.
7 For a thorough look at Americans living and travelling in Paris in the last decade of the nineteenth century, see Levenstein, *Seductive Journey*, pp. 125-213.
8 She was born on 14 January 1870 in Englewood, New Jersey.
9 'May Ellis Maxwell', In Memoriam, *The Bahá'í World*, vol. 8, pp. 631-2; see also Ruhe-Schoen, *A Love Which Does Not Wait*, p. 44.
10 Metelmann, *Lua Getsinger*, p. 11.
11 Nakhjavani, *The Maxwells of Montreal*, forthcoming. See also Ruhe-Schoen, *A Love Which Does Not Wait*, pp. 35-6.
12 Metelmann, *Lua Getsinger*, pp. 11-12.
13 Marian's maternal aunt, Marianne Brown, was probably the first person residing in England to convert to the Bahá'í Faith. This aunt, who never married, took over the care of Marian and her older sister and younger brother when they lost both parents while young. Miss Brown was born in Aycliffe, Durham in about 1827, the eldest child of Reverend James H. Brown and his wife, Marianne Brown. Marian's aunt passed away in 1903 in Watford, Hertfordshire (1841, 1851, 1861, 1871, 1881, 1901 England Censuses and Death Index of England and Wales). Miss Brown's sentiments regarding the Bahá'í Faith at the time of her death are unknown. The honour of being considered the first English believer residing in England was later bestowed upon Ethel Rosenberg.
14 Metelmann, *Lua Getsinger*, pp. 9-10.
15 ibid. p. 10.
16 For a general discussion of Mary Virginia Thornburgh-Cropper and her many contributions to the development of the British Bahá'í community, see the article published shortly after her death in the In Memoriam section of vol. 8 of *Bahá'í World*, pp. 649-51. Unfortunately, many of the biographical details in the article are not correct; nonetheless, her overall accomplishments are set forth accurately.
17 Most British public records list her as Virginia Shepherd Cropper. She was born in Marysville, California on 29 May 1857.
18 The area is now West Virginia, not Virginia. (That part of Virginia broke away during the US Civil War because its residents sided with the Union.) See 'The Bay of San Francisco', online article from the biography (1892) of Morgan Kroesen Thornburgh, brother of William B. Thornburgh, vol. 2, pp. 569-70. The Thornburgh brothers were raised on a farm.
19 Harriet Thornburgh was born in the small port town of Maysville, Kentucky on the Ohio River on 19 October 1838. The 1860 US census gives Iowa as her place of birth but on her US passport application, dated 2 February 1899, no. 379 issued by the US consulate in Nice, Harriet gives her birthplace as Maysville, Kentucky. It is possible that her parents were only briefly in Kentucky. (There was a mass migration of Iowa settlers to California in 1850. McDougall, *Throes of Democracy*, p. 291)

20 William and Harriet Thornburgh married on 5 February 1856 in the town of Marysville.
21 1860 and 1870 US censuses.
22 W. H. Blauvelt, 'Banking', pp. 624-5. Mark Twain (Samuel Clemens) wrote about doing business with that bank.
23 The Ballard family bought the estate, thus for some years the castle was known as the Ballard House. When the house burned down in 1901, the famous Claremont Hotel was built on the site.
24 Davis, '"We are All Americans Now!" Anglo-American Marriages in the Late Nineteenth Century', p. 27.
25 The presiding clergyman was the Ret. Reverend William Ingraham Kip, first Episcopal Bishop of California and noted author and church historian. The Episcopal Church is the American branch of the Anglican Communion (that is, the Church of England). The official witnesses to the marriage were two local politicians. See the California marriage certificates included in the Cropper divorce papers available through National Archives of the United Kingdom.
26 Information on the marriage comes from the *Sacramento Bee* newspaper online archives. The notice of the family sailing to England comes from the online archives of the *New York Times*.
27 The extended Cropper family lived in the Dingle Bank section of Liverpool.
28 There is much information on Denman Cropper's parents and grandparents on a variety of websites on the Internet, including genealogical sites, sites discussing the history of the abolitionist movement, and sites discussing the history of the Dingle Bank section of Liverpool where the Cropper family had their homes, and the Swaylands estate in Kent where Denman grew up.
29 He did have one uncle, however, who was a Rear-Admiral in the Royal Navy.
30 One of the grounds for the Thornburgh–Cropper divorce was adultery. See the court records of the Cropper divorce. The National Archives (United Kingdom).
31 The information in this paragraph comes from public records, including the court records of the Cropper divorce which was finalized in 1897.
32 This is the year that The Married Women's Property Act was passed in England. For the first time, the property of married women no longer belonged to their husbands. Perhaps Denman reasoned that, since Minnie then had complete control of any remaining inheritance she had received from her father, he no longer owed her anything, even though they continued to be legally married. He may have been unaware that the Thornburgh estate was mired in a law suit.
33 Harriet Thornburgh, letter to Phoebe Hearst dated Thanksgiving Day, 1895 from the Crown Hotel, Westerham, Kent, England. PAH papers, Bancroft Library
34 The Crown Hotel was, according to a brief mention in one of Minnie's letters, run by her former cook. It was near to where she had lived while still with her husband and was directly across from the local railway station, thereby affording her easy access to London.
35 One way in which Minnie outwardly maintained her dignity was by continually searching for a house to rent, all the while knowing that she did not have the means to pay for one even if an acceptable residence could be secured. Phoebe had apparently offered to help with rent because Minnie's letters to her are full

of specific property possibilities. Certainly, as long as it looked to her friends that her hotel residences and small rented flats were temporary, it was easier to hold her head up.

36 The estate was paid about US $25,000 just from life insurance policies, not to mention other assets such as interests in mines (*New York Times* archives). In the probate of the will of her husband in 1878, Harriet Thornburgh asked the court for a monthly allowance of $1,000, a sum that would have allowed her to live more than comfortably. I am indebted to Roger Dahl for furnishing me with a copy of the California court probate records.

37 See undated letter of Harriet Thornburgh to Phoebe Hearst, PAH papers, Bancroft Library. Phoebe went with Harriet to the court on at least one occasion and most likely was as outraged by the outcome of the case as were the Thornburghs. Her sense that there had been a miscarriage of justice may in part explain her largesse to the Thornburghs.

38 Harriet Thornburgh, letter to Phoebe Hearst written at the Crown Hotel, Westerham, Kent, 3 January 1896. PAH papers, Bancroft Library.

39 Minnie had to endure the humiliation of having her divorce reported in a number of newspapers on both sides of the Atlantic.

40 Minnie carried out this service for friends without any compensation other than the actual out-of-pocket expenses incurred by the young ladies. See the correspondence of Harriet Thornburgh and Mary Virginia Thornburgh-Cropper to Phoebe Hearst, PAH papers, Bancroft Library.

41 Blomfield, *The Chosen Highway*, pp. 234-5.

42 The US passport application of Harriet Frances Thornburgh, no. 379, issued 2 February 1899 by the US consulate in Nice, states that she left the United States on 6 October 1898.

43 Phoebe was underwriting an international architectural competition to design a new campus for the University of California at Berkeley. The European entries were put on public display in Antwerp, Belgium during the early weeks of October 1898. She must have taken a side trip from Paris to view them, which could explain why she was not listed among those studying the Faith with Lua in Paris.

44 Lua Getsinger papers, USBNA.

45 Menand, *The Metaphysical Club*, pp. 103-16, 139-40.

46 Metelmann, *Lua Getsinger*, p. 8.

47 It is interesting to note that May Bolles's uncle, Benjamin Ellis Bolles, and his wife published a book in 1899 entitled, *Stones of Paris in History and Letters*. Uncle Ellis loved to write about Europe and undoubtedly the timing of this publication was probably meant to coincide with the large influx of tourists to Paris for the 1900 World's Fair.

48 Interestingly, Nell Hillyer and Ella Goodall would attend one of the final court hearings of the Dreyfus trial during their time in Paris in 1899, while returning home from 'Akká. 'Abdu'l-Bahá also was also aware of the Dreyfus Affair because when he met the first French believer, Hippolyte Dreyfus, he asked if he was related to *the* Colonel Dreyfus. (He was not.) For one look at the Dreyfus Affair and its effect on France during this time, see Tuchman, *The Proud Tower*, pp. 171-226._

49 Quoted from Lua Getsinger's 1898 journal as reproduced by Metelmann, *Lua Getsinger*, p. 8. 'Queen Anne' was Anne Apperson.
50 Provisional translation from the French by Mae Nieland. Some words, despite the beautiful penmanship, were illegible.
51 Helen Hillyer to Phoebe Hearst, letter dated 3 December 1898 written in New York. PAH papers, Bancroft Library.
52 From Ella Goodall Cooper's unpublished notes about the history of the Bahá'í Faith in California. Cooper papers, USBNA, p. 2.
53 Telegram from 'Abdu'l-Bahá for Ella and Nell. Cooper papers, USBNA.
54 Helen Hillyer, letter to Phoebe Hearst, 22 December 1898. PAH papers, Bancroft Library.
55 While the Thanksgiving holiday in America has a religious overtone because it is a day set aside to give thanks to God for His bounties, it is also a harvest festival with historic roots dating to the earliest days of English colonization of North America and to similar festivals celebrated in Europe. It became a national holiday through presidential decrees and acts of Congress. It is celebrated with a feast that always includes turkey and usually corn, pumpkin, and cranberries – foods native to North America. All Americans of every ethnic and religious background participate in this holiday held on the fourth Thursday of November.
56 Journal of Lua Getsinger, Lua Getsinger papers, USBNA; see also Metelmann, *Lua Getsinger*, p. 8.
57 Edward wrote in his unpublished memoirs (p. 35) that it was decided that he and Lua would leave first and that Phoebe and her entourage would follow a few days later. Edward said also that the delay in the group following them was necessitated by business Phoebe had to attend to in Paris in her role as a Regent of the University of California.
58 Journal of Lua Getsinger, Lua Getsinger papers, USBNA; see also Metelmann, *Lua Getsinger*, pp. 8-9.
59 Most of the Americans passed through Egypt on their way to Haifa and recounted with much gratitude the warm hospitality they received from the Bahá'ís resident in Egypt. Even though language differences kept them from conversing freely, they would sit together and smile at each other.
60 Journal of Lua Getsinger, Lua Getsinger papers, USBNA; see also Metelmann, *Lua Getsinger*, p. 9.

Chapter 5 The Master and Kheiralla

1 Visitors to the House of 'Abdu'lláh Páshá no longer enter through the gate at the eastern end of the south wall, but through a newer one at the far western end of that wall.
2 Townshend, *'Abdu'l-Bahá, The Master*, p. 45.
3 The following brief summary of the life of 'Abdu'l-Bahá from His birth until the arrival of the Hearst pilgrimage in 1898 is taken primarily from the following sources: Balyuzi, *'Abdu'l-Bahá: The Centre of the Covenant of Bahá'u'lláh*; Mírzá Abu'l-Faḍl, *The Bahá'í Proofs and a Short Sketch of the History and Lives of the Leaders of this Religion*; Perkins, *Servant of the Glory: The Life of 'Abdu'l-Bahá*; Phelps, *The Master in 'Akká*. This last book is especially significant because it contains the recollections of Bahíyyih Khánum of her older brother's life and

was for many years one of the few sources the English-speaking believers had for Bahá'í history. And, of course, the incomparable series by Taherzadeh, *The Revelation of Bahá'u'lláh* (all four volumes).

4 This title had been bestowed by the Báb. Bahá'u'lláh's given name was Mírzá Ḥusayn 'Alíy-i-Núrí.

5 For more about Ásíyih Khánum, often called by the title 'Navváb', see Ma'ani, *Leaves of the Twin Divine Trees*, pp 85-126.

6 Ḥájí Mírzá Ḥaydar-'Alí, *Stories from the Delight of Hearts*, p. 10.

7 This city is now better known by its Turkish name, Edirne.

8 For an account of the life and marriage of 'Abdu'l-Bahá's wife, see Munírih Khánum, *Munírih Khánum: Memoirs and Letters*. See also Phelps, *The Master in 'Akká*, pp. 110-20; Perkins, *Servant of the Glory*, pp. 73-77, 85; Taherzadeh, *The Revelation of Bahá'u'lláh*, vol. 2, pp. 204-9; Ma'ani, *Leaves of the Twin Divine Trees*, pp. 309-359.

9 The Bahá'í teachings forbidding polygamy were not widely known or understood among the believers during that period.

10 In his memoirs Ḥájí Mírzá Ḥaydar-'Alí records Bahá'u'lláh as saying, 'In Adrianople We used to meet with some of the people and gave permission to some to attain Our presence. But while in the Most Great Prison We did not meet with anyone and have completely closed the door of association with the people. Now the Master has taken upon Himself this arduous task for Our comfort. He is a mighty shield facing the world and its peoples, and so He has relieved Us [from every care]' (quoted in Taherzadeh, *The Covenant of Bahá'u'lláh*, p. 138).

11 Shoghi Effendi, 'The Dispensation of Bahá'u'lláh', in *The World Order of Bahá'u'lláh*, p. 135.

12 ibid. pp. 135.

13 ibid. pp. 135-6.

14 Taherzadeh, *The Covenant of Bahá'u'lláh*, pp. 116-17.

15 ibid. pp. 117-18, 136. Bahá'u'lláh took as a third wife a believer who served in His household as a maidservant because of the insistence of her family during the last days of His residence in Baghdád. She did not follow him into further exile for many years, but stayed behind in Baghdád. When she was facing difficulties in Iraq, he arranged for her to come to live in 'Akká. This wife bore him one daughter and her grandchildren and great-grandchildren would create great problems for Shoghi Effendi. See Ma'ani, *Leaves of the Twin Divine Trees*, pp. 251-258.

16 'Abdu'l-Bahá's mother predeceased Bahá'u'lláh by about six years, passing away in 'Akká in 1886. Bahá'u'lláh was with her at the end. He promised her that she would be His consort throughout all the worlds of God.

17 Bahá'u'lláh, Kitáb-i-'Ahd (Book of the Covenant), para. 9, in *Tablets*, pp. 221-2; also in Shoghi Effendi, 'The Dispensation of Bahá'u'lláh, in *The World Order of Bahá'u'lláh*, p. 134.

18 Shoghi Effendi, ibid.

19 For a thorough discussion of the rebellion of the half-brothers of 'Abdu'l-Bahá, see Shoghi Effendi, *God Passes By*, pp. 244-51; Taherzadeh, *The Covenant of Bahá'u'lláh*, part II; Taherzadeh, *The Child of the Covenant*, pp. 130-254.

20 Shoghi Effendi, *God Passes By*, p. 255.

21 11 November was the eve of the Birth of Bahá'u'lláh, but that Holy Day was not celebrated on that date in the Holy Land. To the present day, the celebration of that particular Holy Day is observed in the Holy Land according to the lunar calendar, and so it moves through the year. Hence, Kheiralla made no mention of it.
22 ibid. p. 274.
23 Attachment to Anton F. Haddad, *An Outline of the Bahai Movement in the United States.*
24 ibid.

Chapter 6 Arrival in the Most Great Prison: 'Akká

1 Lua Getsinger, undated letter (c. December 1898) to the Assembly in Chicago. USBNA, transcribed from the original; alternative transcription in Metelmann, *Lua Getsinger*, p. 15.
2 Edward Getsinger more accurately estimated the distance as eight miles, but most people estimated it as nine. The length of the journey varied depending on whether the carriage had to detour inland to cross the two rivers by bridge rather than ford them at their openings to the sea. The bridges were often necessary during the rainy winter months.
3 Paragraph break added for the ease of the reader.
4 Lua Getsinger, undated letter (c. December 1898) to the Assembly in Chicago. USBNA, transcribed from the original; alternative transcription in Metelmann, *Lua Getsinger*, pp. 15-16.
5 Johnson, *History of the American People*, p. 613. See also Traxel, *1898: The Birth of the American Century*, passim.
6 Maxwell, *An Early Pilgrimage*, p. 12.
7 It is impossible to determine who the fourth person was. Most likely, it was Kheiralla, who would have had to accompany Phoebe, Minnie, and Phoebe's maid, Emily, in order to translate for them.
8 Mrs Thornburgh-Cropper, letter to Lady Blomfield, in *The Chosen Highway*, pp. 235-6.
9 Marian Kheiralla, letter to the Bahá'ís of Chicago, written in Haifa, February 1899. USBNA.
10 Ella Goodall, unpublished journal of her 1899 pilgrimage, and letter written to her mother from 'Akká, 9 March 1899, Cooper papers, USBNA; also the journal of Helen Hillyer, Hillyer papers, USBNA.
11 Edward Getsinger brought a camera to 'Akká but the Master refused to allow His picture to be taken. This refusal continued unabated for years as other pilgrims arrived with cameras. When the Master landed in Europe in 1911, He was greeted by hordes of reporters with their cameras and of course He was in no position to insist that these journalists not take His picture. So He gave in to the entreaties of the friends and went to photography studios during His journey so that dignified formal portraits could be taken. These are the images of the Master that are best known to posterity – the elderly man in His late sixties. His visage from His early twenties until old age is lost to us. It seems that May and Harriet viewed a photo of 'Abdu'l-Bahá as a young man during their stopover in Egypt.
12 Actually, His eyes were blue.
13 At this point in the original, Ella begins a new paragraph. For the ease of the

reader, the sentence has been kept with the earlier paragraph.

14 Ella Goodall, letter to her mother written from 'Akká, 9 March 1899. Cooper papers, USBNA.

15 Lua Getsinger, letter to Thornton Chase written from 'Akka, 15 February 1899. Lua Getsinger papers, USBNA, transcribed from the original; alternative transcription in Metelmann, *Lua Getsinger*, p. 22.

16 The lower south section also had a room in which the Master established a small school for the children of the believers, and a few other rooms used for washing, bathing, storage and the like. It should be noted that most of the male pilgrims from the East stayed at an old caravanserai, the Khán-i-'Avámíd, near the port. This antiquated khan served as a Bahá'í pilgrim house of sorts from 1870 until 1910. The Hearst party pilgrims make no mention of it in their accounts. If any of them did visit that caravanserai, it likely would have been either Ibrahim Kheiralla or Edward Getsinger, as they would have had more association with the male pilgrims from the East than the other Western pilgrims.

17 Ella Goodall, letter to her mother written from 'Akká, 9 March 1899. Cooper papers, USBNA.

18 The groups that arrived in February first met the Master in Haifa at a house He had by then rented for them.

19 Lua Getsinger, letter to Thornton Chase written from 'Akká, 15 February 1899. Lua Getsinger papers, USBNA, transcribed from the original; alternative transcription in Metelmann, *Lua Getsinger*, pp. 20-23.

20 Ella Goodall, letter to her mother written from 'Akká, 9 March 1899. Cooper papers, USBNA.

21 It has often been erroneously assumed that Robert Turner accompanied Phoebe to 'Akká in December 1898. But his services were probably needed more in Egypt where he could look after Phoebe's young charges, Anne and Agnes, in her absence. She relied upon his good sense and trustworthiness. All the available documents, especially the Cooper papers, lead to the conclusion that he only visited 'Akká in February 1899.

The exact date of the arrival in Haifa and 'Akká of Phoebe, Minnie and Emily is subject to conjecture. Minnie applied for and obtained an American passport while in Cairo on 17 December 1898.

22 The exact location of the house is no longer known, but it was about a block from the beach not far from the dock constructed for the Kaiser's visit, and was located on or near Jaffa Road, just east of the end of the main street of the German Colony. The house served not only as a hostel for visiting Bahá'ís, but also as a Haifa residence for 'Abdu'l-Bahá to facilitate His supervision of the construction of the Shrine of the Báb. Within the next year, the Master would also rent two other buildings in Haifa for the same reasons. Their locations, close to the beach, made it easy for Him to discreetly come and go without entering the city of Haifa itself. When He was put under house arrest in 1901 and was no longer able to travel to Haifa, He allowed the leases on the three residences to lapse. I am grateful to Dr Moojan Momen for sharing his knowledge of those buildings. See also Gail, *Summon up Remembrance*, pp. 110-11.

23 Emogene Hoagg, undated letter (1899) to Phoebe Hearst. PAH, Bancroft Library.

24 Brenetta Herrman's exact age remains a mystery. She could have been born in either 1873, 1875 or 1876, depending upon whether her passport application, death certificate or other records are examined.

25 This information comes from a list compiled by May Bolles which was graciously shared with the author through the literary executors of the estate of Amatu'l-Bahá Rúḥíyyih Khánum. See also US passport application of Brenetta Herrman, no. 9825, 22 April 1896.

26 May Bolles, undated letter to Phoebe Apperson Hearst, written in Paris (probably in January, 1899). PAH papers, Bancroft Library

27 Maxwell, *An Early Pilgrimage*, pp. 9-10.

28 ibid. p. 13.

29 ibid.

30 ibid.

31 This evening conversation is mentioned in some of Ella's later notes in which she was trying to outline the chain of events of the pilgrimage. Cooper papers, USBNA.

32 Ella wrote about this incident to her mother on 4 March 1899 from Haifa but said the steamer had been held for a day because of mechanical trouble. Both young ladies considered it little short of miraculous that they did not miss their steamer to Haifa. Cooper papers, USBNA.

33 Brown, *For My Children and Grandchildren*, p. 36.

34 The February group of American pilgrims (Anne, Harriet, May, Julia and Robert) planned to meet Phoebe at the port of Jaffa to join her and the rest of her party for the Mediterranean cruise.

35 There were two layers of walls on the three sides of the city facing the land which were separated by a dry moat.

36 For the general background of 'Akká see Dichter, *Akko: Sites from the Turkish Period*, passim.; Ruhe, *Door of Hope*, pp. 13-17; Balyuzi, *Bahá'u'lláh: The King of Glory*, pp. 271-6.

37 From the late 1870s 'Abdu'l-Bahá was allowed some freedom to move about the region – even to make brief journeys to Beirut and Damascus – but beginning in 1901, He was again put under house arrest and so was not allowed to venture forth beyond the city walls again until 1908, the year of the Young Turk Revolution. At the time the first Western pilgrims were there, they were surprised and pleased to find that His confinement was not as strict as they had anticipated. This freedom resulted not from any change in the decrees issued in Istanbul – the orders continued to require strict imprisonment – but from the high regard in which He was held by the local officials charged with enforcing the orders from the capital. 'Abdu'l-Bahá's final emancipation was really a process, rather than a fixed point in time, that unfolded between the overthrow of the Sultan in 1908 and His vacating of the House of 'Abdu'lláh Páshá and move to Haifa in August of 1910.

38 Ella Goodall, letter to her mother written from 'Akká, 9 March 1899. Cooper papers, USBNA.

39 Maxwell, *An Early Pilgrimage*, pp. 19-20.

40 Lua Getsinger, letter to Thornton Chase written from 'Akka, 15 February 1899. Lua Getsinger papers, USBNA.

41 ibid., transcribed from the original; alternative transcription in Metelmann, *Lua Getsinger*, pp. 20-21.

42 The Americans would have assumed, based upon their own culture, that 'Abdu'l-Bahá's wife was the 'lady of the house' and undoubtedly had to adjust their thinking to the realities of the household of the Holy Family. This would not have been difficult because both the Greatest Holy Leaf and the Holy Mother were exceedingly loving and self-effacing.

43 Lua Getsinger, undated letter (c. December 1898) to the Assembly of Chicago. USBNA; see Metelmann, *Lua Getsinger*, p. 16.

44 Paragraph break added for the ease of the reader.

45 This last sentence appears in a margin of the original, apparently to be inserted at the point where it is found here. I have added a paragraph break for the ease of the reader.

46 'Abdu'l-Bahá was referring the story of Mary and Martha recounted in the Bible at Luke 10: 38-42. 'Now as they went on their way, he entered a village; and a woman named Martha received him into her house. And she had a sister called Mary, who sat at the Lord's feet and listened to his teaching. But Martha was distracted with much serving; and she went to him and said, 'Lord, do you not care that my sister has left me to serve alone? Tell her to help me.' But the Lord answered her, 'Martha, Martha, you are anxious and troubled about many things; one thing is needful. Mary has chosen the good portion, which shall not be taken away from her.'

47 Ella Goodall Cooper, handwritten text of a tribute to the Greatest Holy Leaf presented at the Geyserville School, in California, in 1942 as a supplement to Marion Holley's talk on 'Immortal Bahá'í Women'. Goodall papers, USBNA.

48 During a later pilgrimage, 'Abdu'l-Bahá called Edward Getsinger 'his son' to signal to the members of His household that Edward should be treated as one of the few men allowed to enter the section of the home reserved for the ladies. This comes from a handwritten note by ECG on the back of a Tablet from 'Abdu'l-Bahá addressed him (1901) translated on 4 October 1907.

49 In addition to Bahíyyih Khánum and Munírih Khánum, they included the Master's four surviving daughters (two of whom were married), Munírih Khánum's sister, and several other ladies resident in the household.

50 Unpublished 1899 journal of Ella Goodall, typed version, pp. 3-4. Cooper papers, USBNA.

51 ibid. pp. 6-7.

52 Here Ella is undoubtedly referring to fifteenth- to eighteenth-century European paintings of young children which often portrayed them idyllically. From a letter from Ella Goodall to Helen Goodall, 9 March 1899. Cooper papers, USBNA.

53 Rabbaní, *The Priceless Pearl*, pp. 5-6.

54 Maxwell, *An Early Pilgrimage*, p. 14.

55 ibid. p. 15.

Chapter 7 Paying Homage at the Sacred Spot

1 In the Kitáb-i-Aqdas, Bahá'u'lláh has enjoined pilgrimage upon His followers, either to the House of Bahá'u'lláh in Baghdad or to the House of the Báb in

Shiraz. However, after the passing of Bahá'u'lláh, 'Abdu'l-Bahá designated the Shrine of Bahá'u'lláh at Bahjí as an additional place of pilgrimage. In a Tablet, He indicates that the 'Most Holy Shrine, the Blessed House in Baghdád and the venerated House of the Báb in Shiraz' are 'consecrated to pilgrimage', and that it is 'obligatory' to visit these places 'if one can afford it and is able to do so, and if no obstacle stands in one's way' at least once in a lifetime. No rites have been prescribed for pilgrimage to the Most Holy Shrine at Bahjí. Shoghi Effendi explained that other sites associated with the lives of the Manifestations of God could be visited. Bahá'u'lláh, *The Kitáb-i-Aqdas*, pp. 192-3, notes 54, 55, 154.

2 The stream has also been called the Belus River.

3 Oliphant, *Haifa, or Life in Modern Palestine*, p. 104.

4 For a general overview of the Riḍván Garden and its history see Ruhe, *Door of Hope*, pp. 91-8; for a first-hand account of it see Oliphant, op. cit. pp. 103-4.

5 Abu'l-Qásim was not the first gardener at the Riḍván Garden. That honour belonged to 'Abdu'l-Ṣáliḥ, who predeceased Bahá'u'lláh. See 'Abdu'l-Bahá, *Memorials of the Faithful*, p. 27.

6 Taherzadeh, *The Revelation of Bahá'u'lláh*, vol. 4, pp. 30-32.

7 Maxwell, *An Early Pilgrimage*, pp. 32-4. Transliteration added for 'Abu'l-Qásim'.

8 While agreeing with May's version of the story in essentials, the two versions differ in some particulars.

9 Ella Goodall, unpublished 1899 journal, typed version, unnumbered insert after page 7. Cooper papers, USBNA.

10 Lua Getsinger, undated letter (c. December 1898) to the Assembly in Chicago, written from 'Akká. USBNA, transcribed from the original; alternative transcription in Metelmann, *Lua Getsinger*, p. 18.

11 This was the only surviving daughter of Bahá'u'lláh's second wife.

12 It is unclear from the accounts whether the place where these first Western pilgrims rested and were served tea was what is at present referred to as the Bahjí Pilgrim House or whether it was the building called the Tea House, a small building near the southern entrance to the property.

13 Ella Goodall, unpublished 1899 journal, typed version, pp. 8-9. Cooper papers, USBNA.

14 Lua Getsinger, undated letter (c. December 1898) to the Assembly in Chicago, written from 'Akká. USBNA, transcribed from the original; alternative transcription in Metelmann, *Lua Getsinger*, p. 18.

15 Maxwell, *An Early Pilgrimage*, p. 35.

16 ibid. p. 36.

17 This is a reference to the Tablet of Visitation, a specific prayer often recited at the Shrine of Bahá'u'lláh and the Shrine of the Báb and usually included during commemorations of the anniversaries of Bahá'u'lláh and the Báb.

18 'The Holy City', a ballad by Stephen Adams and F. E. Weatherly, and 'Nearer, My God, to Thee', a popular Christian hymn, were frequently sung in Protestant churches in America at the time. Both Lua and Anne had trained singing voices.

19 Maxwell, *An Early Pilgrimage*, pp. 36-8.

20 Lua Getsinger, undated letter (c. December 1898) to the Assembly in Chicago, written from 'Akká. USBNA, in Metelmann, *Lua Getsinger*, pp. 18-19.

21 Maxwell, *An Early Pilgrimage*, p. 38.

22 Ella Goodall, unpublished 1899 journal, typed version, p. 9. Cooper papers, USBNA.
23 Lua Getsinger, undated letter (c. December 1898) to the Assembly in Chicago, written from 'Akká. USBNA, transcribed from the original; alternative transcription in Metelmann, *Lua Getsinger*, p. 19.
24 This is a reference to Ṭáhirih, the great woman of the Báb's dispensation, a poet, advocate for the rights of women, and one of the Báb's staunchest disciples, the only woman designated a Letter of the Living. She was rejected by her family and martyred because of her faith. She was given the titles Qurratu'l-'Ayn (Solace of the Eyes) and Zarrín-Táj (Crown of Gold).
25 Ella Goodall, unpublished 1899 journal, typed version, pp. 9-10. Cooper papers, USBNA.

Chapter 8 The Master Speaks

1 See her letter to the Chicago community on p. 62 in which she promised to record everything.
2 Edward recorded his memories of the pilgrimage in his 1908 memoirs but wrote little in that work about what the Master said. Lua wrote lengthy letters to the believers in the United States during the pilgrimage, but set forth only general summaries of the teachings they were receiving rather than reports of specific talks of the Master.
3 Ella Goodall, letter to Helen Goodall written at Ain Sobhar, Syria, 1 April 1899. Cooper papers, USBNA.
4 Marian Kheiralla, letter to the believers in Chicago written from Haifa, February 1899. Typed version, USBNA.
5 Paragraph break added for ease of reading.
6 Here, the Master must have been referring to a Zoroastrian.
7 Ella Goodall, unpublished 1899 journal, typed version, pp. 1-3. Cooper papers, USBNA.
8 Marian Kheiralla, letter to the believers in Chicago written from Haifa, February, 1899. Typed version, USBNA.
9 This refers to other members of the Master's household, primarily female family members.
10 Here Lua writes in a Biblical style.
11 Lua Getsinger, undated letter (c. December 1898) to the Assembly in Chicago, written from 'Akká. Lua Getsinger papers, USBNA, transcribed from the original; alternative transcription in Metelmann, *Lua Getsinger*, pp. 17-18.
12 Maxwell, *An Early Pilgrimage*, pp. 23-5.
13 The notes of American pilgrims who visited 'Akká over the next decade indicate that polar exploration was a topic the Master talked about a number of times. Interestingly, during the Master's visit to the United States in 1912-13, He had the opportunity to meet Admiral Peary at a reception given in 'Abdu'l-Bahá's honour in Washington, D.C. The Admiral had just won a court case in which he had been formally declared the one who first reached the North Pole. When the Master was introduced to the renowned explorer, he remarked that Admiral Peary had done the world a great favour because before, many people had long been concerned about the North Pole, but now that he had proven that there was nothing there,

people need not worry over it any more, thus he had performed a great public service. The Admiral apparently looked like a balloon that was suddenly deflated after this remark. Thompson, *The Diary of Juliet Thompson*, pp. 272-3.

14 Ella Goodall, unpublished 1899 journal, typed version, pp. 5-6. Cooper papers, USBNA.

15 ibid. p. 7.

16 ibid. pp. 10-11.

17 Muḥsin Effendi, who was married to 'Abdu'l-Bahá's daughter Ṭúbá Khánum, was related to the Báb. He remained a steadfast, devoted believer to the end of his life and is primarily remembered for donating his home, No. 4 Haparsim Street, in Haifa to be used as the first pilgrim house for Western believers. Even though his wife and children eventually turned against Shoghi Effendi and were expelled from the Faith, he did not live to see that happen and died a Bahá'í in good standing. Note that Muḥsin Effendi's name is misspelled in the notes of the pilgrims.

18 Ella Goodall, unpublished 1899 journal, typed version, p. 13. Cooper papers, USBNA.

19 Helen Hillyer, handwritten 1899 pilgrimage journal. Brown papers, USBNA. This episode explains why Charles Mason Remey in his memoirs says that Edward Getsinger gave a talk while in Paris in which he said definitively that the Faith espoused reincarnation. This probably occurred while he and Lua were travelling en route to 'Akká for their second pilgrimage in 1900. Certainly, on their return home they would have corrected this misunderstanding with the Paris believers because they were both always willing to be guided by 'Abdu'l-Bahá. See Remey, *Reminiscences*, pp. 45, 53-54; Stockman, *The Bahá'í Faith in America*, vol. 2, p. 153 and note 297.

20 Ella Goodall, unpublished 1899 journal, typed version, p. 16. Cooper papers, USBNA.

21 Marian Kheiralla, letter to Mrs Herron, 20 June 1900. Printed version, USBNA.

22 This passage probably refers to the central hall of the ladies' section of the apartment, and not to the small room where the Master usually dined with the Western pilgrims. The February group was the largest, thus it is easy to assume that they required a larger space. This central hall was nearer to the family's kitchen and the bedrooms of the family opened onto it. At one end was a long flight of stone stairs leading to the roof. The large banquet hall of the North Wing of the building, visited today by pilgrims, was not rented by 'Abdu'l-Bahá until several years later.

23 Maxwell, *An Early Pilgrimage*, pp. 29-30.

24 Helen Hillyer, handwritten 1899 pilgrimage journal. Brown papers, USBNA.

25 Ella Goodall, unpublished 1899 journal, typed version, pp. 17-19. Cooper papers, USBNA.

26 ibid. pp. 19-20. After she left the Holy Land and was travelling in Syria, Ella recounted this conversation with the Master in a letter to her mother. She was determined to try to apply what he had said about developing her mind as well as her heart: '. . . I am going to begin to learn just as fast as I can and it gives me a new impetus to go at my music for I asked especially about that, and also to learn everything else I can, history sciences and all that. I thought it would be a good scheme for you and me to get a good teacher in history for instance and have a

little class all by ourselves, on botany or biology which is intensely interesting you know, and feel that we are putting in our time that way as well as teaching the truth when we can.' Letter to Helen Goodall written at Ain Sobhar, Syria, 1 April 1899. Cooper papers, USBNA.

27 Brown, *For My Children and Grandchildren*, Introduction by Phoebe H. Brown.

28 Helen Hillyer, handwritten 1899 pilgrimage journal. Brown papers, USBNA.

29 Ella Goodall, unpublished 1899 journal, handwritten version. Cooper papers, USBNA.

30 Extracts of Marian's notes also appear in May's booklet, *An Early Pilgrimage*, pp. 20-22, 26-9, 39-40.

31 Original handwritten 'Notes of the Conversation between the Master and Miss Julia Pearson recorded by Marian Kheiralla, 26 February 1899', USBNA. It was printed as *Conversation February 26, 1899, at Acca.: Answers in Reply to Various Questions*. The printed edition was edited.

32 There is no evidence that Julia ever made a second visit to 'Akká. Sometimes when the Master referred to people 'visiting' He meant that they came in the spirit, not in person.

33 Original handwritten 'Notes of the Conversation between the Master and Miss Julia Pearson recorded by Marian Kheiralla, 26 February 1899', USBNA.

34 ibid.

35 ibid.

36 ibid.

37 ibid.

38 Even though the Kheiralla daughters were in the Holy Land throughout the period of the pilgrimage with their father, none of the Americans seem to have considered them to be part of the pilgrim group. Apparently their interest in the Faith was shallow and the result only of trying to please a long-absent father. Once they left the Holy Land, their connection to the Faith was short-lived.

39 Maxwell, *An Early Pilgrimage*, pp. 20-21.

40 Myron Phelps was an American lawyer who was interested in the Faith, yet who never became a Bahá'í. When he visited 'Abdu'l-Bahá in 1902, he heard a story about a wealthy woman who had brought along her maid when she visited the Master. The maid stood behind her mistress' chair during meals, which made 'Abdu'l-Bahá very uncomfortable. Finally, 'Abdu'l-Bahá had a chair placed by His side at the table and insisted that the maid sit next to Him. He then directed His comments to that maidservant, 'telling her, among other things, to be content; that those who served were often more loved by God than those whom they served' (Phelps, *The Master in 'Akká*, p. 137). While Phelps does not give the name of either the mistress or the maid, it is possible that they were Phoebe and Emily, though the following year several other American ladies also brought their maids with them during their pilgrimages to 'Akká. See also Emogene Hoagg's recollections of her first pilgrimage in the Hoagg collection, USBNA.

41 Maxwell, *An Early Pilgrimage*, p. 26.

Chapter 9 A Surprise Arrival amidst Farewells to 'Akká

1 Lua wrote about this day, 20 March, in a letter written in Cairo on 4 April 1899 to undisclosed recipients in the United States. Lua Getsinger papers, USBNA;

Metelmann, *Lua Getsinger*, p. 24.

2 'That the launching of one of these fundamental activities to be conducted by your Assembly during the present year – the commencement of the interior ornamentation of the Mother Temple of the West – should have so closely synchronized with the placing of the first two contracts for the completion of the Sepulcher of the Bab, as contemplated by 'Abdu'l-Bahá, is indeed a phenomenon of singular significance. This conjunction of two events of historic importance, linking, in a peculiar degree, the most sacred House of Worship in the American continent with the most hallowed Shrine on the slopes of Mount Carmel, brings vividly to mind the no less remarkable coincidence marking the simultaneous holding, on a Naw-Rúz Day, of the first convention of the American Bahá'í Community and the entombment by the Center of Bahá'u'lláh's Covenant of the remains of the Bab in the newly constructed vault of His Shrine. The simultaneous arrival of those remains in the fortress city of 'Akká and of the first pilgrims from the continent of America; the subsequent association of the founder of the American Bahá'í Community with 'Abdu'l-Bahá in the laying of the cornerstone of the Báb's Mausoleum on Mount Carmel; the holding of the Centenary of His Declaration beneath the dome of the recently constructed Ma<u>sh</u>riqu'l-A<u>dh</u>kár at Wilmette, on which solemn occasion His blessed portrait was unveiled, on western soil, to the eyes of His followers; and the unique distinction now conferred on a member [William Sutherland Maxwell of Montreal] of the North American Bahá'í Community of designing the dome, envisaged by 'Abdu'l-Bahá, as the final and essential embellishment of the Báb's Sepulcher – all these have served to associate the Herald of our Faith and His resting-place with the fortunes of a community which has so nobly responded to His summons addressed to the 'peoples of the West' in His Qayyúmu'l-Asmá' (Shoghi Effendi, *Citadel of Faith*, pp. 52-3).

3 'In the same year that this precious Trust reached the shores of the Holy Land and was delivered into the hands of 'Abdu'l-Bahá, He, accompanied by Dr. Ibráhím <u>Kh</u>ayru'lláh, whom He had already honoured with the titles of 'Bahá's Peter', 'The Second Columbus' and 'Conqueror of America', drove to the recently purchased site which had been blessed and selected by Bahá'u'lláh on Mt. Carmel, and there laid, with His own hands, the foundation-stone of the edifice, the construction of which He, a few months later, was to commence' (Shoghi Effendi, *God Passes By*, pp. 274-5).

4 Edward most likely made this suggestion to Phoebe while in Egypt when he went to escort her to Haifa. At the time he already had reservations about Kheiralla, but may not have seen any alternative. It seems that Edward thought a trust fund would be used to assist other teachers of the Faith, in addition to Kheiralla.

5 Edward Getsinger, unpublished memoirs, ch. 3, pp. 10-12. Getsinger papers, USBNA. See also the handwritten note to Albert Windust dated 30 Sept. 1930, Windust papers, USBNA.

6 According to Ella's 1899 pilgrimage journal, Dr Sadris had a most interesting background. Born in Iran to a Muslim family, he converted to Catholicism while in Italy and later to Protestant Christianity. While in Italy he learned of the Persian colony of Bahá'ís in 'Akká and decided to move there where he could be with fellow countrymen. He became attracted to the Bahá'í Faith and loved

'Abdu'l-Bahá very much. It appears from Ella's account that Dr Sadris, being removed from close contact with the Bahá'í community in Haifa and 'Akká, had not acquired a deep knowledge of the Faith. Apparently his primary role in California was as Persian translator and correspondent with 'Abdu'l-Bahá.

7 Ella records in her diary that the order came from Constantinople. Typed pilgrimage journal, p. 12.

8 Edward was already in 'Akká on that day.

9 Helen Hillyer, handwritten 1899 pilgrimage journal. Brown papers, USBNA.

10 Ella Goodall, unpublished 1899 journal, typed version, p. 12. Cooper papers, USBNA.

11 Helen Hillyer, handwritten 1899 pilgrimage journal. Brown papers, USBNA.

12 Apparently, she went by the nickname 'Maggie'. 1870 US Census. Most of the information about Margaret Peeke comes from a book written by her son, Hewson L. Peeke, *A Standard History of Erie County, Ohio*, vol. 1, pp. 464-6; 'Margaret Peeke', in Willard and Livermore, *Great American Women of the 19th Century: A Biographical Encyclopedia*, p. 570; 'New Publications', *Star of the West*, vol. II, no. 14, 23 November 1911, p. 16; and from the US Censuses. In addition, there is information about her husband available on the Internet, various web sites, especially those devoted to the history of the Reformed Dutch Church.

13 Shoghi Effendi, *God Passes By*, p. 257. Edward Getsinger includes Margaret Peeke in his list of those who took part in the pilgrimage. Edward Getsinger papers, unpublished memoirs, ch. 3, p. 7, USBNA.

14 George Peeke graduated from Rutgers College in 1857 and its theological seminary in 1860. Hewson L. Peeke, *A Standard History of Erie County, Ohio*, vol. 1, p. 464.

15 Margaret Peeke was born on 8 April 1838, the daughter of Garry Marshall Peck and Narcissa Benedict.

16 Willard and Livermore, *Great American Women of the 19th Century*, p. 570.

17 ibid.

18 1880 and 1900 US Censuses. Note that in 1900 only two of her six children were still living and of those two, her daughter Grace, a poet and nurse, would die a year later from a disease contracted as a result of her nursing duties. ibid. pp. 464-6.

19 In 1902 she became the head of the Martinist movement in the United States.

20 Her books include *Zenia the Vestal or the Problem of Vibrations* and *Numbers and Letters or the Thirty-two Paths of Wisdom*. Several of her books, more than 100 years later, remain in print.

21 Margaret B. Peeke, *My Visit to Abbas-Effendi in 1899*, p. 4.

22 ibid.

23 ibid. p. 5.

24 ibid. pp. 8-9.

25 According to the dates given by Ella, she, Nell and Lua came back to 'Akká late in the evening of the day of Maggie's last visit to 'Abdu'l-Bahá. This was the same day that the three rushed to 'Akká fearing to be turned away by government officials. Edward does mention in his memoirs being present during Maggie's interview.

26 ibid. pp. 9-10.

27 ibid. pp. 10-11.
28 At that time, even Professor Browne was unaware that 'Abdu'l-Bahá was the author of *A Traveller's Narrative*.
29 ibid. p. 10.
30 ibid. pp. 11-12.
31 ibid. p. 12.
32 ibid. p. 13.
33 The identity of the second woman is unknown.
34 ibid. p. 13-14.
35 A 'stockgilly' is a nineteenth-century name for a carnation/dianthus flower. Stockgillies were the annual variety of that type of flower.
36 Peeke, op. cit. pp. 14-15.
37 ibid. p. 18.
38 Metelmann, *Lua Getsinger*, p. 25.
39 Gail, *Summon up Remembrance*, p. 147. For example, during his years as a resident of Palestine, 'Abdu'l-Bahá always attended the Friday prayer service at either the main mosque of 'Akká or Haifa. This was discontinued by Shoghi Effendi.
40 The Muslim month of Ramadan floats around the solar calendar because the Muslim calendar is lunar.
41 Having returned from Nazareth, Ella and Nell celebrated the Bahá'í New Year with the Haifa community. The two young ladies purchased sweetmeats as their contribution to the occasion.
42 Lua Getsinger, letter written in Cairo on 4 April 1899, pp. 5-6. Lua Getsinger papers, USBNA. Alternative transcription in Metelmann, *Lua Getsinger*, p. 26.
43 ibid, p. 3 of the original letter.
44 Maxwell, *An Early Pilgrimage*, pp. 39-40, based on notes taken by Marian Kheiralla (see above, pp. 138, 313, note 30).
45 Ella Goodall, unpublished 1899 journal, typed version, pp. 20-21. Cooper papers, USBNA.
46 Maxwell, *An Early Pilgrimage*, pp. 41-3.
47 Edward celebrated the Bahá'í New Year in Haifa.
48 The account of the Getsingers' last two days in 'Akká and their departure from the Holy Land comes from the letter written by Lua in Cairo on 4 April 1899 to undisclosed recipients in the United States. Lua Getsinger papers, USBNA; Metelmann, *Lua Getsinger*, pp. 24-29.

Chapter 10 An Egyptian Education

1 Ella Goodall, letter to her parents and brother from Syria, 31 March 1899. Cooper papers, USBNA.
2 Ella Goodall, letter to Helen Goodall written at Ain Sobhar, Syria, 1 April 1899. Cooper papers, USBNA.
3 Ella Goodall, unpublished 1899 journal, typed version, p. 24. Cooper papers, USBNA.
4 The information about this side trip comes from both Ella's 1899 pilgrimage journal (typed and handwritten) and her letter of 31 March 1899 to her mother. There are a number of letters from Anton Haddad to Helen Goodall written over the course of the next few years in which he expresses his gratitude for the

assistance given to him and his family. He repaid their kindness with his untiring efforts to teach the Faith in the United States and to conscientiously translate the correspondence between the Master and the American believers.

5 Ella Goodall, unpublished 1899 journal, typed version, pp. 24-5. Cooper papers, USBNA.

6 Apparently, for at least the first year there was no one in either the Holy Land or Egypt with English skills at the level required to translate the correspondence between the Master and the Western believers. Fortunately, many of the Americans were fluent in French.

7 'Ella Goodall Cooper', In Memoriam, *The Bahá'í World*, vol. 12, p. 682. This Tablet was first translated into English by Anton Haddad.

8 Ella Goodall, letter to her mother from Ain Sobhar, Syria, 1 April 1899. Cooper papers, USBNA. The translator's name is unknown.

9 ibid.

10 Abu'l-Faḍl, *Bahá'í Proofs*, p. 13.

11 ibid. pp. 8-23. See also Balyuzi, *Eminent Bahá'ís*, pp. 263-5.

12 Abu'l-Faḍl, *Bahá'í Proofs*, p. 20.

13 ibid. p. 264.

14 Ella Goodall, unpublished 1899 journal, typed version, p. 25. Cooper papers, USBNA.

15 Helen Hillyer, handwritten 1899 pilgrimage journal. Brown papers, USBNA.

16 Ella Goodall, undated note headed 'Private' to an unnamed party – most likely her mother. Cooper papers, USBNA.

17 Ella Goodall, unpublished 1899 journal, handwritten version. Cooper papers, USBNA.

18 May Bolles, letter to Julia Pearson from Dinard, Ille et Vilaine, France (a seaside resort in Brittany), 1 August [1899?]. Maxwell papers, USBNA. May's mother and brother were at the time indifferent, perhaps even hostile, toward the Faith, but years later both would become believers. Her brother's primary contribution would be the English translation of the French footnotes of *The Dawn-Breakers.*

19 ibid.

20 ibid. The five were Lua, May, Anne, Julia and Brenetta Herrman.

21 Provisional translation, Bahá'í World Centre. This Tablet was copied and inserted with the letter from May Bolles to Julia Pearson (see note 18 above). Pearson papers, USBNA.

22 The Master generally declined to have his picture taken by Edward or any other photographer. A few years later he did allow a different, very persistent Western pilgrim to photograph his extended hand. Edward took very few photographs that included people during the period of his first pilgrimage.

23 The Greatest Holy Leaf also apparently spoke into the phonograph, and Ella and Nell sang into it. The wax disk is now held by the USBNA.

24 This is probably a reference to the Kitáb-i-Aqdas, the Most Holy Book, which became fully available in an authorized English translation in 1992.

25 Ella Goodall, private note to an unknown recipient (Helen Goodall?). Cooper papers, USBNA.

26 Agnes Lane Leonard, letter to Ella Goodall Cooper. Cooper papers, USBNA. It is a mystery why the younger pilgrims did not teach this teenager about the

Bahá'í Faith, though it is unclear whether any of the others made the attempt. Agnes gave all the credit to Harriet. Perhaps Phoebe was concerned about how Agnes's parents would react to her converting to a religion that was not Christian. The Thornburghs and Lanes must have been longtime friends from San Francisco because some years later Minnie would be the guest of Agnes's mother while visiting California. Thornburgh-Cropper correspondence, PAH papers, Bancroft Library.

27 In a note at the bottom of the page, Emogene Hoagg notes that the women had decided to go directly to London on the advice of a physician.

28 Emogene Hoagg, undated letter to Phoebe Apperson Hearst from Milan, Italy. PAH papers, Bancroft Library. In a later note in her handwritten pilgrimage journal, Emogene Hoagg lists the names of two of the three and says that all three had since passed away. It is not clear when that note was penned, but most likely it was less than ten years later. Hoagg papers, USBNA.

29 May Bolles, letter to Julia Pearson from Dinard, Ille et Vilaine, France, 1 August [1899?]. Maxwell papers, USBNA.

30 Edward Getsinger, unpublished memoirs, ch. 3, p. 13.

Chapter 11 Igniting Europe

1 See also above, p. 102. Brenetta Herrman was born in Toledo, Ohio and was in Paris to work and study painting under eminent artists such as James Whistler. She married Earl Stetson Crawford, another American artist studying in Paris. There is no information as to how long she retained an interest in the Bahá'í Faith. She passed away in 1956 in California.

2 Edith later married Dr Joseph de Bons, a dental surgeon. The couple were early pioneers of the Bahá'í Faith in Switzerland; their daughter, Mme Haenni de Bons, continued that service. Balyuzi, *'Abdu'l-Bahá*, p. 400; Mona Haenni de Bons, 'Edith de Bons and Joseph de Bons', *The Bahá'í World*, vol. 13, pp. 878-81.

3 Mona Haenni de Bons, op. cit. p. 878. Shortly after Edith became a believer, her American mother residing in Paris, Marie Louise MacKay, also became a Bahá'í. This mother and daughter made a pilgrimage to 'Akká in 1901. Marie Louise MacKay was born in New York in 1847. Her husband, John MacKay, was born in Ireland but became an American citizen. See Marie Louise MacKay US Passport Applications for 1889, 1915, 1916, 1919, 1923.

4 In other words, this was one of many instances when 'Abdu'l-Bahá knew something without being told.

5 This probably refers to the United States. During the time the pilgrims spent in 'Akká, 'Abdu'l-Bahá spoke to them repeatedly about the special destiny of the United States.

6 May Bolles, letter to Julia Pearson written from Dinard, Ille et Vilaine, France, 1 August [1899?]. Maxwell papers, USBNA. 'Abdu'l-Bahá specifically requested that May remain in Paris for an indefinite time.

7 It is possible that Ethel knew Harriet and Minnie from their social circles in England, since most of her clients for portraits came from their social strata. Furthermore, Ethel had an aunt living in the same neighbourhood of Kent where the two Americans were residing. Harriet mentions 'Miss Rosenburg' in two undated letters to Phoebe that seem to have been written prior to the pilgrimage,

but it is impossible to date these two pieces of correspondence. Thornburgh correspondence, PAH papers, Bancroft Library. I am indebted to Robert Weinberg for information about Ethel Rosenberg's aunt.

8 Mary Virginia Thornburgh-Cropper, letter to Phoebe Hearst, London, 1899. PAH papers, Bancroft Library.

9 Inexplicably, Minnie did not accompany her mother and Ethel on that 1901 pilgrimage. Perhaps part of the reason was that her former husband was wounded during December of 1900 during the Boer War and was brought back to England. He died of complications from his wounds (pneumonia) in April of 1901. As neither had remarried, she may have had to assume some responsibilities for him.

10 Harriet Thornburgh, undated letter to Phoebe Hearst. Thornburgh correspondence, PAH papers, Bancroft Library. Harriet Thornburgh also wrote to 'Abdu'l-Bahá about her daughter's illness, Mrs Hearst's assistance to her and that Minnie had gone to California as Phoebe's guest. She says that she is certain her daughter will be able to assist with the teaching work in California while there and also hopes that she will continue her study of Arabic while in the United States. Bahá'í World Centre Archives, Summary of a letter from Harriet F. Thornburgh to 'Abdu'l-Bahá dated 30 August 1902, provided in an attachment to a letter dated 21 December 2008 written on behalf of the Universal House of Justice to Kathryn J. Hogenson.

11 Joseph Estlin Carpenter, eminent scholar at Oxford as well as a Unitarian clergyman and theologian, would preside over the gathering at Manchester College in 1912, as head of that college, when 'Abdu'l-Bahá was the guest speaker. Professor Carpenter was the author of numerous publications on Christianity as well as works on comparative religion and biographies. He came from a distinguished family of thinkers and social reformers, including his paternal grandfather, who was a notable Unitarian theologian, and his father, William Benjamin Carpenter, who as a physiologist and naturalist became one of the founders of the important principle in the modern field of psychology of the adaptive unconscious. His aunt was the outstanding education and social reformer, Mary Carpenter.

12 Ethel J. Rosenberg, letter to 'Abdu'l-Bahá written in London, 12 February 1903. Bahá'í World Centre Archives, quoted in an attachment to a letter dated 21 December 2008 written on behalf of the Universal House of Justice to Kathryn J. Hogenson.

13 Ethel J. Rosenberg, letter to 'Abdu'l-Bahá written in London, 13 February 1903. Bahá'í World Centre Archives, summarized and quoted in an attachment to a letter dated 21 December 2008 written on behalf of the Universal House of Justice to Kathryn J. Hogenson.

14 ibid.

15 On 27 March 1903 Ethel Rosenberg wrote to 'Abdu'l-Bahá from London that she wanted to return to 'Akká, but lacked sufficient money to travel and besides which felt that she should remain in London to take care of the teaching work until Mary Virginia Thornburgh-Cropper returned. Ethel J. Rosenberg, letter to 'Abdu'l-Bahá, written in London, 27 March (year most likely 1903, though not stated). Bahá'í World Centre Archives, summarized in an attachment to a letter dated 21 December 2008 written on behalf of the Universal House of Justice to Kathryn J. Hogenson.

16 Ethel J. Rosenberg, letter to 'Abdu'l-Bahá written in Paris, 19 January 1905. Bahá'í World Centre Archives, summarized in an attachment to a letter dated 21 December 2008 written on behalf of the Universal House of Justice to Kathryn J. Hogenson.

17 Sara, Lady Blomfield, originally from Ireland, was the very capable widow of the distinguished British architect Sir Arthur William Blomfield. She became a devoted, active believer who was able to raise the status of the British Bahá'í community through her high social standing and hard work. She is best remembered for her book, *The Chosen Highway*, which recounted the history of the Faith primarily through the eyes of the women of the Holy Family; and above all for her part in making available 'Abdu'l-Bahá's talks in Paris (*Paris Talks*, originally published in 1912).

18 Ethel Rosenberg, the first British believer residing in England, would serve the Faith tirelessly for the rest of her life, both in England and the Holy Land. She wrote introductory works about the Faith and assisted both 'Abdu'l-Bahá and Shoghi Effendi with the work of translating the Bahá'í Writings into English. For a comprehensive and engaging look at this significant servant of the Faith, see Weinberg, *Ethel Jenner Rosenberg: The Life and Times of England's Outstanding Bahá'í Pioneer Worker*.

19 Ethel J. Rosenberg, letter to Helen Goodall, dated 24 October (no year). Goodall papers, USBNA.

20 ibid.

21 This was carried out by one of Minnie's solicitors.

22 'Abdu'l-Bahá, untranslated Tablet in Persian to Mary Virginia Thornburgh Cropper, most likely written in 1905. Bahá'í World Centre Archives, summarized in an attachment to a letter written on behalf of the Universal House of Justice to Kathryn Hogenson dated 23 February 2009.

23 Harriet Thornburgh, letter to Phoebe Hearst written from Paris, Easter Day 1903. PAH papers, Bancroft Library.

24 Gail, *Summon up Remembrance*, p. 137.

25 Harriet Thornburgh, letter to Phoebe Hearst written from Paris, Easter Day 1903. PAH papers, Bancroft Library.

26 Phoebe Hearst, letter to Clara Anthony written from London, 21 May 1904. PAH papers, Bancroft Library.

27 Shoghi Effendi created a list of nineteen names of early Western believers whom he wished to honour and designated them 'Disciples of 'Abdu'l-Bahá'. He cut cameos of their pictures and had them published in *The Bahá'í World*, vol. 3. All nineteen were named posthumously. In his first publication of the list, he put in Harriet's portrait and her name as Mrs Thornburgh with no first name. The second time he published the list of Disciples of 'Abdu'l-Bahá was shortly after the passing of Ethel Rosenberg. He may have decided to honour her with the title, but did not wish to lose the numeric symbolism of the number nineteen. So the second version continued to include the portrait of Harriet, but the name given on the caption is Ethel's. The Guardian knew Ethel when he was an adult and so knew what she looked like. The lady whose face is in the photograph, in the full picture, has the 3-year-old Shoghi Effendi perched on her lap. Shoghi Effendi also had the same nineteen pictures copied and placed in buildings at the

Bahá'í World Centre. In some, the same lady is labelled H. Thornburgh and on others it is labelled E. Rosenberg. In addition to those in the nineteen portraits, he also mentioned at a later time that Juliet Thompson and George Latimer were also Disciples of 'Abdu'l-Bahá. Ella's mother, Helen Goodall, is among the nineteen. See *The Bahá'í World*, vol. 3, pp. 84-5, and vol. 4, pp. 118-19. There is also some indication that he also named Mary Virginia Thornburgh-Cropper as a Disciple. A similar confusion in the lists of Disciples of 'Abdu'l-Bahá concerns two of the German believers; Consul Schwarz and Artur Brauns.

28 Whitehead, *Some Bahá'ís to Remember*, p. 30.

29 Letter on behalf of Shoghi Effendi to Lady Blomfield, 26 March 1938. Bahá'í World Centre Archives, provided in an attachment to a letter written on behalf of the Universal House of Justice to Kathryn Hogenson dated 23 February 2009.

30 Remey, *Reminiscences and Letters*, typed multi-volume autobiography, pp. 43-4.

31 ibid. p. 45.

32 ibid. p. 46.

33 Herbert W. Hopper was born on 12 February 1874 in Blair, Nebraska. US passport application, no. 1071, issued 29 July 1901 at US Embassy in Paris, France. By the age of 6, he was being raised by his maternal grandparents on a farm, thus it appears that he was orphaned at a young age (1880 US Census). He arrived in Paris to study architecture in 1898 and met Remey shortly thereafter. He was living on a very tight budget, but nonetheless was able to enjoy exploring the region during free time with Remey. He had worked for an architectural firm in Nebraska prior to coming to study in Paris.

34 Remey, ibid. p. 46.

35 ibid. p. 47.

36 The omission of Brenetta Hermann is a mystery.

37 The believer who found the Faith in New York City. (Her first name is unknown.)

38 Marie Lorraine Squires was taught the Faith in Paris by May in early 1900 after first being introduced to it by Mason Remey. Born in New York in 1874, she grew up in Dixon, Illinois. Remey's parents were old friends of her family. Through Remey she also met Herbert Hopper. Herbert and Marie married on 19 May 1902 in London. Their only child was born in Paris. When their daughter was still an infant, the family returned to Omaha, Nebraska where Herbert worked as an architect for the firm that had employed him previously. All of the members of this family remained active, steadfast believers. I am indebted to Rodrigo Tomas for sharing the information in his possession about the Herbert family which is in part based upon the memoirs of Charles Mason Remey.

39 ibid. p. 49.

40 ibid. p. 56.

41 A dance for which everyone came in costume.

42 Marion Jack, letter to Jeanne Kauz, 9 May 1937. Marion Jack collection, Bahá'í World Centre Archives; quoted in Jasion, *Never Be Afraid to Dare*, pp. 19-20.

43 See Stockman, *The Bahá'í Faith in America*, vol. 2, pp. 153-4, and note 299, pp. 467-8. This Tablet of 'Abdu'l-Bahá, translated by the Research Department of the Bahá'í World Centre, is to an unidentified person, although internal evidence suggests it was to Mírzá Abu'l-Faḍl.

44 ibid. p. 154.

45 Elsa's mother, Alice Pike Barney, was a distinguished portrait artist, many of whose works are on display in important museums. Elsa's sister, Natalie, was a well-known poet who wrote both in English and French and was notorious in her day for her wild parties and excessively unrestrained lifestyle. Mother and sister were among the social circle surrounding the Paris believers though neither ever accepted the Faith.

46 For a heart-felt appreciation of the life and accomplishments of this first native French believer by Shoghi Effendi see *The Bahá'í World*, vol. 3, pp. 210-11, 214. For basic facts on Hippolyte Dreyfus, see Peter Smith, *A Concise Encyclopedia of the Bahá'í Faith*, p. 126. There are many other publications which include information about Hippolyte Dreyfus, but most are available only in French.

47 Sigurd Russell's parents did not live together. Edith Jackson (see p. 184), who it seems had no children of her own, took the young 15-year-old into her home as a sort of foster child. Sigurd's father was an actor in New York and his mother was an elocution teacher who coached many renowned stage actors. Gail, *Summon up Remembrance*, p. 119.

48 This pilgrimage during the winter of 1901 lasted several months and one short account provides glimpses of Harriet Thornburgh. She became friends with the young Persian who served as the English translator during her second visit to 'Akká, Ali-Kuli Khan, even nursing him during an illness. She was, however, becoming deaf, so he had to consciously work to make himself understood to her. She thought he was mumbling deliberately and complained to 'Abdu'l-Bahá that she was feeling left out of the conversations. Undoubtedly, her poor hearing affected her ability to interact with people, and thus to teach the Faith. Gail, *Summon up Remembrance*, p. 137.

49 Charlotte Dixon was one of the preeminent early believers in the United States. Raised on a plantation on the Eastern Shore of Maryland in a prosperous family, through her father she was exposed to the Millerites and their ideas about the imminent return of Christ. She was widowed while pregnant with her second child. Through both her intense faith in God and mystical experiences, she was led to the Bahá'í Faith while living in Chicago. She brought her brother and sister-in-law into the Faith. The latter, Isabella Brittingham, went on to become one of the most noteworthy spokesmen for the Faith in the United States during the first decades of the twentieth century and was named a Disciple of 'Abdu'l-Bahá by Shoghi Effendi. Charlotte herself established the Faith in a number of communities and is especially known as the 'mother' of the Washington, D.C. Bahá'í community. Stockman, *The Bahá'í Faith in America*, vol. 1, pp. 117-21.

50 Bertha Lexow was from Tompkinsville near New York City. Remey, *Reminiscences*, p. 56.

51 Agnes B. Alexander, quoted in Honnold, *Why They Became Bahá'ís*, pp. 4-10.

52 May Ellis Bolles, letter to 'Abdu'l-Bahá written in Paris, France, 13 April 1900. Bahá'í World Centre Archives, summarized in an attachment to a letter written on behalf of the Universal House of Justice dated 21 December 2008 to Kathryn J. Hogenson.

53 'Abdu'l-Bahá, Tablet to May Ellis Bolles Maxwell, 24 January 1901. Provisional translation. Bahá'í World Centre Archives, attached to a letter written on behalf of the Universal House of Justice dated 21 December 2008 to Kathryn J. Hogenson.

54 Edith's sister had married the wealthy merchant R. H. White of Boston, who owned a large department store.

55 Thomas was a naturalized United States citizen. This information comes from his application for a US passport submitted on 9 August 1901 at the US embassy in Paris.

56 Breakwell left the United States on 29 March 1901, and after time in England, arrived in Paris in July where he was staying at the Hotel Dijon.

57 Lakshman-Lepain, *The Life of Thomas Breakwell.*

58 Maxwell, 'A Brief Account of Thomas Breakwell', p. 707.

59 ibid.

60 ibid.

61 ibid.

62 ibid.

63 ibid. p. 709. May's mother, at the end of her life, became a Bahá'í. May's brother, Randolph, became a Bahá'í many years later, as did his wife and daughter.

64 ibid.

65 In 2000, the French Bahá'í community paid loving homage to Thomas Breakwell by erecting a befitting monument over his resting place.

66 Ruhe-Schoen, *A Love Which Does Not Wait*, p. 49. May was not the first Bahá'í to reside in Canada. Also, a number of the Bahá'ís residing in the United States at the time were natives of Canada.

67 May Bolles Maxwell, letter to 'Abdu'l-Bahá written in Montreal, Canada, 9 July 1903. Bahá'í World Centre Archives, summarized in an attachment to a letter dated 21 December 2008 written on behalf of the Universal House of Justice to Kathryn J. Hogenson.

68 This is the building which for a time served as the Seat of the Universal House of Justice and as the offices of the International Teaching Centre.

69 As an elderly man, the strong ego of Remey finally overwhelmed his better qualities. Following the passing of Shoghi Effendi, he claimed in 1960 to be the second Guardian. Consequently, he was expelled from the Faith, thereby forever tarnishing – expunging – a lifetime of distinguished service. For a brief review of his life, see Harper, *Lights of Fortitude*, pp. 287-306.

70 The others were George Townshend and John Esslemont. Shoghi Effendi, *Unfolding Destiny*, p. 377.

71 'Swiss Bahá'ís Celebrate 100 Years of Contribution to World Civilisation', posted on the official web site of the Bahá'í Community of Switzerland, http://www.bahai.ch/english/centenary_interlaken.html (visited September, 2008).

72 I am indebted to Rodrigo Tomas for furnishing this information about the Hopper family. Email to the author from Rodrigo Tomas dated 18 October 2009.

73 Harper, *Lights of Fortitude*, pp. 292-93.

74 Edith, her mother and her sister, Sybil, had moved to Paris in order to promote her sister's career as an opera singer. Interestingly, Sybil Sanderson was William Randolph Hearst's first serious love interest. From published reports available on the Internet, it seems that Sybil's mother was responsible for ending the romance because she feared it would destroy her daughter's career as a singer. Phoebe was reportedly relieved to see the romance end, given her son's young age and her ambitions for him.

Chapter 12 Kheiralla's Downfall

1 Hollinger, 'Ibrahim George Kheiralla and the Bahá'í Faith in America', p. 113.
2 ibid.
3 ibid. This exceptional early believer made at least eleven pilgrimages to the Holy Land.
4 Shoghi Effendi, the eldest grandson of 'Abdu'l-Bahá, was appointed in his Will and Testament as the Guardian of the Faith, in which office he was the Head of the Faith and the Interpreter of its Writings. Following Shoghi Effendi's passing in November 1957 and his inability to appoint a successor, it fell to the Universal House of Justice, after its election in 1963, to consider the situation. After prolonged consultation it found that 'there is no way to appoint or to legislate to make it possible to appoint a second Guardian to succeed Shoghi Effendi'. This meant that there was, henceforth, no institution or individual who could issue authoritative interpretations of the Bahá'í Sacred Scriptures. This situation had been anticipated by 'Abdu'l-Bahá in a Tablet in which he stressed the authority of the Universal House of Justice: 'My purpose is this, that ere the expiration of a thousand years, no one has the right to utter a single word, even to claim the station of Guardianship. The Most Holy Book is the Book to which all peoples shall refer, and in it the Laws of God have been revealed. Laws not mentioned in the Book should be referred to the decision of the Universal House of Justice. There will be no grounds for difference . . . Beware, beware lest anyone create a rift or stir up sedition. Should there be differences of opinion, the Supreme House of Justice would immediately resolve the problems' (*Messages from the Universal House of Justice*, no. 5 (6 October 1963), and no. 23.11 (9 March 1965).
5 In an undated letter to an unnamed recipient from Marian Kheiralla written some time after the pilgrimage, there is a handwritten note [penned by Ella Goodall Cooper?] identifying the author as 'divorced wife of Dr Kheiralla by permission of 'Abdu'l-Bahá'. There are handwritten small notes among the Ella Goodall Cooper papers about the Kheiralla marital problems and Ella also writes of them to her mother. In her 15 February 1899 letter to Thornton Chase, Lua Getsinger says, 'Mrs Kheiralla will not return to America with the Doctor but will go to England for a time and then return to Acca. The Gr. Br. ['Abdu'l-Bahá] invited her to stay here for one year or longer if she wished. He has showed her great honours and called her the "White Pearl of the Kingdom". Her health is much improved and she is very happy.' Edward also mentions the problems of the Kheirallas in his memoirs and talks of the Getsingers' role in getting Marian to 'Akká. Additional information about this episode is from Hollinger, 'Ibrahim George Kheiralla and the Bahá'í Faith in America', p. 115.
6 Haddad, *An Outline of the Bahai Movement in the United States*, pp. 11-13. Kheiralla later denied that he had made direct contact with Muḥammad-'Alí or his cohorts, though it seems likely that he did, given how easily he was able to persuade them to send someone to assist him in the United States within the next year. Smith, 'The American Bahá'í Community, 1894–1917', p. 94.
7 Anton Haddad, letter to Helen Goodall from New York, 18 May 1899. Goodall papers, USBNA.

8 Lua Getsinger, letter to Thornton Chase written from 'Akká, 15 February 1899. USBNA, transcribed from the original; alternative transcription in Metelmann, *Lua Getsinger*, p. 21.
9 Anton Haddad, letter to Helen Goodall from New York, 18 May 1899. USBNA.
10 Lua Getsinger, letter to Thornton Chase written from 'Akká, 15 February 1899. USBNA; also in Metelmann, *Lua Getsinger*, p. 22. See also Edward Getsinger, unpublished memoirs, ch. 3, p. 16.
11 Edward Getsinger, unpublished memoirs, ch. 3, p. 16.
12 Anton Haddad, letter to Helen Goodall from New York, 18 May 1899. USBNA.
13 Stockman, *The Bahá'í Faith in America*, vol. 1, pp. 163-4.
14 Lua Getsinger, letter to Thornton Chase written from 'Akká, 15 February 1899. USBNA, transcribed from the original; alternative transcription in Metelmann, *Lua Getsinger*, p. 22.
15 Anton Haddad, letter to Helen Goodall from New York, 1 June 1899. Goodall papers, USBNA.
16 This provisional translation was submitted by the Secretary of the Bahá'í Publishing Society to the Librarian of the House of Spirituality in 1905. There is no indication who translated it. It was sent to Kheiralla by 'Abdu'l-Bahá in 1899. USBNA.
17 See Luke 18: 25, Mark 10: 25, Matt. 19: 24
18 Edward Getsinger, unpublished memoirs, ch. 3, p. 16.
19 ibid. p. 17.
20 Phoebe A. Hearst, letter to Helen Hillyer written in Washington, D.C., 5 July 1899. Hillyer papers, USBNA. Haddad did try to contact Helen in Paris, but missed her.
21 Lua Getsinger, letter to a recipient named Helen [most likely Helen Hillyer] written at the Washington, D.C. home of Mrs. Phoebe Hearst, undated except for '1899'. Getsinger papers, USBNA. See also Metelmann, pp. 30-31.
22 Edward Getsinger, unpublished memoirs, ch. 3, pp. 18-19.
23 Stockman, *The Bahá'í Faith in America*, vol. 1, p. 169.
24 This confusion about the station of the Master would linger among the Western believers of Christian background long after Kheiralla was no longer a factor in the Bahá'í community. After all, 'Abdu'l-Bahá was very Christ-like. Bahá'u'lláh Himself had said that if one wanted to know what Jesus was like, look to the Master. Yet this was not 'Abdu'l-Bahá's station nor did He claim it for Himself. He constantly emphasized that his name was 'Abdu'l-Bahá – that is, Servant of the Glory. His station was 'Abdu'l-Bahá, His glory was as 'Abdu'l-Bahá. Shoghi Effendi's master work, *The Dispensation of Bahá'u'lláh,* published in 1934, would finally dispel this confusion. See Smith, 'The American Bahá'í Community, 1894–1917', pp. 100-103.
25 Edward Getsinger, unpublished memoirs, ch. 3, pp. 19-20.
26 Hollinger, 'Ibrahim George Kheiralla and the Bahá'í Faith in America', p. 117. See also Stockman, *The Bahá'í Faith in America*, vol. 1, p. 162.
27 Lua Getsinger, letter to Mrs [Rufus?] Bartlett in Chicago, written from Detroit, 18 August 1899. Printed in full in Metelmann, *Lua Getsinger*, p. 33.
28 ibid. pp. 33-34.
29 ibid.
30 ibid. p. 35.

31 Haddad, *Message from Acca* (c. 1900). PAH papers, Bancroft Library. Available online at Bahá'í-Library.org. (October 2008).
32 Haddad, *An Outline of the Bahá'í Movement in the United States,* p. 14.
33 ibid. p. 16.
34 The exact date of his return is unknown. This estimate is by Stockman, *The Bahá'í Faith in America*, vol. 1, p. 167.
35 Haddad, *An Outline of the Bahai Movement in the United States,* p. 16.
36 Hollinger, 'Ibrahim George Kheiralla and the Bahá'í Faith in America', p. 117.
37 Stockman, *The Bahá'í Faith in America*, vol. 1, p. 170.
38 Metelmann, *Lua Getsinger*, p. 33.
39 Edward Getsinger, unpublished memoirs, ch. 3, p. 25.
40 Stockman, *The Bahá'í Faith in America*, p. 174.
41 ibid. p. 176.

Chapter 13 The Sun Comes Out after the Storm

1 Stockman, *The Bahá'í Faith in America*, vol. 1, pp. 177-8.
2 Haddad, *Message from Acca* (1900), pp. 1-2. Available online at http://bahá'í-library.com/pilgrims/message.haddad.html (October 2008).
3 ibid. p. 2.
4 ibid. p. 3.
5 ibid. pp. 4-5.
6 This story is also given in a Tablet from 'Abdu'l-Bahá to an individual believer, in 'Abdu'l-Bahá, *Selections*, no. 144, p 169.
7 Haddad, *Message from Acca*, pp. 5-6.
8 Undoubtedly a reference to the Hand of the Cause of God Ḥájí Mírzá Muḥammad Taqíy-i-Abharí (known as Ibn-i-Abhar), whom some of the pilgrims met during their time in 'Akká in March 1899. See Chapter 12, note 3.
9 Haddad, *Message from Acca*, pp. 6-7.
10 Bahá'u'lláh, Súriy-i-Haykal, paras. 148-9, in *Summons of the Lord of Hosts*, p. 78.
11 ibid. paras. 150-51, pp. 78-9.
12 This is a reference to the story of the crucifixion of Christ as recorded in the New Testament: 'One of the criminals who were hanged railed at him, saying, "Are you not the Christ? Save yourself and us!" But the other rebuked him, saying, "Do you not fear God, since you are under the same sentence of condemnation? And we indeed justly; for we are receiving the due reward of our deeds; but this man has done nothing wrong." And he said, "Jesus, remember me when you come in your kingly power." And he said to him, "Truly, I say to you, today you will be with me in Paradise".' (Luke 23: 39-43).
13 Haddad, *Message from Acca*, pp. 12-14. Haddad comments on this quotation: 'These are the translated words of our Lord spoken to me in response to the information I gave Him regarding the difficulties among the American believers. These notes were afterward corrected by His own hand, and may God help you to accept and practice them.'
14 See Luke 8:21: 'But he said to them, "My mother and my brothers are those who hear the word of God and do it." ' See also Matt. 12:50, Mark 3:35.
15 Haddad, *Message from Acca*, pp. 14-15, part of the notes corrected by'Abdu'l-Bahá; see note 13.

16 Bahá'u'lláh, quoted by Shoghi Effendi in *God Passes By*, pp. 189-90.
17 Stockman, *The Bahá'í Faith in America: Origins*, vol. 1, p. 167.
18 Edward Getsinger, unpublished memoirs, ch. 4, pp. 2-3. See also Hollinger, 'Ibrahim George Kheiralla and the Bahá'í Faith in America', p. 119. Apparently, throughout most of Kheiralla's remaining years, he depended in large measure on financial support from his family. He married a fifth time. His last bride was one of the former Bahá'ís who had followed him and renounced 'Abdu'l-Bahá. For a year or so after he publicly declared that he no longer accepted 'Abdu'l-Bahá as the Head of the Bahá'í Faith or as one with a special station bestowed by God, he established a 'Behaist' church in the Chicago area. But his charisma was not enough to hold his congregation for long, and it soon disbanded.
19 Hollinger, 'Ibrahim George Kheiralla and the Bahá'í Faith in America', p. 120.
20 Edward Getsinger, unpublished memoirs, ch. 3, pp. 21-2.
21 'Abdu'l-Bahá, Tablet to Dr Edward Getsinger, received about September 1901. Getsinger papers, USBNA. Provisional translation, Bahá'í World Centre.
22 Emogene Hoagg recalled that after Kheiralla left the Faith, many of the friends in the United States were no longer able to teach others about the Faith because they had no substitute for Kheiralla's lesson plans, which they had learned, to their sorrow, were incorrect. Emogene Hoagg's typed recollections. Hoagg collection, USBNA.
23 Houses of Spirituality were the precursors of Local Spiritual Assemblies.
24 Lua Getsinger, letter to the 'brothers and sisters in Chicago' written from Haifa, Syria, 19 October 1900; see also Metelmann, *Lua Getsinger*, pp. 28-9.
25 ibid.
26 Thornton Chase characterized Marian Kheiralla as a 'Covenant Breaker' in a letter to Isabella Brittingham dated 1 February 1903 (Stockman, *The Bahá'í Faith in America*, vol. 1, pp. 238-9, fn. 41). Nevertheless, the preponderance of the evidence is that Marian remained faithful to 'Abdu'l-Bahá. See for example, Gail, *Summon up Remembrance,* p. 161. Letters from various early believers hint that Marian became disenchanted with the Bahá'í Faith about 1903, though the cause is unstated and seems unrelated to her former husband. It is known that prior to 1916 she served as a Christian missionary in China and Japan. She returned home to her sister and relatives in England in that year and then moved within a year to Glossop, England where she resided in the Beth Rapha Hostel, a facility run by a Christian group – her last known address. In the end, Marian Miller fades into history and the circumstances of her later life and death remain a mystery. See: Marian Augusta Miller (Kheiralla) petition for reinstatement of her British citizenship, 1916 and attendant papers, National Archives, United Kingdom, file: HO 144/1465/320962. The petition was granted in 1917.
27 Smith, 'The American Bahá'í Community, 1894–1917', pp. 94-5.
28 Marian Kheiralla, letter to Ella Goodall written at the home of Miss Sarah Farmer at Eliot, Maine, dated 24 May, no year. Cooper papers, USBNA. Sarah Farmer had established the Green Acre retreat with the assistance of Phoebe Hearst before either ever encountered the Bahá'í Faith. Each found the Faith independently of the other. Sarah became a devoted believer and ultimately gave Green Acre to the Faith. She would be among those named a Disciple of 'Abdu'l-Bahá by Shoghi Effendi. In her letter, Marian writes of Sarah's desire to begin

including talks about the Bahá'í Faith in the Green Acre summer programme. Apparently Marian spent the summer (1901?) at Green Acre.

29 Gail, *Summon up Remembrance*, p. 164.
30 Stockman, *Thornton Chase*, pp. 160-61.
31 ibid.
32 He took a side trip to London where he was invited to dine with Minnie Thornburgh-Cropper. See Gail, *Summon Up Remembrance*, p. 155. He had become a friend of Harriet Thornburgh's while she was on her second pilgrimage that same year, taking care to ensure that this hard-of-hearing lady was included in conversations. Harriet, in turn, had treated him like a son. See Gail, ibid. p. 137.
33 ibid. pp. 156-7.
34 ibid. pp. 178.
35 Mírzá Abu'l-Faḍl, *The Bahá'í Proofs* (1983 edition), p. 31.
36 Gail, *Summon Up Remembrance*, p. 171.
37 Letter from Thornton Chase to Albert Windust written in Chicago, 9 June 1903. Windust papers, USBNA.

Chapter 14 Keeping the Candles Ablaze

1 Ella Goodall, letter to Mrs Ellsworth written at 72 Adelaide Road, London, NW, 8 June 1899. Cooper papers, USBNA.
2 Ella Goodall, letter to Helen Goodall written at Ain Sobhar, Syria, 1 April 1899. Cooper papers, USBNA.
3 Because Ella and Nell did not overlap with most of the Hearst party during their time in Haifa and did not visit Paris en route to the Holy Land, their visits to Paris and London afforded them their first opportunity to meet some of the other Western pilgrims.
4 Edward Getsinger, unpublished memoirs, ch. 3, p. 13.
5 This perception was not entirely true. William Randolph Hearst was able to make both the *San Francisco Examiner* and the *New York Journal* profitable after liberal infusions of cash to improve them. He especially spent large sums on state-of-the-art printing presses and salaries for top-notch journalists.
6 Nasaw, *The Chief*, pp. 151-52; Whyte, *The Uncrowned King*, pp. 451, 454-55.
7 PAH, letter to Clara Anthony from Paris, 6 June 1899. PAH papers, Bancroft Library.
8 Brown, *For My Children and Grandchildren*, p. 37.
9 Ella Cooper, letter to Anne A. Flint, 28 November 1943. Cooper papers, USBNA.
10 Brown, *For My Children and Grandchildren*, p. 37.
11 There are hints that Agnes Lane, most likely with Julia Pearson accompanying her, returned to the United States ahead of Phoebe because of her chronic health problems. The fact that Agnes isn't mentioned in the accounts of Anne's presentation at court would tend to substantiate this.
12 Burgess (1866–1951) is perhaps best known for his 'purple cow' ditty which goes

I never saw a purple cow
I never hope to see one;
But I can tell you, anyhow,
I'd rather see than be one!

Among his many published works was an article that introduced the 'cubist' movement of twentieth-century artists to the American public for the first time. He also coined the word 'blurb'. He was already a popular author when Nell and Ella met him in London.

13 Onions (1873–1951) wrote best-selling novels; his most popular were ghost stories. At the time he met Ella and Nell, he was not yet a well-known published writer.
14 Brown, *For My Children and Grandchildren*, p. 39.
15 ibid. p. 40.
16 An early history of the Bahá'í Faith in the British Isles summarizing the memories of Mary Virginia Thornburgh-Cropper, Ethel Rosenberg, and Lady Blomfield, compiled and written by 'Mother George' (Prudence George) and to be found in handwritten form among the Balyuzi papers. I am truly grateful to Dr Moojan Momen for sharing this document with me prior to its publication in *Bahá'í Studies Review* (May 2009).
17 Helen Hillyer, letter to Phoebe Hearst from Paris, 7 July 1899. PAH Papers, Bancroft Library. Interestingly, in the same letter Nell relates that Aḥmad Yazdí, in a letter to her from Egypt, discouraged her from learning Arabic.
18 Helen Hillyer, letter to 'Abdu'l-Bahá, 1 June 1899 (location unknown, but probably Paris). Bahá'í World Centre Archives, furnished as an attachment to an email dated 21 December 2008 to Kathryn J. Hogenson written on behalf of the Universal House of Justice.
19 ibid.
20 'Abdu'l-Bahá. Tablet to Ella F. Goodall sent in 1899, provisional translation by Marzieh Carpenter [Gail] in 1938. Cooper papers, USBNA.
21 Brown, *For My Children and Grandchildren*, p. 40.
22 ibid.
23 Newspaper report of the Hillyer–Brown wedding dated 8 March 1900, reproduced as the frontispiece of *For My Children and Grandchildren,* by Helen Hillyer Brown. It should be noted that, at that time, the American Bahá'ís knew little or nothing about the Bahá'í wedding ceremony. It would be some decades later before they would be asked to adhere to that spiritual law.
24 Charlotte Blake Brown (1846–1904) was one of the first female physicians on the West Coast of the United States and a founder of the San Francisco Hospital for Children, later known as the California Pacific Medical Center. She and her colleagues established the first centre for training nurses on the West Coast within that hospital. The daughter of a Presbyterian clergyman and missionary, she was educated at Elmira College and Women's Medical College of Philadelphia. Not only did her son, Philip King Brown, follow in her footsteps as a doctor, so did one of her two daughters, Adelaide Brown, who was an outstanding physician and a leader in public health.
25 Arequipa Sanitorium papers, PAH papers, Bancroft Library
26 'Wedding under Waving Palms: Miss Anne Apperson becomes Bride of Dr. Marshall Flint in the Home of Mrs. Phoebe Hearst, Hacienda del Poso de Verona, Pleasanton', *Oakland Tribune*, 15 September 1903, p. 12.
27 'Bay Area Rite is Set for Hearst Relative', *The Fresno Bee*, 30 July 1970, f. 3-C. See also the Connecticut Death Index. Anne Apperson Flint died in Fairfield, Connecticut.

28 Julia Pearson Hunt died in August 1970 in Cambridge, Massachusetts. Social Security Death Index.
29 Tablet from 'Abdu'l-Bahá to Ella F. Goodall, dated 1903. Cooper papers, USBNA. The name of the translator is not given. Printed here with the permission of the Bahá'í World Centre.
30 Tablet from 'Abdu'l-Bahá to Ella Goodall, dated 1904, translated by Manshadi. Cooper papers, USBNA. Tablet from 'Abdu'l-Bahá to Helen S. Goodall, dated 1905, translated by M. Ameen U Fareed. Goodall papers, USBNA.
31 During the period covered by this work, the women of the United States were still denied the vote. Ironically, Robert Turner, born into slavery, could vote, but his employer, Phoebe Hearst, could not.
32 Helen Hillyer, 1899 handwritten journal. Brown papers, USBNA.
33 Anne A. Flint, letter to Ella G. Cooper from New Haven, Connecticut, 20 March 1944. Cooper papers, USBNA.
34 Ella Goodall Cooper, letter to 'Abdu'l-Bahá written in San Francisco, 19 August 1905. Bahá'í World Centre Archives, summarized in an attachment to an email dated 21 December 2008 to Kathryn J. Hogenson written on behalf of the Universal House of Justice.
35 Ella Goodall Cooper, letter to 'Abdu'l-Bahá written in Oakland, California, 25 January 1903. Bahá'í World Centre Archives, summarized in an attachment to an email dated 21 December 2008 to Kathryn J. Hogenson written on behalf of the Universal House of Justice.
36 Helen Hillyer Brown, letter to 'Abdu'l-Bahá written 'en route Pullman Private Car', 3 October 1912. Bahá'í World Centre Archives, summarized in an attachment to an email dated 21 December 2008 to Kathryn J. Hogenson written on behalf of the Universal House of Justice.
37 Parsons, *'Abdu'l-Bahá in America: Agnes Parsons' Diary*, p. 128.
38 This Tablet from 'Abdu'l-Bahá to Ella Goodall was written in 1902 and re-translated by Dr Ameen'ullah Fareed in Chicago on 12 June 1907. Cooper papers, USBNA. Provisional translation in Bahá'í World Centre Archives.
39 Ella Goodall Cooper, letter to 'Abdu'l-Bahá written in Oakland, California, 25 January 1903. Bahá'í World Centre Archives, summarized in an attachment to an email dated 21 December 2008 to Kathryn J. Hogenson written on behalf of the Universal House of Justice.
40 Report of the Goodall/ Cooper nuptials in the *Oakland Tribune*, evening edition, 11 May 1904, p.1.
41 'Abdu'l-Bahá, Tablet to Mrs Ella G. Cooper dated 18 October 1904. The translator of this typed tablet is unknown. Provisional translation in Bahá'í World Centre Archives.
42 Ella Goodall Cooper, letter to 'Abdu'l-Bahá written in San Francisco, 19 August 1905. Bahá'í World Centre Archives, summarized in an attachment to an email dated 21 December 2008 to Kathryn J. Hogenson written on behalf of the Universal House of Justice.
43 The provisional version used here was a re-translation by Dr Ameen'ullah Fareed dated 5 June 1907, Chicago. Bahá'í World Centre Archives; Cooper papers, USBNA.

44 Cover letter from Ahmad Sohrab to Helen S. Goodall and Ella G. Cooper written at Bahjí, Acca, Palestine, 31 October 1918, enclosed with a Tablet addressed to the same believers from 'Abdu'l-Bahá .

45 Shoghi Effendi in *God Passes By* (p. 333) designates 1925 as the year of the formation of the first National Spiritual Assembly in North America. See Whitmore, *The Dawning Place*, p.122, for an explanation. The first two attempts to elect a National Spiritual Assembly in the United States did not accord with the teaching of the Faith regarding elections, most likely due to ignorance of those principles. It seems as if those placed on the 'National Spiritual Assembly' during those first two years were really being honoured for their services by their fellow believers rather than elected to make decisions, and that the body did not function as an administrative institution in the sense that it did after 1925.

46 She was also elected the following year (1923) to the first National Spiritual Assembly of the Bahá'ís of the British Isles. See Whitehead, *Some Bahá'ís to Remember*, p. 28.

47 See Afroukhteh, *Memories of Nine Years in 'Akká*, and Gail, *Summon up Remembrance* (Marzieh Gail was the daughter of Ali-Kuli Khan).

48 Tablet from 'Abdu'l-Bahá sent care of Ella Goodall and addressed to Mrs Helen Brown, dated between 1902 and 1904. Cooper papers, USBNA. Provisional translation, Bahá'í World Centre.

49 Typed notes about the history of the Faith in California, by Ella Goodall Cooper, Cooper papers, USBNA

50 Ella Goodall Cooper, letter to 'Abdu'l-Bahá written in San Francisco, 19 August 1905. Bahá'í World Centre Archives, provided in an attachment to an email dated 21 December 2008 to Kathryn J. Hogenson written on behalf of the Universal House of Justice.

51 Margaret B. Peeke, letter to 'Abdu'l-Bahá written in Florida, 25 February 1904. Bahá'í World Centre Archives, quoted in an attachment to an email dated 21 December 2008 to Kathryn J. Hogenson written on behalf of the Universal House of Justice.

52 Margaret B. Peeke, letter to 'Abdu'l-Bahá written in Sandusky, Ohio, 13 January 1907. Bahá'í World Centre Archives, quoted in an attachment to an email dated 21 December 2008 to Kathryn J. Hogenson written on behalf of the Universal House of Justice.

53 Margaret B. Peeke, letter to 'Abdu'l-Bahá written in St Augustine, Florida, 4 March 1905. Bahá'í World Centre Archives, quoted in an attachment to an email dated 21 December 2008 to Kathryn J. Hogenson written on behalf of the Universal House of Justice.

54 *Tablets of Abdul-Baha Abbas*, p. 719.

55 ibid. p. 718.

56 'New Publications', *Star of the West*, vol. 2, no. 14, p. 16.

57 Provisional translation of a Tablet revealed by 'Abdu'l-Bahá in honour of Mrs Peeke in 1909, Bahá'í World Centre Archives, quoted in an attachment to an email dated 21 December 2008 to Kathryn J. Hogenson written on behalf of the Universal House of Justice. According to lists of believers in Ohio published in *Star of the West*, Margaret Peeke's son, Benedict Peeke, did become a believer. His wife, Dr Pauline Barton-Peeke, was a leader of the Faith at the national level

for many years. Tragically, even though Margaret bore many children, apparently she never had any grandchildren.

58 *Tablets of Abdul-Baha Abbas*, p. 725.

59 Jeanne Ruhangiz Bolles, letter to Amatu'l-Bahá Rúḥíyyih Khánum, written at Washington, Connecticut, 15 October 1954. Estate of Amatu'l-Bahá Rúḥíyyih Khánum.

60 Anne Apperson Flint, letter to Emogene Hoagg written in Florence, Italy, 14 February 1929. Hoagg papers, USBNA.

61 This may indicate that she didn't see the toddler Shoghi Effendi during her visit. He was a few months shy of two during February of 1899.

62 Anne Apperson Flint, letter to Emogene Hoagg written at Vienna, Austria, 28 January (no year but probably about 1930). Hoagg papers, USBNA.

63 Emogene Hoagg, typed recollections of her first years associated with the Bahá'í Faith, p. 4. Emogene Hoagg papers, USBNA.

64 Ella Goodall Cooper, letter to 'Abdu'l-Bahá written in Oakland, California, 13 February 1906. Bahá'í World Centre Archives, provided as an attachment to an email to Kathryn J. Hogenson written on behalf of the Universal House of Justice.

65 Emogene Hoagg, typed recollections of her first years associated with the Bahá'í Faith, p. 5. Emogene Hoagg papers, USBNA.

66 Ella Goodall Cooper, letter to 'Abdu'l-Bahá written in San Francisco, California, 19 August 1905. Bahá'í World Centre Archives, provided as an attachment to an email to Kathryn J. Hogenson written on behalf of the Universal House of Justice.

67 'Abdu'l-Bahá, Tablet to Ella Goodall Cooper dated 21 June 1921, provisional translation by Aziz'Ullah S. Bahadur at Haifa, Palestine. Bahá'í World Centre Archives.

68 For a general summary of the life and achievements of Ella Goodall Cooper, see In Memoriam, *The Bahá'í World*, vol. 12, pp. 681-84.

69 Letter written on behalf of Shoghi Effendi to Ella Cooper dated 17 November 1947, Cooper papers, USBNA. Printed here with permission of the Bahá'í World Centre.

70 Message from Shoghi Effendi dated 18 July 1951 upon the passing of Ella Cooper, *Citadel of Faith*, p. 162. There is no record as to what Ella's father and brother thought about the ladies of the house opening the family home to a continuous stream of visitors in order to spread a new religion. Apparently neither became a believer, though they must have tolerated Bahá'í activities. Her brother's children attended Bahá'í children's classes and youth activities. The prayer much beloved by Bahá'í children, which begins 'O God, guide me, protect me . . .', was written for her 4-year-old relative, Sheldon Goodall Cooper (1904–1990), by 'Abdu'l-Bahá. Tablet transmitted through Mirza Monier Zain to Mrs. Ella Goodall Cooper, translated on 23 March 1909 by M.A. Esphahani in Washington, D.C. Cooper papers, USBNA.

Chapter 15 Lives of Service Together and Apart: The Getsingers

1 Metelmann, *Lua Getsinger*, p. 37.

2 In a Tablet to Helen Adelaide Hillyer from 'Abdu'l-Bahá included in a letter

received during January 1902 but probably written before that, most likely in 1899 or 1900, the Master spoke of Phoebe as 'thy kind mother, and the Mother of the Faithful, the radiant Leaf, and the pearl of mercy, Mrs. Hearst'. Provisional translation by Aḥmad Yazdí and Marzieh Gail. Cooper papers, USBNA. See also the Sarah Farmer letters to Phoebe Hearst, PAH papers, Bancroft Library; and *Tablets of 'Abdul-Bahá Abbas,* pp. 291-3.

3 The Master accepted the donation because it was sincerely given but purchased an expensive ring for a modest price and sent it to Phoebe. He did not want her to think He was in her debt. *Maḥmúd's Diary*, p. 24.

4 Gregory, 'Robert Turner', pp. 28-29. See also Thomas, 'The "Pupil of the Eye"', pp. 23-5.

5 For an excellent discussion of Phoebe and her role in the Faith following her pilgrimage, see Gail, *Arches of the Years*, p. 52 and passim. Mrs Gail's father, Ali-Kuli Khan, was employed by Phoebe for several years and he remained her friend to the end of her life.

6 An example of her discretion is the letter that she sent to 'Abdu'l-Bahá at the time that she sent Anton Haddad to the Middle East to report on Kheiralla's growing rebellion and to obtain guidance. In the letter she states that she will not give the Master any details in writing but instead hopes that 'Abdu'l-Bahá will allow Haddad to come to 'Akká to make an oral report on her behalf (Phoebe Hearst, letter to 'Abdu'l-Bahá written in Washington, D.C, 5 July 1899. Bahá'í World Centre Archives, summarized in an attachment to a letter dated 21 December 2008 written to Kathryn J. Hogenson on behalf of the Universal House of Justice).

7 Many years later, Anne Apperson Flint wrote to Ella Cooper about this affair. Ella shared the two letters with Anne, who had known about them but never seen them. Anne said that they were not like any of her aunt's writings and that her aunt did not sign her name in the manner in which it was affixed to the letters. Anne explained to Ella what she thought had happened and well remembered how upset her aunt had been at the time (Anne A. Flint, Note included in a letter to Ella Cooper, 19 January 1944. Cooper papers, USBNA. See also notes penned by Ella relating what she had been told by Edward Getsinger. Cooper papers, USBNA). The two letters in question were quoted by Shoghi Effendi in his history of the Faith, *God Passes By* and also reproduced in several editions of *The Bahá'í World.*

8 'Abdu'l-Bahá, Tablet to Edward Getsinger translated by Munavvar Khánum (the date 7 February is on the translation without a year, most likely 1902) and Edward's handwritten notes on the translation. Edward said that he did nothing to cooperate with the reporters. Getsinger papers, USBNA.

9 Clipping of the newspaper article, dated 9 March 1901. PAH papers, Bancroft Library.

10 In the provisional translation of a Tablet from 'Abdu'l-Bahá to Edward Getsinger received on 15 October 1902, the Master wrote:

> Relax thou not in affairs (business), for verily relaxation causes laziness and vexation. Verily Thy Lord will bestow upon thee an ample provision from when thou expectest it not, and He will strengthen thee in that by which thy heart will be at rest through the favors of the Kingdom of El-Abha!

Provisional translation by M. Ahmad Esphahani, 5 October 1907. Getsinger papers, USBNA. Printed here with permission of the Bahá'í World Centre.
11 Afroukhteh, *Memories of Nine Years in 'Akká*, p. 154.
12 Gail, *Other People, Other Places*, p. 186.
13 Provisional translation of an undated letter from 'Abdu'l-Bahá to Dr Getsinger, translated by A. K. Khan, 25 January 1903, Getsinger papers, USBNA.
14 Ella Goodall, letter to Helen Goodall written at Ain Sobhar, Syria, 1 April 1899. Cooper papers, USBNA.
15 Handwritten note by Edward Getsinger on the back of a typed page titled, 'About Daniel and John Returing in their Personality', Getsinger papers, USBNA. See also, 'Statement and Charge to the Custodians of the N.S.A.' by Edward C. Getsinger, Windust papers, USBNA.
16 'Abdu'l-Bahá, Tablet to Dr Getsinger, translated in Washington, D.C. by A. K. Khan on 28 December 1901. Getsinger papers, USBNA. The translation contains a handwritten note in Edward Getsinger's handwriting which states: 'Three tablets like these were received telling me to get out of business and into my research work. ECG.'
17 When Edward Getsinger began to devote his time completely to writing about the oneness of science and religion, for several years he was supported financially by a wealthy believer in Boston, Henry Randall, with the approval of 'Abdu'l-Bahá, who was anxious to keep Edward constructively busy. The Master also said to Harry Randall that in the future Edward's book on science and religion would be widely known. See Randall-Winckler, *William Henry Randall: Disciple of 'Abdu'l-Bahá*, pp. 124-5.
18 Helen Goodall, who had been financially underwriting many of Lua's travels for the Faith, established a trust fund to support the Getsingers during their time in India. It was administered by reliable friends in Egypt who dispatched a stipend to them every month.
19 He may have needed to leave when he did in that ethnic Germans in India were being rounded up and imprisoned by the British because of the outbreak of World War I. Lua, as an American whose parents were native born and of Anglo-Saxon stock, would not have faced the same risk. See Lua Getsinger, letter to Helen Goodall, 1 January 1915, in Metelmann, *Lua Getsinger*, p. 291.
20 See Lua Getsinger, letter to Elizabeth Nourse, in Metelmann, ibid. p. 286.
21 ibid. pp. 194-5.
22 ibid. pp. 406-7 (note 45). Translated by the Research Department of the Universal House of Justice, Bahá'í World Centre.
23 ibid. p. 349.
24 'Abdu'l-Bahá, Tablet addressed to Dr Getsinger, care of Mr Hannen, Washington, D. C., Haifa, Palestine, 31 May 1919. Translated by Shoghi Rabbani. Getsinger papers, USBNA; Bahá'í World Centre Archives.
25 Metelmann, *Lua Getsinger*, p. 352.
26 See, for example, Edward Getsinger's correspondence with Albert Windust (USBNA, passim); and Hollinger, *Community Histories*, pp. xxii-xxiii.
27 'Abdu'l-Bahá, Tablet addressed to Dr. Getsinger, translated by Ahmad Esphahani. No date is given. Getsinger papers, USNBA.
28 See the collection of letters written by Edward Getsinger to Albert Windust

during the last decade of Edward's life. Windust letters. USBNA.

29 Hatch, 'Edward Christopher Getsinger', In Memoriam, *The Bahá'í World*, vol. 6, pp. 493-6.

Chapter 16 Mother of the Faithful

1 'Abdu'l-Bahá, Tablet to Edward Getsinger, translated by Munavvar Khanum. The date 7 February is on the translation without a year, most likely 1902. Edward's handwritten notes are on the translation. Getsinger papers, USBNA.

2 This is undoubtedly a reference to Hooper Harris who was to travel not only to 'Akká but also to Iran.

3 Phoebe Hearst, letter to Helen Goodall, 19 July 1902. Goodall papers, USBNA.

4 Inventory of her bedroom. PAH papers, Bancroft Library.

5 Gail, *Summon Up Remembrance*, p. 177.

6 As a native German speaker, Emily Bachrodt added extra 'r's to some words, like 'her,' and had difficulty with English spelling.

7 Amalia Bachrodt, letter to Phoebe Hearst, written in San Francisco, 13 February 1901. PAH papers, Bancroft Library. In the same letter, Amalia says that, 'I was so pleased to hear from Mrs. Kheiralla, will you kindly give my love to her.'

8 Ella Goodall Cooper, handwritten note on her working papers about the 1898–1899 pilgrimage. Cooper papers, USBNA. I am indebted to Roger Dahl for providing me with the official information on Amalia Bachrodt, based upon his extensive research into government and newspaper records. Email from Roger Dahl to author dated 1 July 2008.

9 Gregory, 'Robert Turner', pp. 28-9. See also Thomas, 'The "Pupil of the Eye" ', pp. 23-5.

10 Clara Reed Anthony, undated letter to PAH. Item #23, PAH papers, Bancroft Library.

11 In response, the Master included in a letter to Ali-Kuli Khan a brief message to be conveyed to Robert. It said, 'Be not grieved at your illness, for thou has attained eternal life and hast found thy way to the World of the Kingdom. God willing, we shall meet one another with joy and fragrance in that Divine World, and I beg of God that you may also find rest in this material world' (Gail, *Arches of the Years*, p. 54).

12 'Abdu'l-Bahá, Tablet to Robert C. Turner, provisional translation, 17 August 1909 in Chicago by Mirza Ahmad Sohrab. Goodall papers, USBNA; Bahá'í World Centre Archives.

13 For example, Dr Alonso Taylor mentions in a letter how taken his small son was with Robert and how the boy mentioned Robert whenever Phoebe was called to mind. Letter from Alonso Taylor to Phoebe Hearst, written from San Francisco, 4 December (no year). PAH papers, Bancroft Library.

14 Ella Goodall Cooper, typed manuscript entitled 'The First Pilgrimage to 'Akka from the Western World'. Cooper papers, USBNA.

15 Harriet Thornburgh, letter to Phoebe Hearst, undated. PAH papers, Bancroft Library.

16 Gail, *Arches of the Years*, p. 55. See also Stockman, "Robert Turner: A Door to the Kingdom', pp. 3 & 11.

17 I am indebted to Rodrick Haake for sharing his information about his grandfather,

Henry Keeling, who was that chauffeur and also a firm, life-long Bahá'í. After returning to the Holy Land, 'Abdu'l-Bahá sent Henry Keeling a short, touching message saying that even though their time together was brief, it was both a spiritual and physical meeting. He assured him of His love and that he was always in His thoughts. He told Henry that even though he was unable to make a pilgrimage to the Holy Land, he was counted among those who were present there. Email from Violette Haake dated 20 November 2009 to Kathryn Hogenson.

18 *Maḥmúd's Diary*, p. 327.

19 Ella Goodall Cooper, letter to Horace Holley, 16 February 1946. Cooper papers, USBNA. It appears that 'Abdu'l-Bahá met Charles Tinsley at his home in San Francisco rather than at the Hearst Pleasanton home. Ella also recounts that Charles Tinsley regularly attended Bahá'í gatherings at her home until he became partially paralysed and had to use a wheelchair.

20 *Maḥmúd's Diary*, p. 331.

21 See the letters of Emma Cecilia Thursby to Phoebe Hearst. PAH papers, Bancroft Library.

22 Cameron and Momen, *A Basic Bahá'í Chronology*, p. 247.

23 This detail comes from Marzieh Gail's memory of Ella Cooper telling of this incident. Gail, *Arches of the Years*, pp. 99-100.

24 Ella Goodall Cooper, summary and extracts from a letter to 'Abdu'l-Bahá written in 1919 reporting the passing of Phoebe A. Hearst. Bahá'í World Centre Archives, attached to a letter dated 21 December 2008 written on behalf of the Universal House of Justice to Kathryn J. Hogenson.

25 ibid.

26 ibid.

27 ibid.

28 'Abdu'l-Bahá, Tablet addressed to Ella Goodall Cooper, San Francisco, California, dated 2 June [1919], translated by Shoghi Rabbani, Haifa, Palestine. Cooper papers, USBNA; Bahá'í World Centre Archives.

29 'Abdu'l-Bahá, Tablet dated 2 June 1919, translated by Shoghi Rabbani, Haifa, Palestine. Cooper papers, USBNA. Provisional translation also provided as an attachment to a letter dated 21 December 2008 written on behalf of the Universal House of Justice to Kathryn J. Hogenson.

30 Ella Goodall Cooper, letter to 'Abdu'l-Bahá, written in 1919. Bahá'í World Centre Archives, summarized and quoted in an attachment to a letter dated 21 December 2008 written on behalf of the Universal House of Justice to Kathryn J. Hogenson.

31 May Bolles Maxwell, undated handwritten note on the letterhead of the Hotel Seville, New York. Estate of Amatu'l-Bahá Rúḥíyyih Khánum. I am indebted to the literary executors of the estate, Mrs Violette Nakhjavani and Miss Nell Golden for providing this document.

32 May Bolles Maxwell, letter to Katherine Page of East Detroit Michigan, written in Portsmouth, New Hampshire, 9 September 1930. Estate of Amatu'l-Bahá Rúḥíyyih Khánum. I am indebted to the literary executors of the estate, Mrs Violette Nakhjavani and Miss Nell Golden for providing this document.

33 ibid.

Annex 2

1 *Tablets of Abdul-Baha*, vol. 2, pp. 291-3. The translation is dated 13 September 1902. The Universal House of Justice has stated: 'The individuals referred to in the fourth paragraph are "Robert", "Alice", and "Louise". The remaining two individuals mentioned are "Apperson" and "Cropper". Concerning the title "Mother of the Faithful", an individual wrote to Shoghi Effendi on this question and was informed, in a letter written on his behalf, that it may refer to Mrs Hearst but that he declined to state this of a certainty without seeing the original of the Tablet' (letter to Kathryn J. Hogenson, 6 January 2010).

Index